D1542237

Love and Politics

and Lesbian Theories

Love and Politics

Radical Feminist and Lesbian Theories

Carol Anne Douglas

ism

press

San Francisco

Library of Congress Cataloging-in-Publication Data

Douglas, Carol Anne.
Love and politics : radical feminist and lesbian theories / by
Carol Anne Douglas.
p. cm.
Includes bibliographical references.
ISBN 0-910383-18-9 :   —   ISBN 0-910383-17-0 (pbk.) :
1. Feminism—Philosophy.   2. Lesbianism   3. Radicalism.
I. Title.
HQ1206.D67   1990
305.42′01—dc20   90-4218
                                                          CIP

ism press, inc.
P.O. Box 12447
San Francisco, CA 94112

4i

Thanks to Barbara Smith, Jill Johnston, Laurel Holliday, Barbara Grier, Dana Densmore, Susan Cavin, Charlotte Bunch, Rita Mae Brown, and Ti-Grace Atkinson, for permission to reprint excerpts from their works.

Also, thanks to the following authors and publishers, for permission to reprint excerpts: From BEYOND GOD THE FATHER by Mary Daly, Copyright © 1973 by Mary Daly, reprinted by permission of Beacon Press. From A PASSION FOR FRIENDS by Janice G. Raymond, Copyright © 1986 by Janice G. Raymond, reprinted by permission of Beacon Press. From THE POLITICS OF REALITY, Copyright © 1984 by Marilyn Frye, reprinted by permission of The Crossing Press. From SEXUAL POLITICS, Copyright © 1970 by Kate Millett, reprinted by permission of Doubleday. From TOWARDS AN ANTHROPOLOGY OF WOMEN, Copyright © 1975 by Rayna R. Reiter, reprinted by permission of Monthly Review Foundation. From THE DIALECTIC OF SEX, Copyright © 1970 by Shulamith Firestone, reprinted by permission of William Morrow & Co. From OF WOMAN BORN, Copyright © 1976 by Adrienne Rich, reprinted by permission of W.W. Norton & Co. From BLOOD, BREAD AND POETRY, Copyright © 1986 by Adrienne Rich, reprinted by permission of W.W. Norton & Co. From THE FIRST SEX, Copyright © 1971 by Elizabeth Gould Davis, reprinted by permission of the Putnam Publishing Group. From THE SECOND SEX, Copyright © 1968 by Simone de Beauvoir, reprinted by permission of Random House. From WOMAN'S WORTH, Copyright © 1981 by Lisa Leghorn and Katherine Parker, reprinted by permission of Routledge & Kegan Paul. From AGAINST OUR WILL, Copyright © 1975 by Susan Brownmiller, reprinted by permission of Simon & Schuster. From THE POLITICS OF REPRODUCTION, Copyright © 1981 by Mary O'Brien, reprinted by permission of Unwin Hyman Ltd.

Table of Contents

4. Male Biology as a Problem 64

5. Men and Women: Same Species 83

Part Three

Love, Sex, and Sexuality in Radical Feminist Politics 107

---

6. Love: Can it be Good? 109

7. Sex: Will it Exist After the Revolution? 130

Acknowledgments

I wrote this book without any financial assistance or help in research. Getting it published has required years of work and almost staggering persistence.

If I had focused only on this book, I think the difficulties would have been overwhelming. Fortunately, I have cast my lot as a feminist as a member of the collective that produces the newspaper *off our backs*, so I had much other work that demanded my attention. I am proud to say that I don't think my work on *off our backs* ever suffered during the years that I was writing this book.

I am genuinely sorry for feminist writers who do not belong to an ongoing political group. Working in a feminist collective does not preclude doing individual work; both collective and individual work are important. I am glad that I have the experience of editing, typing, and proofreading other women's work as well as writing my own.

I want to thank many individuals who helped me along the way.

I thank Virginia Cerello for giving me my first model of an intellectual woman.

I want to thank the members of Boston Female Liberation, my first feminist group. It was the conflict between women in that group who saw themselves as activists (some of whom were lesbian) and those who saw themselves as lesbian/cultural, that started me thinking about the divisions in the movement that I discuss in this book. I always liked women in both groups.

I thank Tacie Dejanikus for her long years of political support and her constant emphasis on the importance of writing clearly. I am grateful to Alice Henry for her continuing supportive criticism of my work. I am especially grateful to Tricia Lootens, for her encouragement while I was trying to find a publisher. I thank Ti-Grace Atkinson, Pauline Bart, and Angela Miles for their interest in the book.

I want to thank Liz Quinn for her personal and political support during the struggles over this book.

I also thank Daniel Fogel of ism press for his helpful suggestions and willingness to leave the ultimate responsibility for content to the author.

I thank Joan E. Biren for her help in selecting from among her wonderful pictures for use in this book.

Most of all, I thank all of the women in the feminist movement for reading, writing, and acting.

Dedication

To the collective of the feminist newspaper *off our backs*, who gave me a political context for life as a feminist during the years that I worked on this book: Tacie Dejanikus, Nancy Fithian, Adriane Fugh-Berman, Farar Elliott, Alice Henry, Angela Johnson, Janis Kelly, Denise Kulp, Vickie Leonard, Tricia Lootens, Fran Moira, Debra Ratterman, Jennie Ruby, Lorraine Sorrell, Joanne Stato, June Thomas, and Ruth Wallsgrove—and especially to Vickie Leonard, for political and personal friendship.

Introduction

What is radical feminism? A whole book seems scarcely long enough to delimit radical feminism. It is hard to find one single definition that encompasses radical feminism, and lesbian feminism, which has stemmed from it.

The purpose of this book is to try to clarify radical feminist theory (or theories) and lesbian feminist theory (or theories), to understand the assumptions behind them, and to discuss how compatible some of the ideas expressed in these theories are with one another.

When I say that I am writing about feminist theory, I am using the term "theory" loosely to mean any ideas or sets of ideas that try to explain the world and suggest ways to change it. The term "feminist theories" probably is more appropriate than "feminist theory." There are many feminist theories. There is even a wide variety of radical feminist theories. Using the term "theory" rather than "theories" could suggest that the theories are in agreement with one another, which often is not the case.

Feminist theory is, in the broadest sense, the body of ideas held by feminists. Feminists create feminist theory or theories as we think, talk and act, although more consciously articulated theory does play a major part in developing and spreading ideas.

This study is confined to feminist theories that have developed in the United States, with a few discussions of important developments by French feminist theorists whose works are read by North American feminists.

I am not focusing equally on socialist feminism because I believe it has been more adequately described than radical feminism, by writers such as Zillah Eisenstein, Heidi Hartmann, and Alison Jaggar.[1] Also, socialist feminism is less confusing. Although socialist feminist writers vary considerably, they tend to agree more on basic principles than do those who describe themselves as radical feminists or lesbian feminists. I will refer to some socialist feminist theorists whose work is too important to be left out of any general discussion of feminist theory.

1

I do not suggest that there is some absolute division between radical and lesbian feminists and socialist feminists. There have always been many similarities, and the theories may be becoming more similar. Probably there are radical feminists who feel closer politically to some socialist feminists than to some others who define themselves as radical feminists. (That is, some radical feminists who do not see women as inherently different from men may feel closer to socialist feminists than to radical feminists who do see women as different).

The word "radical" means going to the root of things. Political radicals believe there is oppression in society and try to look in radically new ways to understand this oppression, its causes and ways of ending it. There is great disagreement about what is truly radical, and that is why there are many kinds of radicals—radical feminists, anarchists, communists, socialists—and why there are many kinds of radical feminists.

Part One of this book discusses various definitions and schools of radical and lesbian feminism, and their relationship to socialist feminism. It looks at some basic assumptions in radical feminist theory and at various other theories, such as existentialism, marxism and anarchism, which have contributed to the eclectic theories of radical feminism.

Women who define themselves as radical feminists and lesbian feminists have a wide variety of views on the origins of women's oppression, which are discussed in Part Two of this book. The impetus for radical feminism developed among women who believed that women's and men's biological differences did not determine personality traits and should not be socially significant. These feminists looked forward to a society where all distinctions based on gender would be eliminated. Since then, other women who also see themselves as radical feminists or as radical lesbians have suggested that there may be socially significant biological differences between women and men—or that, even if there are no inherent differences determining women's and men's behavior, there is a culture that has developed among women that has aspects worth preserving.

Although some of these ideas seem absolutely to contradict each other, in many cases there is not a clear distinction between "biological" and "non-biological" theories. Virtually all discussion of women's oppression under patriarchy involves some discussion of biological differences, even if the question is merely whether men used those differences in order to gain power over women. There is a continuum of ideas on sex differences. Some of the ideas seem to be synthesized by several feminist theorists' suggestions in the 1980s that there is a connection between practice and biology, or that people's perceptions of their biology are an aspect of biology. Human practice affects what biology is.

I suggest that perspectives on biological differences, although they may affect feminists' perceptions of other political issues, are not in themselves adequate information to predict a given feminist's other political ideas or actions.

Radical and lesbian feminists also have a wide range of ideas on love and sexuality, which are discussed in Part Three. An early radical feminist focus on love as a means of enslaving women by men or as a destructive delusion gave way to a discussion that focused more on the politics of sexuality than on love. Radical and lesbian feminists have advocated as most liberating for women everything from celibacy, to heterosexual monogamy, to bisexuality, to lesbian monogamy, to multiple lesbian partners. Lesbian feminists have criticized the compulsory nature of heterosexuality in patriarchal societies. Some celibate and lesbian feminists have criticized heterosexual women as collaborators in patriarchy, and some heterosexual feminists have replied that they don't want to be told what to do, even by other feminists.

In the 1980s, divisions over sexuality within the feminist movement shifted from a lesbian/heterosexual split, to a new divide: those who focus on a critique of sexuality as it often is practiced in today's society, including pornography, prostitution, most heterosexual relationships and role-based lesbian relations—and those who suggest that repression is a greater danger than any kind of sexual expression. This division crosses heterosexual and lesbian lines.

Some lesbian feminists are writing about love and suggesting that it is possible to love in an unoppressive, enriching way. They are suggesting that love and friendship may be similar and overlapping, not different. Others suggest that even in lesbian relationships intimacy still brings problems.

Radical and lesbian feminist ideas on goals, strategies and tactics also differ considerably; these are discussed in Part Four. Goals range from (1) integration with men in a non-sex-differentiated society, to (2) an egalitarian society with a permanent or long-range independent power base for women, to (3) separate societies for those women who want them, to (4) a society where women predominate in numbers and/or political power. The first two goals mentioned are probably more widely held, but the second goal is not necessarily incompatible with the third goal, some form of separatism.

Some of those differences in goals may be differences between long-term goals, short-term goals, and strategies. For instance, separatism of women from men can be either a long-term goal, a short-term goal, or a strategy. Virtually all radical feminists and lesbian feminists accept it at least as a significant tactic for contemporary feminist political groups (that is, they believe there should be all-women political groups).

If the end of patriarchy or male dominance is defined as the goal of radical and lesbian feminists, then all radical and lesbian feminists have a similar goal though they may differ about what truly is a society without patriarchy. Most radical and lesbian feminists would go further and say that a society without any form of oppression or power over others is their goal; feminists and lesbians with very different politics see that as a goal.

Great differences over strategy should not obscure the similarity in goals.

Many radical feminist theorists have not written about strategy and tactics. Analysis of existing conditions and their origins and, less commonly, visions of possible futures, have attracted more theorists' attention than have specific ways of ending oppression. This does not mean that no feminists have talked about action or taken action. Theorists and activists are not always the same women, although often they are.

The relative lack of strategic thinking, particularly in the 1970s, probably has affected the level of activism. At the same time, obstacles to activism, such as the need to focus on dramatic personal-life changes resulting from feminism, the amount of criticism often levelled at particular actions, the frustration at meager results or at having to fight the same battles repeatedly, and the frequency of intragroup and intergroup movement tensions, may paralyze strategic and tactical thinking as well as activism.

Since the late 1970s and particularly in the 1980s, there has been a resurgence of calls for action by feminist writers and of activism itself. The visibility of action-oriented Women of Color, the anti-pornography movement, and many diverse feminists' alarm over the Reagan/Bush administration are causes of the renewed focus on activism and hence on strategy and tactics.

There are, of course, many disagreements over strategies and tactics. Even if there were a consensus that the movement needed more public activism, a consensus about what form that activism should take is a much more remote possibility.

Nevertheless, there are many tactics that a variety of feminists would agree are desirable, even though not everyone wants to, or can engage in them. All feminists probably would agree about the desirability of clerical workers' organizing, for instance, and can support that organizing in some ways even though not everyone is involved in that activity. Many kinds of work could be complementary, although it is true that they "compete" for feminists' time.

This book is an attempt to point out both common ground and differences. My hope is that feminists and lesbians can find more common ground, look at differences honestly, overcome or tolerate those political differences that can be accepted, and deal honestly and nonabusively with any political differences that seem unacceptable.

In the 1980s, feminists have become more aware of differences. In addition to differences in race, class, ethnic background, and sexuality, the movement needs differences of opinion. This book is a plea for acceptance of plurality of opinions; not for a liberal tolerance that assumes that differences in ideas are acceptable because ideas don't matter, but for a dynamic diversity of thought and action that looks forward to a plurality of outcomes as well as a plurality of tactics. I doubt that there can be societies where women and men are really equal unless there are opportunities for women to be women-centered and separate; I doubt that there can be societies where women are women-centered and separate unless women have a stronger position in mixed societies and more egalitarian personal and political relationships with men.

Part One

What is Radical Feminism?

7

Chapter 1

Defining Ourselves

There is no one criterion that adequately describes the differences between various feminist perspectives. One might try, as Maggie McFadden does, to categorize feminist writers by their emphasis on biological differences between women and men, or their rejection of those differences[1]; but one would thereby group together feminists who ascribe to very different strategies. If one bases a categorization on "woman-centeredness," as Hester Eisenstein does,[2] that also can lead one to group together feminists who put forth quite different strategies.

This book will look at several different aspects of radical feminists' and lesbian feminists' thought: ideas on the origins of male dominance in human societies; ideas on love and sexuality; and ideas on goals, strategies and tactics. The writings of individual feminist writers and tendencies or factions in the feminist movement can be understood only if all of these ideas are taken into account.

My discussion links radical feminism and lesbian feminism because the ideas are linked historically and epistemologically. Both sets of ideas assume that men form a class or caste that is separate from women in virtually all societies, that the class or caste of men oppresses women, and that women can and should try to change that.

Both theories are political theories that consider how power is distributed in society or how decisions are made in a society. Both use political language, such as "oppression," "domination," and "liberation." (Even writers, such as Mary Daly, who do not care for these terms, choose other terms that have a similar meaning; she uses terms like "sadosociety" and "sparking.") They use a political framework that, like marxism, sees society as divided into classes and opposes this division, rather than striving for or justifying stratified harmony.

Another basic area of agreement has been the idea that the domination of one group by another on one level of society (e.g., the family), fosters the practice of domination on other levels of society (e.g., government and the workplace). Most feminists thus believe it is impossible to have a society that is personally authoritarian yet politically democratic, or vice versa. Most radical and lesbian (and socialist) feminists see their goal as an end not only to male domination over women, but to all patterns of domination.

Radical feminists did not invent the idea that the personal was the political; Aristotle and Confucius thought the personal was political, too. But for these and subsequent patriarchal philosophers, that meant that the father's control in the family and the ruler's position over the people reinforced each other and that this was desirable.

Within the general outlines of radical and lesbian feminist theory, many differences have developed. Some, but by no means all, may be connected with the differences between those who see themselves as radical feminists and those who see themselves as lesbian feminists. (Not everyone is able to make this choice. For instance, I see myself as both.) A lesbian feminist may simply be a radical feminist who sees lesbianism as an act of resistance against male supremacy and a major element in overthrowing it. I see lesbian feminism as generically a part of radical feminism, but some lesbian feminists may feel that such a designation does not put enough emphasis on lesbianism.

There has been a tendency since the development of lesbian feminism for some lesbians to see radical feminism as subsumed under lesbianism, or simply replaced by lesbianism. This tendency ignores the historical development of radical feminism, the variety of radical feminists (many are not lesbians), and the variety of radical feminist theory or theories.

There are many political differences that cannot be described just by using the words "radical feminist" or "lesbian feminist." Certainly not all political differences are connected with sexual identity.

Although this book is subtitled "Radical Feminist and Lesbian Theories," I do not think the terms "radical feminist" or "lesbian feminist" are the most appropriate designation for every single one of the writers discussed. Some of them do not call themselves "radical feminists" or "lesbian feminists." In order to show the spectrum of contemporary lesbian thought that intersects with and generally is a part of the feminist movement, I am including both lesbian feminists whose theory is basically radical feminist, and some lesbians who do not use the term "feminist" to describe themselves because they feel the designation "lesbian" stands on its own.

Nor would I call every single idea mentioned "feminist." For instance, at one point Laurel Holliday suggested that boys may need more mothering than girls because males are less resilient — an idea which hardly seems feminist. (See Chapter 13). On the other hand, Catharine A. MacKinnon goes too far when she suggests that all who believe that men may be inherently different from women cannot be radical feminists.[3] For such a definition could exclude many feminists, such as Mary Daly, who see women as an oppressed class and are intently focused on ending women's oppression. Many of the women whom I call "classic" radical feminists would say that women who believe in inherent biological differences are not radical feminists.

It seems to me that lesbian writers who do not choose to use the word "feminist" to describe themselves, and who do not propose theories that address the situation of nonlesbian women, are properly called lesbian rather than lesbian feminist writers.

Speaking very broadly, it might be possible to say there are two "kinds" of radical and lesbian feminists. The first group could be called the "classic" radical feminists, those whose politics are most similar to the radical feminist politics articulated in the late 1960s by such groups as New York Radical Women, the Feminists, and Redstockings and by individuals such as Shulamith Firestone, Kate Millett, and Ti-Grace Atkinson (although there are many and major differences between Firestone, Millett, and Atkinson).

That "classic" radical feminist politics — or "concentrate-on-the-enemy" politics — is that basically men and women are more similar than they are different, and that men used the differences that exist in reproduction to oppress women and define them as inferior. Love and sexuality have been defined by men to suit their interests. Women have been injured by not being allowed to do the kind of work that men have done. Women must confront men by direct action and fight for an end to male supremacy. A society in which there is no socially recognized difference between women and men is the goal.

The second position was developed in the early 1970s, often, although not always, by lesbians. This group or position, which might be called the "focus on women" or "biological differences" position, holds that there are greater differences between women and men than the classical radical feminist position maintains. Some even suggest that men are inherently more violent than women. Women's reproductive capacity is not a burden in itself, as some of the classic radical feminists seem to imply. Women's experience as mothers has not been entirely negative because women have developed a culture that is separate from male culture and more nurturing. Women can gain more from being with one another than with men. Women are not more limited than men and do not need to learn from them. Perhaps there are some differences that should be preserved.

Some of these women believe that the goal should be creating societies separate from men, or perhaps ruling them—in a gentle, matriarchal way. The appropriate tactic is building separate, independent women's communities, not confrontation with men. Confrontation might be seen as acting in a male manner, or as being trapped into always reacting to men's actions rather than creating independently.

Writers who seem to hold some variety of these ideas include Mary Daly, Susan Griffin and Sally Gearhart. Of course, they differ greatly from one another and may endorse confrontation in particular instances.

Sometimes, members of these groups fear each other. Members of the focus-on-women group may feel that those who belong to the classic or concentrate-on-the-enemy group are caught up in reacting to men, rather than acting on their own initiative. Members of the confront-the-enemy group may feel that the focus-on-women group spends its time in "fun" activities such as cultural events, avoiding activities such as demonstrations, simply because they are less entertaining.

Significantly, each group fears that the members of the other group *will not be radical enough.*

Not all "heterosexual" radical feminists have a classic radical feminist position. Susan Brownmiller, for example, has contributed to the view that men are more violent than women.

Not all lesbian feminists hold the "biological differences" position. Charlotte Bunch, for instance, seems closer to the classic group.

Not all radical or lesbian feminists identify with either group. However, many do tend toward one or the other. Such tendencies often affect which books and periodicals a woman reads, as well as which discussions and concerts she attends. Many keep informed only of ideas developing within their own part of the movement. Sometimes there is little overlap between the groups.

In the city where I live, Washington DC, members of the two groups have attended the same cultural events in the past several years only when the events have featured Women of Color or Jewish women. The desire to acknowledge and learn about the oppression of Women of Color and Jewish women is bringing radical and lesbian feminists of many ethnic backgrounds and diverse politics closer together politically. The 1980s books by Women of Color and Jewish women[4] may be the first books in years that virtually all members of various movement political tendencies have read.

Many of us, even if we are somewhat drawn to one point of view, also have been deeply influenced by some of those who represent another point of view. I feel quite influenced by both schools.

Many writers have tried to develop a synthesis of different male-originated theories, such as freudianism and marxism or marxism and existentialism. I don't want to attempt another synthesis of those ideas: I want to know whether it is possible to synthesize Ti-Grace Atkinson's thought and Mary Daly's without distorting either. I want to try to reconcile the various, apparently contradictory ideas of the radical and lesbian feminists who have affected me. I want to learn whether there is some way that these different theories form a coherent tradition.

The comparisons in this book will not provide a complete analysis of the work of any one theorist, but should give an idea of the range of thinking in the feminist movement. Some writers' work will suffer more than others' from this sort of treatment, since not all feminist writers have emphasized the kinds of ideas that I am going to analyze. In particular, the work of Simone de Beauvoir is much more than the sum of its parts as discussed in these comparisons. Beauvoir is being included not because she is precisely a radical feminist—which may be a matter for debate—but because she has been the immediate inspiration for many radical feminists.

The work of feminist writers whose style is poetic and is an integral part of their message, such as Mary Daly, also is likely to appear at a disadvantage in the sort of point-by-point comparison that I am doing.

Psychological Analysis

Although some socialist feminists such as Juliet Mitchell have called radical feminism "psychological" in its approach,[5] I would suggest that any theory that proposes a psychological or individual solution to the problem of women's oppression is not radical feminist. Even the most "psychological" statement by radical feminists, the 1969 New York Radical Feminists' manifesto "Politics of the Ego," which says that men oppress women primarily to gain ego satisfaction, calls for an end to the sex class system and challenges the family as an institution. It thus envisions social and political solutions, not individual ones.[6]

On the other hand, the work of feminists such as Dorothy Dinnerstein and Nancy Chodorow[7] focuses on psychology in a way that many radical feminists think is not radical. They tend to explain undesirable male behavior as a result of treatment within the family, particularly on the fact that women do all "mothering." Their major solution to the problems in the relations between women and men is increased child care by fathers. Sometimes they imply that having a male active in child care is necessary to producing balanced human beings who do not see people delineated by sex roles—hardly a solution that offers promise for lesbian mothers.

Radical feminists such as Pauline Bart[8] have criticized this emphasis on psychology as depoliticizing. It treats men as individuals rather than a class and recommends a course of action that women must take individually rather than collectively. The emphasis on the psychologically injurious effects of the nuclear family tends to treat women and men as equally injured by the sex class system.

The appeal that the Dinnerstein/Chodorow theory has for many women may be that it suggests that they can change the world by marrying a liberal man rather than by engaging in political activity.

Class and Race

Many, but not all radical feminists believe that the oppression of women by men is the "primary" human oppression in that it occurred first historically; is the first oppression that an individual human being learns about and participates in; and is the most widespread oppression, occurring in virtually every human society and placing nearly every human being in an oppressed or oppressing sex class.

Virtually all radical feminists acknowledge that race and economic class oppressions also exist and that they may have a harsher impact on a particular individual or group than sex oppression. For instance, radical feminists know that Jewish women were not incinerated by the Nazis just because they were women, although some aspects of their torture may have been different from the torture of Jewish men.

Sex oppression probably is always intertwined with race and class oppressions, and women who are oppressed because of class or race are oppressed by a particular kind of woman-hating classism or racism in addition to facing the classism and racism that men of their class and race experience. Sex oppression also may affect men of oppressed races, when men of oppressing races perceive them as sexual threats to their race power. Radical feminists such as Andrea Dworkin[9] and Catharine A. MacKinnon[10] have alluded to this intertwining of oppressions, but most white radical feminist theorists have not written about it in much detail.

Some radical feminists and many socialist feminists believe that sex, race and class oppressions are so intertwined that it makes no sense to say that any of them is "primary" and that focusing on one of those oppressions as "primary" is an insult to women who are oppressed by racism and classism as well as patriarchy.

A few radical feminist works include class and race in an integral way. Catharine A. MacKinnon's study of sexual harassment, for example, shows how class or workplace dominance and sexual harassment are intertwined aspects of pleasure for the boss who demands sexual acts from a female worker.[11]

Discussion of race and class in the contemporary feminist movement focuses on white racism as it has evolved in western civilization and class oppression that has developed under capitalism, the forms of race and class oppression that prevail in western society and have extended their influence over many other parts of the world. A historical discussion might discover origins of racism far back in history, whenever human beings first began perceiving neighboring peoples as different and killing and enslaving them. A historical discussion might define capitalism as one form of the economic oppression that has existed since human beings first tried to appropriate other human beings' labor, as slaves, servants, subordinates—or wives. A thorough discussion of economic oppression would need to include economic systems in which bureaucratic classes control the labor power of most workers and reap a disproportionate share of the rewards.

A complex view that includes race and class oppression also must accept that women can reap some benefits from connections with men of a society's dominant race and class. Feminists disagree about whether women can be actual members of upper classes or whether white women can be oppressors in the same sense that white men can be, but virtually all would agree that women can participate in oppressive behavior or that they can identify with an oppressor class, even if their sense of identity is based on a delusion.

Is Feminism for All Women?

Although most late 1960s American radical feminist theorists were white, they assumed that radical feminism was a theory that could aid the liberation of women of all races and classes. The earliest anthologies, such as *Sisterhood is Powerful* and *Radical Feminism*,[12] and journals carried articles on colonized women and women in national liberation movements. Women in China, Vietnam, and Cuba often were cited as examples of radical courage. Early anthologies and journals also include some, although not many, articles on and by Black women in the United States (three in *Sisterhood is Powerful*, one in *Radical Feminism*). *Sisterhood is Powerful* included one article by a Chicana woman.

The 1968 "Redstockings Manifesto," typical of women's liberation statements in this regard, says,

> We identify with all women. We define our best interest as that of the poorest, most brutally exploited woman.
>
> We repudiate all economic, racial, educational or status privileges that divide us from other women. We are determined

to recognize and eliminate any prejudices we may have against other women.[13]

The 1971 "Fourth World Manifesto" by Barbara Burris and Kathleen Barry and others maintained that women everywhere have parallel cultures that can be a bond between them; that they form another "world."

> We identify with women of all races, classes, and countries all over the world. The female culture is the Fourth World.[14]

By the late 1970s, many Black feminists and other feminists of Color were saying that white feminists had not sufficiently lived up to this ideal of dealing with racism and creating a feminism by and for all women. However, I think it is important to point out that radical feminists did at least start by thinking of the variety of women and hoping for connections, although that was not enough.

African-American feminist writer Audre Lorde, in her 1980 "Open Letter to Mary Daly," pointed out that Women of Color experience an intensified form of patriarchal oppression, and that writings by white feminists often have not discussed this difference specifically:

> ...Differences expose all women to various forms and degrees of patriarchal oppression, some of which we share and some of which we do not. For instance, surely you know that for non-white women in this country, there is an 80% fatality rate from breast cancer; three times the number of unnecessary eventurations, hysterectomies and sterilizations as for white women; three times as many chances of being raped, murdered or assaulted as exist for white women.[15]

The dialogue between feminists of Color and white feminists over redefinitions of the movement was one of the central features of the movement in the 1980s.

Adrienne Rich has noted, "The radical feminist claim to identify with all women was to undergo severe challenge. To believe that it was right to identify with all women, to wish deeply and sincerely to do so, was not enough."[16]

Writing this book raises questions about race and language. Using a racial designation to describe a Black feminist but not a white feminist accepts the perspective that people are white unless otherwise specified, that white is the norm and other races are not normal. On the other hand, "Black feminist" is also a political designation that many women have chosen specifically, whereas "white feminist" is not. I am using language that most of the time does not designate white feminists as such and does identify Black feminists, but I am skeptical of the implications of this language and I invite the reader to question it, too.

So that whiteness will not be seen as the norm, I shall note here that many of the women discussed in this book are white —including Ti-Grace Atkinson, Simone de Beauvoir, Rita Mae Brown, Susan Brownmiller, Charlotte Bunch, Susan Cavin, Mary Daly, Elizabeth Gould Davis, Christine Delphy, Andrea Dworkin, Shulamith Firestone, Marilyn Frye, Susan Griffin, Sarah Lucia Hoagland, Laurel Holliday, Jill Johnston, Lisa Leghorn, Catharine A. MacKinnon, Kate Millett, Janice Raymond, Adrienne Rich, Kathie Sarachild, and Monique Wittig. I am white, as well.

Women of Color often have chosen to identify themselves primarily by that term or by terms such as "Black feminist," "Black lesbian," or "Asian feminist" rather than using or primarily using terms such as "radical feminist" or "socialist feminist." Some have chosen politics that seem closer to socialist feminism than radical feminism, while others have politics that seem closer to lesbian feminism or radical feminism. By including these Women of Color in chapters that focus on radical feminism and lesbian feminism, I do not mean to imply that they all identify more closely with radical or lesbian feminism than socialist feminism. Merle Woo, for instance, describes herself as a socialist feminist and lesbian activist.

However, writings by many Women of Color, in their focus on personal experience and passionate expression, seem closer to many white radical feminist and lesbian feminist writings than to socialist feminist writings.

How one chooses to organize materials by Women of Color is also significant. I decided to group ideas by Women of Color in each Part in order to show, for instance, the unity of Women of Color in opposing biologically determinist theories of origins— and, in another instance, the variety of Women of Color's ideas on sexuality. Another option would have been to disperse their comments throughout the chapters. I do not mean to suggest by my method of organization that white women and Women of Color have not discussed these issues with each other.

Methods in Feminist Theory

Why am I emphasizing theory as different sets of more or less coherent ideas, influenced by other theories? Haven't radical feminists generally said that consciousness-raising was our basic method of learning about the world and that our lives are the basis of our theory? The "Redstockings Manifesto" said:

> We regard our personal experience, and our feelings about that experience, as the basis for an analysis of our common situation. We cannot rely on existing ideologies as they are all products of male supremacist culture.[17]

A decade later, socialist feminist Nancy Hartsock wrote,

> The practice of small-group consciousness raising, with its stress on examining and understanding experience and on connecting personal experience to the structures that define our lives, is the clearest example of the method basic to feminism.[18]

Isn't that so? What role does theory have outside the consciousness-raising (c-r) group?

For one thing, the c-r group is limited in its membership. No one c-r group—nor all c-r groups that have yet existed—has contained all of the varieties of women's experience that exist in the world today. It can be useful to take what one has learned in the c-r group and go to learn more about women's lives, then report back to the rest through writing. Books on forced prostitution, battering, incest and the whole range of women's oppression widen our understanding of women's oppression.

One of the earliest sharp differences in the movement was connected with the extent to which one relies on consciousness-raising as the basis for theory. The early radical feminist group Redstockings, which originated consciousness-raising, strongly emphasized c-r's importance. It does not seem coincidental that Redstockings insisted that what most women would say they want—monogamous, committed relationships with men—is what they should get. Similarly, what most American workers would say they want probably would be more respectful bosses, shorter hours and higher salaries. Most people—in the United States, at any rate—will say what they want most are improvements in their immediate conditions, not revolution.

Some of the early radical feminists involved in c-r did decide they wanted feminist revolution; most of them, to be sure, had already been radicals before becoming feminists. Consciousness-raising in itself might not necessarily have that effect on a woman who was not already used to thinking of radical social change, although it would make her more aware of mistreatment.

Theory is a way of stretching the imagination, of trying to make generalizations about our individual experiences, trying to visualize how the world can be changed so that oppressive structures are eliminated. Ti-Grace Atkinson's late 1960s ideas were very different from Redstockings' ideas, in part, because Atkinson emphasized theory more.

Political theorizing often is radicalizing. The process of imagining that the world could be different and trying to figure out how to get there destroys apathy and passivity. In societies that have longer and more significant radical traditions than the United States, such as France or Italy, political theory plays a much larger role in politics than it does here.

I stress the imaginative aspect of theory because marxists or some radical feminists, such as the French writer Christine Delphy, have emphasized its basis in material reality, in real life; theory usually also describes what has not yet taken place. Marx wasn't just describing the world when he wrote about "the dictatorship of the proletariat," and we aren't just describing what exists when we write about "feminist revolution" or a "lesbian nation."

Perhaps few women could have imagined radical or lesbian feminism just by looking at our lives unless we had contact with radical feminist or lesbian feminist ideas.

In her 1989 book, *Talking Back: Thinking Feminist, Thinking Black*, African-American feminist theorist Bell Hooks suggests that feminists too often assume that looking at our own lives is enough to enable us to understand our political situation and provide us with a strategy.

> To take woman to the self as starting point for politicization, woman who, in white-supremacist, capitalist patriarchy, is particularly made, socially constructed, to think only me—my body—I constitute a universe—all that truly matters. To take her—this woman—to the self as starting point for politicization is necessarily risky...

[If you say] 'The personal is the political,' [there may be] no sense of connection between one's person and a larger material reality—no sense of what the political is. In this phrase, what most resonates is the word—personal—not the word political. Unsure of the political, each female presumes knowledge of the person—the personal. No need then to search for the meaning of political, simpler to stay with the personal, to make synonymous the personal and the political...[19]

Many women engaged in feminist movement assumed that describing one's personal experience of exploitation by men was to be politicized. Politicization necessarily combines this process (the naming of one's experience) with critical understanding of the concrete material reality that lays the groundwork for personal experience.[20]

But feminist theorists have not been uncritical of theory. Ti-Grace Atkinson wrote,

All that I have said so far is 'theory' in the worst sense. It assumes concepts as fact, any one of which, if false, would challenge what followed. I 'assume' that it is 'natural' to human nature to desire satisfaction (but what about the death wish and *angst*?). I 'assume' that such a major cultural reversal is possible as to radically change the source of identity from outer-directed to inner-directed. (What kind of evolutionary theory would be consistent with that?) I 'assume' that human nature could function so as to fuse one's self-interest with the interests of others in a categorical imperative. (Where is the evidence for any of this?) It is one of the many nightmares of feminism, that to even conceive of what could count as significant changes for women, one must begin by jumping off one cliff after another. And I haven't even considered, here, how such changes could possibly be implemented.[21]

Not all feminist theorists have acknowledged how many assumptions we are making. In a number of radical feminist and lesbian writings, much is implicit or unstated rather than explicit. It is very difficult even to compare and group feminist writers into different schools, as I have tried to do, because sometimes very basic points, such as the author's ideas on whether there are major inherent differences between the sexes, are not stated. Some radical feminist and lesbian writers leave their goals, and perhaps their strategies and tactics, implicit rather than explicit.

Diverse Theories

There are many different feminist methods—we draw on many sources in our writing. For instance, Ti-Grace Atkinson has been influenced by studying philosophy, and argues against the Aristotelian notion that people have different functions in society and are defined by that function (wife, mother, father, slave, master). Mary Daly has been influenced by years of studying philosophy and theology when she was a Catholic theologian. In her book *Gyn/Ecology*, she even manages to turn the Catholic concept of the seven deadly sins against men, pointing out men's eight deadly sins.[22] Susan Griffin is a poet and writes like a poet. The writing of Shulamith Firestone and a number of others is influenced by marxism.[23]

However, many different feminists writers have in common an emotional intensity of style. The work is not divorced from their personal feelings. Writers as different as Atkinson and Daly mention how painful it is to focus on women's oppression in their work. No one could imagine that feminist writers are detaching themselves from their subject.

Radical feminist and lesbian theory is passionate. The real pain of real women covers almost every page. The work of writers such as Adrienne Rich, Audre Lorde, Mary Daly and Janice Raymond also vividly conveys women's experiences of joy.

I am trying to discover what our assumptions are and to make the implicit or unstated as explicit as possible, so that all of us can better evaluate the feminist and lesbian ideas.

The purpose of this book is not to substitute for reading the original works, but to move us to look at them. Some of them have not received the attention they deserve, even within the feminist movement. I am a little surprised at how little analysis we have done of our growing body of theory. Certainly marxists have been analyzing Marx for a century and show no signs of slowing down. Although radical and lesbian feminists, fortunately, have no one writer who is seen as being as central to us as Marx is to marxism, we do have a body of work that is worth discussing.

Our work is notable for its diversity, its pluralism, the lack of a single leader from whom all thoughts flow. Imagine calling feminism "Firestonism," or even "Beauvoirism," and assuming that one writer's ideas were the standard for evaluating everyone else's!

That is absurd. There is no single theory to which one must adhere or one single group to which one must belong to be included in the realm of politics.

Our flexibility is our strength. Feminists will never be shamed by the equivalent of the 1939 Hitler/Stalin non-aggression pact, a strange policy suddenly foisted by leaders on followers who must adhere to it. Feminists will never be in the position of the ex-Communists described in Vivian Gornick's *The Romance of American Communism,* who felt that there was no point in participating in politics if they could no longer belong to the Communist Party because they saw that party as the only people's revolutionary party.[24] Feminists who disagree with a group's ideas or process just form another group.

Although it is fortunate that none of our theorists are canonized, more detailed familiarity with the various ideas could be useful. Some very important feminist books, particularly Ti-Grace Atkinson's *Amazon Odyssey* but also the more widely circulated *The Dialectic of Sex* by Shulamith Firestone have gone out of print, are often left off women's studies reading lists, and women who have joined the movement in recent years often have not read them.

Also, some feminist writers do not credit the sources of their ideas, while others such as Mary Daly and Adrienne Rich credit most of their sources. Some feminists quote Beauvoir's ideas and phrases without giving her name. The Redstockings have complained about how often their ideas are used without credit. But I think that those whose ideas are most commonly used without attribution or acknowledgement are Ti-Grace Atkinson and the early 1970s lesbian feminist group the Furies. In everyday conversations, this doesn't matter so much. We don't have to footnote our conversations. But a writer has a responsibility not to take credit for the ideas of others. I doubt it is entirely a coincidence that it is often the most radical books that become least accessible and are least often cited.

Chapter 2

The Sources of Feminist Theory

What are the sources of feminist theory? Feminists have used almost every possible source of inspiration. For example, seventeenth-century British women arrived at feminism both by the route of Catholicism and the route of radical Protestantism, as Dale Spender describes in her book *Feminist Theorists: Three Centuries of Women Thinkers*.[1] Contemporary radical feminists also have drawn on a wide variety of sources, including marxism, anarchism, existentialism, nineteenth-century feminism, the Black liberation movement, and the Ashley Montague/Robert Graves school of twentieth-century male writers who suggested that women really are better than men because women's behavior is less violent.[2]

Is one of these more of a source than others? Are the sources mutually contradictory? Is it logically inconsistent to try to fuse them?

Although some writers have tried to fuse marxism and existentialism, are they really compatible? Marxism and anarchism are somewhat incompatible, and both of them seem incompatible with the liberalism that is the basis of much nineteenth-century feminism. The Montague/Graves biological superiority views are clearly incompatible with the other views, and I shall not deal with them further here.

Nineteenth-century feminism has influenced twentieth-century feminism. Most contemporary feminists have not looked extensively into their forebears' work, in part because many works went out of print and were not common knowledge until current feminist scholars resurrected them. Books by Dale Spender, Zillah Eisenstein, and Josephine Donovan discuss this history.[3]

African-American Movements

Another influence on feminist thought and practice has been the Black movement, both the Civil Rights movement and Black nationalism. A number of early radical feminists, such as Kathie Sarachild and Carol Hanisch of Redstockings, had worked directly in the Civil Rights movement in the South. From the Civil Rights movement, the mostly white women who formed the first specifically women's liberation groups (radical Black women also were working politically at this time, but most of them did not specifically define themselves as women's liberationists, although some, such as Cellestine Ware, did) learned that it was possible for large numbers of people to become politically active about the oppression in their daily lives. *Both* the theory of non-violence as developed in the Civil Rights movement and the idea of armed resistance ("by any means necessary") of some parts of the Black Nationalist movement have influenced the strategies of, respectively, pacifist and non-pacifist radical and lesbian feminists.

Perhaps the most striking effect of the African-American movement on the feminist movement was the example of Black separatism, or the decision by many that only Blacks could decide the direction of their own movement, and that they need independent all-Black organizations. This example legitimized the idea of separatism, or of creating women-only groups, for many women of different races.

It is understandable if Black people sometimes see that borrowing from their movement as a rip-off, but it is also possible to see this learning from the African-American movement as merely good political sense.

White feminists have not always acknowledged the extent to which ideas have been borrowed or derived from Black movements.

Existentialism, Anarchism, Marxism

Existentialism, marxism and anarchism all see the world as susceptible to change, not static, not a given, endlessly repeating *status quo*. People, either as individuals (existentialism, anarchism) or as members of a group (marxism, some varieties of anarchism) can act, can change, can make changes. All of these philosophies see the world as imperfect, not as good as it could be. The world as it is, is not the best of all possible worlds. Their task is not to justify the existing world, but to change it.

Actually, both marxism and existentialism recognize that there is a human "essence" or nature, as well as existence. As Adam Schaff, a Polish marxist philosopher, has written, if all human beings simply reflected the historical and class conditions under which they were born, we would have no chance of understanding people born in different eras or circumstances. But, because we do have various similarities with them (desire for human contact, need for material well-being, etc.), we can have some understanding of them.[4]

The existentialist point is not that there is no human nature or essence, but that "existence precedes essence," as Jean-Paul Sartre wrote in "Existentialism is a Humanism." There was no idea or ideal of what people should be like that existed before people existed. What people's nature is—what traits they have or don't have, what human society or societies are or can be like—is something we learn from looking at people. We learn whether people can fly by trying to fly. We learn how much people can cooperate by looking to see how much they do cooperate, and by trying to cooperate.

This does not rule out a human nature that determines whether or not people can fly—or under what circumstances they will need tools to do it—or whether and under what circumstances they can cooperate. Our first guesses about whether people can fly, or whether they can work cooperatively, may be wrong—if we look only at whether they are *already* doing those things, rather than trying to see whether they can expand their capacities. People have many capacities—that is one thing we do know.

Although many proponents of these philosophies might deny it, the philosophies do envision some sort of "eternal truth," even if the "eternal truth" is simply that the human condition is important and that human life has value.

Marxism, anarchism, and existentialism are all philosophies that put a value on this world and the individuals living in it. All value freedom, although existentialism puts its greatest emphasis on *individual* freedom and marxism emphasizes *collective* freedom, while most currents of anarchism emphasize both. Marxism based on Marx's early writings, however, does go back to individual, as well as collective, freedom. All of these theories include self-expression and even happiness among their goals.

Marxism, anarchism, and existentialism all are philosophies of action: They assume that human beings must act, they focus on human action rather than on simple existence (if there is such a thing as simple existence devoid of action). They assume that human beings are capable of affecting the world around them and one another, by making choices among different courses of action. Although existentialists generally emphasize the elements of individual choice involved in action, while marxists may emphasize the impact of historical situations on action, both see action as possible and necessary. Even those marxists who say that actions are governed by historical inevitability would admit that many people may betray their class or not have the proper class-consciousness, which means that they in fact can choose whether or not to act in a way that will benefit their class.

Marxism and anarchism emphasize changing "the world," while existentialism focuses on creating the self through action, which may include collective action. All of these involve action, not just thought.

Feminism also is a philosophy of action, which focuses on both collective and individual action, on changing all levels of power relationships in the world and on changing selves as well. When a feminist writer such as Mary Daly writes about "be-ing," she is not talking about "being" as opposed to "action," but about action. "Creative be-ing," she calls it, which we could call "be-ing that acts." Following Beauvoir, many feminists, including Daly and Dworkin, have used the term "becoming," again meaning a kind of action as well as thought.

As far as I know, no one has ever suggested that feminism is a philosophy of pure thought, or that one could be a feminist without taking actions that involve other women.

Like marxism and radical anarchism, feminism is a theory about and for people as social beings. Being a feminist involves developing ideas about, and actions toward women as a group.

A woman is not a feminist if she does not think about women in general, if she merely says, "*I* am as good as a man or better, and will act in a way that shows I know it."

One can be an existentialist of a sort without being necessarily linked to other existentialists: Even if one must act, one can act individualistically rather than collectively.

Existentialism emphasizes what could be called "negative" freedom, or the freedom to resist or reject.[5] An example of the extreme to which this idea of freedom can be taken is Sartre's comment that he was never freer than when France was occupied by Germany. That is, he had more to resist. People active in the Resistance felt they had made a true choice. But an extreme lack of freedom created that situation.

A marxist notion of freedom would involve more control over a situation: ownership of the means of production, control over one's own working conditions.

As writers who have sought to fuse marxism and existentialism have suggested, the two kinds of freedom both have value.

Simone de Beauvoir's Existentialism

Existentialism was brought to feminism by Simone de Beauvoir. Or did existentialism bring Beauvoir to feminism? Was the existence of a philosophy such as existentialism a necessary condition for the creation of feminism as a theory? Or, as the French feminist theorist Michèle Le Doeuf and the American Ti-Grace Atkinson have suggested, is existentialism so fundamentally different from feminism that Beauvoir had passed beyond it before she created her feminist theory? Atkinson suggests that pre-feminist existentialism—that is, Sartre's existentialism as formulated before Beauvoir's *The Second Sex* was published in the late 1940s—is more negative than feminism, and less concrete, since it focused more on individuals than on any type of class and did not offer a theoretical basis for collective organizing. Human beings were supposed to develop themselves and act as if they were freed, but it was not clear how.[6] (In his 1960 book, *Critique of Dialectical Reasoning*, Sartre made more of an attempt to discuss how people could work together in groups).[7]

Le Doeuf has pointed out how Beauvoir used existentialism—and went beyond existentialist concepts—to create her feminism. In *Being and Consciousness*, Sartre says that "all feelings of inferiority derive from free choice. Nothing external has determined what we feel."[8] In other words, other people can't really subjugate a person. A person can always make choices. This would seem to deny the validity of the concept of any oppression, including that of women by men. However, as Le Doeuf says,

> Beauvoir uses the existentialist ethic of authenticity as a theoretical lever to render women's oppression obvious...de Beauvoir had a strange but operative insight: 'Each time the transcendence of the Subject collapses back to immanence, there is degradation of existence into an in-itself. This collapse is a moral fault if it is consented to by the Subject; if it is inflicted on the Subject, it is an oppression.'[9]

In other words, if the "Subject" is hampered in its intrinsic existential striving for free choice, it (she) is oppressed.

> The Subject, defined by its transcendence, is neither a describable being nor a determinable nature...There is no such thing as an 'eternal feminine' because there is no such thing as 'human nature'...[10]

Beauvoir believed there was no fixed nature, just "becoming," so women can become whatever they choose—if they succeed in overcoming those who illegitimately block their "becoming."

Many feminist theorists use existentialist expressions such as "becoming." The concept that human beings can choose to shape themselves in fundamental ways, and that they have an obligation to do so, has been derived from existentialism. Ti-Grace Atkinson and Mary Daly, whose theories differ in many respects, both emphasize possibilities of self-creation that seem derived from existentialism. For example, in *Beyond God the Father*, Daly wrote about "becoming": "This becoming who we really are requires existential courage to confront the experience of nothingness... The only alternative is self-actualization in spite of the ever-present nothingness."[11]

Do a few expressions taken from existentialism, marxism or any other philosophy or theory make a theory existentialist, marxist or connected to the earlier theory? Is feminism logically dependent on existentialism? Certainly it is dependent on having some idea that considerable change is possible, but perhaps marxism could have provided that. However, traditional marxism does not emphasize the voluntary (rather than historically necessary) element of this change as existentialism does.

Anarchism and Feminism

What concepts have radical feminists derived from anarchism? Have borrowings from anarchism been conscious or mostly unconscious?

Anarchist thought, or at least its diffused influence within the New Left of the 1960s, contributed to the development of radical feminism, particularly much of its group structure.

There are two basic types of anarchism: right-wing anarchism, which focuses solely on the freedom of individuals and which usually includes the idea that large businesses can be left intact although government should be dismantled—and left-wing, radical or social anarchism, which sees cooperative groups as well as individuals as basic to society. Social anarchists are just as opposed to capitalism as they are to the state. While right-wing anarchists gravitate to the politics of the Libertarian Party, social anarchists (in the United States at this time) generally focus on organizing collectives and cooperatives. (In other places and times, such as pre-revolutionary Russia, left-wing anarchists have undertaken other revolutionary tactics, such as bombings, as well as building workers' and peasants' cooperatives).

Basic concepts of social anarchism include the idea that different levels of power, in all kinds of social interactions, from the public to the personal, are inherently oppressive. People should make as directly as possible all decisions affecting their own lives, either individually or collectively, depending on the nature of the decision. Human beings are capable of living and working together cooperatively and equally. There is no inherent, necessary drive for power. (But who created the unequal social conditions?) The state, the corporations, the patriarchal family, all must be replaced with more cooperative voluntary associations.

Often, social anarchists adopt the strategy of creating cooperative communities or businesses as examples of the ways that people can work and live together when there are no artificial distinctions between them. There is an emphasis on changing the individual's own attitudes and practices, as well as those of society at large.

In the United States, anarchism is a much less respected idea than, say, marxism, which is hardly given great respect. Universities teach courses on marxism, but rarely on anarchism. Anarchist books are difficult to obtain.

Anarchist ideas spread, nevertheless, sometimes without the label "anarchist." The ideas of establishing collective organizations without leaders; of creating social change primarily through small groups in which each individual can play a large part in determining the group's direction; of creating social change primarily through alternative institutions; and of making one's personal relations as egalitarian as one's political relations, are anarchist in inspiration. (The last often has been espoused by socialists as well). All of these ideas have been adopted by many radical feminists.

Emphasis on change through local community pressure rather than traditional legal institutions is another anarchist concept. When someone says, for example, "Let's deal with rape, woman abuse, or pornography without involving the state, because the state is racist, classist, and prone to censorship. Let's get the community involved in these problems so that men who abuse women in these ways will be censured by their own communities"—she is advocating an anarchist solution. Generally, relying on direct action by individuals rather than on the enforcement of laws by police is an anarchist approach.

Anarchist tactics can be either violent or non-violent. Spontaneous mass revolts, planned sit-ins, and takeovers of buildings all can be anarchist tactics. So can building alternative community services.

Radical feminism focuses more specifically on the oppression of women than does anarchism. Although left-wing anarchists certainly mention patriarchy and oppression within the family, the anarchists' message is less clear because it may focus on the institution of the family as oppressive without identifying who (men) is doing the oppressing.

An article by Temma Kaplan on pre-Civil War Spain shows how this lack of clarity was a weakness in the anarchist movement there. Anarchists suggested that the family was oppressive and ought to be abolished, but opposed women's entry into the workplace as a threat to male workers—thus leaving women with no options. The women turned away from anarchism, understandably.[12]

Radical feminist writers who emphasize the end of oppression or of relations of dominance as such, not simply of men by women, are expressing an anarchist principle. These writers include Ti-Grace Atkinson, Adrienne Rich, and many others (see

Chapter 12). The many radical feminists who emphasize working in small groups and developing the collective process are espousing anarchist principles.

Anarchist feminist writers, such as Carol Erlich and Peggy Kornegger, have emphasized small groups, collective process, a rejection of relationships based on dominance, and community work or direct action to change society. Kornegger has written that women seem almost intuitively to form nonhierarchical, informal groups,[13] a concept similar to the idea of worldwide women's culture expressed in the radical feminist "Fourth World Manifesto" and in Lisa Leghorn and Katherine Parker's 1981 book, *Woman's Worth*.[14]

Marxism and Radical Feminism

What has *radical* feminism derived from marxism? I am not at the moment asking what socialist feminism has gained from marxism.

Radical feminism has derived several concepts from marxism: the idea that there are groups or classes of exploiters and exploited, or oppressors and oppressed; the idea that this situation is not permanent, that the oppressed can fight against and overcome not only individual oppressors but whole class systems; and the concept of dialectics as means of explaining this process of change.

Virtually all radical feminists define themselves as anti-capitalist. Many could call themselves socialist in the sense that they want means of production to be socially owned. Owned *collectively*, but not necessarily by the state—or, many radical feminists would say, definitely not by the state. Radical feminist theory is a development of socialist theory (as well as of anarchist theory) which incorporates aspects of the socialist theoretical tradition.

Marxism defines the oppressed group, the proletariat, in its present condition, primarily in negative terms. The group is defined by its oppression. In order to overcome this oppressed and inferior state, it must end its definition as a separate class by ending the whole class system.

The branch of radical feminism that maintains that it is necessary to end the whole sex class system, to end all distinctions between women and men, has an intellectual link, then, to marxism. There is also a similarity in that members of this branch, such as Shulamith Firestone and Ti-Grace Atkinson, tend to define women's current and past historical condition as a degraded state. To be a woman to these feminists means simply to be oppressed.

Socialist feminism takes various forms. Some socialist feminists view economic class as the primary or key oppression to fight, but are very concerned about the oppression of women. Other socialist feminists and some radical feminists say they see sex and class, or sex, class and race, as equally key, and say the oppressions must be worked on simultaneously. However, socialist feminists use the vocabulary and generally the methodology of marxism (a model focused on economic class) as their main means of analysis. They have already decided that marxism is the most appropriate radical system of thought and seek to modify it, sometimes extensively.

Radical feminists generally have not yet decided that one particular method or system of thought is a more appropriate tool or method of analysis than others. They may write in more varied styles than socialist feminists. Radical feminists sometimes use methods or styles derived from marxism, but they also use many others.

Radical feminists who have used marxist terminology include Shulamith Firestone, who discussed sex as dialectic and began by paraphrasing Friedrich Engels.[15] (See page 50, below). Kate Millett also takes Engels as a point of departure, both praising his analysis of patriarchal marriage and the family and criticizing his explanation of the patriarchal takeover as inadequate.[16] Other early radical feminists, such as Ti-Grace Atkinson and the members of Redstockings, frequently used the concept of class, taken from marxism, to apply to the relations between women and men, and brought a socialist or marxist concept of class struggle to feminism.

One fundamental marxist concept that radical feminists have used is alienation, which was the subject of some of Karl Marx's early writings that were not accessible until the 1930s or widely read until the 1950s. Orthodox marxists still discredit these works, saying that Marx hadn't really found himself at the time, but rediscovery of this writing has formed the core of contemporary European (both western and eastern) marxism.

For Marx, the concept of alienation meant that all human beings have a particularly human capacity to do creative work consciously, with a goal in mind, but that some people have taken control of the work of others, alienating them from it. The ability to do creative, purposeful work was what he considered the central human quality. Other areas of life, such as sexuality, he saw as more "animal." Certainly, a feminist can be critical of this mind/body dichotomy that belittles both sexuality and reproduction.[17]

However, the concept of alienation can be useful for feminists. Almost all aspects of most women's lives—production, reproduction, sexual expression—have been alienated under male supremacy. Women's capacities have been used to profit others. What women have created has been taken from them, alienated from them, considered more important than women who produce it are in themselves: the production of children, domestic services and sexual services often are valued more than the women who provide them. This is alienation.

Catharine A. MacKinnon has used Marx's concept of alienation to discuss sexuality. She suggests, "Sexuality is to feminism what work is to marxism: that which is most one's own, yet most taken away."[18]

Not all radical feminists agree with MacKinnon that sexuality in feminism is analogous to work in marxism. Some see sexuality and work as equally important human capacities that can be alienated or suppressed. Radical feminists like Lisa Leghorn and Christine Delphy have focused on economics.[19]

One might ask whether the difference between radical feminism and socialist feminism is primarily a question of method and whether the two theories have the same long- and short-term goals.

If the goal is a society in which resources are shared collectively, the division of labor based on sexual differences is eliminated, women and men are integrated, and the social importance of gender roles is eliminated, then many radical and socialist feminists have similar long-term goals. However, those lesbian feminists whose long-term goal is to have a separate women's society or to give women more power than men in the long run have a more serious difference with socialist feminists.

In short-term goals, more radical feminists than socialist feminists emphasize establishing independent power bases for women as women. The radical feminist emphasis is more likely to be on women as a class seizing power from men as a class.

However, some socialist feminists have acknowledged the need for a greater power base for women than exists in any socialist countries.

Strategic emphasis tends to be different. Radical feminists are more likely to focus on violence against women, on fostering lesbianism and critiquing heterosexuality, or on working primarily on issues such as reproductive control and housework that relate to women's oppression as women. They may put more emphasis than socialist feminists on having all-women's organizations in all work on feminist issues. However, some socialist feminists also work on issues such as violence against women and reproductive freedom.

Socialist feminist thinking is growing increasingly similar to radical feminism. Socialist feminist Zillah Eisenstein now uses the idea of "sex class" as well as economic class.[20] In *The Radical Future of Liberal Feminism*, she says that all feminism has a radical basis in its assumption that there are classes in society, that men as a class oppress women as a class. "All feminism is also radically feminist in that women's identity as a sexual class underlies this claim [that women are independent from men]."[21]

Socialist feminists such as Heidi Hartmann in her essay, "The Unhappy Marriage of Marxism and Feminism: Towards a More Progressive Union," have recognized that it is possible for a "socialist" system to be patriarchal. (That is, it is possible for a country that publicly espouses socialism to be patriarchal; this does not mean that a country could be truly socialist and also patriarchal). Hartmann recognizes that men have a considerable amount of power through patriarchy; they may prefer this power to changing radically. "Men have more to lose than their chains."[22]

With all of these sources of thought—the Black movement, existentialism, anarchism, marxism, and others—the idea that feminists should either ask marxist questions or, as Juliet Mitchell suggests, come up with marxist answers ("We should ask the feminist questions but try to come up with Marxist answers").[23] too rigidly predetermines what feminism shall be. Marxism is only one of the sets of ideas that has contributed to the development of feminism.

Radical feminist theorist Catharine A. MacKinnon suggests in a 1983 *Signs* article that "socialist feminism has often amounted to socialism applied to women, liberal feminism has often amounted to liberalism applied to women. Radical feminism is feminism applied to women."[24] She calls radical feminism "feminism unmodified." One could either say, like MacKinnon, that it is unmodified, or one could say that it has been modified, or affected by, or has borrowed from practically every other progressive theory—which may amount to an independent, and idiosyncratic, theory.

There are many indications that the different theories of feminism are converging. Socialist feminists are more ready to criticize the state and to work on issues not primarily concerned with jobs or labor. Radical feminists talk about class—as indeed, they always have, but more so. Lesbian feminists demonstrate against Reagan/Bush administration policies. This growing similarity does not mean that convergence will or should be complete. It is implausible for a large movement to have a single focus or ideology. The existence of such a single focus or ideology probably would be an indication that a movement or group is being controlled from a single center, which no part of the feminist movement is.

Theory Under Fire

In the 1980s, some feminists have become uncomfortable with feminist theory or the very idea of theory. Theory involves abstraction: it discusses people as groups as well as individuals.

Susan Griffin has expressed discomfort with theory, or, as she says, with ideology. (One person's theory is another person's ideology).

In a 1982 *Signs* article, Griffin wrote:

> But a speculation about dialogue is also a speculation about ideology. For so often we speak as if my questions and your answers, my statements and your responses, were all written down somewhere in a great codicil of conversations...as if it were recorded that there must be an 'I' and a 'you,' the 'you' corresponding to the inevitable 'other': the enemy.
>
> What if all our efforts toward liberation are determined by an ideology which despite our desire for a better world leads us inevitably back to the old paradigm of suffering?
>
> And now I begin to suspect that all ideology must share a hidden tendency. For beyond a just description of the truth, an ideology holds the promise that one may control reality with the mind, assert the ideal as more real than reality, or place idea as an authority over nature...

And with this promise, always, inevitably, no matter what the ideology, the idea of the other is born. For another must become a symbol and a scapegoat for the ideologist's own denied knowledge that this ideology is not more real than reality...

And moreover ideology makes over the real, material enemy —one who has actual power over our lives, or who actually poses a danger—into an inhuman entity...[25]

Griffin has long been wary of categorizing. In her book *Women and Nature*, she says it is men who categorize. However, it is not clear how one can discuss society without developing categories —or recognizing categories that have been imposed on us. To call others "categorizers" or "ideologists" is also to categorize.

In recent years, feminists have increasingly been criticized— with some of the criticism coming from within the ranks—for "universalism." "Universalism," to critics, means assuming that women's situation is either the same or similar in all societies. White western feminists have been particularly likely to believe that all women are like them, critics say.

Some feminists see generalization as suspect, as universalism.

For instance, Chandra Malpede Mohanty of Cornell University, speaking at the "After *The Second Sex*: New Directions Feminist Theory" conference at the University of Pennsylvania in 1984, said that such terms as "division of labor" and "production" and "reproduction" were western-biased and might not be useful for analyzing non-western societies.[26] One should not have an *a priori* assumption that women are unequal to men in societies outside one's own, Mohanty said.

But feminists have challenged the assumption that it is possible to look at anything objectively, without assumptions. To conceal or repress one's assumptions will not remove them. Trying to formulate and make public as many of one's assumptions as possible at least allows others to evaluate them.

Eliminating such analytical concepts as "division of labor" could leave us without a means of learning whether there is inequality in a society, not only inequality based on gender roles but also based on economic class or race or ethnicity.

Generalization is a necessary part of analysis. Eliminate generalization and the world becomes a cluster of confusing, unrelated facts. There is some difference, however, between descriptive and *pre*scriptive generalization. Of course, all generalizations are in a sense normative. Labeling an act "rape," for instance, is descriptive but also implies that the act is undesirable. Words are not neutral.

Most feminists—of all races—assume that in many, most, or virtually all societies, women work at particular forms of labor because they are women and are often confronted with particular forms of violence because they are women. It is not clear how feminists could unsay this assumption in the interest of abandoning universalism.

Descriptive universalism might say that women in most societies face many forms of control over their work and sexual lives —with variations, of course. Prescriptive universalism would say that all women must follow the same strategy, such as lesbian separatism or taking up arms, to overcome these conditions.

Caroline Whitbeck wrote in a 1984 paper that when we as feminists use the term "we," the term really should include only those who have the opportunity to criticize what is said. Otherwise, feminists may not see other women as selves, she writes.[27]

But there are some women whom feminists must speak for, until they are in a situation where their voices can be heard. Some women in the rich northern countries as well as Third World countries have no access to the media, and live in such controlled environments that they cannot get out of their houses. Only people with a greater share of liberty may be able to say publicly what these women need to live. We must speak out, and later they can tell us if we were wrong in some ways.

A major task of developing both philosophy and politics—and political and social theory—is to determine what human beings need to live and how those needs can be satisfied. We cannot give up these tasks, even if they may seem universalist. Saying that genocide or rape is universally wrong is universalist, but necessary.

We must, it seems to me, make even more speculative assumptions based on our own experience. Western feminists have had opportunities for choices that few women have ever had, and we must share what we have learned from these experiences.

For instance, some of us can assert that it is a loss in women's lives not to be able to choose whether to have deep sexual relationships with women, to have only socially prescribed sexual roles. (Certainly there has been freedom to do this in some Third World societies, as in some African marriages between women. But as far as we know, such opportunities are the exception, as are societies that offer them.) We owe it to other women to tell them about possible choices that they may not yet perceive as choices.

Although northern feminists legitimately have ideas to share, there also is a need to respect the priorities of Third World women. Women who need food and shelter or an end to neo-colonial warfare in their countries need support, as do those who want to have fewer children. Feminist theories are not really universal unless they take into account the situation of all women.

There are many feminist theories, even within radical feminism and lesbian feminism. There are far more if one includes the many theories of socialist, anarchist and liberal feminism.

All of these feminisms should be universal. *Each* of them should be universal. That is, all of them should address the situation of all women in some way. Theories about violence against women, theories of coalition politics, lesbian separatism, anarchist feminism, theories of reform—all should address how their theory will affect women of all nations, races, classes and ages, or how they could fit into a theory that includes all women.

Not every woman can follow every theory or strategy. A strategy is not necessarily invalid because not all women want to or could follow it. But proponents of every strategy can be aware of other strategies and evaluate whether other theories can be complementary on a strategic level.

Ultimately, the only way to create theories that approach understanding women's condition universally is for women from all over the world to create the theories. The problem of universalism is not so much a flaw in generalization *per se* as in who is creating the theory. This is changing as Women of Color living in northern countries and women in Third World countries develop theories. Sharing access to ideas and research resources is the responsibility of northern feminists.

Feminist theory is diverse both in its origins and its contents, as this chapter has shown. Given this background, it is likely that feminist theory will become even more diverse as more women participate in shaping it.

Part Two

The Origins of
Male Dominance

Chapter 3

Against Gender

Feminists, who agree that women are and have been oppressed by men, differ greatly in their explanations of the origins of that oppression. Simone de Beauvoir offered several possible explanations. Socialist feminists often say that there was an original harmony between the sexes that was shattered by the discovery of paternity and the development of private property, but they emphasize the particular development of women's oppression in the industrial era under capitalism. They generally maintain that women in pre-capitalist societies had more productive work and more dignity.

Radical feminists have two basic approaches which differ greatly; in fact, they are almost opposite. Radical feminists of the late 1960s maintained that women have always been oppressed by the categorization of the human species into men and women; the categorization is unnecessary and it serves male domination.

Some lesbian feminist and radical feminist writers have suggested, on the other hand, that the old idea that men are biologically more violent and aggressive is true. Conservative (usually male) sociobiologists say that men are basically more aggressive, but they maintain that this aggressiveness is desirable for the species. Lesbian and radical feminists who say that men are more aggressive than women see aggression as undesirable and highly destructive to humanity.

Not all of the women who maintain that men are more violent (or more capable of violence) are lesbians; not all of those who maintain that there is no essential difference, but only socially created differences, are heterosexual. Among those who maintain that men are fundamentally different from women due to biology, some believe that women were always oppressed by men—but many believe that women had an earlier period of power. Not all of those who believe that there was once a time when women had more power or a period of matriarchy are biological determinists.

Individual feminist theorists have developed a variety of approaches. A study of these approaches in contemporary theory properly begins with Simone de Beauvoir.

Simone de Beauvoir: Ambiguous Cause

Simone de Beauvoir's assertions about the origins of oppression and sex differences, as stated in *The Second Sex*, are dual: She believes that women's biology is a real handicap that has adversely affected women's position in the world, but she also believes that "woman" is only an idea, a category created by men in order to have someone to oppress.

Beauvoir sees the idea of femininity as a destructive myth, like racist and anti-semitic myths about Blacks and Jews. She does not deny that there are "women" in the world today, but she does deny that "woman" is an eternally valid category, that there will always be something called "woman." Such socially created groups exist now and must work to end their existence as "others."

> To decline to accept such notions as the eternal feminine, the Black soul, the Jewish character, is not to deny that Jews, Blacks, women exist today—this denial does not represent a liberation for those concerned, but rather a flight from reality.[1]

Beauvoir asks whether there are women.

> ...Every female human being is not necessarily a woman; to be considered so she must share in that mysterious and threatened reality known as femininity. Is this attribute secreted by the ovaries? Or is it a Platonic essence, a product of the philosophic imagination?[2]

Beauvoir does see the creation of woman as a product of the imagination. Her existentialist background leads her to disbelieve in "essences" (intrinsic qualities). She sees "femininity" as artificial because it must be inculcated.

UPI/BETTMAN NEWSPHOTOS

Simone de Beauvoir (1974)

According to Beauvoir, social differentiation based on sex was not necessitated by inherent differences. Nor is such differentiation—even in its physical aspects—a biological necessity for a species, she points out. It is only one possible adaptation. (Granted, it is the only adaptation taken by mammals, or most vertebrates).

> The perpetuation of the species does not necessitate sexual differentiation... We can imagine a parthenogenetic or hermaphroditic society.[3]

Even if there is no biological necessity for "women," Beauvoir suggests there may have been psychological necessity—or perceived necessity—for their creation by men. She suggests that there is an instinctive social need to differentiate, and hence to define, to perceive as lesser, to oppress. She does not say that men inherently have more of this instinct than women, but that they were able to make use of it because of women's child-bearing. The existence of this inherent instinct she derived, apparently, from the work of her existentialist companion, Jean-Paul Sartre.

She uses Sartre's category of "the Other":

> The category of the *Other* is as primordial as consciousness itself. In the most primitive societies, in the most ancient mythologies, one finds the expression of a duality—that of the Self and the Other. This duality was not originally attached to the division of the sexes; it was not dependent upon any material facts.[4]

Here Beauvoir seems to assume that there are some "essential," inherent, permanent, rather abstract features of human nature—the sort of thing she said she didn't believe in: Self and Other.

Not only are there individuals who differentiate between Self and Other, but these individuals band together in groups, finding it more comfortable to believe that there are other individuals with whom they have something in common, and thus establishing another group that does not possess whatever the selected traits are.

> ...No group ever sets itself up as the One without at once setting up the Other over against itself...Things become clear...if, following Hegel, we find in consciousness itself a fundamental hostility toward every other consciousness; the subject can be posed only in being opposed...[5]

So, Beauvoir maintains that consciousness is basically hostile, rather than altruistic or cooperative.

According to Hegel's "master/slave" dialectic, which Beauvoir apparently accepts, a person asserts his consciousness by becoming someone else's master. He cannot be complete without someone to observe his mastery. He risks his life to obtain this status; presumably, the slave has not been willing to risk his or hers, and that is why he or she is a slave. (Although she feels that this framework may be more accurate to describe the condition of women than of slaves, Beauvoir may not have taken note of the racist and insulting tones of this perception of slaves). Beauvoir sees women as resisting less than male slaves have:

> The advantage of the master, he says, comes from his affirmation of Spirit as against Life through the fact that he risks his own life; but in fact the conquered slave has known the same risk. Whereas woman is basically an existent who gives Life and does not risk her life; between her and the male there has been no combat.[6]

Her acceptance of this line of reasoning may show why Beauvoir seems to apportion a share of the blame for women's situation to women: Sartre had maintained that, if a person is operating "in good faith," she or he must always see that there is some choice. Thus, for an existentialist, the slave has no excuse *not* to reject slavery and operate as a free being—even if the price is death.

Despite the apparently active, conquering model of the master and slave, Beauvoir does not believe that a particular action or series of actions led to men's domination of women, their establishing Woman as the Other. Rather, the process evolved with human consciousness itself.

> Throughout history they have always been subordinated to men, and hence their dependency is not the result of a historical event or a social change—it was not something that *occurred*. The reason why otherness in this case seems to be an absolute is in part that it lacks the contingent or incidental nature of historical facts. A condition brought about at a certain time can be abolished at some other time.[7]

This sort of insistence that the establishment of women's oppression did not happen in history is one reason why socialist feminists have charged some radical feminists with being "ahistorical," lacking a sense of history. This idea that women's oppression always was present, can be traced to Beauvoir.

If the oppression of women did not happen in time, or in history, then can men be held responsible for it? Although existentialists are often concerned with questions of individual and collective responsibility, Beauvoir does not seem to be blaming men much more than women.

On the one hand, she says:

Why is it that women do not dispute male sovereignty? No subject will readily volunteer to become the object, the inessential; it is not the Other, who, in defining himself as the Other, establishes the One.[8]

That is, women have not created male dominance. Men have, and they will not give it up.

Even more critically, she writes:

If woman seems to be the inessential which never becomes the essential, it is because she herself fails to bring about this change.[9]

But this situation is not hopeless; Beauvoir does foresee a political solution:

The reason for this is that women lack concrete means for organizing themselves into a unit which can stand face to face with the correlative unit [men]. They have no past, no history, no religion of their own...They live dispersed among the males...[10]

She outlined the basic obstacles, although perhaps underestimating the common history that women share.

Beauvoir has many negative feelings about women, in fact sees them as inferior to men in some ways. However, she believes women are capable of change.

...When an individual (or a group of individuals) is kept in a situation of inferiority, the fact is that he *is* inferior. But the significance of the verb *to be* must be rightly understood here; it is in bad faith to give it a static value when it really has the dynamic Hegelian sense of 'to have become.' Yes, women on the whole *are* today inferior to men; that is, their situation affords them fewer possibilities. The question is: Should that state of affairs continue?[11]

Of course, she thought it should not:

This accounts for our lengthy study of the biological facts; they are one of the keys to the understanding of woman. But I deny that they establish for her a fixed and inevitable destiny. They are insufficient for setting up a hierarchy of the sexes; they fail

to explain why woman is the Other; they do not condemn her
to remain in this subordinate role forever...the human species
is forever in a state of change, forever becoming.[12]

This emphasis on "becoming," on flexibility, is one of Beauvoir's
gifts to feminism.

French radical feminist writer Michèle Le Doeuf comments in
a 1979 paper that *The Second Sex* does not adequately describe the origins of women's oppression:

> ...Judging by the way de Beauvoir treats this problem the
> oppression of women is a scandal so unthinkable that she cannot
> arrive at assigning it an origin or a sufficient cause. Take the
> procedure of Part I: she examines in succession three possible
> explanations—and rejects them all. She eliminates in turn
> ...first biology, then psychoanalysis, finally historical material-
> ism,...as all these explanations prove successively inadequate...
>
> One ends up, then, with the magic of an oppression without a
> fundamental cause...because women's oppression is not foun-
> ded on anything, it has thus become necessary to invent a host of
> devices and institutional props to create and maintain it.[13]

Le Doeuf suggests that Beauvoir deduced women's oppression
from her own experience, rather than primarily from theoretical
work.

Shulamith Firestone: Origins of 'Otherness'

In her book *The Dialectic of Sex*, Shulamith Firestone took
Beauvoir as her starting point. Firestone suggests, however, that
there is no primordial concept of Otherness, but that the idea of
Otherness arises from the woman/man relationship. Firestone
thus sees Otherness as more of a group than an individual
consciousness. Rather than a collection of selves bristling with
hostility, ready to dominate other selves, there were men who came
to see that they could dominate women and to feel superior to
them. (Without the postulate of an uneasy individual self, however,
why the assertion of domination at all?)

Firestone writes:

> The immediate assumption of the layman that the unequal
> division of the sexes is 'natural' may be well-founded...Unlike
> economic class, sex class sprang directly from a biological
> reality: Men and women were created different, and not equally

privileged. Although, as de Beauvoir points out, this difference of itself did not necessitate the development of a class system—the domination of one group by another—the reproductive *functions* of these differences did. The biological family is an inherently unequal power distribution.[14]

She is saying that bearing children is no privilege—freedom from bearing them is. The organs don't produce the sex class system, the use of them does. Having a uterus is not the problem; being a member of the only group that bears children is.

She sees the family as both oppressive and universal.

...The biological family that we have described has existed everywhere throughout time. Even in matriarchies where woman's fertility is worshipped, and the father's role is unknown or unimportant, perhaps not the genetic father, there is still some dependence of the female and the infant on the male.[15]

For Firestone, biology does play a part in women's oppression. Biology is not neutral: It can be painful, even oppressive, although it evolved rather than being the product of conscious decision. She speaks of the "oppressive power structure set up by Nature and reinforced by man."[16]

For Firestone, bearing a child without conscious choice, even though biologically "natural," is oppressive for a conscious being. Pregnancy and birth are painful.

From biological differences grew the division of labor, and hence classes that were more or less privileged.

...The natural reproductive difference between the sexes led directly to the first division of labor based on sex, which is at the origins of all further division into economic and cultural classes and is possibly even at the root of all caste (discrimination based on sex and other biologically determined characteristics such as race, age, etc.).[17]

From the creation of the first classes, women and men, grew other classes. The origins of the oppression of women are the origins of oppression *per se*, Firestone writes.

Women's oppression has been so tied to biology—so "natural" —that Firestone sees the possibility of ending this oppression arising only with the development of technology, such as birth control:

Though there have always been women rebels in history, the conditions have never before existed that would enable women to effectively overthrow their oppressive roles. Women's capacity for reproduction was urgently needed by the society and even if it hadn't been, effective birth control methods were not available.[18]

If oppression was as inevitably linked to women's biology as Firestone says, how can men be much to blame? Did men have any alternative but to oppress women? But one does not generally speak of an act as oppressive if it is necessary. I am uncomfortable with the idea that this structure of relationships was necessary.

Even if biological differences were the basis of women's oppression, Firestone does not feel this means that differences between women and men are eternal. Even if they always existed, they do not always have to exist:

> But to grant that the sexual imbalance of power is biologically based is not to lose our case. We are no longer just animals. And the kingdom of Nature does not reign absolute. As Simone de Beauvoir herself says:
>
> 'The theory of historical materialism has brought to light some important truths. Humanity is not an animal species, it is a historical reality.'

Firestone then concludes, "Thus, the 'natural' is not necessarily a 'human' value. Humanity has begun to outgrow nature."[19]

Like Beauvoir, Firestone tends to see women as not having done the most important work of humanity. She quotes Beauvoir as saying, "Perhaps, however, *if productive work had remained within her strength*, woman would have accomplished *with man* the conquest of nature..."

Firestone adds, "Thus it was woman's reproductive biology that accounted for her original and continued oppression, and not some sudden patriarchal revolution."[20]

Also like Beauvoir, she sees the oppression of women as something that was not caused by a dramatic series of actions, but rather as something happening far back in pre-history.

Unlike some later writers, Firestone is totally critical of the idea that a matriarchy ever existed, that there was a time when women were free, or that such an alternative could be a solution for the future.

> Matriarchy is a stage on the way to patriarchy, to man's fullest realization of himself; he goes from worshipping Nature through women to conquering it.

Though it's true that woman's lot worsened considerably under patriarchy, she never had it good; for despite all the nostalgia it is not hard to prove that matriarchy was never an answer to women's fundamental oppression. Basically it was no more than a different means of counting lineage and inheritance, one which...did not allow women into the society as equals. To be worshipped is not freedom; for worship still takes place in someone else's head, and that head belongs to Man.[21]

Beauvoir and Firestone could be seen as ambivalent on the question of inherent sexual differences, although they both deny that sexual differences need to be a permanent aspect of human life. In fact, they believe it is crucial to end them. But if differences go further back than recorded history, if the different functions or division of labor based on these differences was inevitable throughout most of human history, is this so unlike a concept of inherent differences?

Differences Not Innate

Some other early radical feminists said more absolutely that behavioral differences between women and men were not inherent, but were class differences, created by culture. Kate Millett advocates this position in her book *Sexual Politics*:

Patriarchal religion, popular attitude, and to some degree, science as well assumes these psycho-social distinctions to rest upon biological differences between the sexes, so that where culture is acknowledged as shaping behavior, it is said to do no more than cooperate with nature. Yet the temperamental distinctions created in patriarchy ('masculine' and 'feminine' personality traits) do not appear to originate in human nature, those of role and status still less.

The heavier musculature of the male, a secondary sexual characteristic and common among mammals, is biological in origin but is also culturally encouraged through breeding, diet and exercise. Yet it is hardly an adequate category on which to base political relations *within civilization*. Male supremacy, like other political creeds, does not finally reside in physical strength but in the acceptance of a value system which is not biological. Superior physical strength is not a factor in political relations — vide those of race and class.[22]

If superior physical strength is seen as including superior weapons, it is indeed a factor in political relations, including race and class.

Millett thinks it is possible that patriarchy was preceded by some other social form, which she says would mean that physical strength was not a sufficient reason for the origin of patriarchy. She says that "conjecture about origins is always frustrated by lack of certain evidence. Speculation about prehistory...remains nothing but speculation."[23]

She thinks the discovery of paternity may have been crucial to the origins of patriarchy.[24] This is Engels' position.

Like Beauvoir and Firestone, Millett sees the female role as more stultifying than the male role, more animalistic and less human because it emphasizes breeding rather than more abstract activities.

> The limited role allotted the female tends to arrest her at the level of biological experience. Therefore, nearly all that can be described as distinctly human rather than animal activity (in their own way animals also give birth and care for their young) is largely reserved for the male.[25]

Millett was among the first feminists to describe contemporary male domination as patriarchy, rather than reserving that term for societies that are more literally father-dominated.

> ...Our society, like all other historical civilizations, is a patriarchy. The fact is evident at once if one recalls that the military, industry, technology, universities, science, political office, and finance—in short every avenue of power within the society, including the coercive force of the police, is entirely in male hands...The principles of patriarchy appear to be twofold: Male shall dominate female, elder male shall dominate younger.[26]

Millett takes a "common sense" approach toward differences between the sexes: It is impossible to know what is intrinsic until you have tried to change it. Only after male supremacy is ended will it be possible to tell whether there are any differences of behavior or preference that were not created simply to foster male supremacy.

> Whatever the 'real' differences between the sexes may be, we are not likely to know them until the sexes are treated differently, that is alike.[27]

Millett is one of those who had the radical feminist idea that male domination was and is the model for other kinds of domination.

> However muted its present appearance may be, sexual dominion obtains nevertheless as perhaps the most pervasive ideology of our culture and provides its most fundamental concept of power.[28]

The "Redstockings Manifesto" is perhaps the clearest statement of that belief that women's oppression is the key to the origins of oppression.

> Male supremacy is the oldest, most basic form of domination. All other forms of exploitation and oppression (racism, capitalism, imperialism, etc.) are extensions of male supremacy: men dominate women, a few men dominate the rest. All power structures throughout history have been male-dominated and male-oriented.[29]

Redstocking Barbara Leon expresses (in a 1973 essay) the idea that women are a class created by men, and sees them existing as a group only because of men.

> Feminists see women as an oppressed class, a class which can only exist in relation to another oppressing class, men, and only for a purpose—the exploitation of labor, which in the case of women also means reproductive labor. The only radical goal is the elimination of all classes.[30]

The late 1960s radical feminists generally did not think men were inherently more violent than women. Men had learned to become violent in their role as oppressors. As Boston radical feminists Roxanne Dunbar and Lisa Leghorn wrote:

> Females or black people who are programmed to a similar [to white males] aggressiveness are as thoroughly diseased and maddened as males in those roles. So neither racial inferiority nor male genes can account for the white man's sickness.[31]

Some radical feminists did see men using force as an original means of obtaining control over women, as this excerpt from an essay by Dunbar illustrates:

> What was restricted for women was not physical labor, but mobility.
> Because women's reproductive capacity led to her being forced into sedentary (immobile, not inactive) life, the female developed community life...

In a very real sense, the hunter was less civilized than the female. He had little political (governing) experience. The experience of the hunter had led him to value dominance; he had become unsuited for living as equals in the community, because he knew only how to overpower and conquer the prey. Other masculine values, formed in the transient existence as hunters, included competition (with the prey) and violence (killing the prey)...Though hunters worked together and developed a sense of brotherhood, their brotherhood developed outside community life.

Gradually in some cases, but often through violent upheaval, former hunters took over female communities, suppressing the female through domination and even enslavement.[32]

Ti-Grace Atkinson: Male Behavior *is the Enemy*

The radical feminist Ti-Grace Atkinson wrote that "I always understood that it was male *behavior* that was the enemy..." rather than men as biological beings.[33] Atkinson asserts that men are not inherently more aggressive or oppressive than women—but her stated reasons for this belief are not attempts to prove that it is true, but to point out how difficult solutions would be if it weren't true.

Some people say that men are naturally, or biologically, aggressive. But this leaves us at an impasse. If the values of society are power-oriented, there is no chance that men would agree to be medicated into an humane state.

The other alternative that has been suggested is to eliminate men as biologically incapable of humane relationships and therefore a menace to society. I can sympathize with the frustration and rage that leads to this suggestion.

But the proposal to eliminate men, as I understand it, assumes that men constitute a kind of social disease, and that by 'men' is meant those individuals with certain typical genital characteristics...It may be that as in other mental derangements, and I do believe that men behave in a mentally deranged manner toward women, there is a biochemical correspondence, but this would be ultimately behaviorally determined, not genetically.

I believe that the sex roles—both male and female—must be destroyed, not the individuals who happen to possess either a penis or a vagina, or both, or neither. But many men I have

spoken with see little to choose from between the two positions
and feel that without the role they'd just as soon die.[34]

Although Atkinson sometimes used the term "roles," she did not
equate the male and female role or imply that men and women
were equally restricted. To emphasize roles too much would be to
de-emphasize class.

Even the outspoken Atkinson was perhaps pulling her punches
here. Marxists do not refer to capitalists as "the capitalist role" or
speak of "capitalist behavior." It is possible to say that one
opposes capitalists without it being assumed that one believes
that capitalists are biologically inferior. Why can't one say the
same about men, that as a class they are at present the enemy,
without being perceived as saying that they are genetically inferior or deserving of extinction? They simply hold unjust power.

The Feminists, a group of which Atkinson was an active member, put out a statement saying:

> THE FEMINISTS discarded the notion generally accepted by popu-
> lar feminism that the sex-role system defines the oppression of
> women or that our enemy is the male role. The inadequacy of the
> sex-role theory of oppression becomes obvious when one consid-
> ers its implication: that both men and women are oppressed by
> their respective sex-roles. Which is comparable to: both slaves
> and masters are oppressed by the slave system. By adopting this
> theory the women's movement has managed to skirt the issue of
> power and its relationship to oppression...
>
> Men, as the only possible embodiment of the male role and as
> the first embodiment of the Oppressor role, are the enemies and
> Oppressors of women. The female role is the product of the
> male role: It is the female's self-defense against the external
> coercions imposed by the male role. But because the female role
> is the internal adjustment of the female to the male role, the
> female role stabilizes the role system. Both the male role and
> the female role must be annihilated.[35]

To Atkinson, sex in itself was not a sufficient reason for the
original division of people into groups. Unlike Firestone and
Beauvoir, she imagines, at least for the sake of argument, a society
in which women were not yet oppressed by men.

> It is reasonable to assume that at some period in history the
> population was politically undifferentiated; let's call that mass
> 'Mankind' (generic).

The first dichotomous division of this mass is said to have been on the grounds of sex: male and female. But the genitals *per se* would be no more grounds for the human race to be divided in two than skin color or height or hair color. The genitals, in connection with a particular activity, have the *capacity* for the initiation of the reproductive process. But, I submit, it was because one half the human race bears the *burden* of the reproductive *process* and because man, the 'rational' animal, had the wit to take advantage of that, that the child-bearers, or the 'beasts of burden,' were corralled into a political class. The biologically contingent burden of childbearing was equivocated into a political (or necessary) penalty, thereby modifying those individuals' definition thereby defined from the human to the functional—or animal.[36]

In other words, at some point men used women's biology—their child-bearing capacity—as both a reason for, and a means of enslaving them.

Atkinson does not underestimate the difficulty of overthrowing classes, but she sees attributing differences to changeable class structures as more ethically acceptable than the idea of destroying human beings without leaving open the possibility that they might be able to give up their class allegiances.

What is extremely difficult...but necessary, is for the Oppressed to cure themselves (destroy the female role), to throw off the Oppressor, and to help the Oppressor to cure himself (to destroy the male role). It is superhuman, but the only alternative—the elimination of males as a biological group—is subhuman.[37]

When she talks about changing men, Atkinson is not talking about hand-holding and affectionate persuasion, as is clear from the tone of her work.

Like Beauvoir, Atkinson sees the origins of oppression in fundamental human impulses. Although Atkinson no doubt derives her ideas from Beauvoir, she emphasizes fear of being alone as a reason for human aggression and the search for an "Other," while Beauvoir emphasizes hostility. Atkinson writes:

We see another human being as physically complete and autonomous (powerful) and ourselves as abbreviated thus incomplete (powerless)...

Man feels the need of something, like Himself, as an 'extension.' This presents a problem since *all* Men [she means women, too] suffer this same need. All Men are looking for potency—the substantive power to close the gap between their bodily and mental powers. It seems clear that, once the resolution takes this external direction, some Men—ideally half (thus, one for each)—would have to catch *other* Men in some temporary depression of consciousness...and at some physical disadvantage. This temporary depletion of Self provides the opportunity to simultaneously devour the mind of a member of the selected class and to appropriate their substance to oneself.

It is this process that I call 'metaphysical cannibalism'...This process absorbs the free will of the victim and destroys the evidence that the oppressor and the victim are the Same. The principle of metaphysical cannibalism seemed to meet both needs of Man: to gain potency (power) and to vent frustration (hostility).[38]

The oppressor does not resolve his aloneness by metaphysical cannibalism, but only increases his appetite for more control.

Metaphysical cannibalism does not solve the dilemma posed by human rationality for either the Oppressor or the Oppressed. The Oppressor can only whet his appetite for power by external measures (like drugs to dull the symptom of pain) and thus increases his disease and symptoms. The Oppressed... [is] rejecting life but not quite dead, sensible enough to still feel the pain.[39]

Atkinson expands Beauvoir's theory that "woman" is male-created:

The class of women is one-half of a dichotomized class definition of society by sex. The class of women is formed by positing another class in opposition: the class of men, or the male role. Women exist as the corollaries of men, and exist as human beings only insofar as they are those corollaries...

Since the very definition of women entails that only one other class could be relevant to it, only one other class could possibly be oppressing women: the class of men...[40]

Similarly, Atkinson maintains that Blacks and other racially oppressed groups were created as groups only by white supremacists. The feminists' dilemma is that:

...It is as women—or 'females'—that women are persecuted, just as it was as slaves—or 'blacks'—that slaves were persecuted in

America. In order to improve their condition, those individuals who are today defined as women must eradicate their own definition. Women must, in a sense, commit suicide, and the journey from womanhood to a society of individuals is hazardous.[41]

For Atkinson, the oppression of women serves as a sort of model for a study of oppression because of the group's size, dispersion and prolonged history.

The class of women has several peculiar political characteristics:

(1) the class of women, or the female role, is generally agreed to be the largest single political class in history; (2) the oppression of the class of women *qua* women is stable historically and similar geographically; (3) the political class of women, or the female role, is generally agreed to be the earliest political class in history, therefore all known cultures are constructed with the oppression of women as the major foundational ingredient (i.e., the class of women is the key functional unit in all of our social, economic and political institutions and values); (4) the class of women has been dispersed over time, thereby further suppressing it, throughout later class systems: e.g., chronological, familial, religious, racial, economic.[42]

Of course, the points that Atkinson says are generally agreed are not necessarily.

Although Atkinson sees oppression as grounded in basic human fears, she does not seem to see it as inevitable. She does not blatantly say it was "necessary" or "unnecessary" in so many words, but she seems to allow for the possibility of choice. Nor does she say that men were innately more predisposed to oppress, more violent; she does say that men had the *opportunity* to oppress, because they took advantage of women's disability during childbearing. They chose to take this opportunity, and presumably did not have to do so.

Atkinson does not see the use of women by others to provide the function of childbearing and rearing as ever having been a necessary or ethically acceptable social choice. She constantly maintains that no one (and no group) has a right to use another as a mere function. This rejection of functionalism or use of other human beings as less than human, free agents is a hallmark of Atkinson's philosophy.

Female Culture

Women in the feminist movement began to become critical of entirely negative descriptions of women in contemporary and earlier societies. The "Fourth World Manifesto," written by Barbara Burris, Kathleen Barry, *et al.* in 1971, was an early expression of pride in some of the attributes that women had developed even in an oppressed condition, an assertion that inferiority of status did *not* lead to completely inferior characteristics.

The manifesto maintains that a female culture has developed—globally—and that it has desirable attributes.

> We are proud of the female culture of emotion, intuition, love, personal relationships, etc., as the most essential human characteristics. It is our male colonizers—it is the male culture—who have defined essential humanity out of their identity and who are 'culturally deprived.'
>
> We are also proud as females of our heritage of known and unknown resistance to male colonial domination and values.
>
> We are proud of the female principle and will not deny it to gain our freedom. It is only by asserting the long suppressed and ridiculed female principle that a truly human society will come about. For the split between the male and the female will only be bridged and a fully human identity developed...when the female principle and culture is no longer suppressed and male domination is ended forever.[43]

Later, the authors added a postscript insisting that their concept of the female culture did not refer to inherent characteristics. Yet, with the spread of such ideas as "the female principle" through the feminist movement, the emphasis on femaleness as good also spread:

> The female culture and the male culture are not natural; they are artificial creations of a male-dominated world. The artificial split between what has been defined as female and what has been defined as male has nothing to do with the inherent nature or potential of females or males...
>
> This 'Manifesto' was never intended to be a glorification of the female principle and culture...It would be a tragedy if women were to make our oppressed state into a virtue and a model of humanity and the new society...

Neither the male culture nor the female culture is a model for human society.[44]

But there are those who differ, who maintain that female culture is a positive model for society.

Early Mary Daly and Andrea Dworkin

In *Beyond God the Father*, published in 1973, Mary Daly maintains that men's oppression of women is not biologically inherent. Daly quotes New York radical feminist Anne Koedt as saying that "biology is not destiny, and that male and female roles are learned—indeed that they are male political constructs."[45] Daly then saw sexual differences as artificial impositions of male supremacy:

> The roles and structures of patriarchy have been developed and sustained in accordance with an artificial polarization of human qualities into the traditional sexual stereotypes. The image of the person of authority... has corresponded to the eternal masculine stereotype, which implies hyper-rationality (in reality, frequently reducible to pseudo-rationality), 'objectivity,' aggressivity, the possession of dominating and manipulative attitudes toward persons and the environment, and the tendency to construct boundaries between the self and 'the Other.' The caricature of human being represented by this stereotype depends for its existence upon the opposite caricature—the eternal feminine.[46]

"Androgyny" was how she then defined the appropriate human condition or the solution. Later her perception changed (see pages 79-81, below). In *Beyond God the Father*, Daly saw women or women's conditioning as bearing *some* of the responsibility for their oppression.

> The exploitative sexual caste system could not be perpetuated without the consent of the victims as well as of the dominant sex, and such consent is obtained through sex role socialization—a conditioning process which begins to operate from the moment we are born, and which is enforced by most institutions.[47]

In her mid-1970s book, *Woman Hating*, Andrea Dworkin says that "the culture" is the determining factor, providing sex roles that we are forced to fit into. This culture, Dworkin points out, is perpetuated by myths and fairy tales. She does not, however, delve into the origins of this woman-hating culture. Her discussion of world history begins less than a thousand years ago, with Chinese foot-binding and the burning of European women as witches.[48]

Dworkin does say that she sees man's separation of himself from nature as the source of oppression. "The separation of man from nature, man placing himself over and above it...may lead to the extinction of many forms of life."[49] She compares man's arrogance toward nature with his arrogance toward woman. In her discussion of man's attitude toward nature, she was among the first feminist theorists to allude to the possibility of nuclear destruction.

In *Woman Hating* she saw men and women as basically similar, perverted by culture. In a brief allusion to possible ways of life of tribal societies, which she admits she does not know, she imagines a time "when people functioned as part of the natural world, not yet over against it; when men and women, male and female, were whatever they were, not polar opposites, separated by dress and role into castes, fragmented pieces of some not-to-be imagined whole."[50] In other words, she thinks that early women and men did not have sex roles, that sex roles are not natural. All early myths were myths of a primal androgyne, which later myths corrupted and distorted.[51]

Subsequently, Dworkin said that the division of labor based on sex was *necessary*: "We see that the first division of labor based on biological sex originated in a fundamental survival imperative."[52] However, she felt that women's power of giving life—and the high mortality rate in childbirth—frightened men, leading to practices of protection, segregation, and slowly increasing social restriction. Men thus began to experience power by excluding women from community life, then developed a myth of female evil to justify "laws, rites and other practices which relegated women to pieces of property."[53]

Dworkin wrote that "man" and "woman" are fictions, caricatures, cultural constructs: "As models they are reductive, totalitarian, inappropriate to human becoming."[54] She therefore follows Beauvoir, without mentioning her, in seeing "woman" as a created being.

However, Dworkin adds that if there *were* two distinct, discrete biological sexes, it would be appropriate to have two discrete, sex-determined modes of human behavior. "One might argue for a liberalization of sex-based roles, but one cannot justifiably argue for their total redefinition"[55] if one accepts the premise that there are two biological sexes, she wrote. (A dangerous comment for a feminist; why should the burden of proof be on feminists to show that there aren't two sexes? Why should rights and responsibilities in society be based more on sex than on any other characteristics?)

In *Woman Hating*, she sees transsexuals, hormone research and test-tube babies as proof that there are not two, but many sexes.[56] However, in her 1983 book, *Right-wing Women*, Dworkin takes a more critical stance toward reproductive technologies, warning that women might be treated even worse by men than they already are, if women became no longer necessary for reproduction.[57]

Chapter 4

Male Biology as a Problem

Other writers came to focus on male rather than female biology as a source of problems.

Elizabeth Gould Davis, in her posthumous book *The First Sex*, states that women are by nature more intelligent than, and less violent than men. Davis had labored alone, not as part of the feminist movement. Yet her book immediately achieved considerable popularity in the movement, although it also had many critics. Essentially, Davis said that sexual differences were real and that the old division of traits into female and male represented reality (except that men had not credited women with all of the positive traits they really possess).

> Woman...is a practical idealist, a humanitarian with a strong sense of *noblesse oblige*, an altruist rather than a capitalist.[1]

Davis sees the old idea that woman is closer to nature as true, and a positive source of good.

> Woman...is the ally of nature, and her instinct is to tend, to nurture, to encourage healthy growth, and to preserve ecological balance. She is the natural leader of society and of civilization, and the usurpation of her primeval authority by man has resulted in the uncoordinated chaos that is leading the human race back to barbarism.[2]

> Man is the enemy of nature: to kill, to root up, to level off, to pollute, to destroy are his instinctive reactions.[3]

She does not see women's biology as a liability.

That woman is handicapped by her womanhood is the fault of society and not of nature.[4]

Elizabeth Gould Davis: Males as Mutants

Davis suggests that one sex *is* biologically inferior—the male. Drawing on the discovery that fetuses are initially female, she suggested that males are mutants, unnecessary genetic mistakes.

> It seems very logical that this small and twisted Y chromosome is a genetic error—an accident of nature, and that originally there was only one sex—the female...
>
> The first males were mutants, freaks produced by some damage to the genes caused perhaps by disease or a radiation bombardment from the sun.[5]

Davis does not emphasize the point that all vertebrate species undergo this "mutation" or development of two sexes.

> ...The extra X chromosome in females accounts not only for the greater freedom of girls from birth defects and congenital diseases...but also for the superior physiological makeup and the superior *intelligence* of women over men.[6]

However, she did not think that all of men's negative traits were inherent.

> Only masculine ego, an acquired characteristic not an innate one, stands in the way of a decent society [she means one ruled by women].[7]

In fact, Davis maintains that men initially accepted rule by women, which provided a better, less violent society. Male violence was less developed then, so it is not unchanging.

> Contrary to the popular impression that our early ancestors lived on warfare and violence, all the evidence, historical as well as archeological, points to the fact that man was pacific and warfare unknown before the patriarchal revolution.[8]

Davis calls killing and eating animals "a fall, or original sin."[9] She links the development of violence and oppression to killing and eating animals, which she assumes began significantly later than the development of human consciousness.

> The killing and eating of animals by man is a recent phenomenon and is related in time to the patriarchal revolution.[10]

Even before the development of patriarchy, however, men were violent, according to Davis. She quotes Robert Briffault as saying that "the male of the species was 'a marauding beast' and 'woman was his sexual prey'." She argues that "women, in order to protect themselves and their children from these marauding beasts, soon banded together and formed the first communities—manless except for the young boys of the group.[11]

Davis says the mother and child relationship is the core of civilization, the initial relationship around which civilization was founded, and the initial experience of human love; she draws on the work of Johann Jacob Bachofen (a man) to substantiate her point:

> The relationship which stands at the origin of all culture, of every virtue, of every nobler aspect of existence, is that between mother and child.[12]

Clearly, quoting men and believing their arguments was no problem for her.

Davis set up matriarchal society as a political model:

> Patriarchal peoples place more importance in property rights than in human rights and more emphasis on rigid moral conformity than on concepts of justice and mercy. Matriarchal societies, as studied by scholars from Morgan and Bachofen to Malinowski and Mead, are characterized by a real democracy in which the happiness and fulfillment of the individual supersede all other objectives of society.[13]

She maintains that the principles of justice and democracy were better served under matriarchy. She suggests that society as a whole, men included, would be better served if women ruled. This is very different from the goal of equal participation, even equal participation in revolution.

Davis sees feminism not as elimination of the oppression of women as a class and the end of all class divisions in society, but as fidelity to "the female principle," or the good attributes associated with women. Of course, she intends to end the oppression of women, but not the existence of women as a group.

> To the 'feminist' of both sexes, femininity is synonymous with the eternal female principle, connoting strength, integrity, wisdom, justice, dependability, and a psychic power foreign and therefore dangerous to the plodding masculists of both sexes.[14]

This idea of the female principle was very different from the early radical feminists' idea that sex classes were entirely male-created. However, there are points in common, in that both seek to end male domination and both are critical of the "male behavior" men have developed while in the dominant political position.

Davis' stature and the quality of her research are points of considerable controversy. Some radical feminists have suggested that Davis seemed interested only in the possible achievements of women in the distant past. Redstocking Kathie Sarachild wrote:

> Although touted as returning woman to her rightful place in history, *The First Sex* actually does much to deprive women of their place in history. Only a pre-history is discovered for women. When recorded history begins, it's all downhill. The book completely leaves out any record of the feminist struggle and advance in the 19th century.[15]

Another disturbing aspect of Davis' ancient matriarchs is that they are all Celtic and blue-eyed, wherever in the world they appear. African and Asian women did not need "white goddesses"; they had plenty of their own.

Jill Johnston: Separate Species

In 1971, following Davis, lesbian writer Jill Johnston asserted that women and men were biologically different and that biology was destiny. Male biology was linked to oppressive impulses.

> The feminist rhetoric is steeped in a denial of biological destiny. For if they can deny the biological forces that created the cultural conditions of oppression, they can start with the culture and work from the top as it were to reform things where they appeared to go amiss, and thus retain the man... But biology is not simply ancient or primeval history. Biology is right now. One can observe the constant renewal of biological imperatives creating their novel if always patriarchal forms of cultural oppression. It is impossible to disentangle biology and culture. The cultural takeover of the male is biologically motivated. All systems of inequity are rooted in some biological imperative of the male. The female was originally the self-sufficient self-recreating creature, the male one of her offspring... The cultural repression of women is rooted in womb envy.[16]

Initially, Johnston suggested, we were one sex—presumably female—and she suggests that there was a "fall from grace" when two sexes developed. She seems to be referring to biological developments rather than mere changes of definition and perception. She does not say, as Beauvoir did, that the two sexes were an intellectual construct, a male-inspired definition.

> The fall was from some primeval division into two sexes. I think any bio-analytically oriented person knows we were originally one sex.[17]

She calls these two sexes separate species:

> The female became a separate species subdued and subsumed like the other animals in the competition for survival.[18]

She does not ask why other species have two sexes.

Johnston accepts the idea that woman was closer to nature than man:

> ...The woman is parent prime, and the man in his anxiety and to become the master of himself against 'nature' (woman) in his creation of a culture as some kind of monstrous compensation for a real or at least felt inadequacy...Man is completely out of phase with nature. Nature is woman. Man is the intruder. The man who re-attunes himself with nature is the man who de-mans himself or eliminates himself as man.[19]

Johnston accepts the ideas of matriarchy and mother-right, a mother's right to her children. She sees two (presumably separate in time) origins of oppression: the development of separate sexes and a historical defeat of women by men.

> The overthrow of mother-right was *the world historical defeat of the female sex.*[20]

Johnston says she believes that matriarchy or a time of greater power for women existed, and she suggests that a *return* to such an era would be desirable.

> *We're moving backward now. We can't go back fast enough.*[21]

In other words, Johnston here abandons the concept traditionally held by many liberals and radicals, of progress and history as an unfolding of greater potential for freedom.

Johnston maintains that the difference between the sexes is desirable. She specifically rejects the radical feminist idea of ending the distinction between women and men:

I too would not like to see the distinction [between the sexes] abolished.[22]

SCUM: Man, the Incomplete Female

Some of the most intense expressions of rage at males' limitations had been written in 1967 in Valerie Solanis' "SCUM (Society for Cutting Up Men) Manifesto." (Solanis was not an activist in the organized feminist movement. She had worked for, and later shot, pop artist Andy Warhol.)

> Being an incomplete female, the male spends his life attempting to complete himself, to become female. He attempts to do this by constantly seeking out, fraternizing with and trying to live through and fuse with the female...[23]

In the 1970s, other writers followed in Solanis' lead. Particularly close in wording were the women of CLIT (Collection of Lesbian International Terrors), who published three groups of articles.

In CLIT Statement #2, published in 1974, they wrote, "males aren't human."[24]

> ...It is impossible for women and men to become more and more alike because all men are terminally male which means jealous hole/woman killer.[25]
>
> The truth of the matter, which all patriarchies since their conception have tried to suppress, is that women are not only superior sexually to men, but also intellectually and emotionally and every other way except for physical strength.[26]

Others, such as lesbian writer Rita Laporte, used gentler terms but saw men as limited.

> Only by banding together and following a leader can men find strength, for they are emotionally and spiritually weaker, more dependent and sheep-like, than women. This animal-like urge to band into groups, while giving the individual members a feeling of potency, also necessitates fighting to defend the prowess of their leader against other, exactly similar groups...
>
> Women, on the other hand, are determined by no such group pull.
>
> Women who wish to cooperate with other women do so on the human, not the animal, level. Not being pushed by instinct to fall into gangs behind a more powerful woman, they are free to join together intelligently and they are free to leave the group by intelligent choice when they feel the group is up to no good...

This makes it impossible for vast hordes of women to be led into activities destructive to the human race. At the same time it makes agreement harder to come by.[27]

LaPorte is speaking very generally. There is surely less group violence by women than by men, but one could not say that women never join or stay in fascist or violent groups.

Man: The Violent Ape

In the mid-1970s, the tendency to focus on biological sex differences continued to develop among lesbians and some heterosexual radical feminists. The (heterosexual) Susan Brownmiller's book *Against Our Will: Men, Women and Rape* was one of the catalysts in developing this tendency.

Brownmiller saw the male capacity to rape as a central factor in male/female relations, rather along the lines of the old pro-disarmament watchword that people who have a weapon may be tempted to use it.

> ...A human male can evince sexual interest in a human female at any time he pleases, and his psychologic urge is not dependent in the slightest on her biologic readiness or receptivity. What it all boils down to is that the human male can rape.
>
> Man's structural capacity to rape and woman's corresponding sexual vulnerability are as basic to the physiology of both our sexes as the primal act of sex itself...The human sex act accomplishes its historic purpose of generation of the species and it also affords some intimacy and pleasure. I have no basic quarrel with the procedure. But, nevertheless, we cannot work around the fact that in terms of human anatomy the possibility of forcible intercourse incontrovertibly exists. This single factor may have been sufficient to have caused the creation of a male ideology of rape. When men discovered that they could rape, they proceeded to do it.[28]

The comment that she has "no basic quarrel with the procedure" seems dubious considering the rest of her arguments—that "the procedure" is uniquely suitable for force.

Brownmiller sees rape as a form of social control of women by men.

Women have been raped by men, most often by gangs of men, for many of the same reasons that blacks were lynched by gangs of whites: as group punishment for being uppity, for getting out of line...[29]

Man's discovery that his genitals could serve as a weapon to generate fear must rank as one of the most important discoveries of prehistoric times, along with the use of fire and the first crude stone axe. From prehistoric times to the present, I believe, rape has played a critical function. It is nothing more or less than a conscious process of intimidation by which *all men* keep *all women* in a state of fear.[30]

Brownmiller says that rape as a form of social control is present in many societies. She cites Dr. Margaret Mead's studies of the Mundugumor and Iatmul of New Guinea and some American Plains Indians as examples of societies where rape is used to put down recalcitrant women. She also cites Robert Murphy of Columbia University on the Manduruca Indians of Brazil.[31] However, she quotes Mead as saying that the Arapesh of New Guinea did not rape, though they knew that other peoples did.[32]

Brownmiller says that obtaining a male protector was the only means of escape that women had from rape by many.

One possibility, and one possibility alone, was available to woman. Those of her own sex whom she might call to her aid were more often than not smaller and weaker than her male attackers. More critical, they lacked the basic physical wherewithal for punitive vengeance; at best they could maintain only a limited defensive action. But among those creatures who were her predators, some might serve as her chosen protectors... Female fear of an open season of rape, and not a natural inclination toward monogamy, motherhood or love, was probably the single causative factor in the original subjugation of woman by man...[33]

Some lesbians, like Adrienne Rich in "Compulsory Heterosexuality and Lesbian Existence," have criticized Brownmiller's dismissal of the possibility that women could have supported one another against men.[34]

Brownmiller sees rape and male dominance as model concepts for oppression. "Concepts of hierarchy, slavery and private property flowed from, and could only be predicated upon, the initial subjugation of woman."[35]

Away from Androgyny

Unlike Brownmiller, many who focused on men's aggressive behavior were lesbians and considered a description of men as violent to be part of lesbian feminist theory.

Many women proclaimed that not only were men oppressive, they were just plain worse than women. Men did not possess desirable qualities worth emulating. The human ideal was not an "androgynous" conglomerate of "masculine" and "feminine" characteristics. Women in their current state already had the traits they needed to cultivate. They did not need to imitate men.

As Susan Leigh Starr wrote in the lesbian magazine *Sinister Wisdom*:

NOTHING ABOUT ME IS MALE. I do not need anything masculine or male in order to be whole. I do not have *any* male qualities to actualize—I have certain female potentials that while living under a male system have not flourished...

I have scars and a deep anger about that in me which has been fought or raped by men, by their world. Removing the scars, the split, is my self-loving task as a lesbian feminist.

The result will *not* be more than woman, more than man—but fully Woman for the first time.[36]

Androgen and Aggression

Laurel Holliday, one of the former editors of the lesbian magazine *Amazon Quarterly*, wrote the book *The Violent Sex* in 1978, which expresses the idea that men are inherently more violent than women. Holliday accepts without question the research of male psychologists who maintain that girls and boys have intrinsically different interests—and of male anthropologists, like Lionel Tiger, who have written that male dominance is the rule in nature (*in order to justify it*). She does not even mention the work of women in those fields who have had different findings. (However, Holliday now says she has a somewhat different perspective of biology, although she has not written about it).[37]

"From conception on," Holliday argues, "there are physiological differences between the two sexes which shape their physiological development."[38] She cites studies on rats saying that "androgen level is a key to aggression and dominance."[39]

Like Davis, Holliday connects the development of male violence with hunting and meat consumption: "The beginning of large game hunting marked the beginning of sexually dimorphous roles."[40]

But she does not mention that there some other primates that are highly sexually differentiated, with the males much larger than the females. They do not engage in large game hunting. Gorilla males average 200 pounds more than females, but gorillas are vegetarian. Chimpanzees have relatively equal sex roles, but they hunt and eat meat.[41] Feminist anthropologist Leila Leibowitz's article, "Perspectives on the Evolution of Sex Differences," published in the 1975 book *Toward an Anthropology of Women*, discusses the variety of physiological sexual differences and sex-role behavior among apes.[42]

According to Holliday, women's "biology" made it less likely that they would hunt:

What prevented women from taking the male path to violence? Our biology, simply put.[43]

By this, she means that women had children and "stayed at home." She is counting child-rearing as well as child-bearing as part of biology. Women who were disposed to hunt, she says, would have lost out in natural selection.

Even if a few early women had refused to stay at home and had joined the hunt, their likelihood of producing children, and thus of contributing their cantankerousness to the gene pool of the group, would have been greatly diminished because of their higher exposure to death, to miscarriage, and to the loss of their children, had they taken them along.[44]

Like Davis, Holliday assumes that most women in early hunter-gatherer societies deliberately rejected meat because they had moral objections to eating it.

When they began to hunt for meat, men denied their primate heritage and took power over other animals.[45]

...The decision to kill damaged all of men's relationships—to themselves, to other animals, other men, women, children, and eventually the cosmos.[46]

...If there was a 'Fall,' if Adam sinned, surely it was then [when men ate meat].[47]

In other words, she suggests—like Davis—that animals, not women, are history's first victims, and that hunting was the first oppression. Why human killing for food is morally different from other animals' doing so is not explained. Nor do these writers suggest that early men kept all or most of their meat for themselves, refusing to share it among women and children.

Holliday suggests that the social patterns formed in hunting were not models for cooperative society:

> But was cooperation between males really what resulted from large game hunting?...'Cooperation' consisted mostly of the ability to form a tight chain of command, and, in fact, *dominance* and *submission* insured concerted group action rather than voluntary cooperation.[48]

Holliday takes Brownmiller's argument about the historical importance of men's capacity to rape a bit further, suggesting that male sexuality and violence are intrinsically related:

> Sex and aggression would appear to be inextricably connected in our primate and primitive heritage.[49]

She has said that violence came from killing animals, that killing animals for food was a departure from primate "heritage," and then that sex and violence are linked for primates. These ideas are inconsistent.

Despite Holliday's argument that there are profound biological differences between the sexes, she nevertheless maintains, like the late 1960s radical feminists, that biology is not destiny. Human beings can bring about change.

> Human biology is not destiny, however, for unlike all other living creatures we have a degree of consciousness which permits us to overrule negative programming, whether it be genetic or the result of adverse conditioning.[50]

What *is* is not inevitable, she says, even if it is produced by hormones:

> ...We are experiencing the final throes of an *unnatural development*, a *maladaptive selection* which we must consciously come to recognize as such and vigorously try to overcome.[51]

The "unnatural development" or "maladaptive selection" apparently is the development of violent men. But even if men have certain predispositions that are dangerous for the species, Holliday maintains, these predispositions can be discouraged.

The more violence a child experiences at the hands of his parents, the more violent he is likely to be to others as an adult...[52]

Susan Cavin: Too Many Men

Another lesbian writer who has focused on trying to determine the origins of women's oppression is Susan Cavin, the author of *Lesbian Origins*, a book that was published in 1985 but was printed in part in periodicals much earlier and influenced Adrienne Rich's well-known article on compulsory heterosexuality. (Rich was one of Cavin's dissertation advisers).

Even Cavin, who sees differences between women and men as being so great that she advocates that the number of men in a society should be considerably smaller than the number of women, does not see male dominance as biologically determined.

All anti-patriarchal theorists (marxist, feminist, lesbian feminist, matriarchist) agree that *women's oppression is not a biological construct, but rather a social variable*...[53]

The key words here may be "women's oppression." That is, Cavin may not be rejecting the idea that men and women have inherently different personality traits, but rather saying that any such difference does not necessarily mean that men will automatically be able to control women.

Cavin criticizes many other theories about the origins of women's oppression. Theories devised by heterosexual feminists "fail to reach theoretical clarity regarding male supremacy" or its origins because they assume heterosexuality as universal. Susan Brownmiller's theory (page 71, above) emphasizes early women's fear of an open season of rape driving them to submit to "protective mating" and thus to subjugation; Cavin suggests that this scenario does not account sufficiently for the existence of lesbian and celibate women.

She is far more critical of the theory (which she identifies with the patriarchal school of thought) that the "immobilizing" effects of pregnancy on women led "naturally" to male dominance: "The presumptions that all women are both heterosexual and continuously pregnant," Cavin notes, "are erroneous."[54]

It may be true that many feminist theorists have not thought adequately about relations between women in prehistoric societies—but assuming that men were able to coerce women into compulsory relations hardly seems heterosexist. And assuming that women were often pregnant does not necessarily mean that they *wanted* the heterosexual relations that made them pregnant.

Cavin says the transition from an original gynocracy composed primarily of women and children to patriarchy is characterized by "*a mass societal shift from the original high-female/low-male sex ratios to the historical high-male/low-female sex ratios of early patriarchy, then later to the near equal sex ratios of established and late patriarchy. The transition is accompanied by decreasing female/increasing male social space...*"[55]

In other words, Cavin believes that women together with their children formed the first societies. Women first expelled their adolescent sons from society, then, in a later era, took their sons as lovers (rather than having relations with random males encountered briefly, which she says women had been doing until then). Entrance of adult sons into society gave males more power relative to females, and gradually non-kin adult males were accepted who eventually sought and acquired positions of dominance.[56]

Cavin's perception of the behavior of other primates is central to her theory. She suggests that apes tend to live in high female-to-male ratio groups to provide greater safety for females and their offspring from males.[57] Her argument suggests that most ape societies are predominantly female in numbers, are formed by sisters and have a low incidence of male dominance over females. This description does not fit any apes (chimpanzees, gorillas, orangutans, gibbons) very closely, although it does come closer to describing the group structure of many "old world monkeys," or cercopithecidae. Of the apes, orangutans may be closest to Cavin's model, although most commonly females live alone with their young rather than banding together. Males are usually solitary.

Cavin does not draw on Jane Goodall's work on chimpanzees, which was published years before Cavin's book was presented as a doctoral thesis, although Cavin does quote other works on chimpanzees. Cavin also does not use the work of Sara Hrdy on langurs and baboons or Dian Fossey's work on gorillas, although their books were published well before *Lesbian Origins*.[58] Fossey's book *Gorillas in the Mist* suggests that male gorillas really do dominate groups, though there are usually more females than males. Males try to keep females from leaving—and often succeed. Female gorillas in a group generally are not related to each other.

Male chimpanzees are less dominant than male gorillas, but the females in a group are less likely to be related to each other than the males are, Goodall says. Females form much closer ties to their offspring than to other adult females.

Fossey's work suggests that young primate males, such as gorillas, may be driven away not by females wanting more "female space" but by adult males wanting less competition.

Cavin challenges the common feminist theory that sex separation, and the division of labor by sex, are inherently oppressive to women. In her cross-cultural survey of sex separation practices around the world, she finds that many African and Pacific island cultures segregate adolescent boys from females and impose post-partum sex taboos, whereby a man must refrain from sexual contact with his wife for a matter of months, or even years after she has given birth. Suggesting that adolescent sex separation and post-partum sex taboos might favor women's autonomy and power, Cavin turns the schemas of sex segregation and integration on their heads: "Women's oppression is directly tied to the mass physical *integration* of adolescent and adult males into female social networks...The entrance of the mass of males into everyday residential contact with female society brings dominance hierarchies into society...These male dominance hierarchies economically, socially, and politically segregate the mass of women from positions of power in society. Vertical social segregation, not horizontal physical segregation, characterizes patriarchal formations."[59]

Division of labor by sex, in Cavin's view, may have favored women in original human societies, in which she says they outnumbered men by a large margin*—but only *became* oppressive after men overturned, and integrated themselves into, women's societies:

> I see the sexual division of labor as the classic form of homosexual segregation. There is little that is heterosexual about it, except the role play...

---

*Cavin does not prove that original human societies were largely female. Indeed, no one can prove or disprove such a theory, although speculation about the origins of society can be interesting.

I challenge the notion that the division of labor by sex is originally based on the heterosexual act. No doubt the sex stereotypical occupations assigned to women and men in patriarchal society resemble heterosexual femme/butch roles. I contend that the patriarchal sexual division of labor does not represent the sexual division of labor in original society. The division of labor by sex has more to do with homosex grouping and homosex relations than it does with the heterosexual act of coitus.[60]

Woman the Natural

It has become increasingly common and often accepted for feminists to suggest that women do—presumably because of their biology as well as their lives, because they bear and rear children—have some closer relation to nature than men do. This idea had been utterly rejected by the late 1960s radical feminists.

Susan Griffin's book *Woman and Nature* sees women as closer to nature and men as having rejected nature. Griffin says that man perceives himself as apart from nature, while woman is part of it.

It is decided that matter is transitory...it is decided [man decides] that the nature of woman is passive.[61]

She continues her description of men's views.

...The demon resides in the earth...women are closer to the earth...Women are 'the Devil's gateway.'[62]

Furthermore, "Women are more sensual ... the senses are deceptive..."[63]

She adds that men see women and nature as representing death and cruelty: "Nature lives and breathes by crime... [woman has the] cunning suppleness of a beast of prey."[64]

Also, she says that men are angry that women do not always yield and the earth does not always bear fruit. "He wants her to produce at will."[65]

She sees women as having escaped this divorce from nature.

We know ourselves to be made from this earth. We know this earth is made from our bodies. For we see ourselves. And we are nature. We are nature with a concept of nature. Nature weeping. Nature speaking of nature to nature.[66]

Griffin does not directly address the question of whether men are more violent by nature, but she does seem to see women as more nurturing by nature. Her book is written in more poetic than analytic form.

Mary Daly: More on Sex Difference

Mary Daly's ideas on sex differences—as expressed in *Gyn/Ecology*, published in 1978—are not completely clear. Daly quotes from sources as divergent as Valerie Solanis and George Gilder to say that men are basically passive, with an inner barrenness, dependent on the structure of society to define their role.

In *Gyn/Ecology*, Daly also identifies women and nature—or men's treatment of women and their treatment of nature. "Women and our kind—the earth, the sea, the sky—are the real but unacknowledged objects of the attack, victimized as The Enemy of patriarchy—of all its wars, of all its professions."[67]

Daly rejects the conventional ideas of "masculinity" and "femininity." She says that the "feminine" and "masculine" roles, stereotyped sets of characteristics, "are essentially distorted and destructive to the Self and to her process and environment."[68]

However, Daly seems to see a distinction—perhaps an inherent distinction—between women and men. In fact, part of her basis for rejecting the ideas of femininity and masculinity seems to be that they can be used to cloak real differences between women and men.

> Male propagation of the idea that men, too, are feminine— particularly through feminine behavior by males—distracts attention from the fact that femininity is a man-made construct, having essentially nothing to do with femaleness. The seductive preachers of androgyny, of 'human liberation,' dwell upon this theme of blending.[69]

In other words, men lure women away from real change by a few changes in "masculine" behavior, although "masculinity" is merely an archetypal concept they created in the first place. They are not changing anything real, so they are not changing anything.

In a 1979 interview with *off our backs*, in response to my question about whether there were inherent biological differences between women and men, Daly said perhaps there were.

> ***oob***: Do you think that part of the problem with men is so basic that it goes back to biological-chemical differences?

Daly: I'm inclined to think that. I'm not about to go out and have dogmas about that. I always like Elizabeth Gould Davis' remark in *The First Sex* that men are mutants. The Y chromosome is like a shrivelled X chromosome. And we all know that everyone is female for starters, as a fetus. And truly if there is a mutant, it's not the female. If there's one original sex, it would be the female. That's a difficult thing to say when you can't ground it all in absolute evidence. Mutations have a way of dying out. So maybe mutations will manage to kill off themselves eventually.

It's an easy cop-out to say it's only the patriarchal male, with a different society it might be different. For centuries men called women misbegotten males, so we shouldn't be afraid to speak out our intuition that men are misbegotten females— which would be much closer to the truth.[70]

In *Pure Lust*, her 1984 book, Daly carries further her suggestion of the differences between women and men.

[Under Aristotle's philosophical system] women were said to belong to the fixed species called MAN.

Metamorphosing women are not flattered but rather horrified at the idea of such belonging. Moreover, the experience of such a woman is that she does not 'belong'...

Macroevolution is defined as 'evolutionary change involving relatively large and complex steps (as transformation of one species to another).' Such evolution is now intended, with varying degrees of explicitness, by many Crones [a designation for women that Daly proudly reclaims]. Metapatriarchal women experience as ineffably accidental our connection with the species that has planned and executed witchcrazes, death camps, slavery, torture, racism in all of its manifestations, world famine, chemical contamination, animal experimentation, the nuclear arms race. This difference is affirmed by a series of conscious choices...

The traditional concept of 'species,' especially 'the human species' does not adequately encompass the differently oriented lines supposedly contained therein. I refer primarily to its grotesque blurring of differences between those whose intent and behavior is radically biophilic and those whose desensitized/ decentralized, soulless and berserk (dis)-orientation manifests 'gross inability to communicate' and fundamental enmity toward Life itself.

Daly adds:

> Wise readers will recognize that this sort of distinction is not a
> simplistic bifurcation on the basis of gender. Patriarchy here is
> seen as a disease attacking the core of consciousness in females
> as well as males.[71]

In other words, women such as Margaret Thatcher who support the arms race presumably are, like most men, a different
species from biophilic (life-loving) women. It's not clear where this
leaves women who just vote for men who support evils such as
the arms race. Are Republican women a different species? Don't
women share some responsibility for slavery, racism, etc.?

It is not clear whether Daly believes men can gain the biophilic
virtues that she says women tend to possess.

In *Pure Lust*, Daly writes that radical feminist women really
are *Other*—radically other from either men or the role women
are supposed to play in patriarchy. "The starting point of a
woman's metapatriarchal Metamorphosis is an ontological intuition of her Otherness in relation to all of the shapes imposed
upon her by patriarchy." Women need to realize—in the sense of
acting as well as knowing—this Otherness, Daly writes.[72]

Daly is using the word "other" in a different sense than Beauvoir
did. Beauvoir meant the non-subject who is acted-upon. Daly, in
one of her many reversals of language, is using the word "other" to
mean something like *subjectivity*—a different sort of subjectivity
from that experienced by men in patriarchy who use subjectivity to
see others as objects.

Daly is not the only radical feminist who has, with time, become
more inclined to consider the possibility that men may be inherently more violent than women. In 1989, long-time radical feminist Robin Morgan for the first time began speaking of such a
possible difference. In an interview in *off our backs*, she said:

> If it turns out that there is a real biological difference—and we
> still don't know—between men and women—if it turns out that
> it's like the old feminist joke that men are suffering from
> testosterone poisoning—then we have to put our minds to
> solving that problem.

That does not mean androcide and it does not mean doing to men all of the things that men have done to women. But it does mean that if some people happen to be more prone to violent means of problem-solving, then those people should be less empowered to have access to the means by which they can harm everyone. In other words, if it does turn out that anatomy is destiny, that's all the more reason for women to have power.[73]

However, some radical and lesbian feminists are critical of the idea that women are closer to nature than men.

Marilyn Frye is one lesbian feminist who does not equate women and nature. In her 1983 book, *The Politics of Reality*, she says:

What we may do when we try to imagine *ourselves* independent is just slip ourselves into his [man's] shoes and imagine ourselves the center of the universe, the darlings of Mother Nature and the cherished sisters of all other women.[74]

If we try to interpret "nature" in a way that fits in with a political theory—to make other species into symbols for us rather than beings in their own right—we may be failing to see the variety that exists.

Chapter 5

Men and Women: Same Species

There are lesbian feminist writers who disagree with the concept that men are inherently different from women.

Like many lesbian feminists, Charlotte Bunch has suggested that the origins of male dominance were in specific violent actions by men. In "Lesbians in Revolt," an essay, she wrote:

> The first division of labor, in pre-history, was based on sex: men hunted, women built the villages, took care of children, and farmed. Women collectively controlled the land, language, culture, and the communities. Men were able to conquer women with the weapons they had developed for hunting, when it became clear that women were leading a more stable, peaceful, and desirable existence. We do not know how this conquest took place, but it is clear that the original imperialism was male over female: the male claiming the female body and her service as his territory (or property).[1]

Bunch rejects the idea that men are innately oppressive. At the 1979 New York University feminist theory conference commemorating the 30th anniversary of the publication of Beauvoir's *The Second Sex*, Bunch said, "[Another panelist] has said that women and men are different sorts of beings. Is that so? I do find that idea seductive. I feel my experience of life is different from men's, but I'm not sure that we are different sorts of beings."[2]

Some Black and Jewish feminists have spoken strongly against the "biological flaws" theory from the perspective of their respective histories. The Combahee River Collective's "Black Feminist Statement" of 1977 says,

> But we do not have the misguided notion that it is their male-ness, *per se*—i.e., their biological maleness—that makes them what they are. As Black women we find any type of biological determinism a particularly dangerous and reactionary basis upon which to build a politic.[3]

Andrea Dworkin wrote about her reaction as a Jew to the biological differences argument in *Heresies* #6:

> I am a Jew who has studied Nazi Germany, and I know that many Germans who followed Hitler also cared about being good, but found it easier to be good by biological definition than by act...
>
> I would not be associated with a movement that advocated the most pernicious ideology on the face of the earth. It was this very ideology of biological determinism that has licensed the slaughter and/or enslavement of virtually any group one could name, including women by men...Recently, more and more feminists have been advocating social, spiritual and mythological models that are female supremacist and/or matri-archal. To me, this advocacy signifies a basic conformity to the tenets of biological determinism that underpin the male social system...
>
> Wherever power is accessible or bodily integrity honored on the basis of biological attributes, systematized cruelty perme-ates the society and murder and mutilation contaminate it. We will not be different.[4]

Martha Shelley, also speaking as a Jew, criticized the idea of women's biological superiority.[5] (See page 154, below).

It is interesting that those women who belong to racial or ethnic groups that have been stigmatized are particularly critical of the use of arguments that apparent differences between people are biologically based. However, an evocation of genocide may be somewhat unfair to those who argue that women are less destructive than men. As a group—albeit a varied group—most of the women who believe that men are more violent than women strongly identify themselves as non-violent and, in fact, identify women as having better values than men because women act in a less violent way. By definition, women who maintain that women are innately less violent are unlikely to call for the violent elimination of men.

African-American feminists, although they disagree on some points, have consistently rejected the idea that behavioral differences between women and men are innate. In the introduction to *The Black Woman*, an anthology she edited, Toni Cade (later Toni Cade Bambara) writes,

> It seems not to occur to these scientists (white, male) that the behavioral traits they label 'basic' and upon which the psychologists breezily build their theories of masculine/feminine are not so 'basic' at all; they do not exist, after all, in a context-free ether. They may very well be not inherent traits but merely at-the-moment traits.[6]

Cade, like many other African-American feminists, has expressed the idea that male supremacy was a European or Christian invention.

> ...I am convinced, at least in my readings of African societies, that prior to the European obsession of property as a basis for social organization, and prior to the introduction of Christianity, a religion fraught with male anxiety and vilification of women, communities were egalitarian and cooperative. The woman was neither subordinate nor dominant, but a sharer in policy making and privileges...And while it would seem she had certain tasks to perform and he particular duties to attend, there were no hard and fixed assignments based on gender...[7]

In her 1978 book, *Black Macho and the Myth of the Superwoman*, Michele Wallace wrote that male supremacy was brought to Africans by the white slave trade:

> Though originally it was the white man who was responsible for the black woman's grief, a multiplicity of forces act upon her life now and the black man is one of the most important of them.[8]

Other Black feminists have put more emphasis on male supremacy as a widespread phenomenon, and as the origin of other forms of oppression.

In a 1970 essay, Kay Lindsey wrote,

> The original sin...was the separation of the sexes, which on the surface appeared to be merely a division of labor, with respect to each sex's capacity to do certain types of work...

The temporary incapacity of women in pregnancy and childbirth offered men the opportunity to use women as their own extensions...From females, man moved on to children; out of this grouping the family evolved. From protection and defense of his property, man moved on to the seizure of the land of others and his prisoners of war became his slaves.[9]

In an article for the lesbian publication *The Ladder*, Anita Cornwall wrote:

To put it bluntly, patriarchy is the root cause of all the major ills in the world today. For as long as men are able to keep half of the population in chains (us Sisters that is), they going to be forever trying to enslave the other half.[10]

In her essay, "Lesbianism: An Act of Resistance," Cheryl Clarke describes male domination as the original oppression.

Gender oppression (i.e., the male exploitation and control of women's productive and reproductive energies on the specious basis of a biological difference) originated from the first division of labor, *viz.*, that between women and men, and resulted in the accumulation of private property, patriarchal usurpation of 'mother right' or matrilineage, and the duplicitous, male-supremacist institution of heterosexual monogamy (for women only)...The ruling class white man had a centuries-old model for his day-to-day treatment of the African slave.[11]

In her 1981 book *Ain't I a Woman*, Bell Hooks (Gloria Watkins) wrote that African women were subjugated by men before whites appeared in Africa.

Black male sexism existed long before American slavery. The sexist politics of white-ruled and colonized America merely reinforced in the minds of enslaved black people existing beliefs that men were the superiors of women...[12]

However, in her 1987 book *Feminist Theory: From Margin to Center*, Hooks had changed her perspective somewhat:

While we know that sex role divisions existed in the earliest civilizations not enough is known about these societies to conclusively document the assertion that women were exploited or oppressed ...The sexism, racism and classism that exist in the West may resemble systems of domination globally but they are forms of oppression which have been primarily informed by Western philosophy. They can best be understood within a Western context, not via an evolutionary model of human development.[13]

None of these women cite a more aggressive male nature as a reason for male supremacy.

Hooks writes in *Feminist Theory: From Margin to Center*:

...Feminist ideology tends to equate male development and perpetuation of oppressive policy with maleness; the two things are not synonymous. By making them synonymous, women do not have to face the drive for power in women that leads them to strive to dominate and control others.[14]

In her 1989 book *Talking Back*, Hooks says,

Contemporary feminist thinkers...suggest that differentiation of status between females and males globally is an indication that patriarchal domination of the planet is the root of the problem...Ideologically, thinking in this direction enables Western women, especially privileged white women, to suggest that racism and class exploitation are merely the offspring of the parent system: patriarchy. Within feminist movement in the West, this has led to the assumption that resisting patriarchal domination is a more legitimate action than resisting racism and other forms of domination. Such thinking prevails despite radical critiques by black women and other women of color who question this proposition. To speculate that an oppositional division between men and women existed in early human communities is to impose on the past, on these non-white groups, a world view that fits all too neatly within contemporary feminist paradigms that suggest man as the enemy and woman as the victim.[15]

Hooks suggests a different paradigm:

Thinking speculatively about early human social arrangement, about women and men struggling to survive in small communities, it is likely that the parent-child relationship with its very real imposed survival structure of dependency, of strong and weak, of powerful and powerless, was a site for the construction of a paradigm of domination. While this circumstance of dependency is not necessarily one that leads to domination, it lends itself to the enactment of a social drama wherein domination could easily occur as a means of exercising and maintaining control. This speculation does not place women outside the practice of domination, in the exclusive role of victim. It centrally names women as agents of domination, as potential theoreticians, and creators of a paradigm for social relationships wherein those groups of individuals designated as 'strong' exercise power both benevolently and coercively over those designated as 'weak.'

...Such thinking enables us to examine our role as women in the perpetuation and maintenance of systems of domination. To understand domination, we must understand that our capacity as women and men to be either dominated or dominating is a point of connection, of commonality.[16]

The concept that children's situation is the paradigm for oppression calls into question a great deal of feminist theory, including much feminist writing on mothering. The idea that mothers can freely oppress children is questionable; in many societies, including many tribal societies, women have less power over male children than over female children.

Recognition that women have the capacity to oppress does not require a theory that sees children as the paradigm of oppression.

Chicana lesbian feminist Cherríe Moraga writes of the oppressor's psychological need to brand and scorn Women of Color and other minorities as "the other":

...It is not really difference that the oppressor fears so much as similarity. He fears he will discover in himself the same aches, the same longings as those of the people he has shitted on. He fears the immobilization threatened by his own incipient guilt. He fears he will have to change his life once he has seen himself in the bodies of those he has called different.[17]

A few lesbian separatist Women of Color question whether men are fundamentally different from women. For example, a story by Juana María Paz suggests that men are mutants.[18]

Cultural Doesn't Mean Biological

Not all feminists who have focused on women's culture explain that culture as a result of biological differences with men. In her 1986 book *A Passion for Friends*, Janice Raymond writes that she does not believe that concentrating on women's positive qualities implies a belief that those qualities are biologically infused.

Women have no biological edge on the more humane qualities of human existence, nor does women's uniqueness proceed from any biological differences from men. Rather, just as any cultural context distinguishes one group from another, women's 'otherness' proceeds from women's culture.[19]

Raymond believes that women's earliest significant relationships (historically) were with one another, and that if women recover their true selves they will be more oriented to women.

Adrienne Rich was one of the first radical feminists to divorce herself from the Firestone tradition of seeing women's biology as inherently oppressive. In *Of Woman Born*, published in 1976, she distinguishes between "the *institution* [of motherhood], which aims at ensuring that that potential—and all women—shall remain under male control" and "the *potential relationship* of a woman to her powers of reproduction," which Rich does not see as inherently oppressive.

> ...In certain cultures, the idea of woman-as-mother has worked to endow all women with respect...and to give women some say in the life of a people or a clan. But for most of what we know as the 'mainstream' of recorded history, motherhood as an institution has ghettoized and degraded female potentialities.[20]

Rich's theory of the origins of the oppression of women, as stated in *Of Woman Born*, is that it is connected with "the male mind...haunted by the idea of *dependence on a woman for life itself*..."[21]

She sees patriarchy as *"power over others*, beginning with a woman and her children...Each colonized people is described by its conqueror as weak, feminine, incapable of self-government, ignorant, uncultured, effete, irrational, in need of civilizing."[22]

Rich appears to see some possible legitimate power in matriarchy. She cites Robert Briffault as saying that "the matriarchal elements in any society have a *functional* [Rich's italics] origin" and that this power of women has "organic authority."[23]

Is "organic" power nonoppressive? Couldn't the father's authority be called "organic" also?

She cites Briffault as saying that there is a "free consent to the authority of women in a matriarchal society."[24] How does one determine when political consent is given freely?

Rich points out that whereas Helen Diner (author of *Mothers and Amazons*) and Davis say woman's motherhood is a source of power that led to gynocracy, others "including Simone de Beauvoir and Shulamith Firestone deny that either a 'matriarchal' or 'gynocratic' order ever existed and perceive women's maternal function as...the root of our oppression." Rich's comment is,

"Whatever the conclusion drawn, there is an inescapable correlation between the idea of motherhood and the idea of power."[25] Perhaps—but there is a considerable difference between seeing motherhood as one's source of power and seeing it as one's source of vulnerability.

Rich sees the existence of past matriarchy as an indication or proof that women need not remain powerless "if female biology was ever once a source of power, it need not remain what it has since become: a root of powerlessness."[26]

However, Rich says,

> ...It can be dangerously simplistic to fix upon 'nurturance' as a special strength of women, which need only be released into the larger society to create a new human order. Whatever our organic or developed gift for nurture, it has often been turned into a boomerang...[27]

In *Of Woman Born*, Rich did not discuss specifically the question of whether men are inherently more aggressive. There is no indication in *Of Woman Born* that she thought they were. In April 1981, I asked her whether she believed that men were inherently dangerous or biologically inclined to be oppressive, and she said that she was not inclined to focus on biology to that degree.[28]

In her 1980 article, "Compulsory Heterosexuality and Lesbian Existence," Rich expresses interest in Susan Cavin's idea that initially women banded together with their children, and that it was rape of the mother by the sons that made patriarchy possible.[29]

However, when Rich wrote her 1984 essay, "Notes Toward a Politics of Location," she had revised her opinion about theories of origins.

> I've been thinking a lot about the obsession with origins. It seems a way of stopping time in its tracks...We can't build a society free from domination by fixing our sights backward on some long-ago tribe or city.[30]

Biology as Creativity

Yet feminists have continued developing more theories of the origins of male supremacy.

Irish-Canadian socialist feminist Mary O'Brien, in the 1981 book, *The Politics of Reproduction*, suggests that the origin of women's oppression is in men's desire to control paternity. This is somewhat similar to Rich, but O'Brien, a former midwife, has more of a biological focus. Men want to do this not so much to pass on property, as Engels said, as to try to appropriate the product of reproduction, the child, because they cannot bear not being fathers. Men are alienated from reproduction because they have no part to play once the "seeds" have left their bodies until after the baby is born, O'Brien says. For that reason, a man feels he must ensure that the child is his. She implies that men could not help oppressing women, because "for men, physiology is fate."[31]

O'Brien criticizes Beauvoir and Firestone for their completely negative perception of pregnancy and childbirth. She suggests that such attitudes stem from the ideology of male supremacy, in which men belittle childbirth because their own part in reproduction is so small. She goes so far as to write that "for women, anatomy is creativity."[32]

Although O'Brien would strongly disagree with those who argue that women are better than men and should not associate with them, she has in common with many of them a tendency to see biological differences as having a *necessary* influence in shaping the history of women's and men's relations.

Original Harmony

Socialist feminists generally say that there was an original harmony between women and men. Only with the knowledge of paternity, the growth of private property, and the urge to pass it on to their sons did men become oppressive. Many of their writings even imply that women were not so greatly oppressed until industrial capitalism moved much production out of the home.

Elizabeth Fisher, the late author of *Woman's Creation*, is a strong exponent of the original harmony thesis.

> ...Humanity, being based on co-operation, has its origins in primitive egalitarianism and...this egalitarianism may even apply to the sexes...The earliest humans shared tasks... Dominance is inherent neither in the animal world nor in humanity.[33]
>
> Dominance, after all, is a laboratory concept. It simply means that when a piece of food is thrown before two animals, one of them often defers to the other...[34]

Fisher says the men in the family did not become oppressive until the state was created and became a model for oppression. Fisher sees the patriarchal family as the authoritarian state in microcosm rather than its model. The state developed in Sumer around 6,000 years ago.[35]

> The authoritarian state was the model from which individual fathers derived power.[36]
>
> Integral to the success of the first organized bureaucracies was the distortion of human sexuality into actual and symbolic production, the repression of female sexuality, and the linkage of war and sex for men. With the worship of material accumulation, people were reified to be used as tools and frequently were treated as possessions themselves.[37]

Fisher suggests that even rape was not practiced until after men became herdsmen. She says introducing forced coitus in animal breeding may have given men the idea of rape.[38] She ignores anthropological studies describing rape in hunter/gatherer societies, such as those cited in works like Gayle Rubin's article, "The Traffic in Women."[39]

Fisher suggests that worshipping fertility did not mean worshipping women, but was anti-woman.

> Fertility worship led to the forced breeding of women; more important, it signified the perversion of sex from pleasure to procreation.[40]

Fisher does not believe that women and men are inherently different. She suggests that any sex hormones can increase the amount of aggression in an animal or person.

> What is clear is that sex is energizing, be it testosterone or estrogen. When that energy finds no outlet, it gets displaced into irritability and, on occasion and in some species, into fighting behavior.[41]

She adds,

> We are told that ingesting testosterone makes a female more aggressive; we are not told that ingesting estrogen is also likely to make her more aggressive.[42]

Woman: A Bargain Commodity

However, Gayle Rubin, a socialist feminist anthropologist, sees violence against women as a major factor in pre-agrarian societies.

In the Amazon valley and the New Guinea highlands, women are frequently kept in their place by gang rape when the ordinary mechanisms of masculine intimidation prove insufficient. 'We tame our women with the banana,' said one Mundurucu man (Murphy, 1959:195).[43]

She sees paternity and patriarchy as inadequate concepts to explain male oppression of women.

Many New Guinea societies...are viciously oppressive to women. But the power of males in these groups is not founded on their roles as fathers or patriarchs, but on their collective adult maleness, embodied in secret cults, men's houses, warfare, exchange networks, ritual knowledge, and various initiation procedures.[44]

Rubin develops anthropologist Claude Lévi-Strauss' concept of the exchange of women between men, which he saw in a matter-of-fact way, as the basic model or paradigm of women's oppression. Men took women in marriage not just for the sake of obtaining the women themselves—but to become kin to other men, to establish bonds between men. Rubin sees this as the reason for the incest taboo.

'What, would you like to marry your sister? What is the matter with you? Don't you want a brother-in-law?...With whom will you hunt, with whom will you garden, whom will you go to visit?' (Arapesh, cited in Lévi-Strauss, 1969:485)...

The 'exchange of women' is a seductive and powerful concept [Rubin says]. It is attractive in that it places the oppression of women within social systems, rather than in biology. Moreover, it suggests that we look for the ultimate locus of women's oppression within the traffic in women, rather than within the traffic in merchandise.[45]

Although Rubin says that the idea of the exchange of women places the problem of women's oppression in the realm of social interactions rather than biology, the idea of the exchange does not necessarily rest on the concept that men and women have no serious biological differences. Indeed, men might treat women as objects for exchange, whether or not they were inherently more aggressive than women.

Rubin, however, maintains that women and men are very similar, and that this similarity has become the ultimate human taboo, or unacknowledgeable reality, because of men's stake in preserving the division of labor.

Women carry the heavy burdens in some societies, men in others. There are even examples of female hunters and warriors, and of men performing child care tasks. Lévi-Strauss concludes from a survey of the division of labor by sex that it is not a biological specialization, but must have some other purpose. This purpose, he argues, is to insure the union of men and women making the smallest viable economic unit contain at least one man and one woman...[he says] the sexual division of labor is nothing else than a device to institute a reciprocal state of dependency between the sexes. (Lévi-Strauss, 1971:347-48).

The division of labor by sex can therefore be seen as a 'taboo': a taboo against the sameness of men and women, a taboo dividing the two sexes into two mutually exclusive categories, a taboo which exacerbates the biological differences between the sexes and thereby *creates* gender...

Gender is a socially imposed division of the sexes...Kinship systems rest upon marriage. They therefore transform males and females into 'men' and 'women,' each an incomplete half which can find wholeness only when united with the other. But they are not as different day and night, earth and sky, yin and yang, life and death. In fact, from the standpoint of nature, men and women are closer to each other than either is to anything else—for instance, mountains, kangaroos, or coconut palms. The idea that men and women are more different from one another than from anything else must come from somewhere other than nature. Furthermore, although there is an average difference between males and females on a variety of traits, the range of variation of those traits shows considerable overlap.[46]*

Rubin also sees forced heterosexuality as an inherent characteristic of male domination and a requirement of the sexual division of labor, or division of roles into male and female.

---

*French lesbian feminist Monique Wittig has identified the taboo against homosexuality or lesbianism as the ultimate taboo, a similar point if it is based on the notion that sex or gender categories are arbitrary.[47]

At the most general level, the social organization of sex rests upon gender, obligatory heterosexuality, and the constraint of female sexuality.[48]

Woman the Artifice

French radical feminists continuing down the path begun by Beauvoir have developed it further. The group associated with *Questions Féministes*,* the theoretical journal that Beauvoir nominally edited, strongly rejects the notion of "woman" as a being with inherent characteristics.

A 1979 *Questions Féministes* editorial stated,

>...Our oppression is not the result of 'not being womanly enough,' but precisely the contrary: from our being *too much so*. We are prevented from leading lives as free and independent individuals...

>...[We] try to take apart the notion of the 'difference between the sexes' which orders and supports this idea of 'Woman,' ...*The social existence of men and women does not depend at all on their nature as male and female, i.e., on the shape of their anatomical sexual organs.*[49]

It is men as a group in power that women must oppose, the editorial says:

>When a group is in power, it is this group which disseminates the ideology and which dictates its categories...

>The theme of difference in itself (whatever the content given to the difference) serves the oppressive group. As long as the oppressor holds the weapons of power, all difference established between him and the others confirms him in the only difference that matters to him—that of holding power.[50]

(But simply because a group in power chooses to proclaim that difference from it indicates inferiority, does that mean that anyone challenging the group must maintain that differences are completely unreal?)

---

*In the fall of 1980, a split in the *Questions Féministes* group over political lesbian theories caused the journal to cease publication. A new journal, *Nouvelles Questions Féministes*, was begun by those who disagreed with lesbian separatism.

Women have no natural characteristics, the editorial says, only responses to oppression.

> ...All so-called natural characteristics attributed to an oppressed group serve to imprison this group in a Nature which, given its status as oppressed, is then confused ideologically with a 'nature' which consists of being oppressed.[51]

The editorial suggests that accepting the idea that woman is closer to Nature involves accepting the idea that men can be equated with culture.

> We are close to Nature? No, they ban us from access to the tools of social mastery, from knowledge of our own bodies, from creation. One kind of creation they let us have—by an ambiguous word-play, the 'creation' of babies.[52]

Christine Delphy, a member of the *Questions Féministes* staff and later of *Nouvelles Questions Féministes*, wrote in the introduction to her book *Close to Home* that she distrusts theories that try to explain the origins of oppression.

> An institution which exists today cannot be explained by the simple fact that it existed in the past, even if this past is recent. I do not deny that certain elements of patriarchy today resemble elements of the 'patriarchy' of six thousand years ago or that of two hundred years ago; what I deny is that this continuation—in so far as it is a *continuation* (i.e. in so far as it really concerns the same thing)—does not in itself constitute an explanation.[53]

Like many socialist feminists, radical feminist Delphy does not feel that historical explanations sufficiently take into account the given conditions of each period. However, Delphy does have ideas about the origins of women's oppression. She points to human practices rather than biology as the cause.

> ...It is *oppression which creates gender*; that logically the hierarchy of the division of labor is prior to the technical division of labor and created the latter: i.e., created the sexual roles, which we call gender. *Gender in its turn created anatomical sex*, in the sense that the hierarchical division of humanity into two transforms an anatomical difference (which is in itself devoid of meaning, like all physical facts) into a category of thought.[54]

ᴊmen and men, we naturalize history, we assume that men and women have always existed and will always exist. Not only do we naturalize history, but also consequently we naturalize the social phenomena which express our oppression making change impossible...instead of seeing giving birth as a forced production, we see it as a 'natural,' 'biological' process, forgetting that in our societies births are planned (demography), forgetting that we ourselves are programmed to produce children, while this is the only social activity 'short of war' that presents such a danger of death.[58]

Some French, Québecoise and American lesbians have construed Wittig's "One is Not Born a Woman" to mean that lesbians should not use the term "woman" to define themselves because "woman" is a socially constructed role that they have rejected.

Beauvoir and Scarcity

Simone de Beauvoir's own ideas did not remain static after publication of *The Second Sex*. She later said that her conception of the origins of women's subjugation had changed to emphasize the importance of scarcity rather than a psychological need for an other. She came to see the scarcity idea as more materialistic.

I believe that the Other is not simply an idealist relationship, it is a material relationship. It is a power relationship, based on scarcity.[59]

What kind of scarcity does she mean? Scarcity of food? Of labor power? She did not develop the idea. Economic scarcity hardly explains why women, in particular, should be an oppressed group.

Is it possible that perceived scarcity of emotional resources could also be a factor? Emotional work takes time. Perhaps men, seeing women care for children, wanted some of that care for themselves. This way of stating the question could be called materialist; the emotional work or nurturance could be broken down into many definable tasks. The idea of emotional resource scarcity, though, is not so far from Beauvoir's original concept of the need for an Other: It retains the focus on men's desire to have someone to control on many levels, not just to produce more tangible goods, such as food, although women did that too. Very likely men also considered sexual intercourse a resource, as North American lesbian writer Joyce Trebilcot has suggested.[60]

How much does it matter that Beauvoir somewhat repudiated the psychological construct (need for an other) on which much later feminist thought has been based? Atkinson sees need for control to escape one's inadequacies as the basis of oppression and attainment of psychological wholeness as a solution. Daly and other lesbian writers see men's lack of wholeness and desire to control "women's energy" as the basis of women's oppression.

Even if Beauvoir were disavowing her earlier construct completely, which is not clear, that would not necessarily mean that it was wrong.

It seems likely that Beauvoir's turn to a theory of scarcity is connected with Jean-Paul Sartre's change to scarcity as a theoretical basis in his 1960 book *Critique of Dialectical Reasoning.* Sartre then wrote that material scarcity, rather than otherness, was the source of alienation.[61] This seems to be a much narrower concept. Do all hunter-gatherer societies experience scarcity? If not, don't they still experience people as others? Scarcity may be a more appealing notion, not only because it sounds more materialist, but because it sounds more curable. But can even the end of scarcity end alienation?

Even Marx's 1844 manuscripts on alienation indicate that he believed that equal distribution was only part of the solution to the problem of alienation. Nothing less than control over one's own work would be enough. If scarcity was the basic problem, why would control of the means of production be so important?[62]

If ending scarcity is not enough to resolve economic class oppression, surely it is not enough to resolve the other aspects of women's oppression.

The Biological and the Social Interact

In the 1980s, feminists are developing the idea that the biological and social environments interact and that the social can affect the biological—or how we construe it—as well as *vice versa.*

When I interviewed her in 1979, Ti-Grace Atkinson expressed ideas somewhat different from her earlier ones.

oob: You don't think it's possible that men are innately more violent than women?

Atkinson: I think it's possible. But I think that if you posit social characteristics as innate, that you get on very, very dangerous

ground in terms of these groups ever living together in any kind
of equity, especially when the people who are more violent have
the power now. I think it's very, very difficult to distinguish environment from biological determination. It has always seemed
to me very possible that culture is inherited in terms of people
growing up in certain societies where femininity is emphasized.
It shows up physically and culturally. These things are all inter-
mixed. So how can you separate them? Even if it's biological in
that sense that doesn't mean it isn't slowly evolved through
time.[63]

In other words, for practical reasons, she feels it is difficult and
dangerous to assume that differences are biological. But if there
are biological differences, these may be aggravated by the system
of male dominance.

Lesbian feminist Marilyn Frye suggests that differences between
women and men are not unchangeable, since most societies have
established codes to penalize those who depart from prescribed
male and female behavior. However, even if those differences are
not necessary, they still may have developed in connection with
biology, because we are whole beings of whom the body is a part,
she writes.

I see enormous social pressure on us all to act feminine or act
masculine (and not both), so I am inclined to think that if we
were to break the habits of culture which generate that pressure, people would not act particularly masculine or feminine.[64]

Furthermore, we are animals. Learning is physical, bodily.
There is not a separate, nonmaterial 'control room' where
socialization, enculturation and habit formation take place and
where, since it is nonmaterial, change is independent of bodies
and easier than in bodies.

Socialization molds our bodies; enculturation forms our
skeletons, our musculature, our central nervous systems. By the
time we are gendered adults, masculinity and femininity are
'biological.'

But now 'biological' does not mean 'genetically determined' or
'inevitable.' It just means 'of the animal.'[65]

Some might assume that saying biology can be changed implies
that women and men should connect to evolve more androgy-
nously together. Frye, however, sees it as a reason for separatism.

...It is no accident that with varying degrees of conscious intention, feminists have tried to create separate spaces where women could exist somewhat sheltered from the prevailing winds of patriarchal culture and try to stand up straight for once. One needs space to *practice* an erect posture; one cannot just will it to happen. To retrain one's body one needs physical freedom from what are, in the last analysis, physical forces misshaping it to the contours of the subordinate.[66]

Radical feminist theorist Catharine A. MacKinnon also sees the social as having an impact on the biological.

It is not because women bear children that women are subordinate or because men have higher testosterone levels that they are more aggressive. I think it may even be the case that men's hormone levels have everything to do with the way they are raised and that the relationship between biological difference and social status is the other way around from what it's supposed to be.[67]

Socialist feminist Alison Jaggar also sees the biological and social bases of sexual relations as interacting—which she sees as primarily a socialist feminist point of view, although as we have just seen, some radical and lesbian feminists share it, while some socialist feminists do not:

We cannot say abstractly that biology determines society, because we cannot identify a clear, non-social sense of 'biology' nor a clear, non-biological sense of 'society.'

In some ethnic groups, there is little sexual differentiation between women and men. Women are as tall as men, have equally broad shoulders and narrow hips, and have breasts so small that it is often difficult to tell an individual's sex...The relatively smaller size of females in other ethnic groups is often due directly to the fact that their nutrition is inferior because of their lower social status. Differential feeding may also have resulted in selection for shorter females...These are some of the ways in which society produces genetically inherited sex differences, as well as sex differences, society.[68]

In some sense, all of the feminist theories discussed have linked the domination of women by men to biology, even those of women such as the *Questions Féministes* writers or many socialist feminists (other than Jaggar) who most strongly repudiate the significance of biological differences. A feminist theory—a theory that says that women and men are in different classes— necessarily recognizes some connection between biological and social categories. At the very least, such a theory must maintain that men have used women's biological capacities as a means of dominating women.

It sounds schizophrenic for a movement to include both those who believe that sex class differences are biologically inherent and those who believe they aren't; but perhaps the split has positive aspects on the level of recruitment. Some women outside the movement may find the approach that women and men are basically the same attractive, while others may find the emphasis on male aggressiveness more compelling. As long as the latter focus does not lead to despair, resignation or inaction, it may not be as unproductive as some classic feminists fear.

There may be no adequate answer to the question of whether women and men are inherently different while their experiences of life differ so greatly. We may have to live with the ambiguity and work around it.

History: Cycle or Progress?

Feminists theorists disagree about history.

A group of feminist theorists maintains that there never was an era in which women were *not* oppressed by men. Soon after human consciousness arouse, men captured the power of women and have been able to create systems that institutionalized and perfected that control.

Another group says that women once had a more powerful position in the world, but were overthrown by men. Some perceive this early period literally as a matriarchy, or a series of matriarchal tribes or societies, in which women had a considerably greater role in decision making than they have had since. Others see this time more generally as an era in which mother goddesses were worshipped and women on earth had more respect.

Most members of both groups of theorists maintain that it makes a great difference which theory of history is correct— which is unfortunate, since it is difficult, if not impossible, to prove what happened in the remote past.

Why does this difference matter? It matters if the two historical theories lead to a different analysis of the present or different strategies for the future.

Basic perceptions of human nature might be affected by one's theory of history. The idea that there was once an actual matriarchy could be used to show that women are capable of running a society, are not bound to be subordinates or victims. But those feminists who disbelieve in the existence of a matriarchy do not believe that women are incapable of running a society or are subordinate or weak by nature. Evidence that there was an era of matriarchal rule might prove that women are not "inferior"—but evidence of the *non*-existence of an era of matriarchy would not prove that women *are* "inferior."

Paradoxically, evidence that there once was a long era of matriarchy would tend to show that men are capable of co-existing with women without ruling them, of living in a less aggressive way. However, evidence that men have always dominated women since the development of human consciousness would not prove that men are incapable of living on an equal basis with women. Most feminists are not so ruled by history that they believe that people are incapable of behaving differently from the way they have behaved in the past.

Those who believe in the era of matriarchy fear that those who do not may fail to see women as strong. Those who reject the idea that there was an era of matriarchy fear that those who accept the idea will see the era as embodying the traditional "female" characteristics of nurturance, tenderness, etc. and will try to "return" to that era, thinking that a return to more open expressions of affection would eliminate the need for other changes. The critics of matriarchy fear a literal return to emphasizing the value of mothers over other women, and/or a total rejection of direct confrontation with men (either of the reformist or radical variety).

But neither tactic, confrontation or non-confrontation, is necessarily linked to the idea that an era in which women were more powerful once existed. Maintaining that an era existed is not necessarily the same as calling for its return.

Part of the dispute is connected with one's intellectual stake in the idea that human history progresses. If one has a strong belief in the idea that only as different stages of technology and production develop can different stages of political, social and mental development be reached, then one is less likely to be comfortable with what could appear to be glorification of previous eras. Yet both Marx and Engels, emphatic and influential believers in stages of development, believed that certain earlier stages, not only primitive communism but also the ancient Hellenic world, had features which had not yet been improved upon by subsequent eras.

Twentieth-century radical or liberal North Americans might forget that many civilizations have believed that history was cyclical and that significant change was impossible, and have literally tried to "recover past glories." At first the word "cyclical" might make women smile and say, "Ah, yes, like a woman's menstrual cycle." But the idea that history is cyclical has a dreadful history. Conservative thinkers do not espouse it by accident.

If no progress is possible, then everything can be reversed. Racial hatred and domination can never be eliminated. A small elite will always gain control of every society. People will never stop valuing the accumulation of material "goods" over other people. Above all, conservative thought from ancient China and India, to European royalists and modern-day conservatives, has propounded the idea that one should accept a stratified universe as the natural order. No radical change will last, because people will tire of it and the old order will creep back or be reimposed.

This cyclical view is frightening, because it is partially true. As marxists theoretically recognize, each idea and every social system carries within itself the potential for its own destruction. New antagonisms will develop as older ones are settled. There are years (and decades) in which "revolutionary conditions are ripe," and everyone is excited about change, and years in which popular movements subside and the powers-that-be herald the return of "the old truths."*

---

*Frederick Engels views history as moving—through struggle, counter-struggle, setback, and advance—in an *upward spiral*, negating itself only to come round and negate itself again, but on a higher plane. (Marx and Engels took their "negation of the negation" concept from Hegel's dialectics, giving it materialist content). Engels endorses Lewis Henry Morgan's forecast that the future, liberated society "will be a revival, in a higher form, of the liberty, equality and fraternity of the ancient gentes [communal clans]."[69] Yet Engels, who holds that early human societies were woman-centered and matrilineal (with descent and inheritance passing from mother to children), stops short of asserting that the future, communal society will *also* revive matrilineage. —Editor (Daniel Fogel).

Feminists have a personal, collective, material, intellectual stake in fundamental change in all aspects of society—change in a feminist direction, of course. They cannot deny that retrogression or reaction is possible—the nineteenth-century feminist movement and the reaction against it are too fresh in everyone's minds. All feminists have a stake in believing that change is possible, and need to formulate theories with this in mind. (Obviously, if you theorize that change or progress is impossible, you cannot promote it effectively). The possibilities of both progress and reaction need to be taken into account. Those who theorize that there was once an era of matriarchy must not reject the idea of progress—nor must those who theorize that women have always been oppressed by men but are slowly beginning to challenge that oppression reject either the possibility of progress, or the possibility of reaction.

These two branches of radical feminism, the "differences" and the "no-differences" groups, are derived from different premises, from different intellectual traditions. The idea that human beings are perfectible and the idea that they (or some group of them) are irredeemably, congenitally flawed, spring from different perspectives, with different histories. Generally, radicals with a socialist perspective and liberals have believed in humanity's capacity for self-development. Conservatives and reactionaries have generally been the chief proponents of the congenital flaw idea: They have maintained that women of all races, and dark-skinned peoples, are biologically flawed.

Can the Oppressed Oppress?

The question of whether men's oppression of women is linked to men's biological traits, is connected with the question of whether the oppressed can become the oppressors. Certainly, the example of the Russian revolution and the later rise of Stalinism indicates that, among men, it is possible for those who claim to represent the oppressed, or those who lead them, to become oppressors. This process is not necessarily a simple reversal; by "becoming the oppressor," I mean something more than the exercise of some political clout over the former ruling class. It is possible to exercise some coercion over others without depriving them of human rights or political representation. Laws requiring desegregation of public accommodations in the United States, for instance, coerce without disenfranchising oppressors who would be yet more oppressive without those constraints. To become an oppressor means to create a ruling class and a new oppressed class—or continuing the oppression of some already oppressed classes while alleviating the oppression of others.

Participation of women in systems of race and class oppression, or acceptance of those systems, indicates that women are naturally capable of being oppressors.

If one believes that oppressiveness—or a propensity for aggression or control—is linked to male biology, then presumably she would not have to develop many "checks and balances" to prevent women from engaging in oppressive behavior during or "after the revolution." Even a slight familiarity with the feminist movement shows that women have been by no means unconcerned about the possibility that other women could become attracted to power over others or behave in an oppressive way. From the very beginning, feminists have tried to institute ways of preventing the development of oppressive leaders in the movement.

Feminists who are vocal advocates of instituting measures to prevent the development of hierarchy often are the same women who profess the belief that men are oppressive by nature and that oppression is by nature male. I suggest that they don't quite believe this idea. They may believe that men are more oppressive by nature than women, but if they take steps to prevent the rise of hierarchy among women in their groups they must believe that women are capable of being oppressors. Some feminists say that oppressive behavior is imitative of men, or is male-identified, but in order to imitate behavior, women must be capable of it.

If we are to look at history to determine which people are more aggressive or oppressive by nature, it is by no means clear why we should say that the male sex is biologically predisposed to oppress, and not *also* say that the "white" or "caucasian" race is biologically predisposed to oppress.

Women of Color's citing oppressive behavior by white women makes it excruciatingly clear to many feminists that it is possible to be both oppressive and oppressed.

If we see women behave in oppressive ways, we might want to take that into consideration when we try to formulate theories to explain the past.

Part Three

Love, Sex, and Sexuality in Radical Feminist Politics

Chapter 6

Love:
Can it
be Good?

One of the central questions that feminist theory needs to discuss is the question of love as an emotion, an experience—its political, social and theoretical implications for feminism. Feminist theory in some ways focuses on autonomy, on the idea that a person must learn to be alone in the world. Ti-Grace Atkinson, in particular, has stressed the idea that love is a disease, or at least a symptom of "the victim's response to the oppressor," and that self-containment is necessary.

Some other feminists have taken a more optimistic perspective on love, or on certain modes of love. Simone de Beauvoir sees nonoppressive love as a possibility between two human beings who both operate as subjects. Shulamith Firestone sees nonoppressive love as a possibility for women if reproductive patterns change, economic autonomy is assured, and social constraints on sexuality are removed. Lesbian feminists see love between women as a possibility and advocate it as a strategy for social change, as well as a desirable goal in itself.

Like most other writers in contemporary society, feminists generally mean sexual love when they refer to love. Love between parents and children or friends is less frequently discussed.

There are contradictions between an emphasis on love as a goal and/or strategy and autonomy as a goal and/or strategy. If both goals/strategies are pursued, there may be constant tension between the two. Is the desire for another person to love productive and creative, or is it an escape from responsibility for one's own life? Is it not almost impossible to strike a balance between love and autonomy? In Beauvoir's terms, is love a form of transcendence or immanence? How do most feminist theorists perceive it?

Can a goal/strategy that does not include love ever become acceptable to most women?

I am exploring different feminist theorists' concepts of love to see if there has been a change over time in feminist perspectives of love—both perceptions of heterosexual love and of lesbian love. There appears to be a greater change in the perception of love between women than in the perception of love between women and men. To what extent are these seen as different experiences?

Beauvoir: From Flawed to Authentic Love

Mid-twentieth century feminist writings about love began with Beauvoir. She assumes that love as it now exists is deeply flawed, but that an "authentic love" can be salvaged. Love now diminishes and enslaves women, but this is not an inherent or necessary part of love.

Women have not been allowed to love themselves unless a man loves them, she notes. "Only in love can woman harmoniously reconcile her eroticism and her narcissism..."[1] She "abandons herself to love first of all to *save herself*...Everything useless to him she destroys."[2] "Love becomes for her a religion."[3]

Some of Beauvoir's descriptions seem to blame the woman. "She chooses to desire her enslavement so ardently that it will seem to her the expression of her liberty."[4] As an existentialist, Beauvoir says the woman "chooses," but how freely does she choose?

Beauvoir recognizes that a woman is not always able to find a "love on which it is even remotely possible to graft this religious construction. But it often happens that a woman succeeds in deifying none of the men she knows. Love has a smaller place in woman's life than has often been supposed."[5] Or is it possible that none of the men can play the patriarchal role plausibly, rather than that the women want to deify them and yet cannot?

She accuses women of operating in "bad faith"—an existential-ist concept—when they expect men to behave like gods, to be flawless, and will love them only if they are. But surely she must have seen that men had set *themselves* up as gods, defining the situation and the terms. Why are *they* not accused of operating in "bad faith?"

Beauvoir even sees women as operating in bad faith when they expect that men will love the same way they love. "She fancies that the man's love is the exact counterpart of the love she brings to him; in bad faith, she takes desire for love, erection for desire ..."[6] In patriarchal society, it is men who expect to get more from love than they give, not reciprocating fully—as she acknowledges. Why is *this* not bad faith?

Is Beauvoir saying that a man's love only amounts to erection? She does not go that far, but this passage tends in that direction.

In some ways, Beauvoir seems to see men's love as more authentic, closer to what love ideally should be, than women's love. This is one of the points that illustrates her difference—or the difference in *The Second Sex*—from the radical feminists who came later. When men love, she says, "they never abdicate completely...at the very heart of their lives, they remain sovereign subjects."[7] Beauvoir, of course, thinks that remaining a sovereign subject in one's own life is desirable. She suggests that men have succeeded at this better than women.

Woman "remains engulfed in [being] this loving woman whom man has not only revealed, but created. Her salvation depends on this despotic free being that has made her and can instantly destroy her. She lives in fear and trembling before this man who holds her destiny in his hands without quite knowing it, without quite wishing to... [He is an] involuntary tyrant."[8]

But the man is not an "involuntary" tyrant. He only wishes to deny his position, especially if it has become boring to him and he would prefer another object. Is it plausible that anyone but the class of tyrants would have established tyranny? Is it accidental if people are in a situation in which one of them lives "in fear and trembling," even if she must conceal the trembling because it is unbecoming? It is certainly true that the man does not want to feel guilt.

How true is it that men have whole selves that they whole-somely manage to keep intact during love? Are those selves not created in large part by that love from women? Aren't those male selves created by the privilege that there have been and will be women available to bolster their identity, so that they need not hold on so hard to a particular woman? They have created a whole class of women available to them.

"...It is agonizing for a woman to assume responsibility for her own life," says Beauvoir.[9] There is an existentialist emphasis on individual responsibility here. She does not seem to see that men in patriarchal societies have not taken responsibility for their own lives, although they may have taken credit for doing so.

She writes of women's need to be seen through men's eyes, quoting a Colette character in the novel *The Vagabond* as saying, "I admit, I yielded, in permitting this man to come back the next time, to the desire to keep him not a lover, not a friend, but an eager spectator of my life and my person... One must be terribly old, Margot said to me one day, to renounce the vanity of living under someone's gaze."[10]

Beauvoir does not point out that this desire to have a spectator to one's life is at least as much men's as women's. Men have created a whole social order that provides them with a class of spectators. Ti-Grace Atkinson later pointed this out.

Beauvoir says that a man may be tyrannical, but he demands less than a woman does. "A lover who has confidence in his mistress feels no displeasure if she absents herself, is occupied at a distance from him; sure that she is his, he prefers to possess a free being than to own a thing."[11] But she recounts the example of Victor Hugo, a great champion of liberty, who kept his lover in a locked apartment.[12] Beauvoir does not show that man prefers "possessing a free being" to "owning a thing." If a woman worries more about her male lover when he is absent, it is because she knows that he has more freedom to act and less commitment— not necessarily because she is insanely jealous.

Beauvoir does show that the love system as it exists in patriarchal systems has been set up to self-destruct for women: If a woman really loves a man, she may disconcert him, and that will threaten his love for her. "A passionately demanding soul cannot find repose in love, because the end she has in view [repose in love] is inherently contradictory. Torn and tormented, she risks becoming a burden to the man instead of his slave, as she [is it really *she*?] had dreamed; unable to feel indispensable, she becomes importunate, a nuisance...If she is wiser and less intransigent, the woman in love becomes resigned."[13] "The lover seeks his reflection in her, but if he begins to find it altogether too faithful, he gets bored. It is, again, one of the loving woman's misfortunes to find that her very love disfigures her, destroys her; she is nothing more than this slave, this servant, this too ready mirror, this too faithful echo."[14] A woman succeeds in love to the extent that she does not love too much, or is not carried away by love, as Firestone later says more explicitly.

Beauvoir thinks that a more genuine love between women and men is possible (and desirable).

> Genuine love ought to be founded on the mutual recognition of two liberties; the lovers would then experience themselves both as self and as other: neither would give up transcendence, neither would be mutilated; together they would manifest values and aims in the world. For the one and the other, love would be revelation of self by the gift of self and enrichment of the world.[15]

> An authentic love should assume the contingence of the other; that is to say, his lacks, his limitations, and his basic gratuitousness. It would not pretend to be a mode of salvation, but a human interrelation.[16]

However, she does not deny the pitfalls involved in love for women today. "On the day when it will be possible for woman to love not in her weakness but in her strength, not to escape herself but to find herself...on that day love will become for her, as for man, a source of life and not of mortal danger." [Again, she sees love for man more as a source of his life than a way of feeding on another's life.] "In the meantime, love represents in its most touching form the curse that lies heavily upon woman confined in the feminine universe, woman mutilated, insufficient unto herself."[17] She does not quite say that it is one of the institutions that most surely keeps women there.

Beauvoir: Institution of Intercourse

In the context of this perspective on love, Beauvoir's views on sexuality are, not surprisingly, critical. Although Ti-Grace Atkinson is known for calling sexual intercourse an institution, Simone de Beauvoir actually preceded her in naming it an institution. The context was Beauvoir's discussion of marriage.

...Sexual intercourse thus becoming an institution, desire and gratification are subordinated to the interest of society for both sexes; but man...can enjoy contingent pleasures...This sexual frustration of woman has been deliberately accepted by men...[18]

How, then, could men's approach to sexuality and love be authentic? Could deliberately accepting another's sexual frustration be authentic? How can women—or men—be authentic if their sexuality is institutionalized? "...Since the sexual act is regarded as a *service* assigned to woman...it is logical to ignore her personal preferences."[19] Beauvoir refers here to the woman's preference as to which man becomes her husband. But in a context where this preference is constrained, it is reasonable to assume that her choice of particular sexual acts is constrained also.

Beauvoir suggests that a woman must direct her attentions not to an individual she might be most likely to love, but to the man who is most likely to marry and financially support her. "...She [the married woman] must renounce loving a specific individual in order to assure herself the lifelong protection of some male."[20] Woman's sexuality in this situation becomes an instrument to be used for survival, not pleasure.

One's ideas on love are likely to be deeply affected by one's experience of it. Since Beauvoir has published several volumes of autobiography, it is not difficult to see connections between her theories and her experiences. Mary Evans, a British sociologist who wrote a book about Beauvoir, suggests that Beauvoir had to pretend always to be rational about love, could not act as women in love often act, because maintenance of her close relationship to Sartre depended on proving that she was not "just another woman"—an emotional rather than intellectual being—to him. Her freedom to express her feelings in love was confined not by traditional social constraints but by a new set of rules (set by Sartre) by which the couple operated, under which the expression of her jealousy and fear over his affairs with other women was unacceptable. She was a woman in love who couldn't act like a woman in love—and who was sexually rejected by Sartre, though kept on as his intellectual and emotional life-mate, when she was about forty.[21]

Firestone: Men Can't Love

According to Shulamith Firestone, love has been so damaging in the sex/class system that women must consider whether they want to get rid of love. At one point, she goes so far as to say that "men can't love," yet she sees love between women and men as being possible, perhaps only after many changes in class relations (between women and men) have taken place.

Firestone points out that men have used women's emotions to give them strength. "[Male] culture was [and is] parasitical, feeding on the emotional strength of women without reciprocity."[22]

Firestone says that a desire to become part of another self is the basis of love.

> ...Love is not altruistic. The initial attraction is based on curious admiration (more often today, envy and resentment) for the self-possession, the integrated unity, of the other and a wish to become part of this self in some way (today: read intrude or take over), to become important to that psychic balance...Thus love is the height of selfishness: the self attempts to enrich itself through the absorption of another being.[23]

But she does not see this process as inherently wrong.

> Love is being psychically wide-open to another...Anything short of a mutual exchange will hurt one or the other party.
>
> There is nothing inherently destructive about this process. A little healthy selfishness would be a refreshing change. Love between two equals would be an enrichment... Lovers are temporarily freed from the burden of isolation that every individual bears.[24]

She does not see anything wrong with this temporary escape. However, she says that destructive love experiences are much more common than positive ones and may destroy the individual.

It is an unequal balance of power between men and women that corrupts love, Firestone says. "...The destructive effects of love occur only in a context of inequality."[25] Firestone says that it is the distribution of power in the biological family that sets up the conditions for unequal love relationships. In a somewhat freudian turn, she says, "...In the girl, the mother's rejection...produces an insecurity about her identity in general, creating a lifelong need for approval. But because of this early rejection,...the male will be terrified of committing himself... For him to feel safely the kind of total response he first felt to his mother, which was rejected, he must degrade this woman so as to distinguish her from the mother."[26]

It is regrettable that Firestone blames the mother instead of male power. If men dominate the society, it makes sense that women will seek male approval and men will degrade women, no matter how their mothers treated them.

Firestone believes Freud's assertion that the incest taboo is the basic universal taboo. She sees the incest taboo as an instrument that teaches a child very early to "distinguish between the 'emotional' and the 'sexual'."[27] By abolishing the family, she hopes to abolish this distinction, to enable people to connect sexuality and love. Presumably child sexual expression with adults would be one means, although she does not emphasize this.

Firestone, of course, wrote this before a number of women writers revealed how widespread and destructive incest and other forms of child sexual abuse are. Feminists writing today would say that if the child is to love adults, "love" and "sex" would still have to be split to some extent, because adults have too much power over children for children to be free in a sexual relationship with an adult.

Firestone writes, "Men can't love (male hormones? Women traditionally expect and accept an emotional invalidism in men that they would find intolerable in a woman)."[28] But she does not really seem to believe that men cannot love—much less, that they are biologically unable to do so—since she suggests more and various heterosexual arrangements as part of her solution.

If, as she stated earlier, male and female behavior in sexual relationships is primarily shaped by their experiences in the nuclear family, then there would be no reason to assume that men couldn't change. She never suggests the converse, that male inability to love may have *created* the nuclear family, in which the role of "loving one" is allocated to the wife/mother.

Firestone, even more forcefully than Beauvoir, points out that women must be cautious and practical about love (that is, be less than completely open to love and loving), in order to preserve themselves in male-dominated society. While Beauvoir saw this behavior as unauthentic, Firestone sees this caution as reasonable for women.

A man must idealize one woman over the rest in order to justify his descent to a lower caste. Women have no such reason to idealize men — in fact, when one's life depends on one's ability to 'psych' men out, such idealization may actually be dangerous...

But though women know to be unauthentic this male 'falling in love,' all women, in one way or another, require proof of it from the man before they can allow themselves to love (genuinely in their case) in return.[29]

This "male 'falling in love'...acts to equalize the two parties"[30] — but, because the man loves and wants the artifice, it cannot last. "...The woman knows that this idealization, which she works so hard to produce, is a lie, and that it is only a matter of time before he 'sees through her.' Her life is a hell..."[31]

Firestone feels that there would be some idealization of the other person, but not a destructive amount, in love between equals. "It is only the *false* idealization...that is responsible for the destruction. Thus it is not the process of love that is at fault, but its political, i.e., unequal, *power* context..."[32]

Why do women want love? Firestone offers several reasons. In male-dominated society, women are rarely allowed to realize themselves. It is "easier to try for the recognition of one man than of many."[33]

Women also need love "for its natural enriching function."[34] Apparently, she sees this as an inherent need.

Also, women need love because in male-defined society, they require it (from men) "for social and economic reasons."[35] A woman loves in exchange for security, because she must. She "will never be able to love gratuitously, but only in exchange for security..."[36] Firestone thinks it would be wrong to blame women for developing such survival tactics.

The kinds of security a woman needs include:

1) the emotional security, which...she is justified in demanding.
2) the emotional identity which she should be able to find through work and recognition, but which she is denied — thus forcing her to seek her definition through a man.
3) the economic class security that, in this society, is attached to her ability to 'hook' a man.

Two of the three are invalid conditions for love, but are imposed upon it.[37]

There is a valid kind of love, but women are forced into invalid kinds of love, Firestone says: "...In their precarious political situation, women can't afford the luxury of spontaneous love ... [which] would endanger...male approval."[38] Lesbian feminists later said that women could not afford to *deny* themselves this kind of love, and hurt themselves if they do—in conflict with the Firestone/Redstockings position that women involved with men are doing all they can at the present time.

Firestone is one of those who sees it as a sexual problem that "women regard themselves as erotic."[39] "This functions to preserve direct sex pleasure for the male, reinforcing female dependence: Women can be fulfilled sexually only by vicarious identification with the man who enjoys them. Thus eroticism preserves the sex class system."[40] It certainly does, unless those women who find *women* more erotic, act on those impulses and become involved with other women. But this is not the solution Firestone considers. (Even in that case, it would be possible for a woman to see herself as another woman's sexual object, but there might be somewhat less chance of that happening than with a man).

Atkinson: Love is for Victims

Ti-Grace Atkinson sees love as part of women's condition of oppression, not as a salvageable good that had been corrupted. She assumes that men do not love: Her discussion focuses on what love does to women. She sees love as a political institution, necessary to the functioning of male domination.

> I propose that the phenomenon of love is the psychological pivot in the persecution of women. Because the internalization of coercion must play such a key functional part in the oppression of women due to their numbers alone, and because of the striking grotesqueness of the one-to-one political units 'pairing' the Oppressor and the Oppressed, the hostile and the powerless, and thereby severing the Oppressed from any kind of political aid, it is not difficult to conclude that women by definition must exist in a special psychopathological state of fantasy both in reference to themselves and to their manner of relating to their counterclass. This pathological condition, considered the most desirable state for any woman to find herself in, is what we know as the phenomenon of love.[41]

The most common female escape is the psychopathological condition of love. It is a euphoric state of fantasy in which the victim transforms her oppressor into her redeemer. She turns her natural hostility toward the aggressor against the remains of herself—her Consciousness—and sees her counterpart in contrast to herself as all-powerful (as he is by now at her expense).

The combination of his power, her self-hatred, and the hope for a life that is self-justifying—the goal of all living creatures —results in a yearning for her stolen life—her Self—that is the delusion and poignancy of love. 'Love' is the natural response of the victim to the rapist.[42]

Power brings love, she says.

Any theory of attraction could begin with the definition of the verb 'to attract': the exertion of a force such as magnetism to draw a person or a thing...Usually the magnetized moves toward the magnet in response to the magnet's power; otherwise, the magnetized is immobile...Unfortunately, magnetism depends upon inequity.[43]

According to Atkinson, women have not necessarily had a choice about whether to love—or whether to have sexual relations.

Isn't love a transgression of the self? A giving over of what we know will be taken by violence if we don't?[44]

To refuse to name this giving "love" might make it unbearably grim.

Insofar at least as love is inequitable, that is, as long as it is not by definition reciprocal, love will not survive the liberation of women.[45]

Atkinson assumes that love will remain non-reciprocal.

Almost none of Atkinson's definitions of love apply to love between women, which clearly is not the response of the victim to the rapist or a giving over of something that could be taken by force.

What is love but the payoff for the consent to oppression? What is love but need? What is love but fear? In a just society, would we need love?[46]

Atkinson clearly thinks the answer to the last question is "no." If all personal needs are political needs, then in a politically just society there would be no needs. Perhaps this submerges the personal a little too much into the political, the individual into the collective.

An article by the Feminists, which shows Atkinson's work, says:

> We must destroy love (an institution by definition), which is generally recognized as approval and acceptance. Love promotes vulnerability, dependence, possessiveness, susceptibility to pain, and prevents the full development of a woman's human potential by directing all her energies outward in the interests of others...[47]

Unlike Beauvoir and Firestone, Atkinson does not see love as something that can be salvaged, but as a development that was created solely to foster male domination. She sees *autonomy* as the feminist goal, and sees friendship as being more compatible with autonomy than love is.

> *I distinguish between 'friendship' and 'love.' 'Friendship' is a rational relationship which requires the participation of two parties to the mutual satisfaction of both parties. 'Love' can be felt by one party; it is unilateral by nature, and, combined with its relational character, it is thus rendered contradictory and irrational.*[48]

But Atkinson is not recognizing that friendship and "love" may co-exist in the same situation. One friend, for instance, may love another sexually, and the other may not reciprocate in the same sense, but a caring interaction may still be possible. Such inter-relations are common among lesbians. Some kinds of love may be on a continuum with friendship; such a concept is not part of Atkinson's framework in *Amazon Odyssey*.

In a 1979 interview with *off our backs*, Atkinson told me that she had feelings for women that might be called "love," but she would prefer not to use that term. Atkinson said present-day friendship for her generally means friendship among women. Friendship with men, like love, poses dangers.[49]

An article by the Feminists, which clearly reflects Atkinson's touch, says,

> Friendship between men and women, under the present conditions of inequality, is the pretence that equality and mutual respect exists. So long as the male role exists, men have the option of assuming it; therefore, the relationship is one of jeopardy to women. In actuality, friendship serves to reinforce the female role need for approval and support.[50]

Pro-Love Radical Feminists

Certainly not all radical feminists have rejected love as Atkinson did.

Kate Millett sees love as something (presumably positive) that patriarchy is constituted to curtail.

> Most patriarchies go to great lengths to exclude love as a basis of mate selection. Modern patriarchies tend to do so through class, ethnic, and religious factors.[51]

For Redstockings, love was indeed a possible and even necessary goal—love between women and men. If most women wanted it, then it must be a right and a necessary—and feasible—goal, because most women are rational and know what they want. Kathie Sarachild wrote,

> It's not a question of working inside or outside the system...it's a question of whether we want to finally go after what we really want, our own true desires, or whether we are toning down our desires, lying about them, even to ourselves, in order to get favors from men who have power...
>
> It's a question of going after what we really want in our work lives and in our love lives—and as women really know, the two are very related—and only having power will get us what we really want in both...When we have power, men will finally begin to give *us* love rather than the other way around, the real love we've all been longing for all these years, and this will change our relationships with women, too.[52]

Sarachild assumes that men will love women more if women get more power—even at their expense. She therefore assumes that men as well as women are basically rational, that they prefer strength and autonomy (in others) to dependence, that they will prefer equal relationships to relationships in which they hold the greater share of power. Do these ideas prepare women for the kind of opposition they are likely to face? Will men necessarily love autonomous women more? Is it possible that men might hate them more? If they did, would that make autonomy less worthwhile? Which goal—love or autonomy—has priority?

Redstockings thought that men could be politically pressured not only to do housework, but to love more deeply, with greater commitment.

To Redstockings member Barbara Leon, love is legitimate, and men are capable of giving it to women, but they have refused to give it. Somehow they must be pressured to love:

Atlantic City, NJ, September 7, 1968 — Feminists picketing the Miss America pageant, shown here during a break in their protest.

Not the least of the crimes committed against women under male supremacy is that of our emotional abandonment by men... It is this central fact which is a prerequisite for all the other actions taken against us by our oppressors.[53]

Leon suggests that women are fighting to get love from men.

The feminist realization was that you don't get what you want—in this case monogamy, love and commitment—by pretending you don't want it. And you don't get what you want by pretending you already have it. You only get what you want by fighting for it.[54]

There was a feeling that demanding love from men meant you were willing to give up anything for it, when actually demanding love, real love, from men meant no longer giving things up, being ready to stop giving things up...[55]

How men would be persuaded to love more is never explained. Would they give "true love" out of fear of losing access to women if they didn't?

In a 1979 article, Ellen Willis, a radical feminist since the late 1960s who defines herself as heterosexual, wrote that sexual love is *necessary* to happiness: "I believe that sexual love in its most passionate sense is as basic to happiness as food is to life..."[56]

If love is that basic to happiness, what is to become of autonomy? What if the loved person dies or departs? Is happiness then impossible?

Willis suggests that sexuality naturally is not derived from hostility or the desire to dominate, but from affection.

To my mind, [Wilhelm] Reich's most revolutionary assertion was also his simplest (some would say simple-minded): that natural sexuality is the physical manifestation of love.[57]

For Willis, love and sexuality are redeemable from the uses to which they have been put under male domination. But even in conditions of equality, Willis sees love as a possible source of pain.

...There is an inherent, irreducible risk in loving: it means surrendering detachment and control, giving our lovers the power to hurt us by withdrawing their love, leaving or wanting someone else.[58]

Willis feels that love and complete independence are incompatible, but suggests that love can be worth the loss of independence that it necessitates. Although Willis defines herself as heterosexual, she sees heterosexual love as dangerous for women at the present time.

Under present conditions, heterosexuality really is dangerous for women, not only because it involves the risk of pregnancy and of exploitation and marginality, but because it is emotionally bound up with the idea of submission.[59]

Robin Morgan, then married, actually carried the "right to demand love" to the conclusion that every woman had a right to a Great Love.

We have a right, each of us, to a Great Love...By the right to a great love I don't mean romanticism in the Hollywood sense, and I don't mean a cheap joke or cynical satire. *I mean a great love*—a committed, secure, nurturing, sensual, aesthetic, revolutionary, holy, ecstatic love. That need, that *right*, is at the heart of our revolution... Let no one, female or male, of whatever sexual or political choice, dare deny that, for to deny it is to *settle*. To deny it is to speak with the words of the real enemy.[60]

What can the right to a Great Love possibly mean? A claim to have a right to the passionate attention of some other individual is a contradiction in terms. One may have the right to a love free from extrinsic social obstacles, but one cannot have the "right" to another human being's love. Possibly one may have the *need*. Generally, the fulfillment of needs may be a right. But with *this* need, society cannot do much more than to demolish the barriers which patriarchy had set up against fulfillment.

To "settle" is to deny a part of oneself. It may be possible to create a society which minimizes the likelihood that a person will have to "settle" or be celibate, but no society can guarantee an appropriate lover to each member. Even if a Great Love is one goal that is generally considered desirable, either "settling for a less perfect love" or celibacy (if not both) must be options. It is also possible that the expectation that love should be "Great Love" makes it more difficult to cope with actual relationships.

Are feminists setting up women for disappointment if they suggest that a Great Love is possible for most or all of us? If a Great Love is the goal, will people be able to work for a free society? Will their focus be on social change or personal "hunting"?

Only Lesbians Can Love

The late lesbian writer and contributor to the early lesbian magazine, *The Ladder*, Rita Laporte, wrote that men cannot love. Unlike Firestone, she believed it. Laporte believed that love exists and can be positive and mutually beneficial, but that men have no capacity for it. She discussed this idea in an article supposedly written by a visitor from another planet.

> Your males, arrested at the primitive level of genital sexuality, have little or no notion of what love means.[61]
>
> Only your lesbians know the meaning of true love, that mature dedication to another that transcends animal lust and raises sexual expression to total emotional flowering and integrates sexuality into a perfect unity of two human beings profoundly in love. We do not mean to imply that all Lesbians find this transcending love...[62]

Although what Laporte wrote certainly is dramatic and controversial, her tone was not angry.

> What is so sad to us is that many of your 'heterosexual' women are capable of such loving were they not so heavily molded from birth into the conviction that they must love a man... The vast majority of your women still cling to the myth of heterosexual love.[63]

Laporte continues,

> While male and female 'fit' very well in the matter of reproduction, of getting sperm to ovum, this is not true of their sexualities.[64]

She explains,

> The man has a handy, all-purpose organ: it urinates, it impregnates, and it gives him delightful sensations. Women are blessed with three separate organs, a considerable evolutionary advance in complexity: a urethral orifice, a vagina (or sperm conduit), and a remarkable little organ...the clitoris. This organ differentiation in the female has psychological consequences. 'Lovemaking'...is to the woman something very different from what it is to the male. 'Tension reduction' is a phrase a number of male Behaviorists like and that describes male sexual activity very well...[65]

Men are not to blame for not loving better, according to Laporte. They simply cannot.

> Love-making, properly speaking, is something that can take place only between two women whose total sexualities and total beings are united in love.[66]

For Laporte, lesbian coupling is the normal and fullest expression of love.

> Marriage is obsolete, say many heterosexual feminists. I agree as long as they specify *heterosexual* marriage. It was never

anything more than an economic convenience and power necessity for males. It never satisfied the woman's emotional needs, not merely sexual, but the total emotional needs of her sexuality. How could it when woman is basically lesbian?[67]

(Of course, not all lesbians would agree that marriage is an appropriate metaphor for lesbian relationships, or that monogamy should be the ideal for lesbians. There is a considerable range of lesbian opinion on this topic).

Love as a Political Bond—or as Friendship

To Rita Mae Brown, one of the earliest lesbian feminist activists, "love" is not only a potentially positive interaction between individuals, but a means of social change.

Love is the enemy of unequal social structure. When people really love they become disobedient. And by love I don't just mean sex because that's a tiny fraction of the love we are capable of.[68]

By this creative, social-changing love, Brown seems to mean lesbian love, which she sees as getting beyond the class and other boundaries between women. This statement seems strange, since feminists often see love as the cement of unequal social structures. If love reinforces gender hierarchy, can we automatically assume that it undercuts race and class hierarchies, even among lesbians?

For Mary Daly, writing in *Beyond God the Father*, love can be separated into genuine love and love as a political instrument. Genuine love can be positive.

Genuine love, which is not blindly manipulable by political power of domination, seeks to overcome such power by healing the divided self. Sexist society maintains its grasp over the psyche by keeping it divided against itself...[69]

Some desire for unity with others is positive.

It is commonly perceived that on the deepest ontological level love is a striving toward unity, but the implications of this unity have not been understood by the philosophers of patriarchy. It means the becoming of new human beings, brought forth out of the unharnessed energy of psychically androgynous women, whose primary concern is not giving birth to others but to themselves.[70]

In *Gyn/Ecology*, Daly writes that woman-identified (lesbian) love and friendship are not dichotomized, not different from each other but blend into each other. She says that for men, erotic love and comradeship are transitory and involve a loss of identity. "It [erotic love for men] involves hierarchies, ranking roles—like the military—on the model of S and M [sadomasochism]"—as differing from friendship.

> Woman-loving Spinsters/Lesbians who are finding integrity of gynaesthetic experience know that such splitting of erotic love from friendship and likening to warrior-comradeship is symptomatic of the disease of fragmentation...For female-identified erotic love is not dichotomized from radical female friendship, but rather is one important expression/manifestation of friendship.
>
> Women loving women do not seek to lose our identity, but to express it, dis-cover it, create it. A Spinster/Lesbian can be and often is a deeply loving friend to another woman without being her 'lover,' but it is impossible to be female-identified lovers without being friends and sisters.[71]

Daly emphasizes that this bonding or friendship must be between whole, independent selves. Like Atkinson, she sees autonomy as a goal, but she provides more discussion of connections between autonomous women than Atkinson did.

> Out of this strong self-centering bonding can come the physical spaces of which we dream. These will be unlike the earlier attempts to make women's spaces, which have reflected the unsureness of women in earlier stages of the Journey... There is still bonding out of weakness—pseudobonding—when women are afraid to *be* alone. Rather than being empowering, places which reflect pseudobonding become disabling... The Hags... will come together because they are enspiriting, because they know how to be/travel Alone. These seasoned Spinsters will no longer be seeking the solace of domestication. They will be at home on the road.[72]

Daly's perception of love and friendship seems derived from existentialist ideas. Her definition of love may be seen by some women as challenging rather than comforting.

> Sparking is igniting the divine Spark in women. Light and warmth, which are necessary for creating and moving, are results of Sparking. Sparking is creating a room of one's own, a moving time/spaceship of one's own, in which the Self can

expand, in which the Self can join with other Self-creating Selves.

Sparking is making possible Female Friendship, which is totally other from male comradeship... Male comradeship/ bonding depends upon energy drained from women (its secret glue). The bonding of Hags in friendship *for* women is not draining but rather energizing/gynergizing...

The term *comrade* is derived from a Middle French word meaning a group of soldiers sleeping in one room, or roommate. The concept of room here is spatial, suggesting links resulting from physical proximity, not necessarily from choice. The space is physical, not psychic, and it definitely is not A Room of One's Own...The comrades do not choose each other for any inherent qualities of mind/spirit. Although this accidental and spatial 'roommate' aspect does apply to all women insofar as all women are oppressed/possessed, it does not apply to the deep and conscious bonding of Hags in the process of be-ing. Since the core/the soul spark of such deep bonding is friendship, it does not essentially depend upon the enemy for its existence/ becoming.[73]

This emphasis on female friendship was new. Simone de Beauvoir's perception of female friendship was extremely negative.

...Young girls quickly tire of one another. They do not band together...for their mutual benefit; and this is one of the reasons why the company of boys is necessary to them.[74]

Women's fellow feeling rarely rises to genuine friendship, however. Women feel their solidarity more spontaneously than men; but within this solidarity the transcendence of each does not go out towards the others...each is against the others.[75]

In fact, the theme of woman betrayed by her best friend is not a mere literary convention; the more friendly two women are, the more dangerous their duality becomes.[76]

Although radical feminists have used more pro-woman language than Beauvoir, many of them have not talked much about friendship. Such writers as Shulamith Firestone and Kate Millett scarcely deal with friendship between women. Redstockings may write of sisterhood and Ti-Grace Atkinson of class consciousness among women, but they write little on friendship. Susan Brownmiller doesn't say much about it. Rita Mae Brown uses the word "love" much more often than friendship.

However, since the mid-1970s, Mary Daly's comments, Adrienne Rich's discussion of "the Lesbian continuum"—including women's friendships—and, most recently, Marilyn Frye's and Janice Raymond's work—are focusing on women's friendships. (See chapter 11). Perhaps not too much emphasis should be put on the point that many feminist theorists have not written about friendship, since they have used other terms such as sisterhood and have developed ties in consciousness-raising and political groups. Still, the renewed emphasis on feminist friendship—brought up by lesbians—is worth noting.

There are hard questions to be asked. Enthusiastic comments about bonding are not the same as a hard discussion of the boundaries of friendships, of whether relationships between women can be oppressive, whether only "politically correct" women are worthy or capable of friendship, whether friendships entail obligations, or whether friendships develop structures and patterns.

The Maternal Model

There is another model for affectionate relations besides the model of friendship: the mother/child relationship. Feminists who define themselves as matriarchists say that the mother/child relationship is a past and present model for love relationships. Barbara Love and Elizabeth Shanklin, who in the late 1970s published a New York newspaper called *The Matriarchist*, suggested seeing mother/child relationships as exemplary, and matriarchy, a society based on such relationships, as desirable. "By matriarchy, we mean a society in which all relationships are modeled on the nurturant relationship between a mother and child."[77]

Other feminists such as Ti-Grace Atkinson strongly deny that love modeled on a mother's love for her child would be desirable. Atkinson points out that the mother has far more power than the child and sees the relationship as a model of power-based relationships.[78]

Saying that human love may have developed from the mother/child relationship, is not the same as saying that love in the mother/child relationship is a perfect model for all love. The relationship can never be absolutely equal or reciprocal. Even if the child loves the mother and provides for her in old age, it would be difficult to do as much as the mother did for her.

Chapter 7

Sex: Will it Exist After the Revolution?

Radical feminists have not only challenged "love," but also "sex."

Radical feminist Anne Koedt's 1968 article, "The Myth of the Vaginal Orgasm," discussed the clitoris as the center of sexual activity. Although she criticized standard heterosexual intercourse for focusing on a position that is not the most pleasurable for women, she thought that heterosexual relations were redeemable if men responded to demands of women for pleasure.

> We must begin to demand that if certain sexual positions now defined as 'standard' are not mutually conducive to orgasm, they no longer be defined as standard. New techniques must be used or devised which transform this particular aspect of our current sexual exploitation.[1]

Intercourse is for Men

Ti-Grace Atkinson interpreted the "myth of the vaginal orgasm" differently in "The Institution of Sexual Intercourse," written in 1968. Her thesis was that sexual intercourse was an institution created by men to perpetuate male domination. The fact that "the" classically-defined sex act usually does not provide enough clitoral stimulation to give women orgasms shows that it is not an institution that is in women's interests, Atkinson says.

The purpose, i.e., the social function, of the institution [of sexual intercourse] is to maintain the human species.

It used to be that the construct of marriage guaranteed the institution of sexual intercourse...The substitute theoretical construct of vaginal orgasm is necessary only when marriage is threatened...

Vaginal orgasm is, then, a substitute for the construct for marriage. Unfortunately for those women who are accepting the substitute, vaginal orgasm as a political construct is less in their interests than marriage...

The salient feature of both is that both constructs (marriage and vaginal orgasm) are in the interests of the male and against the interests of the female, and both constructs were, not surprisingly, conceived of by men. Both constructs limit a woman's human possibilities (the double standard is built into any double-role theory). Both constructs incorporate attempted justifications (excuses?) for the role assigned to women in sexual intercourse...[2]

Atkinson maintains that,

...The maternal instinct is obviously too indirect an interest to justify sexual intercourse to a free woman... As exterior coercion lessens, it must be projected inside the victim.[3]

Sex Drive to Disappear

Atkinson thinks that the only way to free women—to let them operate as full human beings, not required to be cogs functioning under society's (men's) dictates—is to free them from the function of reproducing the species. Other means must be found, so that women would not be mere instruments. (But, presumably, could still choose to reproduce in the old way. Atkinson apparently does not think they would want to do so.) She writes:

This step alone (ending sexual intercourse as society's means of reproduction) would reduce sexual intercourse, in terms of its political status, to a practice. But the biological theories as well as the psychological ones would fall with the institutional purposes: Sexual drives and needs would disappear with their *functions*. But since a practice must have some sort of structure, and without a social function sexual relations would be individually determined and socially unpatterned, sexual intercourse would not be a practice either.[4]

Although Atkinson thinks sexual drives would disappear if they were no longer necessary for reproduction, she also considers the possibility that they might continue. Only when the system of compulsion is removed, will it be possible to determine what sexual desires exist.

> Having lost their political function, one possibility is that perhaps we could discover what the nature of the human sensual characteristics are from the point of view of the good of each individual instead of what we have now which is a sort of psychological draft system* of our sexualities.
>
> [After the two sex classes no longer existed], sexual organs... would probably not be called that anymore since the term 'sexual organs' assumes two sexes.[5]

Her assumptions about the inextricable connection between genital pleasure and reproduction are heterosexually focused. The clitoris, for instance, does not have a direct reproductive function. Atkinson, in her discussion of what is wrong with intercourse, notes the capacity of the clitoris for nonreproductive pleasure. But she does not consider the independence of the clitoris when she says that sexual organs would wither away, once their reproductive function had disappeared.

Atkinson questions whether, even if physical desires continued after the reproductive function no longer existed, the desires would necessarily be directed toward another person. Would an independent, self-sustaining person really want genital contact with another person?

> Why is it [tactile contact] with another person more pleasurable than auto-contact? In whose interest is this physical contact between two people, and what are the grounds of this interest? If masturbation has such strong arguments in its favor (assuming the sexual organs are a kind of sense organ) such as technical proficiency, convenience, egocentricity, on what grounds is an outside party involved?
>
> Must this alleged pleasure be mutual? and if so, why? What motivates the desire to touch other people? ...Isn't it crucial, to the argument for tactile contact as innately pleasurable, whether or not you can hold the claim that touching the other person is directly pleasurable to the toucher, not only indirectly

---

Draft system refers to military conscription.

pleasurable by witnessing the pleasure of the touched? How could it be claimed that the fingertips are as sensitive as the alleged erogenous areas of the body?[6]

Atkinson apparently does not consider sequential mutuality, or taking turns touching, to be actually mutual; it is not clear why she does not. There is no reason to suspect that there is a power imbalance between the toucher and the touched if neither has the institutionalized role of toucher or touched.

Atkinson suggested that there were better ways of expressing positive feelings toward another person. "Why would such [positive] feelings have to be expressed by touching instead of verbally?"[7]

Celibacy as an Option

Several articles published in the late 1960s and early 1970s by the Boston radical feminist group Cell 16 suggested that celibacy might be a satisfying option for women, a way of freeing themselves from past obsessions and proceeding with life and work.

A 1971 article by Dana Densmore, "Independence from the Sexual Revolution," typifies this approach. "Desires and even needs can be created," Densmore wrote.[8]

Densmore suggests that individualist ideology fosters a compulsive desire to be loved.

The very isolation the individualist ideology imposes makes us desire even more to be loved and accepted, and fear even more being unlovable.[9]

On the other hand, this compulsive need to be loved, though individualistic rather than socially-oriented, has not been based on the cultivation of women's individual qualities but on a kind of self-immolation — and "individualism" without the individual.

The solution offered to all this is often to open yourself up until you can merge selflessly with another person. In many cases it is explicitly sex.[10]

This direction is useful neither for women as individuals nor as a group, she says.

...Many girls who would be most free to fight in the female liberation struggle are squandering valuable energy... They lavish and dissipate their valuable talents and emotional strength on attempts to be attractive to men and to work things out with lovers so that 'love' might be less degrading. And too often all they reap is demoralization, damaged egos, emotional exhaustion.[11]

Densmore suggests that orgasms are no solution.

> Under the banner of 'not denying our sexuality' and pointing to
> repression in the past when women were denied the right to
> any pleasure in their bodies at all, many of us now embrace
> sexuality and its expression completely uncritically. As if
> present excess could make up for past deprivation. As if even
> total sexual fulfillment would change anything... Even with
> perfect sexual fulfillment, mutual guilt-free pleasure, we are still
> oppressed.[12]

Even if men give more sexually than they have been giving, that
does not free women, according to Densmore: "As long as men are
the superior caste and hold the political power in the class
relationship between men and women, it *will* be a favor your lover
is doing you, however imperiously you demand it."[13]

Densmore pointed out how "sexual liberation" as defined by the
"sexual revolution" just put more of a burden on women:

> The right that is a duty. Sexual freedom that involves no free-
> dom to decline sex, to decline to be defined at every turn by sex
> ...Sex is everywhere. It's forced down our throats.[14]

Densmore is somewhat more convinced than Atkinson that
sexual urges are inherent.

> No doubt there are some innate needs, or at least propensities.
> But a propensity can be culturally built into an obsession or
> culturally killed off, sometimes simply by never reinforcing it. I
> personally suspect that some form of sex urge may turn out to
> be innate...[15]
>
> And if it turns out that this urge is not that strong, it might
> still be worth keeping (i.e., reinforcing) if it affords people
> physical pleasure or pleasures of intimacy. But it should be
> taken for granted that it must pleasurable to *both parties*,
> always: which means it must never be institutionalized by law
> or culture. And if it *is* a basic 'drive' felt by both men and
> women, there is no need to institutionalize it to ensure
> survival.[16]

(Lesbian feminist writers would suggest that the fact that
heterosexuality has been institutionalized demonstrates that it is
not inherent).

Densmore asks what it is that people really need.

> What is it we really need? Is it orgasm? Intercourse? Intimacy with another human being? Stroking? Companionship? Human kindness? And do we 'need' it physically or psychologically?
>
> Intercourse, in the sense of the physical act which is the ultimate aim of so much anxiety, plotting and consuming, is not necessarily the thing we are really longing for...[17]
>
> Without denying that sex can be pleasurable, I suggest that the real thing we seek is closeness, merging, perhaps a kind of obliviousness of self that dissolves the terrible isolation of individualism.[18]

Densmore urges women to direct more of their attention and affection to women, to satisfy more of their human needs with women. She assumes that for the most part this increased closeness will not be lesbian (which perhaps she sees as in a genitally-defined way).

> ...Destruction of the sense of isolation through communication, community, human kindness, and common cause are all available from other women as you work together in the struggle against oppression.[19]

Densmore sees seeking better sexual relations with men as politically counterproductive.

> We are not living in an ideal society, and 'post-revolutionary' characters or lifestyles might well hinder revolution or make it impossible. The fact that in a good society women might want to produce children, at least until the perfection of the artificial womb, is no reason for me to take myself out of the struggle by having children now under these conditions. Similarly, the belief that sex would have a place in a good society does not necessarily mean that we must engage in it now.[20]

However, she does not demand that women give up sexual relationships.

> If a particular sexual relationship or encounter is convenient, appropriate, and pleasurable, if it is not demeaning or possessive or draining in any way, you might decide to choose to invest some of your precious self in it.[21]

The burden of proof is on the relationship, to prove that it is constructive.

Densmore assumes that sex is only one aspect of life, not necessarily the most important. She does not believe that all of our energies are derived from it or that other activities are mere substitutes for it.

> ...It is only if we are *merely* sexual beings, *exclusively* sexual beings, that choosing to put our energy elsewhere indicates any kind of denial. (The great scientist or writer who puts all his energy in his work is not *denying* anything...) [22]

The argument that, if a need is not exclusive there is no harm denying it, is not persuasive. Few feminists (if any) would argue that women are exclusively intellectual beings with no interest in interpersonal relations; but all would say that women who have focused *only* on interpersonal relations probably are denying their intellectual needs.

Mary Daly also has noted that sexual interactions and a focus on sex are not necessarily liberating. In *Beyond God the Father*, published in 1973, Daly quotes marxist Herbert Marcuse on how de-sublimated sexuality can be used to "reinforce the *status quo*, keeping people 'happy' with truncated, unrebellious existence." [23]

Although writers like Atkinson and Densmore emphasized celibacy rather than lesbianism, they were similar to lesbian feminists in a number of ways. They for the most part rejected sexuality with men at the present time—and perhaps always—as oppressive to women. They urged women to focus on other women, rather than on men. They suggested that lack of independence or ability to be self-sustaining was basic to the sexual politics of patriarchy.

Celibate feminists continued to speak out in the 1980s in the *Journal of Celibate Women*.

Chapter 8

Lesbianism as a Politics

Lesbian feminist politics is by definition a politics of separatism, in the sense that lesbian feminists assume that the lesbian feminist experience is a unique one which gives rise to theoretical insights that only women who have become lesbians can develop and practice. However, women who are not lesbians can understand lesbian feminist politics and be critical of the institutionalization of heterosexuality—many lesbian feminists assume.

Not all lesbians are lesbian feminists. In fact, many women who had been lesbians before the feminist second wave began in the late 1960s have been uncomfortable with lesbian feminists and have feared that lesbian feminists weren't really lesbian or really attracted to women, but only acting on political ideas. However, for many lesbian feminists, new ideas and new appreciation of and attraction to women were fused.

Debates within the radical feminist movement on lesbianism and heterosexuality have not been mere bickering among factions, personal tensions or differences over tactics: They stem from fundamental philosophical differences in definitions, goals, strategies—nearly everything. Women's theoretical differences on these issues are not always divided according to self-definition as lesbian or heterosexual, although there is often a connection between a woman's self-definition and her theoretical perspective.

Definitions of lesbianism and heterosexuality are connected. If a woman sees lesbianism as a political question, part of the most productive strategy or goal for women, she is likely to see the institution of heterosexuality as oppressive. If a woman does not see the institution of heterosexuality as oppressive to women, she probably will not see lesbianism as an important part of a political solution to women's oppression.

Definitions of lesbianism and heterosexuality may be related to a woman's position on the question of whether there are inherent, inevitable differences between women and men. A woman who does not believe that most behavioral differences between women and men are biologically caused, is not likely to believe that lesbianism is determined genetically or during infancy. However, a woman who believes that there are significant, lasting biological differences between women and men may believe that there are inherent differences between lesbian and heterosexual women — or that differences between women and men are so great that all women, given a real opportunity, would choose to be lesbian.

Generally, only those who believe that lesbianism can be *chosen*, rather than being genetically determined or instilled in infancy, see lesbianism as part of a political solution for women.

The belief that sexual orientation is genetically determined or instilled in infancy is more commonly held by gay men than by lesbians. Lesbians who see their lesbianism as predetermined are more often those who identify as gay women than as lesbian feminists, and they are more likely to belong to gay groups, if they belong to any political groups, than to radical feminist or lesbian feminist groups.

Lesbian writers who believe that lesbianism is a choice for which a woman does not need early "programming" include Charlotte Bunch, Rita Mae Brown, the Furies, Mary Daly, Adrienne Rich, Kate Millett, Audre Lorde, Barbara Smith, Jill Johnston, Rita Laporte, Del Martin, Phyllis Lyons, the CLIT women, Marilyn Frye, Cheryl Clarke, and Janice Raymond. Most of these believe that lesbianism can be political and is a part of radical feminist strategy or a life of choosing women over men.

Other feminists who believe that lesbianism is a voluntary choice include Ti-Grace Atkinson, Robin Morgan, and Shulamith Firestone. Some of them acknowledge lesbianism as having a special political potential for feminists; Firestone did not.

There have been heterosexual radical feminists who have not defined lesbianism as an intrinsic part of feminist politics. Several members of New York's Redstockings do not.

Many lesbians have been seriously hurt by heterosexual women either in feminist organizations, on a personal level, or both, and this had a significant impact on their theory. On the other hand, some heterosexual radical feminists have felt that their feminist work has been unacknowledged and their personal lives over-scrutinized because of their heterosexual relationships.

Negative Perceptions of Lesbianism

There is a history anti-lesbianism in the contemporary women's movement that goes back as far as Simone de Beauvoir. Beauvoir's treatment of lesbians in *The Second Sex* was less than enthusiastic.

> Since she [the lesbian] seeks self-affirmation, it is displeasing for her not to realize wholly her feminine possibilities...in repudiating the limitations implied by her sex, it appears that she limits herself in another way. Just as the frigid woman wants sexual pleasure while she refuses it, so the lesbian may often wish she were a normal and complete woman while preferring not to be.[1]

Beauvoir's treatment of "frigid" women shows that it is not only lesbian sexuality that she sees unsympathetically. Frigidity could be an authentic response to a sexuality that Beauvoir notes is institutionalized. If a lesbian is not a "normal and complete woman," then being a man's sexual object must be the requirement for normality and completion.

In a paper on "Lesbian Attitudes and *The Second Sex*," lesbian feminist Claudia Card points out that Beauvoir recognized that lesbianism is a choice: "The lesbian 'makes herself lesbian.'"[2] However, Card notes that,

> Beauvoir seemed not to see that if 'homosexuality' is a choice, heterosexuality is a choice. To put it in her more specific language, [which Beauvoir used about lesbianism] it [heterosexuality] is an attitude which is not physiologically, psychologically, or economically determined and which likewise can be evaluated according to its authenticity.[3]

Card suggests that a greater thoughtfulness about lesbianism might have changed Beauvoir's theory about the origins of oppression.

Instead of identifying *human* relationships with *heterosexual* relationships and assuming that the significant Other for any consciousness is an Other of the 'opposite' sex, she might have challenged Hegel's assumption of an original hostility in human consciousness toward others...She might have considered whether the tendency of any consciousness to regard another *a priori* as an object of hostility is not rather a *consequence* of oppressive institutions than among the conditions giving rise to them...[4]

Shulamith Firestone's brief treatment of "homosexuality" was somewhat disparaging.

Though few women, because of the excessive pressure on them to conform, actually repudiate their sexual role altogether by becoming active lesbians, this does not imply that most women are sexually fulfilled by interactions with men...

Homosexuals in our time are only the extreme casualties of the system of obstructed sexuality that develops in the family. But though homosexuality at present is as limited and sick as our heterosexuality, a day may soon come in which a healthy transsexuality would be the norm...[5]

Here she apparently means bisexuality, not what we think of today as transsexuals, people who have "sex change" operations.

Atkinson on Lesbianism

Ti-Grace Atkinson initially held a critical view of lesbians, although her position changed later. At first, in 1969, she wrote:

The lesbian solution to the problem of women is to evade it, that is, to opt for an apolitical solution.[6]

At the time, she felt that closet lesbians in the National Organization for Women (NOW) constituted a conservative element because they were threatened by rapid change and the possibility of exposure.

By 1970, Atkinson had modified her position.

I think that lesbianism, to men, is the ultimate political position for women. This is not to say that lesbianism actually is... Given that the male dynamic toward women is sex, he could hardly see any woman without it.[7]

Sometimes I think that lesbianism is just about as apolitical as black nationalism.[8]

However, Atkinson still felt that risk-taking by working in radical groups—not sexuality—was the criterion for radicalism.

> It's true that the very concepts of lesbianism depend upon the positing of that counterclass, men. One *might* want to claim that there is a certain rejection operating here, and that for that reason alone, lesbianism qualifies as a political act.
>
> Still, lesbianism is totally dependent, as a concept as well as an activity, on male supremacy. This fact, alone, should make a feminist nervous.[9]

Presumably she means that lesbianism is dependent on male supremacy because it depends on categorization of people as male and female. Some lesbians, such as Adrienne Rich, do not believe that the concept of lesbianism depends on male supremacy. (See page 254, below). Atkinson continues,

> But lesbianism is based ideologically on the very premise of male oppression: the dynamic of sexual intercourse. Lesbians, by definition, accept that human beings are primarily sexual beings. If this is the case...one would have to grant that women *are*, in some sense, inferior.
>
> 'Sex' is based on the *differences between* the sexes. Sexual intercourse is the interrelation between these two classes, and sexual intercourse, unsurprisingly, is not in the interests of women.
>
> The institution of sexual intercourse is anti-feminist, first, because the source of women's arousal and pleasure is in the clitoris, not in the vagina. And, second, it is anti-feminist, because sexual intercourse is the link between the wife and the mother roles...
>
> A case could be made that lesbianism, in fact *all* sex, is reactionary, and that feminism is revolutionary.[10]

Atkinson was ignoring the fact that "sexual intercourse" between lesbians was not the same as the classic act of intercourse between a man and a woman, and that lesbian sexuality, to the extent that it is genitally focused, is mostly focused on the clitoris. Because she believed that sexual desire existed only to further the use of women in reproduction, and that such desires would wither away if women no longer had to perform that function, she felt that any sexual expression perpetuated women's domination by men. (By this criterion, masturbation, too, would be a reactionary perpetuation of sexual desires that must wither away if women are to be free). She did not sufficiently realize that her paper "The Institution of Sexual Intercourse" described the institution of *heterosexual* intercourse.

In what sense did she think that men were "sexually superior" to women? Was it because they have orgasms more automatically? But she knew of Masters' and Johnson's findings that women were capable of multiple orgasms.

Atkinson's position on lesbianism reflected difficulties she was experiencing in the movement:

> One of the central problems for all members of oppressed groups is self-hatred. To feminists, lesbianism represents a kind of self-identification. If any individual spends most of her time dealing with the ways in which members of her class are abused, it's unlikely that she will be able to maintain too much of a positive attitude either toward herself or toward other members of her class.[11]

Since Atkinson wrote this, there has been a much greater emphasis on bonding with, and enjoying other women. However, the problem that negative personal or political experiences with women may complicate the lesbian feminist's life and feelings is still very much present.

Atkinson wrote,

> Woman's identification must be sought in the eyes of her Oppressor. To turn to other women for ego support is like trying to catch a reflection of herself in a darkened mirror.[12]

Apparently, Atkinson believed that a woman could only become a subject if man acknowledged her as a subject, not as other. But would that not still leave her an object, if her subjectivity depended on his view of her? Surely only a person *herself* or a group *itself* can demand, or achieve, status as a subject.

By the end of 1970, Atkinson recognized the political element in lesbianism more clearly and saw it as an integral feminist "issue."

> Lesbianism, for feminism, is not just 'another' issue...Nor is lesbianism about 'autonomy'...Lesbianism is pretty clearly about 'association,' not about aloneness...It is the association by choice of individual members of any oppressed group—the massing of power—which is essential to resistance...It is this commitment, by choice, full-time, of one woman to others of her class, that is called lesbianism. It is this full commitment, against any and all personal considerations, if necessary, that constitutes the political significance of lesbianism.[13]

However, in her strategic model Atkinson did not see lesbians as necessarily part of the "feminist rebels," but as a sort of "buffer zone":

Lesbianism is clearly the buffer between the male and female classes.[14]

When lesbian "buffers" are attacked by men, she thought that they might or might not support the class of women. But she suggested that feminists must support lesbians and win them over (as if feminists and lesbians were separate groups).

Lesbianism is to feminism what the Communist Party was to the trade-union movement. Tactically, any feminist should fight to the death for lesbianism because of its strategic importance.[15]

Her criterion for lesbians or any women has always been whether they were willing to take risks in the name of women as a class.

I'm enormously less interested in whom you sleep with than I am in with whom you're prepared to die.[16]

Atkinson went further (in the same speech) toward acknowledging lesbianism as a political force. She began using "lesbian" as a positive term for all committed feminists.

There are other women who have never had sexual relations with other women, but who have made, and live, a total commitment to this movement. These women are 'lesbians' in the political sense.[17]

She suggested that all feminists wear a button saying, "I am a Lesbian" and called herself a political lesbian until lesbians told her they felt the term did not recognize the specificity of their experience.

Atkinson was the first non-lesbian radical feminist to acknowledge the political importance of lesbianism in the movement.

Lesbian Self-Definition

In the early 1970s, even radical lesbian feminists generally saw all sexual categories, including lesbianism, as a product of male-defined society. The classic 1970 paper, "The Woman-Identified Woman," by the New York group Radicalesbians, says,

...Lesbianism, like male homosexuality, is a category of behavior possible only in a sexist society characterized by rigid sex roles and dominated by male supremacy...In a society in which men do not oppress women, and sexual experience is allowed to follow feelings, the categories of homosexuality and heterosexuality would disappear.[18]

'Lesbian' is one of the sexual categories by which men have divided up humanity.[19]

Lesbians have become less satisfied with this assumption of innate bisexuality. In 1980, Adrienne Rich wrote that this assumption is just another extension of the assumption that women are innately heterosexual. She calls it "the old liberal leap over the tasks of the here and now" and points out that it is not very positive about women. "It also assumes that women who have chosen women have done so simply because men are oppressive and emotionally unavailable..."[20]

Definitions of a lesbian or lesbianism differ. Some see the lesbian as a woman who is *greater than* other women, some see her as a woman *like* other women, some see her as not being a woman at all by certain definitions of the word "woman." Women can hold any one of these positions and still believe that it would be possible for *all* women to choose to be lesbians. Theoretically, either those who see a lesbian as greater than other women or those who see a lesbian as not being a "woman," could believe that not all women are capable of becoming lesbians.

In a 1977 *Sinister Wisdom* piece, former *Ladder* editor and current publisher of Naiad Press books Barbara Grier wrote:

> In my mind it [a lesbian] means a superior being...a woman of course...but a superior woman, someone beyond and above... almost a goal to be achieved.[21]

Nevertheless, she sees lesbianism as a goal obtainable for all women who can overcome the outside restraints.

> I believe that women would automatically be Lesbians given social choice to be. It is, after all, so preferable a way to be, to live, that I cannot imagine anyone thinking for a moment of any other choice given the facts. What has not been available on a mass scale is this information...this sense of exhilaration.[22]

"The Woman-Identified Woman" by Radicalesbians was the first assertion of the idea that lesbianism can be an expression of feminist politics and a political strategy.

> Until women see in each other the possibility of a primal commitment which includes sexual love, they will be denying themselves the love and value they readily accord to men, thus affirming their second-class status.[23]

Rita Mae Brown wrote, "If you reserve those 'special' commitments for men then you are telling women they aren't worth those commitments, they aren't important."[24]

This analysis of lesbianism as a strategy necessarily implied a critique of heterosexuality as an institution. "The Woman-Identified Woman" said:

For this we must be available and supportive to one another, give our commitment and our love, give the emotional support necessary to sustain this movement. Our energies must flow toward our sisters, not backward toward our oppressors. As long as women's liberation tries to free women without facing the basic structure that binds us in one-to-one relationship with our oppressors, tremendous energies will continue to flow into trying to straighten up each particular relationship with a man...into trying to make the 'new man' out of him, in the delusion that this will allow us to be the 'new woman.'[25]

In 1972-73, a Washington DC lesbian feminist collective, the Furies, continued to develop the ideas put forward in "The Woman-Identified Woman." This is not surprising, since Rita Mae Brown, a former member of Radicalesbians, also was a member of the Furies.

Furies member Charlotte Bunch wrote about lesbianism as a political choice:

Woman-identified Lesbianism is, then, more than a sexual preference, it is a political choice. It is political because relationships between men and women are essentially political, they involve power and dominance.[26]

Some lesbian feminists, such as Charlotte Bunch, emphasized that lesbian feminism was not merely a reaction against men, although many women may have thought the initial political ideas sounded that way.

The Lesbian, woman-identified-woman, commits herself to women not only as an alternative to oppressive male/female relationships but primarily because she *loves* women. Whether consciously or not, by her actions, the Lesbian has recognized that giving support and love to men over women perpetuates the system that oppresses her. If women do not make a commitment to each other, which includes sexual love, we deny ourselves the love and value traditionally given to men. We accept our second-class status.[27]

*Some members of the Furies collective in one of their
group houses in Washington DC, 1971.*

Lesbian writers have pointed out the advantages of lesbianism, as well its possible political benefits.

Wilda Chase (a pseudonym) wrote, in an essay for *The Ladder*,

Lesbians do have definite advantages over heterosexual women. Their less intimate contact with men gives them a margin of protection against the grossest forms of damage. They should guard against complacency, however. Like all female citizens who grow up and live in a male-dominated world, Lesbians also have identity problems.[28]

Martha Shelley wrote in 1969,

The Lesbian, through her ability to obtain love and sexual satisfaction from other women, is freed of dependence on men for love, sex, and money. She does not have to do menial chores for them (at least at home)...She is freed from unwanted pregnancy and the pains of childbirth, and from the drudgery of child raising.[29]

Shelley does not ignore the problems.

On the other hand, she pays three penalties. The rewards of child raising are denied her. This is a great loss for some women, but not for others...

The Lesbian still must compete with men in the job market, facing the same job and salary discrimination as her straight sister.

Finally, she faces the most severe contempt and ridicule that society can heap on a woman.[30]

(In the 1980s, the spread of artificial insemination has made possible what is sometimes referred to as "the lesbian baby boom." Lesbians can now choose whether to bear children.)

Mary Daly sees lesbianism as a refusal to be "the other." In *Gyn/Ecology*, she wrote that women who are present to each other "are no longer empty receptacles to be used as 'the Other'."[31]

Daly quotes lesbian writer Marilyn Frye as saying, "Male parasitism means that males *must* have access to women; it is the Patriarchal Imperative. But feminist no-saying is more than a substantial removal (redirection, reallocation) of goods and services because access is one of the faces of power. Female denial of male access to females substantially cuts off a flow of benefits, but it has also the form and full portent of assumption of power."[32]

When women assume power in this way, they can be subjects rather than objects or "others." How can a woman become a subject unless she rejects a social order that turns her into an object? How can she be a subject if she still accepts man's definition that she is his?

Jill Johnston also had written about rejecting the role of the "other."

> Feminism will no longer need itself when women cease to think of themselves as the 'other' in relation to the 'other' and unite with their own kind or species.[33]

In Johnston's words it sounds as if all of the change will take place in women's unconscious and personal lives, without significant opposition by men.

Lesbian feminists, while seeing lesbianism as a political choice and a political strategy, tried to be careful not to give the impression that being a lesbian was the only political commitment needed.

As Charlotte Bunch wrote in "Lesbians in Revolt,"

> Being a Lesbian is part of challenging male supremacy, but not the end. For the Lesbian or homosexual woman, there is no individual solution to oppression.
>
> The Lesbian may think she is free since she escapes the personal oppression of the individual male/female relationships. But to society she is still a woman...(I've never heard of a rapist who stopped because his victim was a lesbian!)[34]

Political lesbianism was posed as a direct challenge to heterosexual feminists. As Ginny Berson, a member of the Furies and later of Olivia Records, wrote,

> Lesbianism is not a matter of sexual preference, but rather one of political choice which every woman must make if she is to become woman-identified and thereby end male supremacy.[35]

Rita Mae Brown wrote, in "The Shape of Things to Come,"

> If you cannot find it in yourself to love another woman, and that includes physical love, then how can you truly say you care about women's liberation?[36]

Lesbian feminists responded to heterosexual feminists' charges that lesbian feminists were "lesbian chauvinists"—which developed as soon as lesbian feminism developed. Jill Johnston wrote:

> The lesbian denounced as a chauvinist was a neat way of delaying the issue [of a heterosexual feminist's own sexuality].[37]

But some Furies members were trying to discover possible ties with women who did not identify themselves as lesbians. The 1975 introduction to the Furies' collection, *Lesbianism and the Women's Movement*, written by Charlotte Bunch and Nancy Myron, says that:

> Some new bonds are beginning to emerge between Lesbians and single women. We share a common economic and psychological reality: we are solely responsible for our lives—all of our lifetime. We have rejected ownership by men and with it, economic support. We face survival issues without heterosexual cushions ...We must provide for ourselves, our children, and each other —economically, emotionally, and if we organize, politically.[38]

Rita Mae Brown, whose ideas were fundamental to the creation of lesbian feminist theory, wrote that lesbianism was the central women's issue because it dealt with women's relationships to each other. The focus on what happens *between women* rather than between women and men, practically turned the feminist movement around. There had been emphasis on sisterhood before, but the sisterhood was focused outward, against men.

Brown wrote,

> Lesbianism is the one issue that deals with women responding positively to other women as total human beings worthy of total commitment. It is the one area where no man can tread.[39]

The Lesbian: Woman Prime or Beyond Woman

In her book *Lesbian Nation*, Jill Johnston made some of the strongest claims for the inherent lesbianism in all women—and the primacy of the lesbian in radical change.

> It's impossible to separate our oppression as women from our oppression as lesbians. All women are lesbians...
>
> I feel in a position to assert that the lesbian with a political definition is the woman committed woman *par excellence* and that this is the goal of feminist revolution.[40]

Johnston proclaimed,

> Feminism at heart is a massive complaint. Lesbianism is the solution...Until all women are lesbians there will be no true political revolution.[41]

The slogan "lesbianism is the solution" has a very different emphasis from Radicalesbians or the Furies' articles, which carefully pointed out that organized political activities were necessary.

For Johnston, a lesbian is more of a woman than anyone else. She said there is a "female principle," an inherent "womanness," and that the lesbian has more of it. This is different from "The Woman-Identified Woman" or the Furies' articles, which saw divisions between people ("male," "female," "lesbian," "heterosexual") as being male-imposed categories to justify and perpetuate rule.

Johnston wrote,

> The lesbian is woman prime. The woman who maintains or regains her integrity as a woman. By (re)uniting with her feminine principle. The reunion of the mother and the daughter into the true sister principle. The straight woman will discover how she has been colossally duped by being robbed of her womanhood...
>
> The test case of the oppressed woman is the woman who is most woman [Johnston means the lesbian].[42]

The apparent opposite of this concept is an idea posed by French lesbian writer Monique Wittig, who maintains that a lesbian is not a "woman" at all because the social construct or idea "woman" means someone who has sex with men.

In her article "One is Not Born a Woman," Wittig writes,

> The refusal to become (or to remain) heterosexual always means to refuse to become a man or a woman, consciously or not.[43]

Wittig believes that a lesbian is not a woman because she does not play a woman's socially defined role.

But Jill Johnston turns from saying that the lesbian is the most "woman" to saying the lesbian is not a woman, in terms roughly similar to those Wittig used later.

> The liberated political lesbian by this reasoning is of course no longer a woman. Woman being defined as an oppressed person. Defined in other words by men. The language is no longer adequate to signify the liberated sex. The woman identified woman was an excellent phrase to help define the lesbian in

her prime womanhood in distinction to all women who still partake of male privilege through bed, marriage, and fraternization, but 'woman' is too overwhelmingly the name of the sex so called and thus checked and retained by the man. My own use of the word here was convenient to expose the fraud of the 'real woman' and establish the is-ness of the lesbian as the sex with the organs commonly referred to as woman.[44]

To CLIT, writing in 1974, a lesbian is:

...A woman who has broken through the patriarchal confusion of centuries to realize that a brilliant and (fully equipped emotionally and intellectually) species called women have been imprisoned and made to associate with a totally inferior species which attempts to justify this imprisonment by making the prisoners think they are stupid and inferior...[45]

In 1977, *Sinister Wisdom* editor Harriet Desmoines suggested that lesbians were becoming a separate species, apparently because they had the potential to change sexuality and reproduction.

THE REVOLUTION WILL BE IN EFFECT THE CREATION OF A NEW SPECIES: *A SPECIES WHICH REDEFINES SEXUALITY AND REPRODUCTION; THE PRODUCTION AND EXCHANGE OF USE VALUES; AND THE LANGUAGES OF THE CONSCIOUS AND SUBCONSCIOUS.*

THE NEW SPECIES IS ALREADY EMERGING... 'LESBIAN' HAS DENOTED WOMEN WHO HAVE SEXUAL RELATIONS WITH WOMEN; THE NEW SPECIES, THE EMERGING LESBIAN WOMAN, INCORPORATES THE OLD MEANING WITHIN A FULLER MEANING: *LESBIAN*, A WOMAN IN TOTAL REVOLT AGAINST THE PATRIARCHY.[46]

For lesbian writer Bertha Harris, like Monique Wittig, the lesbian refuses to be man or woman. As Harris wrote in 1976,

The lesbian is a new creature, neither man nor woman, but one who takes from both the father and the mother, in order to create work that goes beyond the limits of gender.[47]

She added,

...Born of woman, she consciously rejects *being* a woman— because she does not want to die: to be unable to work is to be dead; the 'man's woman,' because of what has happened to her below the waist, is dead above the neck.[48]

Surely most lesbians can see why heterosexual women became
offended at such remarks.

Harris sees the term "woman" as meaning dependent on man.
As a female becomes independent—presumably by work outside
the home, among other things—she becomes less like the
male-defined idea of a "woman."

> ...The more a woman works, and works to make things happen,
> the less 'woman' she becomes, the more lesbian...
>
> Patriarchy, by inducing fear of the lesbian, induces fear of
> work in all women.[49]
>
> ...By making work (outside the prescribed labors of the female
> role), she has ceased being a woman; she has transgressed
> against the community agreement not to work.[50]

What about the many heterosexual women who have always
worked for wages? Are they lesbians? Or are they still "women," as
Wittig might say, because they still have sex with men?

In "One Is Not Born a Woman," Wittig maintains that it is
possible to give up the categories of male and female, and still be
a lesbian.

> Lesbian is the only concept I know of which is beyond the
> categories of sex (woman and man), because the designated
> subject) lesbian is *not* a woman, either economically, or
> politically or ideologically...For what makes a woman is a
> specific social relation to a man...a relation which implies
> personal and physical obligation...a relation which lesbians
> escape...[51]

In "The Straight Mind," Wittig says the basic taboo in
patriarchal society is against homosexuality and lesbianism.
Domination by men is based on their splitting the world into the
categories of women and men, heterosexual and homosexual.

> In this thought, to reject the obligation of coitus and the
> institutions that this obligation has produced as necessary for
> the constitution of society, is simply an impossibility...
> Thus lesbianism, homosexuality, and the societies that we form
> cannot be thought or spoken of, even though they have always
> existed...
>
> Yes, straight society is based on the necessity of the different/
> other at every level. It cannot work without this concept...
> But what is the different/other if not the dominated? For

heterosexual society is the society which not only oppresses lesbians and gay men, it oppresses many different/others...

...For us, this means there cannot any longer be women and men, and that as classes and as categories of thought or language they have to disappear, politically, economically, ideologically. If we, as lesbians and gay men, continue to speak of ourselves and to conceive of ourselves as women and as men, we are instrumental in maintaining heterosexuality.[52]

Other lesbians in France and Québec adopted Wittig's position that lesbians are not women; these lesbians define themselves as "radical lesbians". Québecoise radical lesbians Ariane Brunet and Louise Turcotte wrote in 1982: "In fact, heterosexuality is the cause of sexism... Heterosexuality is the institution that creates, maintains, and supports men's power."[53] They reject feminism as insufficiently lesbian: "Feminism is neither our politics nor our history..."[54]

These ideas have influenced some lesbian theorists in the United States. Sarah Hoagland wrote in 1988, "...I have become convinced that the concept 'woman' is a created category, like the concept 'feminine,' and is bankrupt."[55] She writes, "The concept of 'woman' includes no real sense of female power."[56] In her book *Lesbian Ethics*, Hoagland sometimes uses terms such as "lesbians and women" or "women or lesbians" to refer to lesbians and nonlesbian women.

One could infer from Johnston, Wittig, the radical lesbians and Hoagland that lesbians need not identify with other women or work with them—unless they, too, choose to be lesbians.

Saying that lesbians are not women or are utterly different from other women may have an intellectual link with the old "third sex" idea espoused by turn-of-the-century sexologists in Europe and the United States. One can find works from that period that refer to lesbians as a separate species. Take, for instance, this excerpt from the 1903 German lesbian novel *Are These Women?* by Aimée Duc,

> ...We are confusing cause and effect if one believes women whom men think very 'feminine' to be so. Quite the contrary. They are 'unfeminine' since they live only for the wishes and pretensions of men. Consequently, the really 'feminine' ones would be those who keep their individuality all for themselves and who form a special species, physically and psychologically.[57]

The resemblance to "The Woman-Identified Woman" is striking until one comes to the mention of a separate species.

Implying that lesbians have no reason to work with other women seems a rather precarious strategy, given the relatively small number of lesbians. How many revolutionary groups announce that they are transcending their class while the oppressor class is still in power? Even if this is the ultimate goal, it seems a shaky immediate strategy at a time when a class, such as the class of women, is trying to develop class consciousness.

Talking about not being women—especially saying that some women have already transcended the category of "women"—hardly seems like an effective tactic at a time when most women have not yet acknowledged that women—as defined by this society—are a class. Wittig *does* believe that women are currently a class.

One could define "women" in so many ways—one could say that women are those who, as a class, are subjected to rape, forced childbearing, and other forms of sexual exploitation by men. This definition would include lesbians, even lesbian separatists with karate black belts. (Of course, some men are raped by other men without being women, but these men are not raped as a class. Gay men are subjected to violence as a group because they are considered traitors to the male class.)

Criticism of 'Lesbian Superiority'

Not all lesbians in the feminist movement endorsed the claim that lesbians are better than heterosexual women.

Martha Shelley wrote, for a 1977 *Sinister Wisdom* discussion:

> Once we start regarding ourselves as a separate species, a new 'übermensch'—superior to males and heterosexual women—we are no better politically than the Nazi Party or the Ku Klux Klan... I have been a lesbian feminist for a long time and in fact was one of the founders of the Gay Liberation Front. I am also a Jew. Whenever I hear this race-species-superiority trip it makes me sick. When I hear it from lesbians, it makes me want to (a) throw up, (b) go straight and have babies, (c) abandon the human race and be a hermit. It makes me sick when I hear stories about anti-Arab racism in Israel. In both cases, I feel somehow involved and responsible, and I ask myself, what were we fighting for.[58]

Brooke, a radical feminist lesbian, wrote in 1975 that not all lesbians with connections to the movement are serious feminists:

> The lesbian version of cultural feminism has two sides to it: 1) Being a lesbian is sufficient in itself for being a feminist. 2) One has to be a lesbian in order to be a feminist...Lesbianism is either confused with feminism or placed above it.
>
> At best this is apolitical...At worst it is an anti-political elimination of feminism with the goal of universal lesbianism substituted for the goal of women's liberation...The function of feminism is to create social change, not social life. Friends, etc., may be an outgrowth of feminism, but not its purpose.[59]

Part of her criticism of the role of lesbian feminism in the feminist movement stems from a concern that some women were becoming lesbians as part of a fad, or out of opportunism, not because they loved women or were committed to remaining lesbians after their initial relationships broke up.

> There are so many fad lesbians running around, it isn't funny. These women have used, hurt and driven many serious lesbians out of the women's movement. Many heterosexual women (who are too honest and not easily intimidated) have left the organized women's movement. (A few [anti-lesbian] bigots have gone, too).[60]

Brooke's criticism of lesbian feminists is not only a political analysis, but also another and different version of the common lesbian fear of being hurt by women not committed to lesbianism. Many separatists also have expressed this fear.

Chapter 9

The Critique of Heterosexuality

One of the major theoretical points of lesbian feminism has been its critique of heterosexuality as an institution. Although the first lengthy radical analysis of heterosexuality was done by Ti-Grace Atkinson in "The Institution of Sexual Intercourse," almost all radical analysis of heterosexuality has been written by lesbians.

Atkinson's position on heterosexuality was uncompromising. She saw (hetero)sexual intercourse as a male-defined act that reinforced male supremacy.

> The determining characteristic of the class of men is their sex characteristic...This could account for the male obsession with sex. Sex acts as a reassuring reminder of his class supremacy. In addition, given the context of class oppression, sex acts as a convenient reminder to the female of her class inferiority.[1]

Atkinson is saying that every time a man has intercourse with a woman he reinforces his belief—and hers—that he, as a man, has a right to women's bodies and that male-defined intercourse is the normative sex act.

Unlike some heterosexual feminists who see "worst cases" such as rape or prostitution as the main target for change in male sexuality, Atkinson focused on marriage because it affects the most women.

> Since the highest incidence of the male-female relationship is in marriage, it should be a primary target.[2]

Marriage, if one examines the laws which define it, is as much if not more in the interests of men than slavery was in the interests of the master. And yet, the aims of the Movement are to get rid of the abuses *within* marriage, *equalize* the roles, but, for *God's* sake, keep the institution. How can you equalize the roles when the essential *nature* of these roles is to be *contrasting*? Could you maintain slavery if you 'equalized' the roles of master/slave to master/master?[3]

Of course she does not think that reforming marriage should be the aim of the Movement. When Atkinson talks about marriage reform being the Movement's aim, apparently she is criticizing groups such as NOW, although the more radical Redstockings might be included.

Atkinson issued a challenge to women:

The price of clinging to the enemy is your life.

To enter into a relationship with a man who has divested himself as completely from the male role as possible would still be a risk.

But to relate to a man who has done any less is suicide.

Women are still operating on a personal rather than a political basis.

The proof of class-consciousness will be when we separate off from men, from these one-to-one units...

There can be no significant improvement in the situation of women until this happens...

I, personally, have taken the position that I will not appear with any man publicly, where it could possibly be interpreted that we were friends.[4]

Lesbian Critiques

Lesbian feminists soon offered critiques of heterosexuality that were similar in many ways to Atkinson's critique, although lesbians saw women as having more desire for sexual contact than Atkinson thought they had.

Given the women's liberation movement's strong emphasis on women speaking from their own experience, what was the justification for lesbians describing, analyzing, and criticizing heterosexuality? Most lesbians have, in fact, had sexual relationships with men, usually before they became lesbians. Most heterosexual women have not had sexual relations with other women.

Rita Mae Brown wrote, "Straight women don't know what our lives are like. They don't think like we do. We understand their lives because we were raised to be straight. It is one-way communication."[5]

But lesbian feminists also have tried to include *all* women in the struggle against the institution of heterosexuality, as Charlotte Bunch and Nancy Myron did in the introduction to *Lesbianism and the Women's Movement.*

> We are less concerned with whether each woman personally becomes a lesbian than with the destruction of heterosexuality as a crucial part of male supremacy. Lesbians have been the quickest to see the challenge to heterosexuality as necessary to feminism's survival. However, straight feminists are not precluded from examining and fighting against heterosexuality as an ideology and institution that oppresses us all. The problem is that few have done so. This perpetuates lesbian fears that women remaining tied to men prevents them from seeing the function of heterosexuality and acting to end it. It is not lesbians (women's ties to women), but women's ties to men, and thus men themselves, who divide women politically and personally.[6]

Like Atkinson, lesbian feminists criticized the structure of heterosexual sex.

Coletta Reid, a member of the Furies, wrote:

> Female sexual passivity is central to heterosexuality... It is no accident that the 'missionary' position is the favored one in advanced patriarchy. The man is 'on top' in bed just as he is in the economy and politics. The woman is pinned down, can hardly move, and has the least chance of having an orgasm. If marriage is legalized prostitution, then heterosexuality is socially approved rape.[7]

Heterosexuality is oppressive not only when it is overtly violent, lesbian feminists said, but also when it is more subtle. The institution operates in many ways.

Furies member Sharon Deevey wrote:

> I realized that *every* fuck is a rape even if it feels nice because every man has power and privilege over women, whether he uses it blatantly or subtly. My 'liberated' husband kept me down not by violence but by making me feel guilty. He wanted me to be a strong woman as long as my main worries were about his feelings, problems and 'oppression.'[8]

Jill Johnston also argued the greater likelihood of satisfaction in lesbianism—and homosexuality for men.

> Not only is the psycho-emotional potential for satisfaction with another woman far greater than that with a man, insomuch as every woman like every man was originally most profoundly attached to herself as her mother, but there is more likelihood of sexual fulfillment with another woman as well since all organisms best understand the basic equipment of another organism which most closely resembles themselves.[9]

In an argument similar to Atkinson's, Johnston suggested that male biology—and the history of men's interpretation of that biology, the history of the use of the penis as a means of domination, makes an "equal" sexual relationship between women and men difficult.

> It is in any case difficult to conceive of an 'equal' sexual relationship between two people in which one member is the 'biological aggressor'...The man retains the prime organ of invasion.[10]

Johnston continues:

> Every woman who remains in sexual relation to man is defeated every time she does it with the man because each single experience for every woman is a reenactment of the primal one in which she was invaded and separated and fashioned into a receptacle for the passage of the invader.[11]

According to this logic, there would seem to be an "out" for the heterosexual feminist trying to end the repetition of the act of penile penetration: Substitute another form of sexual expression, such as oral or manual touching. That heterosexual feminists have not written much about this as a serious strategy, despite their recognition of "the myth of the vaginal orgasm" and the lack of a perfectly effective, safe means of birth control, suggests that they do not really exercise any power in their relationships with men (and know they don't).

Rejecting the Male Model

In her 1974 speech to a NOW conference on sexuality, "Renouncing Sexual Equality," Andrea Dworkin rejects the idea that women should be equal to or the same as men sexually. She sees all relations of dominance as stemming from men's *sexual* relations with women:

The male sexual model is based upon a polarization of humankind into man/woman, master/slave, aggressor/victim, active/passive...The very identity of men, their civil and economic power, the forms of government they have developed, the wars they wage, are tied *irrevocably* together. All forms of dominance and submission, whether it be man over woman, white over black, boss over worker, rich over poor, are tied *irrevocably* to the sexual identities of men and are derived from the male sexual model. Once we grasp this, it becomes clear that *in fact* men own the sex act, the language that describes sex, the women whom they objectify. Men have written the scenario for any sexual fantasy you have ever had or any sexual act you have ever engaged in.

There is no *sexual freedom* or *justice* in exchanging the female role for the male role...There is no *freedom* or *justice* or even common sense, in developing a male sexual sensibility— a sexual sensibility that is aggressive, competitive, objectifying, quantity oriented. There is only equality.[12]

The speech suggests that women's sexuality has been repressed and will need greater expression, but that male sexual styles are no fit model for change.

Dworkin then said that men must change their sexual relations, including their sexual acts. She saw lesbianism as the model for new forms of sexuality.

I think that men will have to give up their precious erections and begin to make love as women do together. I am saying that men will have to renounce their phallocentric personalities, and the privileges and powers given to them at birth as a consequence of their anatomy, that they will have to excise everything in them that they now value as distinctly 'male.'[13]

Specifically, what does this mean? That men should switch entirely to oral and manual sex? To having fewer orgasms or none? At the very least, she must have meant a change in emphasis, so that male satisfaction is no longer the focus and penetration by the penis no longer the standard act. Presumably, she also means emotional change. In saying that men could be capable of relating sexually as lesbians do, she was assuming that their sexuality was not utterly biologically determined.

Anger at Heterosexual Women

Lesbians also analyzed heterosexual privilege and the economics of heterosexual sex. Coletta Reid wrote:

> I realized that when I was married I had been bought off. I had accepted being subservient, sexually available, and keeper of his home in return for some degree of economic security and social acceptance. I had become a fat hen who gave up her freedom for regular corn...
>
> The saddest revelation was that feminists still had a stake in being fat hens. They primarily wanted the farmer to treat them a little better...[14]

(By the 1980s, many lesbian feminists were responding to the demands of fat women by learning to avoid using such fatophobic statements).

Although heterosexual feminists often felt that lesbian feminists were being intolerant, many lesbian feminists felt that any such tolerance would amount to "giving up" on their heterosexual sisters, not caring what happened to them. Furies member Barbara Solomon wrote,

> Heterosexuality insures male supremacy. To say that 'Everybody needs love and I could care less if a woman is fucking a man' is to say 'Any oppressed person needs some payoff to make them preserve their oppression. I could care less if a woman is oppressed, and I could care less if that oppression makes her gang up with that pig to fuck me over.'[15]

Some lesbian feminists express great pain over interactions with heterosexual women. Lesbians are quite aware that they are used as the "extremists" of the women's movement, the threat to make men behave. According to Barbara Solomon:

> Straight women don't want us to fight with men—they just want payoffs from men *and* women...If she stays in middle-of-the-road straight women's liberation, she can play us off against her man and have the best of both worlds. He's going to have to start behaving...
>
> Every lesbian knows through personal experience how straight women sell us out. Each of us at some time has been infatuated with a straight woman and we compromised ourselves, grovelled to be good to her and tried to prove to her that we were better than men, all in hopes that she would love us...She had to betray us...[16]

The 1974 CLIT papers expressed this sentiment even more intensely.

> ...Because they (straight women) pass superficially as women, they are in the position of 'agent' relative to dykes...the result is that these lesbians engage in pointless and energy draining dialogue with them...Straight women are not lesbians. You can't talk to a *potential* anything [some lesbian feminists had suggested seeing heterosexual women as potential lesbians]...
>
> ...The straight woman...acts (what she thinks is) seductive... comes on...then you show interest in her on that level... surprise! she turns off, becomes cool, dissociated, uninterested, perhaps contemptuous...you imagined it all...you back off... then surprise! she turns on again...and the whole drama is repeated again, and again and again and again, until you either get hurt, bored, crazy, or she comes out (probably with someone else)...[17]

The CLIT women moved on from expressing experience-derived pain to giving the ultimate insult—saying that straight women are men, an obvious impossibility, rather than saying that they are male-defined.

> They are males in disguise...
>
> The danger of straight women is their disguise. They look like women.[18]

The CLIT women did admit that male-identification, thinking in a male-ist way, is a problem for lesbians, too.

> ...The real battle is between the dykes and the pricks, the dykes struggling to rid themselves of the prick inside their heads as well as outside...[19]

Heterosexuality as Compulsory

On the other hand, Charlotte Bunch attempted to give heterosexual feminists a framework by which they could understand and work against the institution of forced heterosexuality. In 1975, she wrote:

> Basically, heterosexuality means men first. That's what it's all about. It assumes that every woman is heterosexual; that every woman is defined by and is the property of men. Her body, her services, her children belong to men. If you don't accept that definition, you're a queer—no matter who you sleep with...[20]

Adrienne Rich wrote in her 1980 essay "Compulsory Heterosexuality and Lesbian Existence" that challenging heterosexuality is a fundamental, necessary part of lesbian politics—and ultimately of feminist politics.

> The assumption that 'most women are innately heterosexual' stands as a theoretical and political stumbling block for feminists. It remains a tenable assumption partly because lesbian existence has been written out of history or catalogued under disease, partly because it has been treated as exceptional rather than intrinsic, partly because to acknowledge that for women heterosexuality may not be a 'preference' at all but something that has had to be imposed, managed, organized, propagandized, and maintained by force is an immense step to take if you consider yourself freely and 'innately' heterosexual...To take the step of questioning heterosexuality as a 'preference' or 'choice' for women—and to do the intellectual and emotional work that follows—will call for a special quality of courage in heterosexually identified feminists, but I think the rewards will be great...[21]

Criticism or defense of heterosexual women's individual relationships is not the basic point of criticizing heterosexuality, Rich writes.

> The question inevitably will arise: Are we to condemn all heterosexual relationships, including those which are least oppressive? I believe this question, though often heartfelt, is the wrong question here. We have been stalled in a maze of false dichotomies which prevents our apprehending the institution as a whole: 'good' versus 'bad' marriages; 'marriage for love' versus arranged marriage; 'liberated' sex versus prostitution; heterosexual intercourse versus rape...Within the institution exist, of course, qualitative differences of experience; but the absence of choice remains the great unacknowledged reality, and in the absence of choice, women will remain dependent upon the chance or luck of particular relationships and will have no collective power to determine the meaning and place of sexuality in their lives.[22]

Rich emphasizes the lesbian element in all women who love and bond with each other—rather than restricting the definition of lesbianism to those who express themselves through "sexual act." She writes beautifully of "the lesbian continuum":

> I mean the term *lesbian continuum* to include a range—through each woman's life and throughout history—of woman-identified experience, not simply the fact that a woman has had or consciously desired genital sexual experience with another woman. If we expand it to embrace many more forms of primary intensity between and among women, including the sharing of a rich inner life, the bonding against male tyranny, the giving and receiving of practical and political support...[23]

Rich suggests that heterosexuality is instituted and maintained by force. She points out that lesbian feminists cannot accept the notion that most women will always be heterosexual, and even criticizes the assumption held by many lesbian feminists, including the writers of "The Woman-Identified Woman" and the Furies' articles, that without male domination, everyone would be bisexual.

> The extension of this assumption [of female heterosexuality] is the frequently heard assertion that in a world of genuine equality, where men were nonoppressive and nurturing, everyone would be bisexual. Such a notion blurs and sentimentalizes the actualities within which women have experienced sexuality...[24]

Rich suggested that the institution of heterosexuality is at this time inseparable from violence. She quoted Catharine A. MacKinnon[25] in support of this argument.

> MacKinnon raises radical questions as to the qualitative differences between sexual harassment, rape and ordinary heterosexual intercourse... She criticizes Susan Brownmiller for separating rape from the mainstream of daily life and for her unexamined premise that 'rape is violence, intercourse is sexuality,' removing rape from the sexual sphere altogether. Most crucially she argues that 'taking rape from the realm of "the sexual," placing it in the realm of "the violent," allows one to be against it without raising any questions about the extent to which the institution of heterosexuality has defined force as a normal part of "the preliminaries".' 'Never is it asked whether, under conditions of male supremacy, the notion of "consent" has any meaning.'[26]

Ariane Brunet and Louise Turcotte have suggested that Rich's critique of heterosexuality is actually too tolerant of heterosexuality. They believe that Rich implies that "compulsory heterosexuality and lesbian existence are somehow parallel. According to this thinking, if we have been able to become Lesbians in a heterosystem, then our very existence can be used to validate their assertion that heterosexuality is *their* choice...Once one has recognized the 'compulsory nature' of heterosexuality she's rid of the obligation to follow the norm [heterosexuality]. She can now willingly follow [heterosexuality]...

"...How can one choose between the political institution of the dominators and the power of revolt of the dominated class?"[27]

However, Rich was suggesting that it would difficult to authentically choose heterosexuality in a society in which it is compulsory, not that lesbianism and heterosexuality are parallel choices.

Lesbian Invisibility

Marilyn Frye, in her 1983 book *The Politics of Reality*, points out how invisible lesbians and the possibility of lesbianism have been, how hard for women to discover. She wrote that lesbians do not exist in standard language. Dictionaries have defined sex as penetration with a penis.

> Dictionaries generally agree that 'sexual' means something on the order of *pertaining to the genital union of a male and female animal...*
>
> ...There is nothing women could do in the absence of men that could, without semantic oddity, be called 'having sex.'[28]

Frye suggests that the kind of perception or attention a lesbian gives a woman who is not a lesbian may enable the latter to change her perception of, and attention to women.

> Heterosexuality for women is not simply a matter of sexual preference, any more than lesbianism is. It is a matter of orientation of attention, as is lesbianism...Attention is a kind of passion...
>
> If the lesbian sees the women, the woman may see the lesbian seeing her...The woman, feeling herself seen, may learn that she *can be* seen; she may also be able to know that a woman can see, that is, can author perception.[29]

But can being perceived, however well, be the crucial step in becoming a perceiver, a subject?

Lesbians' feelings about heterosexual women, as we have seen, are often ambivalent—and sometimes quite negative. Not all of the "attention" that lesbian feminists have given heterosexual women has been filled with affectionate concern. Lesbians are not one-dimensional beacons of warmth, nor would Frye suggest that they should be.

Conscious Choice

Lesbian feminist Joyce Trebilcot wrote in a 1983 paper that feminists must take responsibility for their own sexual choices, whatever they are. When heterosexual feminists say their sexuality is determined by an overwhelming physical attraction for men, they are not taking responsibility for their sexuality, she writes.

It is peculiar, Trebilcot says, to assume

> ...that one's feelings must determine one's sexual identity, [i.e.] that one's genital twinges must determine whether one is lesbian, or heterosexual, or both. Granting that some women are sexually aroused only by men, they are not therefore locked into any of the familiar identities or excluded from any. Such women may, in the first place, choose for or against heterosexual *activity*...It is also true that a woman may choose to make love to or with women, even though she is not sexually aroused. A woman's claim that she is not erotically responsive to women but only to men does not in itself limit her choices as between lesbianism, heterosexuality, or bisexuality, or celibacy of whatever variety. Sexuality is socially constructed; in reconstructing it we need not assume either that erotic feelings should lead to love making or that love making ought to occur only where there are erotic feelings.[30]

Does Trebilcot mean to imply that one perhaps *should* engage in sexual activity even without sexual arousal? What lesbian is going to want to have sex with this unaroused woman who is trying to be sexual for nonsexual reasons? And why should either of them want to?

But Trebilcot does not say that it is impossible for feminists to be heterosexual while taking responsibility for their sexuality. She suggests that taking responsibility for heterosexuality means recognizing all of the reasons—social and economic, as well as sexual—that contribute to the choice to continue heterosexual relationships. Realizing that lesbianism is a possible choice, even if one does not choose to pursue it, makes it more likely that a heterosexual woman will be able to avoid heterosex*ism*, Trebilcot writes.

...The physical pleasure [of heterosexual sex] is not after all separable from the economic, emotional, social, and other advantages that she gains from heterosexual relationships...

A woman who has such an understanding... [is] taking responsibility for her own sexuality,... [which] contributes to a greater closeness in the women's community... [and] a lessening of heterosexism...[31]

In other words, choosing to do consciously whatever one does sexually, rather than assuming its inevitability, is taking responsibility for sexuality, Trebilcot says.

Heterosexual Feminists React

Many heterosexual feminists, including radical feminists, have been angered both by analyses of heterosexuality as an institution and by lesbian feminism *per se*. Some heterosexual feminists immediately responded defensively to Atkinson and the lesbian feminists.

In her article, "Lesbianism and Feminism," published not long after "The Woman-Identified Woman," radical feminist writer Anne Koedt wrote that lesbian feminist critiques "lend support to the notion that it *does* matter what the sex of your partner may be... it is oppressive for that very question even to be asked."[32]

There was considerable anger over the idea that feminists were presuming to judge one another's sex lives.

Koedt wrote:

If you are a feminist who is not sleeping with a woman you may risk hearing any of the following accusations: 'You're oppressing me if you don't sleep with women'; 'You're not a radical feminist if you don't sleep with women'; or 'You don't love women if you don't sleep with them.' I have even seen a woman's argument about an entirely different aspect of feminism be dismissed by some lesbians because she was not having sexual relations with women... There is an outrageous thing going on here strictly in terms of pressuring women about their personal lives.[33]

Probably *no* critique of heterosexuality, however politely worded (of course, they weren't all politely worded) would have been acceptable to most 1970s heterosexual radical feminists.

In a 1971 interview, Simone de Beauvoir expressed her reaction to some radical and lesbian feminists' rejection of all sexual relations with men and to the idea that "every fuck is a rape."

Is it true that all sexual relations between a man and a woman are necessarily oppressive? Instead of refusing such relations, could one not work at them so that they are not oppressive? I'm shocked when people tell me that intercourse is rape, basically one is adopting male myths. That would mean that the male sex organ really is a sword, a weapon. It is a question of inventing new, non-oppressive sexual relations.[34]

In her 1972 book *All Said and Done*, Beauvoir defended the vaginal orgasm and criticized feminists who rejected it as entirely a myth.

...The clitoris is intimately connected with the vagina, and it may be that this is the connection which makes the vaginal orgasm possible. However, coition with penetration of the vagina does provide pleasure of an undeniably specific kind, and this is the form that many women find the fullest and most satisfying. Laboratory experiments that isolate the internal sensitivity of the vagina as a whole from its reactions as a whole prove nothing. Copulation is not an intercourse between two sets of genital organs, nor yet between two bodies, but between two persons, and the orgasm is in the highest sense of the word a psychosomatic phenomenon.[35]

(Apparently by a "psychosomatic phenomenon," Beauvoir means a phenomenon connecting mind and body).

To Redstockings, a heterosexual radical feminist group, whatever women did should be accepted as a legitimate and rational survival strategy. To criticize what women did was to be anti-woman.

In "The Marriage Question," an article in Redstockings' book *Feminist Revolution*, Pat Mainardi wrote,

Although most American women are married, will be married, have been married or would like to be married, fashionable women's movement rhetoric classifies women who live with men as 'unliberated' second-class feminists at best, 'collaborators with the enemy' at worst.[36]

Consciousness-raising revealed what most women wanted. To reject what most women said they wanted was to attack most women.

Whereas the leftists [in the Movement] attacked the institution of marriage, the lesbians went one further and attacked any relationships with men. Neither group was interested in finding out the truth about their own and other women's lives—they already assumed they knew it...[37]

Mainardi apparently did not consider valid lesbians' descriptions of their own lives—what they had learned about the possibility of loving other women, how they had been hurt by women who chose men over them, how they had participated in heterosexual relations, then changed.

Actually, the Redstockings were just as angry at Atkinson's belief that women who lived with men were collaborators as with lesbian feminist politics.

Mainardi continued,

> Women who lived with men were 'collaborators with the enemy' went the new line, and they should 'liberate themselves' by leaving. Women began to be pressured to leave their husbands against their wishes and *whatever* the consequences... The group called The Feminists founded by Ti-Grace Atkinson, limited the number of women living with men to one-third of the group because they were supposed to be less militant and radical and would dilute purity. One could no longer testify honestly about one's married life because anything bad would be greeted with 'leave him.'
>
> During this time, feminists still living with a man became less honest about their reasons, and so nothing could be truly resolved.[38]

The perceived pressure to be dishonest was indeed a problem for the movement. Honest discussion is a prerequisite for resolving differences. However, silence at the mere prospect of disagreement should win no political applause.

Mainardi continued that she believed that marriage was both salvageable and desirable.

> To admit that one married out of love for another human being, that one valued the relationship and wished it to continue, and that, even so, one was still determined to force an end to whatever inequality and oppression existed within the marriage, was to open oneself to ridicule and condemnation...
>
> I believe women—and men—would like love, security, companionship, respect and a long term commitment to each other. Women rarely get much of this, in marriage or out, but we *want* it.[39]

Mainardi assumes that women and men ultimately want the same thing—good, mutually supportive relationships. Because most women want these relationships (with men), she feels they should have them—and seems to offer the hope that most women could obtain them.

As lesbians feared being used by the heterosexual women, heterosexual feminists feared being used by lesbians—and simplified lesbians' call for women to band together into a demand that specific women "put out." Mainardi wrote,

> The leftist women thought of us as support troops for their dogma; the lesbians as potential sex partners, the sum of these two attitudes—followers, supporters and sex partners—is exactly the same as men's attitudes towards all women.[40]

Mainardi apparently did not think that the desire for other women to become lesbians was motivated by concern or affection. Nor did Mainardi see that lesbians might be at least as eager to have more lesbian friends and political allies as to have "sex partners."

By 1975, the year that *Feminist Revolution* was published, lesbian feminists such as Charlotte Bunch and Lucia Valeska were encouraging heterosexual feminists to join in the challenge to institutionalized heterosexuality. The Redstockings' members, however, took no part in criticizing heterosexuality as an institution.

However, by the mid- to late 1970s, the debate between lesbian and heterosexual feminists cooled down, or fewer women wrote about it. Lesbians focused more on lesbianism than on heterosexuality, or worked in groups which did not focus on sexuality or lesbian feminism. Few heterosexual feminists wrote about these conflicts.

A few years later, the defense of heterosexuality resurfaced. New York University professor Jessica Benjamin wrote a 1979 paper, "Starting from the Left and Going Beyond," saying,

> The conviction is strong in me that I could never know freedom with a man. The freedom we seek in love, of being known for who we are, of sharing our dreams and visions. I can imagine such freedom only with another woman.[41]

But she goes on to say that she must be heterosexual, and that heterosexual women need a forum:

> It seems to me that the evasion of both personal and political levels of our relationships to men—the reformism of heterosex-

ual women—is motivated by the fear of revealing weakness and facing ambivalence, of losing safety without gaining freedom.[42]

Is it the loss or the *gain* of freedom that is frightening? Benjamin writes:

> Our dependency ties us to those who have oppressed or denied us by the bonds of love...this, our most personal political problem, has been dealt with largely by the strategy of terror, that is moralizing and the strategy of evasion, that is apathy... Both of these approaches have in common the feeling of shame. The shame of this dependency, this weakness, this powerlessness. The last women's group I was in foundered on this shame, on the inability to talk about our relationships with and dependency on men. Heterosexual women have largely retreated into a private struggle around this issue, increasingly unaided by consciousness raising or collective life forms. But this is not merely because women are relieved to slip back into their earlier entrapment, but because we are ashamed of it.[43]

Freedom (which she herself just defined as leaving men) is seen as too heavy a burden—but so is having to face criticism for rejecting freedom.

Canadian socialist feminist Mary O'Brien sees sex in terms of heterosexuality. She criticizes the feminist movement for emphasizing sexual freedom more than reproductive freedom. She says that to expect women to refrain from having sex with men is to expect them to give up sexual pleasure.

> The recurrent masculine dread that women hold a potential political weapon in the withholding of sexual access to their persons belongs in the same conceptual category as the myth of the general strike. It is ultimately anarchic in its divorce from rational cooperation, to say nothing of the prejudiced postulate that women can quite easily forego sexual satisfaction.[44]

She seems to assume, then, that women *should* cooperate with men sexually, and that women will almost be forced by their own desire to do so.

Robin Morgan defended heterosexuality in her 1982 book, *The Anatomy of Freedom*:

> Deep down, heterosexuality is, for a feminist, the desire not to write off the male half of the species completely.[45]

Morgan's comment suggests that the only way of acknowledging men's existence is by having sexual relations with them. The comment ignores the existence of many lesbians who have connections with men as brothers, sons, fathers, friends or political allies.

In 1989, after she had broken up with her husband and become a lesbian, Morgan's perceptions of heterosexuality and lesbianism had changed. She told *off our backs*, in an interview discussing her book *The Demon Lover*:

> ...It was not until I fell in love with a woman that a whole perspective of other kinds of sexuality, an energy of eroticism that was not in some ways self-defeating, became conceivable...
>
> It is extremely difficult at this moment in history for even the most principled woman and the most principled man to speak the same language.[46]

In 1979, the feminist newspaper *off our backs* ran complementary commentaries by a heterosexual radical feminist, Vickie Leonard, and a lesbian radical feminist (myself). A note made it clear that the authors were close friends debating, not playing out a split.

Vickie Leonard wrote:

> My hatred and distrust of men runs deep as does my love and bonding with women...Because of my brothers, I can hate what men do and still like being around them.
>
> For some feminists, realizing how intensely men hate women can be terribly frightening. I grew up with that—it doesn't intimidate or scare me. Also, superficially sucking up to men doesn't appall me either. Those are the facts of life in patriarchy.
>
> I have few, if any, hopes about reforming men. That's prevented me from the pain of isolation or disappointment a feminist might feel if she were attempting to radicalize a man...
> ...Feminists may be heterosexual because they are in a comfortable long-term relationship, one that predates their feminism. They may fear jeopardizing their political and personal relationships with feminists by mixing in the sexual and romantic. Some women still crave male approval. Frankly, I'd rather a woman sought male approval in her personal life than in her feminist group bullying them to work with male-dominated alliances.[47]

This "defense" of heterosexuality is certainly different from most earlier ones by heterosexual radical feminists.

In a responding article, I wrote,

> I have been a heterosexual feminist myself. It does bother me
> when I hear lesbians say 'a straight woman can't be a feminist.'
> Of course she can. Thousands of women, from Elizabeth Cady
> Stanton on down to the present, have been. Of course a hetero-
> sexual woman can realize that women are oppressed as a
> group and can decide to work with other women to end that
> oppression. Like all other feminists, she deserves respect for her
> commitment and work.
>
> I don't think that women who define themselves as hetero-
> sexual should be forced or pressured to change...Every woman
> must make her own decisions...however...
>
> If women in heterosexual relationships were really free,
> would they be risking cancer with the pill, a perforated uterus
> with an IUD or an abortion with any other method simply to
> engage in a practice that does not satisfy them? If men were
> really concerned about changing power relationships, would
> they not concentrate on other sexual acts, equally capable of
> giving them orgasms?
>
> Why would one be more sexually attracted to men than to
> women? Why would more powerful people be more attractive?
> Are such explanations (which I've heard) as 'I like how
> strong/tall men are' another way of being attracted to power?
> Why do women use different intellectual and political standards
> in choosing men than in choosing women friends? Because no
> man would fit the same standards?[48]

Changing Sexuality

It seems necessary to point out that not all of those who
strongly proclaimed themselves to be lesbian feminists and developed a lesbian feminist theory and style that challenge heterosexuality have maintained consistent politics. Some are no longer
lesbians (which does not necessarily mean that their earlier
relationships with women were insincere). Others, like Rita Mae
Brown and Jill Johnston, while staying primarily lesbian, have
modified their politics.

Jill Johnston changed her position to a sort of irritated sarcasm
about issues of lesbian and feminist politics. In a 1979 *Village
Voice* article, she wrote that, "What interests me about my sexual
identity is not having one."[49]

Rita Mae Brown by 1981 was saying that relationships with men as well as women were acceptable. In a 1981 interview with the *Washington Post*, she said, "If I thought I could only respond to half the human race, I'd jump off the Golden Gate Bridge. I love women. I love men. I love everybody. My assumption is that, until proven otherwise, people are pan-sexual."[50]

Both of these writers have often used irreverent styles, so it is perhaps not entirely inconsistent that they eventually were irreverent about lesbian feminist politics.

It is difficult in this society to maintain oneself as a lesbian or to maintain a consistent radical politics of any sort. There are few rewards or reinforcements, except in lesbian circles or circles that share one's brand of radical politics.

In fact, not all of the other writers whose positions on sexual politics are quoted in this book have maintained the same sexual stance that they originally expressed; for instance, not every heterosexual has remained heterosexual. Although she advocates having no personal connections with men, Ti-Grace Atkinson had a close tie to a man, whose fatal injury is mentioned in *Amazon Odyssey*.[51] Most of the writers have, as far as I know, maintained the same sexual orientation as the one described here. (It is possible to change one's sexual behavior without changing one's theoretical perspective; one could have a relationship with a man while still believing it would be more constructive to be lesbian or celibate, for instance. But usually a person's ideas change to match behavior, if behavior doesn't match ideas.)

Perhaps when someone advocates a particularly militant stance—on sex or on other political questions, we might reflect, "yes, but is she really going to carry that out for the rest of her life?" Militancy and consistency are not always firmly united.

There is perhaps a tinge of unreality about some discussions of heterosexual relations. The structure of heterosexuality is oppressive, but relationships carried out within that structure vary. If a major argument for being a lesbian is that men will always behave horribly and that "every fuck is a rape," then a woman may lose some of her commitment to lesbianism when she discovers that some men are unaggressive and behave considerately in personal relations. More persuasive than saying that every fuck is a rape, would be saying that intercourse *has been influenced* by the fact that *many* men rape women. If we exaggerate too much, women with different experiences will not believe us, and we may wind up not believing ourselves. One of the first women to say that "every fuck is a rape" later got married.

Feminists of Color on Sexuality

The thoughts of feminists of color on sexuality have been diverse. African-American women, in particular, have faced not only woman-hating, but also specific devaluation of themselves as Black women in a white-male-dominated society which considers white women more beautiful than Black women.

Early in the movement, Cellestine Ware, a founder of New York Radical Women, wrote,

> The rejection of black women by black men is a phenomenon best explained by the black man's underlying hatred of blackness and by the need to dominate that underlies male-female relationships.[52]

But in her 1970 book *Woman Power*, Ware is critical of feminists who "wish to abolish relationships with men and wifehood and motherhood as roles uniquely oppressive."[53] Ware called the Feminists a group that, "rather than constituting a political organization to annihilate sex roles...is an organization to eradicate sexuality and the emotions." Ware adds that "If we are such stuff as revolutions are willed by, we are also the creatures of our biology"—thus suggesting that sexual expression is necessary and desirable.[54]

Black feminists have considered a number of solutions to sexual oppression. In a 1969 essay, Toni Cade (now Bambara) wrote,

> I tend to agree that celibacy for a time is worth considering, for sex is dirty if all it means is winning a man, conquering a woman, beating someone out of something, abusing each other's dignity in order to prove that I am a man, I am a woman.[55]

A number of Black feminists have advocated lesbianism as a solution. One of the earliest of such essays was "Letter to a Friend," a *Ladder* article by Anita Cornwall:

> Because, honey pie, *never* again will I sleep with any man of color. Men have fucked me over for the absolute last time. And I can say without reservation that *any* woman sleeping with *any* man on a fairly regular basis is prostituting her mind, her body, and her spirit, no matter what the relationship is called—i.e., marriage, living together, shacking up or what the hell—the situation is still the same, she is the slave and he is the king.[56]

In a 1980 article for the anthology *This Bridge Called My Back*, Cheryl Clarke continued the discussion of lesbianism as a political act.

> For a woman to be a lesbian in a male-supremacist, capitalist, misogynist, racist, homophobic, imperialist culture, such as that of North America, is an act of resistance.[57]

Clarke also challenges the institution of heterosexuality:

> The woman who embraces lesbianism as an ideological, political and philosophical means of liberation of all women from heterosexual tyranny must also identify with the world-wide struggle of all women to end male-supremacist tyranny at all levels. As far as I am concerned, any woman who calls herself a feminist must commit herself to the liberation of *all* women from *coerced* heterosexuality as it manifests itself in the family, the state, and Madison Avenue.[58]

In a 1980 speech, Pat Parker extended the criticism of heterosexuality to the nuclear family:

> ...The left must give up its undying loyalty to the nuclear family. In the same way it is difficult for upper and middle class women to give up their commitment to the nuclear family, but the nuclear family is the basic unit of capitalism and in order for us to move to revolution it has to be destroyed.[59]

In her 1978 essay, "Uses of the Erotic: The Erotic as Power," Audre Lorde wrote about the energy that women can obtain from the erotic, which she connects with lesbianism (although she does not say that it is only associated with lesbianism). Lorde writes that the suppression of women's erotic feelings has been a major aspect of women's oppression.

> In order to perpetuate itself, every oppression must corrupt or distort those various sources of power within the culture of the oppressed that can provide energy for change. For women, this has meant a suppression of the erotic as a considered source of power and information within our lives.[60]

Lorde is critical of the ideas of feminists such as Atkinson who see the erotic as a source of power only for men. She sees this rejection of the erotic in women as a reflection of male-dominated society.

> We have been taught to suspect this resource, vilified, abused and devalued within western society...

It is a short step from there to the false belief that only by suppression of the erotic within our lives and consciousness can women be truly strong. But that strength is illusory, for it is fashioned within the concept of male models of power.[61]

Lorde sees the erotic as a source of strength that can enable women to dare to try to enrich our lives in all areas, such as work.

Once we know the extent to which we are capable of feeling that sense of satisfaction and completion, we can then observe which of our various life endeavors bring us closer to that fullness...

Within the celebration of the erotic in all our endeavors, my work becomes a conscious decision...[62]

Lorde is very far from thinking that sexual relationships must be oppressive or unequal. She believes that mutuality is possible.

The sharing of joy, whether physical, emotional, psychic, or intellectual, forms a bridge between the sharers which can be the basis for understanding much of what is not shared between them, and lessens the threat of their differences.[63]

(Of course, if one person is determined to be master of the other, the joy—if in fact it was truly shared—might *increase* the threat of their difference, or of their similarity).

In 1977, Barbara Smith wrote an article that asked why many Black women, despite having close relationships with other women, did not become lesbians. She suggests that the reason is that Black women already bear so many oppressions:

Heterosexual privilege is usually the only privilege that Black women have. None of us have racial or sexual privilege, almost none of us have class privilege, maintaining 'straightness' is our last resort... I am convinced that it is our lack of privilege and power in every other sphere that allows so few Black women to make the leap that many white women, particularly writers, have been able to make this decade.[64]

Of course, not all African-American feminists are lesbians. Michele Wallace, author of *Black Macho and the Myth of the Superwoman*, mentions lesbianism only once in her 1978 book, and the reference is not particularly complimentary.

Some black women have come together because they can't find husbands. Some are angry with their boyfriends. The lesbians are looking for a public forum for their sexual preference.[65]

In her 1981 book, *Ain't I a Woman*, Bell Hooks (Gloria Watkins) pointed out that women have been trapped by male definitions of their sexuality. First, women were trapped by sexual repression, and now women are trapped by increasing exploitation and hostility.

> Now that the pill and other contraceptive devices give men unlimited access to the bodies of women, they have ceased to feel that it is necessary to show women any consideration and respect. They can now see all women as 'bad,' as 'whores,' and openly reveal their contempt and hatred. As a group, white men expose their hatred by increased exploitation of women as sex objects to sell products and by their whole-hearted support of pornography and rape. Black men expose their hatred by increased domestic brutality (white men also) and their vehement verbal denouncement of black women as matriarchs, castrators, bitches, etc.[66]

Nevertheless, Hooks does not agree with lesbian feminist criticisms of heterosexuality.

> Attacking heterosexuality does little to strengthen the self concept of the masses of women who desire to be with men.[67]

Although *Ain't I a Woman* recognizes the work of African-American lesbians such as Audre Lorde and Barbara Smith, it does not discuss lesbianism.

In her 1984 book *Feminist Theory: From Margin to Center*, Hooks says that sexuality is oppressive when a woman is assumed to be the property of a whole group, generally the group of men, although it would also be oppressive to be assumed available for lesbians. Sexuality, says Hooks, will become less oppressive when it is recognized that sexual relations are part of a particular relationship with a particular person—that the choice of a particular man, for instance, does not make a woman available to men in general.

Hooks says that asserting the particularity and specificity of sexual desire, its connection to the set of interactions to another individual, enhances the struggle to end sexual oppression.

> Many women choose to be heterosexual because they enjoy genital contact with individual men. Feminist movement has enriched and added new dimensions to lesbian sexuality and there is no reason it cannot do the same for heterosexuality...

A liberatory sexuality would not teach women to see their bodies as accessible to all men, or to all women for that matter.

Implicit in the idea of sexual preference is the assumption that anyone of the preferred sex can seek access to one's body. This is a concept that promotes objectification... Sexuality would be transformed if the codes and labels that strip sexual desire of its specificity and particularity were abandoned.[68]

It is unlikely that many lesbians think they have an automatic right of access to all other lesbians' bodies.

In her 1989 book *Talking Back*, Hooks suggests that feminists should write more about men. "When one girl in four is a victim of male incest, one woman in three is raped, and half of all married women are victims of male violence, addressing ways men and women interact daily must be a concern of feminists."[69] However, in the next sentence she says, "Relationships of care and intimacy often mediate contact between women and men within patriarchy so that all men do not necessarily dominate and oppress women. Despite patriarchy and sexism, there is potential for radicalization and transformation."[70]

In *Talking Back*, Hooks elaborates on her perspective on heterosexism.

I feel that a critique of heterosexism, to me, is included in the notion of sexism. I don't see heterosexism as a being a separate category, because it seems to me that heterosexism is definitely the child of sexism.[71]

Feminists of Color are continuing to write about the ways that sexuality under white supremacist patriarchy has particularly injured them.

Barbara Omolade's article "Hearts of Darkness," describes the historical and continuing effects of mass rape on black women under slavery.

The racial patriarchy of the white man enabled him to enact the culture's separation between the goodness, purity, innocence and frailty of woman with the sinful, evil strength, and carnal knowledge of woman by having sex with white women who came to embody the former and black women who came to embody the latter.[72]

But Omolade adds that the oppression had not extinguished Black women's sexuality.

If the sexual act between white men and black women was a ritual reenactment of domination, the oppression failed to completely dampen the sexual expression of black women within the black community, which often became a ritual enactment of affirmation of her freedom and happiness...[73]

Latina lesbian Cherríe Moraga, in *Loving in the War Years*, writes how Chicana women are stigmatized as descendants of Malinche, a Mexican Indian woman who supposedly helped the Spanish conquer the Aztecs. Lesbianism is seen as a practice picked up from whites, she adds.

There is hardly a Chicana growing up today who does not suffer under her name [Malinche's] even if she never hears directly of the one-time Aztec princess.[74]

The woman who defies her role as subservient to husband, father, brother, or son by taking control of her own sexual destiny is purported to be a 'traitor to her race' by contributing to the 'genocide' of her people—whether or not she has children. In short, even if the defiant woman is *not* a lesbian, she is purported to be one; for, like the lesbian in the Chicano imagination, she is una *Malinchista*. Like Malinche of Mexican history, she is corrupted by foreign influences which threaten to destroy her people.[75]

Juanita Ramos, in the anthology *Compañeras: Latina Lesbians*, writes, "Being a lesbian is by definition an act of treason against our [Latin] cultural values."[76]

The Critique Continues

Some feminists have continued the critique of sexuality in the 1980s. For instance, Andrea Dworkin wrote in an essay in her 1983 book *Right-wing Women* that sexual intercourse is key to male domination. She continues to develop the ideas that she had set forth in her 1974 speech, "Renouncing Sexual Equality":

Because women are exploited as a sex class for sex, it is impossible to talk about women's sexuality outside the context of forced sex or, at the least, without reference to forced sex...

The force itself is intrinsically 'sexy,' romanticized, described as a measure of the desire of an individual man for an individual woman...

It is through intercourse in particular that men express and maintain their power and dominance over women...[77]

In an essay in her book *Right-wing Women*, Dworkin suggests that there are possibilities for a woman to free her sexuality. This has nothing to do with increasing one's number of orgasms, Dworkin writes.

> There is also, possibly, sexual intelligence, a human capacity for discerning, manifesting, and constructing sexual integrity. Sexual intelligence could not be measured in numbers of orgasms ...It would be in the body, but it could never be in an imprisoned, isolated body, a body denied access to the world... Sexual intelligence would probably be more like moral intelligence than like anything else...[78]
>
> Sexual intelligence in women, that rarest intelligence in a male-supremacist world, is necessarily a revolutionary intelligence, the opposite of the pornographic (which simply reiterates the world as it is for women), the opposite of the will to be used, the opposite of masochism and self-hatred, the opposite of 'good woman' and 'bad woman' both. It is not in being a whore that a woman becomes an outlaw in this man's world; it is in the possession of herself, the ownership and effective control of her own body...[79]

Unlike the Redstockings' idea that women basically know what they want, Dworkin suggests that it is very difficult for women to even have an intelligent estimate of their own desires under male supremacy. Her idea of sexuality seems a little closer to Atkinson's, although Atkinson would not necessarily agree that sexual intelligence was possible.

Dworkin does not explain what the sexuality of a woman who owned herself would be. How would she have sexual relations with others—if she did—without giving up some measure of "ownership"?

Dworkin's 1987 book *Intercourse* continues her critique of intercourse with men, but does not indicate how a better sexuality could develop—nor does she say that lesbianism might be a better alternative. She damns intercourse and its effects even more than in her previous work.

Dworkin suggests that women who have been used as sexual objects may never recover sufficiently to be equal to men. "Equality means physical wholeness, virginity—for the woman, equality requires not ever having been reduced to that object of sensuality in order to be used as a tool of men's desire and satiation in sex. What is lost by the woman when she becomes a sexual object, and when she is confirmed in that status by being fucked, is not recoverable."[80] Undoubtedly, being used as an object is painful and damaging, but the suggestion that women can never recover sounds awfully despairing.

Feminists must be concerned not only with their own sexual integrity but also with other women's, Dworkin suggests. Saying that it is acceptable for some women to be employed in prostitution or pornography is colluding in their oppression, she says in *Right-wing Women.*

> Supporting the use of *some* women in any area of sex exploitation is the willful sacrifice of women on the altar of sex abuse and it is a political repudiation of the sex-class consciousness basic to feminism: it is—whoever does it—antifeminism.[81]

In a 1982 article, feminist theorist Catharine A. MacKinnon, who is closely allied with Dworkin, wrote:

> Sexuality is to feminism what work is to marxism: that which is most one's own, yet most taken away.[82]
>
> Sexuality is that social process which creates, organizes, expresses, and directs desire, creating the social beings we know as women and men, as their relations create society.[83]

Like Dworkin, MacKinnon sees sexuality as the key to male supremacy.

> Women and men are divided by gender, made into the sexes as we know them, by the social requirements of heterosexuality, which institutionalizes male sexual dominance and female sexual submission. If this is true, sexuality is the linchpin of gender inequality.[84]

This is also similar to Atkinson.

MacKinnon continues,

> ...Each element of the female *gender* stereotype is revealed as, in fact, *sexual.* Vulnerability means the appearance/reality of easy sexual access; passivity means receptivity and disabled resistance.[85]

MacKinnon's definition of woman is somewhat similar to Monique Wittig's.

To MacKinnon, alienated sexuality is part of the definition of a woman.

> A woman is a being who identifies and is identified as one whose sexuality exists for someone else, who is socially male. [The latter could be a woman with some share of male power]. Women's sexuality is the capacity to arouse desire in that someone.[86]

MacKinnon suggests that women's sexuality has been so artificially constructed that neither mere absence of oppression nor more expression of the sexuality as it exists can be liberating.

> If being *for* another is the whole of women's sexual construction, it can be no more escaped by separatism, men's temporary concrete absence, than eliminated or qualified by permissiveness...[87]

In MacKinnon's framework, it is possible for a *woman* to be the one for whom another woman's sexuality exists; it is not a true escape to create this situation, she suggests.

In a 1983 interview with *off our backs*, MacKinnon suggested that none of us can trust her own feelings about sexuality.

> Until we confront the ways that both women and men identify ourselves and experience our sexuality as something that is inextricably part of gender inequality—that is, the inequality of women and men or male dominance and female subordination —until we realize that we've eroticized that and that is what gender means, then we're going to keep saying things like 'if I get off on that, how can it be wrong,' as if this is a moral critique, when it isn't.[88]

Sexuality is often coerced in male-dominated society, MacKinnon says. The boundary between rape and non-rape is not easy to determine. Rape is sexuality as well as violence:

> I think the notion that rape is violence not sex comes from women wanting to say that we are not turned on by being violated...
>
> The problem of sexuality as it is presently construed is that force is not seen as force...I also think that men tend to be sexually aroused by dominance in all its forms.[89]

In her 1987 book *Feminism Unmodified*, MacKinnon is pessimistic about the possibility of having nonoppressive sexual relationships in the present day.

Audiences [at her speeches] constantly expressed their desire for sexual connection undominated by dominance, unimplicated in the inequality of the sexes, a sexuality of one's own yet with another...The problem...is that many people want to believe they already have this more than they want to have it... Audiences want to affirm that the sexuality for which we need what we do not have—a society of sex equality—already exists and merely needs to be unearthed...

...Sex feeling good may mean that one is enjoying one's subordination; it would not be the first time. Or it may mean that one has glimpsed freedom, a rare and valuable and contradictory event. Under existing conditions, what else would freedom be? The point is, the possible varieties of interpersonal engagement, including the pleasure of sensation or the experience of intimacy, does not, things being as they are, make sex empowering for women.[90]

Much of MacKinnon's work seems carefully considered over time. However, the sweeping suggestion that sex now cannot be empowering for women recalls the sweeping statements of the early days of the feminist movement.

Chapter 10

Realignment in Feminist Sexual Politics

A lack of discussion of intimate issues of sex and love by many feminists has led to a climate of frustration. When discussion developed, it was not the discussion that some radical feminists wanted. Sex has been discussed far more often than love—as it generally has been in the feminist movement after the earliest days.

The new dialogue has included little discussion of practices such as oral and manual sex (lesbians differ in attachment to these practices, as do women of other sexualities), differences between partners on frequency of sex, long distance relationships and their implications for sexuality, relationships between women who both have little leisure, or most other common sexual problems.

The feminist debate in the 1980s instead often focused on the practice of sadomasochism and on butch/femme sex roles because some lesbians began demanding recognition in the feminist movement for these practices. Some forays on these subjects were made in the 1970s, but the debate did not become movement-wide until the 1980s.

These women often defended, and were defended by, hetero-sexual feminists who felt that many lesbian feminists had been too critical of heterosexuality. Of course, not all heterosexual feminists lined up on this side. Some heterosexual feminists, particularly those involved in working against pornography and violence against women, have joined lesbian feminists in saying that some forms of sexuality can be criticized.

Nor do all lesbians who support butch/femme roles, particu-larly in a historical context, necessarily support sadomasochism. To condemn butch/femme relationships entirely would be to repudiate a large chapter in lesbian history and many courageous women who took great risks to love other women.

Butch/Femme Relations

In 1981, Lesbian Herstory Archives founder Joan Nestle launched a defense of butch/femme love that has been followed by many articles in publications such as *Lesbian Ethics*. Nestle wrote,

> Butch/femme was an erotic partnership serving both as a conspicuous flag of rebellion and as an intimate expression of women's sexuality...
>
> Because of the complexity and authenticity of the butch/femme experience, I think we must take another look at the term *role-playing*, used primarily to summarize this way of loving. I do not think the term serves a purpose either as a label for or as a description of the experience. As a femme, I did what was natural for me, what felt right. I did not learn a part; I perfected a way of loving.[1]

In 1982, the annual feminist conference at Barnard College focused on a critique of the lesbian feminist critique of sexuality (such as heterosexuality and dominance relationships); the con-ference included workshops on the politics of sadomasochism and the practice of butch/femme roles, while major speakers spoke in favor of exploring "sexual danger," which presumably includes or features sadomasochism.[2]

Speakers criticized the critique of sexuality developed in various ways by Ti-Grace Atkinson, lesbian separatists (unnamed), Adrienne Rich, Andrea Dworkin, Susan Brownmiller and Kathleen Barry (who wrote a book on forced prostitution,

Female Sexual Slavery). Some of the women criticized are lesbians, while others are heterosexual or celibate.

There appears to be a realignment on sexuality that cuts across the lesbian/heterosexual division. On the one side are those (generally radical or lesbian) feminists who have presented a critical analysis of sexuality that challenges many norms, such as: the institution of heterosexuality; the influence of the practice of rape on all male/female relations, including those in which the man does not commit rape; the institution of sexual intercourse as a male-defined act; and dominance/submission in sexual relationships generally.

On the other side are women who object to these critiques, suggesting that sexuality is an individual matter and that those who criticize it disregard other women's liberties and passions (including the desire to submit). Perhaps this position could be called the sexual libertarian position.

Many of those who are sexual libertarians have a socialist feminist, rather than a radical feminist analysis of women's situation; that is, they tend to focus more on work than on sexuality as central to women's oppression. This is not to say that all socialist feminists are sexual libertarians.

Sadomasochism

Sadomasochists often refer to themselves as "sexual outlaws," and to other lesbian sexuality as "safe" or "vanilla." But *all* lesbians are criminals in many states. (Perhaps this is an unforeseen result of the occasional glorification of the lesbian as "outlaw": trying to determine who is the "most outlaw").

No feminists have suggested criminal penalties against sadomasochism among women where there is no use of force or injury. Some have said that sadomasochism is not a feminist practice. If one takes the viewpoint that all power over others is ethically wrong and/or likely to reinforce political domination—which has long been a common feminist belief—then celebrating a form of it departs from this belief.

Although discussion of sadomasochism and dominance took a great deal of space in lesbian and feminist publications and attention in the movement in the early 1980s, sadomasochism does not seem to be an issue in most lesbians' personal lives. *The Gay Report* by Karla Jay and Allen Young, published in 1979, said that 2% of lesbians had very positive, and 7% somewhat positive feelings about sadomasochism—while 4% had very positive, and 7% somewhat positive feelings about bondage.[3]

Some terms of the debate are code words for one side or the other, such as "risk" or "danger." Other terms are used by both.

Many feminists in the 1980s use terms made popular by French male sexologist Michel Foucault and say that sexuality is historically constructed in particular eras—not a universal, given practice. But the argument that sexuality is historically constructed can be used to mean almost anything. Sexual libertarians have used it to say, "Sexuality is constructed; practices like sadomasochism have no inherent meaning—they can mean just what the participants want them to mean."

On the other hand, feminists who feel there should be a critique of sexuality sometimes say, "Practices such as sadomasochism are not just games: They arose in connection with, and were constructed by our oppressive situation—so it's reasonable to criticize them as reflections of it."

The Sexual Libertarian Position

In 1981, Amber Hollibaugh and Cherríe Moraga wrote a dialogue in which they complained that lesbianism had been desexualized and that the model they felt had been set up for lesbians had been too rigid. By "desexualized" lesbianism, critics generally mean the political lesbianism developed by groups like the Furies and its heir, the lesbianism described in Adrienne Rich's article on compulsory heterosexuality.

> What grew out of this kind of 'non-sexual' theory was a 'transcendent' definition of sexuality where lesbianism (since it exists outside the institution of heterosexuality) came to be seen as the practice of feminism. It set up a 'perfect' vision of egalitarian sexuality, where we could magically leap over our heterosexist conditioning into mutually orgasmic, struggle-free, trouble-free sex. We feel this vision has become both misleading and damaging to many feminists, but in particular to lesbians... Who can really live up to such an ideal?[4]

Ann Snitow, Christine Stansell and Sharon Thompson, in the introduction to the 1983 book *The Powers of Desire*, also suggest that making lesbianism political desexualized it.

> In pointing to anger rather than eros as the wellspring of lesbianism, the manifesto ['The Woman-Identified Woman'] opened the way for the desexualization of lesbian identity.[5]

Should lesbians *not* have politicized lesbianism? Is that what the authors are saying? Is their message that lesbian feminists' challenge to other women to consider leaving men was misplaced? Should these lesbians instead have argued only that lesbians have better orgasms?

Early lesbian feminists like the Furies had no idea that they were calling for a "desexualized" lesbianism. Consider the fiction of Rita Mae Brown, a member of Radicalesbians and the Furies who helped initiate the call for women to come out; no one could argue that her fiction is desexualized. Furies member Joan E. Biren (JEB) observed at a 1988 lesbian conference, "The idea that we [the Furies] weren't sexual has been greatly exaggerated. We were raunchy."[6]

At the 1982 Barnard conference, Alice Echols suggested that some lesbian feminists, particularly Adrienne Rich, have presented a version of lesbianism that is too sexless.

> ...Lesbian recognition has been achieved by further abstracting it from the realm of sexuality and cloaking it as female bonding...[7]

> ...Women's sexuality is assumed to be more spiritual than sexual, and considerably less central to their lives than is sexuality to men's. For instance, Adrienne Rich describes female sexuality as an 'energy which is unconfined to any single part of the body or solely to the body itself.'[8]

Is Echols criticizing the idea that sexual attraction may develop from, or be connected with experiences that are not totally physical? How could human sexuality be confined to a single part of the body?

Echols feels that Rich's perspective on "the lesbian continuum" desexualizes both lesbian and heterosexual women.

> Rich's expansive definition of lesbianism completely disregards the attraction of heterosexuality. Should not any affectional continuum embrace the full range of erotic and sexual tendencies?[9]

Does this mean that an article focusing on women's feelings for each other is unacceptable? Would it also be unacceptable to write that there may be latent homosexual feelings involved in male bonding? The idea that heterosexuality is an institution, which Rich puts forth, in no way implies that women never have heterosexual desires.

Sexy Roles

Some defenders of the libertarian view suggest that sexuality without roles or acknowledged power relationships would not be "sexy" or erotic. That's just what Atkinson said much earlier, when she asserted that we would be better off *without* sexuality.

Amber Hollibaugh writes:

> ...If you deny that roles, S/M, fantasy or any sexual differences exist in the first place, you can only come up with neutered sexuality, where everybody's got to be basically the same because anything different puts the element of power and deviation in there and threatens the whole picture.[10]

Another argument is what could be called the pressure theory of power. In other words, the desire for power exists, and if you don't vent some of it in a way that's acknowledged, it will leak out in less desirable ways.

Cherríe Moraga argues:

> ...What I think is very dangerous about keeping down such fantasies is that they are forced to stay unconscious. Then, next thing you know, in the actual sexual relationship, you become the capturer, that is, you try to have power over your lover, psychologically or whatever. If the desire for power is so hidden and unacknowledged, it will inevitably surface through manipulation or what-have-you.[11]

One could see power in precisely the opposite way: that the more one has and uses it, the more one wants. Like the exercise of other chosen practices, such as singing or playing tennis, the exercise of power seems likely to create a taste for more of the same rather than diminishing it.

Moraga and Hollibaugh, like other sexual libertarians, defend the practice of heterosexuality.

> By analyzing the institution of heterosexuality through feminism, we learned what's oppressive about it...but we don't learn what's *sexual*. We don't really know, for instance, why men and women are still attracted to each other, even through all that oppression ...There *is* heterosexuality outside of heterosexism.[12]

That women and men are attracted to each other does not contradict the critique of heterosexuality: As Atkinson points out, the attraction is a magnet drawing with *unequal* power. It would be a better defense of heterosexuality to say that tenderness can exist in heterosexual relations.

Some sexual libertarians suggest that the lesbian feminist critique of sexuality is basically a white middle-class critique which is not relevant to Women of Color and working class women. Moraga and Hollibaugh take this position:

> We also believe our racial and class backgrounds have a huge effect in determining how we perceive ourselves sexually... In our involvement in a movement largely controlled by white middle-class women, we feel that the values of their cultures (which may be more closely tied to an American-assimilated puritanism) have been pushed down our throats.[13]

However, Audre Lorde and Alice Walker have criticized sado-masochism; the critique is not exclusively white.[14] Nor is the value that sexual relationships should be egalitarian derived from white American puritanism.

Although they argue against sexual norms, the sexual libertarian feminists seem to assume that having directly sexual relations with other people is a criterion of normality. "It would be a bad defeat if we had to resign ourselves to asexual lives," said Ellen DuBois in a paper at the 1982 Barnard conference.[15] But although many feminists, perhaps most, might feel that celibacy was a defeat, others would not.

The sexual libertarian writers suggest that sexual arousal or excitement is in itself a good thing, perhaps more important than other values. Snitow, Stansell and Thompson wrote:

> ...What is the psychological relationship between sexual taboo and arousal? Does shame reduce, or enhance, erotic excitement? Does sexual excitement depend on creating and recreating taboos? Is there such a thing as a progressive taboo?[16]

Are they suggesting that feminism or feminists should seek to maximize arousal? Or orgasms? Why? Such an idea in a feminist context requires explanation. It does not go without saying that the maximum arousal is the greatest good.

Socialist feminist Gayle Rubin and other sexual libertarians say sadomasochists are a sexual minority who need protection, as did lesbians and gays in pre-gay liberation days. Rubin feels that feminists who criticize sadomasochism do so because they have an unrealistic image of lesbian sexuality as gentle and non-role-differentiated.

Given prevailing ideas of appropriate feminist sexual behavior, S/M appears to be the mirror opposite. It is dark and polarized, extreme and ritualized, and above all, it celebrates difference and power ... This does not mean that sexual behavior should not be evaluated. How people treat each other in sexual contexts is important. But this is not the same as passing judgement on what are essentially cultural differences in sexual behavior. There are plenty of lesbian relationships which are long term and monogamous, in which both partners switch roles or do the same thing, in which all touching is gentle, but in which the partners are mean and nasty to each other ... S/M partners may occupy polarized roles, the touching may be rough, and yet they may treat each other with respect and affection.[17]

Undoubtedly she is right that lesbians who like sadomasochism can be affectionate and that those who do not can be unkind. Structures do not always determine the ease of interactions. A hierarchically organized office in a capitalist company can sometimes have more pleasant outward relations among the staff than a theoretically egalitarian collective. In fact, it may be likely that the collective will be more obviously explosive. Trying to establish egalitarian relationships is never easy.

Sadomasochistic sex roles do not necessarily correspond to roles outside of sex, Rubin says.

Nor are the social relations between tops and bottoms similar to the social relations between men and women, blacks and whites, straights and queers. Sadists do not systematically oppress masochists ... class, race and gender neither determine nor correspond to the roles adopted for S/M play.[18]

Rubin suggests that sadomasochism, which can be heterosexual, homosexual, or lesbian, is not inherently connected with any political position. She is apparently responding to criticisms that sadomasochism is inherently anti-feminist and/or fascist. She points out that fascists have considered gays communists and communists have considered them fascists.

There is nothing inherently feminist or non-feminist about S/M. Sadomasochists, like lesbians, gay men, heterosexuals, etc. may be anarchists, fascists, democrats, republicans, communists, feminists, gay liberationists or sexual reactionaries. The idea that there is an automatic correspondence between sexual preference and political belief is long overdue to be jettisoned.[19]

At the level of articulated political opinion, Rubin is of course correct. People's sexuality and their stated political opinions can occur in almost any combination. This argument does not address the question of whether the sexual politics of one's relationships has an unconscious effect on or reinforces one's public politics, and *vice versa.* Can she believe, for instance, that a person can be utterly patriarchal in sexual relations but utterly democratic in work and politics? Won't a little of the private politics leak out?

Feminists who advocate egalitarian sex roles do so in part because they believe there is a connection between hierarchy in sexual relationships and hierarchy in non-sexual relationships. And, yes, of course, if the hierarchy is expressed in ways totally different from sadomasochism, and, perhaps, totally outside the bedroom, it is still hierarchy. Feminists who present a critique of dominance say we *all*—not just those women who engage in sadomasochism—are apt to fall into hierarchical patterns.

Pornography

The feminist anti-pornography movement is a particular target of the sexual libertarian feminists.

Alice Echols wrote: "The sexual repressiveness of the lesbian cultural feminist's orthodoxy has engendered the heterophobia that is, in turn, vented in the anti-pornography movement."[20] Echols implies that the anti-pornography movement is primarily lesbian in ideology and composition. Apparently she is focusing on highly visible writers such as Andrea Dworkin. In fact, many anti-pornography activists are heterosexual (Susan Brownmiller, for example), and have explicitly heterosexual reasons for opposing pornography.

The Washington area group Feminists Against Pornography (FAP), which was founded in the late 1970s, has always been mainly heterosexual. Such groups as FAP, New York Women Against Pornography, and some others make presentations about pornography to both women and men, because they want men to learn to see sex in non-pornographic ways. This anti-pornography movement is trying to change men more directly than is any other group of feminists.

One FAP founder, a heterosexual feminist, told me she thought it was "lesbian chauvinist" to oppose the anti-pornography movement simply because lesbians don't have sex with the men whose perceptions have been warped by pornography. Lesbians who do not support the anti-pornography movement, in her view, seem unconcerned about what happens to their heterosexual sisters in relationships with men.[21]

Catharine A. MacKinnon has carried this argument further: She suggests that some lesbians may be unconcerned about the injuries to women who work in the pornography trade, because they want to use pornographic materials for their own stimulation.

> Claiming to represent women, these people [women lawyers who say that pornography is free speech] have in effect decided that there will continue to exist an entire class of women who will be treated in these ways so that they can have what they call freedom of speech. Freedom means their free access to women. Speech means women's bodies saying what they want them to say.
>
> Why are women lawyers, feminists, siding with the pornographers?...I don't see a lot of women lawyers, feminist or otherwise, selling their asses on the street or looking for a pornographer with a camera in order to fulfill their sexual agency...[22]

Snitow, Stansell and Thompson, after focusing almost exclusively on the lesbian and other feminists who criticize heterosexuality and pornography, suggest that those feminists and sexual libertarians are *both* guilty of extremism.

> ...Modern feminism has gone from extreme to extreme. Instead of adding each new possibility to the list of sexual gains, we have, rather, traded in the old for the new: the clitoris for the vagina, lesbianism for heterosexuality, sadomasochism for desexualized lesbianism. How much does this extremism reflect a habit with sexual language, as we take illuminating metaphors as literal and comprehensive descriptions: rape for sex with men, friendship for sex with women, vulnerability for victimhood? We oscillate between two perspectives: on the one hand, a self righteous censoriousness; on the other, a somewhat cavalier libertarianism, which deals but minimally with vulnerability?[23]

Is it persuasive to say that both those who criticize power relationships and those who defend them are extreme? What are we left with?

Response to the Sexual Libertarian Argument

Feminists critical of the sexual libertarian attitude have been most especially concerned about sadomasochism. Butch/femme relationships are generally seen, even by somewhat critical radical feminists, in a very different light from sadomasochism. (On the other hand, there are lesbians who see *any* lesbian relationship as better than *any* heterosexual one).

Many feminists see inequality of power as a possibility (or likelihood) in almost all relationships—an undesirable possibility (or likelihood). The idea that a power difference should be institutionalized or celebrated is of particular concern to many feminists.

In 1982, a number of radical feminists published a book called *Against Sadomasochism.* One of the book's selections, a 1975 speech by Ti-Grace Atkinson to gay men, said:

> S/M is the cat the Establishment does not want out of the bag—*not* because it does not understand your blood kinship; but because it does not want women to understand in such overt and brutal terms the very nature of the power relationship. And, I must add, the nature and function of sex itself—at least, as the Establishment would have it.[24]

In the *Against Sadomasochism* collection, feminist philosopher Bat-Ami Bar On wrote:

> By insisting that sexuality is or ought to be a private matter, one joins with the forces that have mystified it...
>
> There is certainly a place and a need for progressive tolerance of the practice of sadomasochism. But feminists who defend the practice call for much more than progressive tolerance. They call for social acceptance and approval.[25]

She writes that consent for masochists is problematic. No one can really consent to give up freedom or to be humiliated and degraded, she said. The nature of sadomasochism is that the rules keep the masochist sufficiently unhurt so that she'll be unavailable again:

> The masochist control rule provides the masochist with the power to limit the behavior and authority of the sadist...
>
> However, these rules do not change the essential quality of the experience...

A sadist with a reputation for non-compliance with the masochist-control rule would probably be hard pressed to find a masochist...

...There is little that is substantive about the consent of participants in sadomasochistic encounters.[26]

On the other hand, Gayle Rubin, a self-identified masochist, wrote:

The silliest arguments about S/M have been those which claim that it is impossible that people really consent to do it... The overwhelming coercion with regard to S/M is the way in which people are prevented from doing it...[27]

However, some women who have been in sadomasochistic relationships have later criticized them. So far, the criticisms seem to come from those who played the role of masochist. *Against Sadomasochism* includes an article by a former masochist who says she was abused and intimidated to keep her from leaving.[28]

Audre Lorde also is critical of sadomasochism. In an interview with Susan Leigh Starr, Lorde said:

If we are to scrutinize our human relationships, we must be willing to scrutinize all aspects of those relationships. The subject of revolution is ourselves, is our lives.

Sadomasochism is an institutionalized celebration of dominant/subordinate relationships. And it *prepares* us either to accept subordination or to enforce dominance. *Even in play*, to affirm that the exertion of the power over the powerless is erotic, is empowering, is to set the emotional stage for the continuation of that relationship, politically, socially and economically.[29]

Many feminists of various political tendencies have taken to heart Lorde's article on the erotic as power. Yet some have chosen to ignore her statements on sadomasochism, continuing to maintain that critics of sadomasochism are puritanical and white.

Some critics say that women involved in sadomasochism can't really be part of the feminist movement. In *Pure Lust*, Mary Daly writes that the differences over sadomasochism and pornography that have emerged are not debates *within* the feminist movement because supporting sadomasochism or pornography is antifeminist and puts one outside the movement.

When women, whether heterosexual or lesbian, whose consciousness has been thus destroyed proclaim themselves pro-sadomasochism, pro-pornography...they may be exercising 'free speech,' but they are speaking neither *as* feminists nor *for* feminists. Since the inherent logic of their position is simply anti-feminist, they do not represent a 'split' or a 'struggle' *within* the feminist movement. Rather, they have become tools of the sadosociety in its continuing effort to destroy female consciousness.[30]

Daly does not account for the fact that some women who have demanded feminist acceptance of sadomasochism, roles and pornography are women who have contributed to the movement on other issues, like Gayle Rubin. It may be possible to have a nonfeminist or even anti-feminist position on some issues while having a feminist position on other issues. Another example might be women who take a feminist position on a number of economic issues but oppose reproductive rights.

By the late 1980s, the debate over sexuality more often focused on pornography. Feminists such as Catharine A. MacKinnon and Andrea Dworkin see pornography as central to women's oppression. Feminists and lesbians who take the sexual libertarian position suggest that some pornography may be beneficial to those women who enjoy looking at it.

MacKinnon and Dworkin drafted a model anti-pornography ordinance that would allow women who have been injured by pornography to sue those who make and distribute it for violating their civil rights. The ordinance was adopted by the city of Indianapolis, Indiana in 1984 but was struck down by an appeals court and that ruling was accepted in a summary judgement (without a hearing) by the United States Supreme Court.

A group called the Feminist Anti-Censorship Task Force (FACT) was formed in New York and other cities to oppose the anti-pornography ordinance. In a brief opposing the ordinance in the *Indianapolis* case, FACT, a group led by sexual libertarian lesbians, said in support of pornography,

Women need the freedom and the socially recognized space to appropriate for themselves the robustness of what traditionally has been male language.[31]

A number of famous feminists, including Adrienne Rich, signed the FACT brief, some of them not because they supported the argument that pornography could be beneficial for women. Some, like Rich, said that any anti-pornography legislation could be misused by the government. Some agree with opposing pornography in other ways, such as by demonstrations.

In a statement on the FACT brief, Rich wrote,

> I brought no automatic assent to the FACT brief, and there are parts of it with which I quarrel. I think it underrepresents the actual toll taken on women's lives by the *actions* associated with sexual slavery, while claiming that actions, not images, are the problem...

> ...I am less sure than Dworkin and MacKinnon that this is a time when further powers of suppression should be turned over to the State.[32]

Even feminists not directly involved in the anti-pornography movement have been very critical of the sexual libertarians. Radical feminist Karen Lindsey writes that the debate has made her feel less at home in the feminist movement. Lindsey concedes that some anti-pornography feminists have been too vituperative in their criticism of those who defend sadomasochism and pornography. Still, it is the defenders of S/M and pornography who trouble her, as they have many others.

> I've always felt that...I could travel any place in the country and find, through the shared name of feminism, women with whom I would have a deep and important bond, whatever our political differences.

> The existence of dedicated feminists who support pornography and celebrate sadomasochism changes all that. Our political work can coexist; our visions can't...What Adrienne Rich so beautifully calls the 'dream of a common language' is gone for me.[33]

Sexual libertarian feminists respond that much of the feminist critique of sexuality—including both criticism of heterosexuality and of sexuality based on dominance—developed from the 1970s trend in feminism that saw men and women as opposites and celebrated what were deemed to be women's traits. Only such a view could make women critical of rough or dominance-based sex, the sexual libertarians argue. Gayle Rubin calls what she considers the women's values approach *"femininism."*[34] Alice Echols also sees this approach as the basis for the critique of dominance and roles.

But, as we have seen, the critique of dominance and sex roles was developed earlier—in the late 1960s—by radical feminists such as Atkinson. The Feminists in 1968 described themselves as an organization dedicated to fighting against sex roles. Some late 1960s heterosexual radical feminists such as Anne Koedt were skeptical of lesbians precisely because of butch/femme relations, which conjured up the image of polarized sex roles. Atkinson and these heterosexual radical feminists strongly opposed the idea that there were inherent differences between women and men, and wanted to end the differentiation of people based on gender. Also, they opposed dominance relations in sex and other areas both for ethical and political reasons—because women were the ones who had been subordinate.

This form of objection to dominance and sex roles existed long before the emergence of lesbian sadomasochism as an issue, before the development of the idea that women's culture had special values and even before the expression of lesbian feminism as a specific politics.

On the other hand, one could conceivably say that the sexual libertarian position is one of the varied descendants of the Redstockings' idea that each woman's interpretation of her own sexual experience is valid and should be accepted. The conflict between this position and the critique of sex roles is one of the most longstanding in the movement.

The "equally valid" approach raises this problem, for butch/femme and sadomasochistic relations as well as for lesbian relations generally: When more than one woman is involved, there may be varied interpretations of the same experience. Some women may interpret their experiences as playful and pleasurable, while others with similar experiences—even those in the same relationship—may interpret them very differently.

Chapter 11

Love and Freedom

Feminists still are only beginning to write much about the difficulties of combining love, sex and freedom for people who are both subjects. How can there be total freedom of action for one person when the other is a subject?

Love, Sex Still Problems

It is extremely common for one person, even if both are women, to seem to feel more affection and/or more desire than another. It is common for one person to wish to end sexual relations at a point when the other does not. It is common for persons involved with each other to want sexual relations at different rates of frequency or to want to experience sex differently. Feminists are only beginning to discuss these questions, as in Tricia Lootens' 1984 *off our backs* article which asks what lesbian lovers who no longer want to make love but want to remain primary to each other can do.

> ...What if you are happy with your lover, and have been for some time, but every time one of you builds up the nerve to try making love, the other one sobs or pretends to be asleep?...
>
> How happy can lovers be if they don't have a sexual relationship? How close does sex bring us? How far apart does it have to drive us?[1]

It is true that the erotic can be strengthening, as Audre Lorde has written, but sexual relations also can produce tension that certainly is not strengthening—at least not in the short run. When relationships end or go through very difficult periods, the erotic energy can turn to an intense form of distress.

Joyce Lindenbaum, a lesbian feminist therapist, suggests in a 1985 *Feminist Studies* article that an unconscious "merging" frightens many lesbian couples, who start feeling loss of self and respond by ending sexual relations or breaking up.

> The crisis occurs when one of the women begins to feel that she has become lost in her partner...
>
> Given that women are the major caretakers in this culture, a love relationship between women has a particular potential to evoke certain aspects of mother-infant intimacy...the lesbian couple's recreation of primal intimacy gives rise to the excruciating terror of primal loss...
>
> Having stirred the memory of primal intimacy and passionately dissolved the boundaries between them, the lesbian couple arrives at...*the sacrifice of sex*. Though it may take weeks or months, sometimes even years, these women gradually stop making love.[2]

Lindenbaum is not suggesting that lesbian relationships have more problems than heterosexual relationships. We may suppose that heterosexual relationships that approach deep intimacy may face similar problems.

Simone de Beauvoir, although she called for sexual relations based on mutual recognition, also suggested in *The Second Sex* that relationships might then become less "sexy" (as did hers with Sartre, who discontinued sexual relations at some point in their relationship).

> ...Erotic attraction dies almost as surely in an atmosphere of esteem and friendship, for two human beings associated in their transcendence...no longer need carnal union...[3]

Most feminists don't think this separation of love and sex should happen, but it often does. Perhaps the phenomenon of losing sexual attraction when love is successful supports the arguments of those feminists who say there is a need to rethink and reshape what people find erotic.

Of course, fear of merging because a relationship is very intimate is not the only reason that sex may become difficult. For many women, sexual abuse in childhood or adult relationships with men still affects their sexuality after the abuse has ended and they are in non-abusive relationships. The journal *Lesbian Ethics* devoted much of an issue to this subject in 1987.[4] A survey by JoAnn Loulan revealed that 38% of all lesbians were abused as children, the same percentage as that of women in the general population studied by Diana Russell.[5]

(Lesbians might note that JoAnn Loulan's books *Lesbian Sex* and *Lesbian Passion*, published in the 1980s, provide a number of suggestions for lesbians having difficulty maintaining the sexual aspect of relationships).[6]

Asking How to Love Well

Lesbian feminists are beginning to discuss how to love well as well as how to relate sexually.

Marilyn Frye thinks it is possible to love without cannibalizing each other. She suggests that people can preserve autonomy while loving each other.

> One who loves is not selfless either. If the loving eye is in any sense disinterested, it is not that the seer has lost herself, has no interests, or ignores or denies her interests. Any of these would seriously incapacitate her as a perceiver. What *is* the case, surely, is that unlike the slave or the master, the loving perceiver can see without the presupposition that the other poses a constant threat or that the other exists for the seer's service; nor does she see with the other's eye instead of her own. Her interest does not blend the seer and the seen, either empirically by terror or *a priori* by conceptual links forged by the arrogant eye. One who sees with a loving eye is separate from the other whom she sees. There are boundaries between them; she and the other are two; their interests are not identical; they are not blended in vital parasitic or symbiotic relations, nor does she believe they are or pretend they are.[7]

But Frye does not discuss why these people want a relationship in the first place. She takes off from Atkinson's discussion of metaphysical cannibalism without considering its first premise.

Feminists asking whether love can be valid and strengthening rather than an escape from freedom might want to consider that neither the emotion of love, nor many of the actions associated with love—being lifted out of oneself—are exclusive to love for persons. One can love a bird or a tree, a book, or a political movement. That is, the person can think about these things affectionately, try to understand them, and try to work for their betterment (preserving the life or the species of the tree or the bird; trying to get the book back into print; working for the movement). These comparisons do not insult or trivialize love; indeed, they may salvage the concept of love from the idea that it is an illegitimately extracted emotion, state of being, or mode of action.

It is possible to love without being oppressed. Many feminists love the feminist movement without being coerced to do so or brought up to believe they should.

But what about love between individuals?

Love sometimes involves taking actions that put someone else's welfare before one's own. Only if this situation is chronic or one-sided is it oppressive. Sometimes, such actions may have to be rather one-sided, as when an adult loves a child and takes care of the child. Even if such actions cannot be justified by an ethic that primarily values autonomy, they can be by an ethic that expects the individual to have some responsibilities—at least chosen ones—to others.

Love is manifested in actions, not just emotions. A fairly consistent pattern of supportive actions can be called "love."

In a 1984 *Hypatia* article, "Love, Knowledge and Transformation," Caroline Whitbeck puts forth a model for a feminist eros that is not necessarily lesbian, although it is based on the awareness developed from lesbian feminism that opposition or being opposite is not a requirement of erotic love, and, in fact, works against one's possibilities of really knowing the other.

In a feminist eros, Whitbeck says, the relation of the self to the other is not to be represented by gender differences (even if the two people are a woman and a man). "...Differentiation does not depend on opposition"; different does not mean opposite.[8]

Whitbeck writes:

> What is distinctive about eros within feminist erotics is that it is a bond to an other who is understood as analogous to the self...Since the other is not viewed as opposite as it is in masculinist ontology and erotics, it is presumably possible to genuinely recognize the characteristics of the self in the other.

Such genuine recognition contrasts with mistakenly attributing the one's own characteristics to the other...[9]

If the lover and beloved were opposite in nature, it could hardly be expected that each would be able to recognize the other for what s/he is.[10]

Like Frye, Whitbeck identifies love with knowing. But Whitbeck does believe that "surprise" over the other person's actions, attitudes or remarks is a major element in eros.

As Claudia Card (personal communication) has observed, surprise is erotic (if it isn't something else). The truth of this observation is explained by the underscoring of the other's otherness in those circumstances: the other's otherness is most vividly experienced in the spontaneous and hence unexpected action of the other.[11]

Whitbeck thinks that erotic *ex statis*—being taken out of one's self, which she sees as desirable in the context of a feminist eros—does not happen only in sexual relationships.[12] She believes it can also happen in the mother/child relationship or between friends. She does not see this going out of oneself as dangerous, if it is done in the context of a feminist eros of really seeing each other for who she is. (But isn't it possible that great injury can be done by a person who really sees one as one is, if that person is not scrupulous?)

Whitbeck goes on to say that familiarity "mutes otherness."

Friendship is something of a problem for an ontology based on a self/other opposition, since friendship turns on *shared* goals and understandings. One response to the difficulty is to deny that friends are distinct beings. Thus Aristotle at one point speaks of friends as one soul in two bodies.[13]

This concept of friendship hardly seems to pose less of a self/other problem than an erotic relationship. In fact, friends sometimes avoid forming sexual relations because they fear they already are "too close" and lesbian couples sometimes stop having sexual relations after they have become "too close," as Lindenbaum and Lootens pointed out.

If one assumes that surprise is a crucial element in eros and that the familiarity of friendship is somehow different, isn't this an argument for maintaining that friends and lovers are distinct categories? Whitbeck suggests that it is good for eros to be based on friendship, yet she also endorses the idea of surprise as erotic.

It is true that surprises can be pleasant as well as unpleasant; but the argument that surprise is erotic, is reminiscent of the fact that *anxiety* is erotic — in the erotics based on tension and antagonism that predominate in contemporary society.

Isn't it possible that development of a feminist eros means development of an eros that does not depend on surprise, or, of course, on anxiety? Why not try to create an erotics based on the predictability that is linked to trustworthiness, on shared experiences and perceptions?

Female Friendship

Although lesbian feminists such as Mary Daly had been discussing friendship between women for some time, the first feminist book on the subject was published in 1986, Janice Raymond's *A Passion for Friends*. (Radical feminist Karen Lindsey wrote an earlier book, *Friends as Family*,[14] that discussed the importance of friendship but did not analyze it much or focus on women).

Raymond sees love and friendship as intertwined. She feels that there should be love within friendship and friendship within love.

She does not much scrutinize the ways that love may have been injurious to women, but looks at the ways that love and friendship between women can be mutually strengthening. She does not look at love or friendship between women and men or focus on asking whether those relations are possible. She says that feminist theory should not focus on women's connections with men. "This definition places feminism at a false starting point, that is, woman in relation to man rather than woman in relation to woman."[15]

Raymond writes that one of the "most devastating consequences" of women's oppression is that it makes "women *not lovable* to their Selves and to other women . . . When a woman sees a sister brutalized . . . and how few women really survive, Gyn/affection is erased from memory."[16]

Raymond suggests that female friendship is what women should be fighting for, a necessary condition of a world in which women are not oppressed. "Women must ask not only what we are fighting against but also what we are fighting for. The destruction of female oppression and the development of female friendship go hand in hand."[17] Raymond says that feminists have not sufficiently stressed friendship as part of the struggle, part of the goal, and an integral part of life.[18] (See pages 298-9, below).

Friendship is both a good thing in itself and a way for women to stay strong enough to keep working for feminism, according to Raymond.

> Friendship gives women a point of crystallization for living in the world. It gives form, shape, and a concrete location to women who have no state or geographical homeland... Friendship provides women with a common world that becomes a reference point for location in a larger world... Thus a sharing of personal life is at the same time a grounding for social and political existence.[19]

Raymond realizes that women face possible disappointments in close friendships, but she suggests that the disappointment that comes from expecting that all women or all feminists will act as friends is more disillusioning than carefully chosen friendships will be. She urges women who have been disillusioned by other women to be forgiving and not turn entirely away from women. She criticizes "...a certain sentimentalizing of female bonding which expected too much and then backed away when it was not delivered... Nihilistic disaffection is the easy way out."[20]

Raymond urges women to develop careful, thoughtful friendships. She refers to both sexual and nonsexual friendships under the name of friendship.

> Friendship is a passion but, in my vision, it is a thoughtful passion. It manifests a thinking heart.[21]

Raymond's "thinking heart" is rather like Marilyn Frye's "loving eye," a capacity for perceiving and caring about the other person. Like Frye and Lorde, Raymond believes that it is possible to love without damaging oneself or the other woman.

> There has been much discussion of passion within the lover relationship, but not much talk of friendship within love. It is my opinion that when a lover finds she is losing her Self in the heightened awareness of and attachment to another woman in a sexually passionate relationship, the friendship is problematic. Either the friendship wasn't strong initially or it got swallowed up in the sexual passion of the lover relationship.[22]

Raymond sees love, sexuality, and friendship as connected. She sees a possibility for passionate friendship without sexual expression, but not for sexuality without passionate friendship.

In any kind of lover relationship that is committed, one's lover should be one's best friend. And if one's best friend is one's lover, she should also be the primary passion of her lover's life.[23]

When Raymond says one's lover/friend should be one's primary passion, presumably she does not mean that a passion for feminism or other life goals should take a back seat.

Raymond sees love and friendship as desirable and necessary, complementary rather than contradictory. Possible injurious effects of love she sees as stemming from a failure by one or both women to love well—thoughtfully—enough, not as an indication that there is anything wrong with love in itself.

As the movement moves from the initial rejection of the control of women's sexuality by men and the affirmation of women's right to love each other, to actually working on trying to create new relationships, the difficulties in life, love, and sex become more perplexing.

There is much disagreement among feminists over what sexuality is and what love is, and also over the role sexuality and love should have in women's lives now and in the future. Perhaps the only common ground is the idea that women need to decide for themselves what role sexuality and love will play in their lives, and that men must no longer control women's sexuality.

*Reproductive rights demonstration, Washington DC, 1979.
Signboards read, (in Spanish) "Abortion, Yes! Sterilization
Abuses, No!" and "Leave Our Clinics Alone."*

Second Annual Michigan Womyn's Music Festival, August 1977.

© 1977 JEB (Joan E. Biren)

Dessie Woods and her daughter head the 1981 "Take Back the Night" march in Washington DC. Woods had served time in a Georgia prison due to an incident in 1976, in which she killed a white man who had kidnapped both her and a friend and was trying to rape her.

August 26, 1981—Member of the Congressional Union, a group organized by Sonia Johnson, chains herself to the White House fence to demand ratification of the Equal Rights Amendment.

New York City, November 18, 1984—"Not in Our Name," a feminist march against capitalism, imperialism and corporate exploitation of women.

August 27, 1983—Audre Lorde (right) speaks at the march marking the 20th anniversary of the civil rights march on Washington led by Martin Luther King, Jr. The woman at left provides sign language interpretation for the hearing-impaired.

March 27, 1982 — Lesbians march on Washington DC in protest against the Reagan administration.

Arlington, Virginia, November 15, 1981 — Women's Pentagon Action, connecting militarism with women's oppression.

Washington DC, May 12, 1984—Feminists protest pornography at "Take Back the Night" march.

Washington DC, July 3, 1986—Lesbians protest the attorney general's Commission on Pornography. Other lesbians and feminists testified before the commission on the harm pornography does to women.

San Francisco, July 15, 1984—Lesbian separatists at the National March for Lesbian and Gay Rights.

Part Four

Goals, Strategies and Tactics: A Radical Feminist Weakness?

Chapter 12

What is the Goal, Anyway?

What are the possible goals of radical feminism? It might be useful to consider all of the *theoretically* possible goals, all of the goals consistent with various theories, rather than confining the discussion at the outset to those goals which seem practically possible. What is practically possible is not always clear. One hundred years ago most of the political movements of this century—the spread of communism, the temporary triumph of fascism, the national liberation movements—probably would have seemed impossible.

Theoretically possible goals include: the abolition of social distinctions between women and men, the end of characterization of people by gender; the end of all forms of male supremacy, class oppression and race oppression; complete integration of women and men; economic and/or political autonomy for women; the establishment of separate nations or nations-within-nations for women; mixed societies ruled by women; and, no doubt, others.

Radical feminists can agree on the goal of ending male supremacy. There also is agreement on many specific goals, such as women's control of their own bodies, an end to rape and all violence against women, freedom of sexual expression, and economic autonomy for all women.

Some goals may seem to cancel each other out: Integration of women with men seems to be a goal that diverges sharply from that of establishing either women's rule over men, or all-female nations. However, if these conflicting goals are envisioned for the *long term*, then cooperation in the *short run* may still be possible.

One key difference between a liberal feminist and a radical feminist might be their time-tables: Does a woman see equality with men as possible at the present time, or only in the distant future? Radical feminists, who believe that male supremacy and other oppressions are deeply entrenched, would be more likely to see women's equality as a long-term goal. Some women who have no interest in working with men in the present, might see the integration of women and men or the abolition of gender as future goals.

Also, the abolition of gender might not just be a goal of those who advocate integrated societies in which women and men are equal. Following a class enemy framework, some women who advocate rule by women over men might see such rule as a way of ensuring the eventual abolition of gender, in the same way that marxists have said that rule by the working class will abolish classes. Whether rule by formerly oppressed classes does indeed abolish class systems is another question; theoretically, some people intend it to have that effect. At any rate, few feminists see women's rule over men as a goal.

Separate women's societies, and societies where women and men are equal, are not necessarily contradictory. They could coexist, even within the same country.

In discussion of goals, the question of "historical inevitability" raises its head. If one thinks, as marxists do, that a particular class embodies the most "progressive" elements in society, does this mean that one believes that this class inevitably will be victorious?

Surely the potential for rebellion always exists. But a look at history may convince us that the "most progressive forces" do not always win. The most radical ideas probably will not prevail, even if the most supposedly radical class appears to succeed. Radical groups sometimes lose outright in overt conflict, as in Spain in the 1930s, but they can also become de-radicalized once they are in power, as happened in the Soviet Union.

If one literally believed in "historical inevitability," there would be little point in formulating goals. Since revolutionaries generally do formulate goals, make plans and try to shape events, they do not believe in historical inevitability in any absolute sense.

Do our goals, the goals of the different branches of radical feminism, differ greatly? Or are they so unclear that it's hard to tell?

Beauvoir: Independence

Simone de Beauvoir's goal for women is independence. In *The Second Sex*, she seems to agree with socialist thought's emphasis on economic independence for women.

> It is through gainful employment that woman has traversed most of the distance that separated her from the male; and nothing else can guarantee her liberty...[1]

However, she says that "working today, is not liberty" in a capitalist system. "Only in a socialist world would women by the one attain the other" [by working for pay, attain liberty].[2]

Beauvoir, who wrote *The Second Sex* when there was no organized feminist movement in her country, did not have much to say about how to reach a socialist world or other goals. But in the 1970s, she endorsed and participated in many feminist actions.

Beauvoir's existentialist goal is for women and men to be "mutually recognizing each other as subjects,"[3] which contrasts with her more immediate goal of economic independence. Could economic independence possibly be enough to ensure that people see each other as subjects, despite the innate human tendencies to treat people as others which she postulates?

Self-Determination and Integration

Shulamith Firestone's goals were:

> 1) *The freeing of women from the tyranny of their biology by any means available,* [she emphasizes extrauterine pregnancy] *and the diffusion of the childbearing and childrearing role to the society as a whole, to men and other children as well as women ...*
>
> 2) *The economic independence and self-determination of all.* Under socialism, even if still a money economy, work would be divorced from wages, the ownership of the means of produc-

tion in the hands of all the people, and wealth distributed on the basis of need...

3) *The total integration of women and children into the larger society.*

4) *Sexual freedom, love, etc.*[4]

Like Firestone, other early radical feminists expressed some goals that applied to everyone, men as well as women. *Lilith's Manifesto*, issued in 1969 by the Women's Majority Union of Seattle, said:

This revolution has got to go for broke: *power to no one, and to every one: to each the power over his/her life, and no others.*[5]

A 1969 statement by Chicago Women's Liberation also stressed self-determination:

What does women's freedom mean? It means freedom of self-determination, self-enrichment, the freedom to live one's own life, set one's own goals, the freedom to rejoice in one's own accomplishments. It means the freedom to be one's own person in an integrated life of work, love, play, motherhood...the right to full self-realization and to full participation in the life of the world...[6]

Kate Millett wrote that an ideal politics "...might simply be conceived of as the arrangement of human life on agreeable and rational principles from whence the entire notion of power *over* others should be banished..."[7]

Millett also emphasizes the role of sex as a means of revolution and as part of the goal:

The goal of revolution would be a permissive single standard of sexual freedom, and one uncorrupted by the crass and exploitative economic bases of traditional sexual alliances.[8]

From the beginning, radical feminists often stressed the need for ending economic and racial exploitation as well as male supremacy. A 1968 leaflet written for New York Radical Women by Kathie Amatniek (later Sarachild) said:

HUMANHOOD IS THE ULTIMATE!

ONLY WHEN ALL THOSE WHO ARE EXPLOITED—WHETHER AS BLACK PEOPLE OR AS WOMEN, AS THE POOR AND UNEMPLOYED, OR AS INDIVIDUAL WORKERS AND CHEAP ORGANIZED LABOR 'THANKFUL' FOR OUR JOBS—ONLY WHEN

WE SEE THAT OUR PERSONAL LIMITATIONS ARE REALLY
PRISONS BUILT BY THE PRIVILEGED...THAT, THEREFORE, THE
WEAK AND EXPLOITED MUST UNITE IN ORDER TO BREAK OUT
OF THE PRISONS—ONLY THEN, CAN THERE BE INDIVIDUAL
FREEDOM FOR ALL PEOPLE AND REAL LOVE BETWEEN MEN
AND WOMEN. IT IS OBVIOUS THAT INTEGRATION FOR FREE MEN
AND WOMEN IS NOT A UTOPIAN GOAL BUT A BIOLOGICAL
NECESSITY. INTEGRATION OF FREE PEOPLE WILL BE THE
ULTIMATE SOLUTION FOR HUMANITY.[9]

Amatniek (Sarachild) called for integration of women and men
as the goal. Perhaps her background in the Civil Rights Movement
contributed to this emphasis.

Atkinson: Self-Justifying Life

Ti-Grace Atkinson is critical of "equal rights" as a goal.

The traditional feminists want equal rights for women with men.
But on what grounds? If women serve a different *function* from
men in society, wouldn't this necessarily affect women's rights?
For example, do *all* women have the 'right' not to bear children?
Traditional feminism is caught in the dilemma of demanding
equal treatment for unequal functions, because it is unwilling to
challenge political (functional) classification by sex.[10]

The whole structure of society would have to be redefined—in
fact, biological functions might have to be redefined—in order for
women and men to be equal. This perspective of Atkinson's does
not mean that she disavows the idea that at some point all
human beings would be equal. More tersely, she put it:

Obviously, if feminism has any logic to it at all, it must be
working for a sexless society.[11]

Atkinson sets up a model for a utopian, egalitarian society:

A community, as an entity, entails certain activities peculiar to
societies: community work (e.g., collecting garbage, farming,
child care), and community legislation and commitment priorities (e.g., regulation of exchange, community investment). The
community as a whole (one individual, one vote) determines
what the community requires in terms of goods and services.
The production of the items from these categories would be
divided into the significantly creative and those items not
considered by the community as creative. (Each member must
vote on the basis of whether *it* would choose to be employed in

its spare time at that task.) All noncreative tasks would fall into the category of 'community work.'[12]

Atkinson's ultimate goal is even more ambitious: a self-justifying life for all.

Removing oppression at this late date requires no less than an elaborate and intact theory restructuring life as self-justifying in and of itself.[13]

Atkinson's understanding of women's oppression is taken from Beauvoir's concept of the search for an Other to use to keep one from fearing death and emptiness. Atkinson's solution, then, is that all people must learn not only to function autonomously but to be truly able to satisfy themselves. She sees dependence on others as a motivating force and justification for slavery of all kinds.

It seems to me that aesthetic theory might be of help... If the act of creation and the act of appreciation are combined, we might have the circular, self-contained structure we need. At present, identity is built from the outside. We are dependent for our very existence on recognition. But what if identity were built from the inside? What if one's life were like a work of art, created by dialogue with one's surroundings...[14]

Perhaps artists, though, care more about having their work seen by at least a few other people than Atkinson suggests. Perhaps a model of perfect autonomy is unobtainable. Moreover, what would be the attraction of revolutionary community if people wish to be utterly autonomous?

Women's Rule

Unlike Firestone, Sarachild and Millett—who speak of eventual integration with men as the goal—and Atkinson, who assumes it, other feminists have different visions.

Valerie Solanis' 1967 SCUM (Society for Cutting Up Men) Manifesto has probably more often been considered a "mood" piece expressing anger, than a serious plan of action.

Life in this society being, at best, an utter bore and no aspect of society being at all relevant to women, there remains to civic-minded, responsible, thrill-seeking females only to overthrow the government, eliminate the money system, institute complete automation, and destroy the male sex.[15]

SCUM will kill all men who are not in the Men's Auxiliary of SCUM. Men in the Men's Auxiliary are those men who are working diligently to eliminate themselves...[16]

After the elimination of money there will be no further need to kill men; they will be stripped of the only power they have over psychologically independent females...[17]

This goal accomplished,

...Women will be busy solving the few remaining unsolved problems before planning their agenda for eternity and Utopia— completely revamping educational programs so that millions of women can be trained within a few months for high-level intellectual work...[18]

Elizabeth Gould Davis' stated goal was not to eliminate men, but merely to obtain their worship.

She who was revered and worshipped by early man...will once again be the pivot—not as sex but as divine woman—about whom the next civilization will, as of old, revolve.[19]

She does not seem to sense that worship can be ambivalent or double-edged, that it may co-exist with hatred or foster it.

Lesbians for Self-Determination

When lesbian feminism developed, lesbian feminist goals did not always sound that different from early radical feminist goals, especially when stated in the most general terms.

The introduction to the Furies' book, *Lesbianism and the Women's Movement*, said,

As we [lesbian feminists] work to destroy that male power and gain female self-determination...[20]

Self-determination is a commonly stated goal for feminists.

In the 1970s, radical feminists came to believe that "equality" in an unequal system was an absurd goal, and to emphasize self-determination instead.

As Mary Daly wrote in *Beyond God the Father*,

Radical feminists know that '50/50 equality' within patriarchal space is an absurd notion, neither possible nor desirable...The notion of a 50% female army, for example, is alien to the basic insights of radical feminism.[21]

In her 1974 speech "Renouncing Sexual 'Equality'," Andrea Dworkin said,

> Others of us, and I stand on this side of the argument, do not see equality as a proper, or sufficient, or moral, or honorable final goal. We believe that to be equal where there is not universal justice, or where there is not universal freedom is, quite simply, to be the same as the oppressor.[22]

Presumably, she is talking about white women's equality with white men. If everyone were equal, there would be no oppressor.

Ending the Class

Radical feminists generally speak of ending male power, or the class of men as being separate from and above women, rather than of gaining power over men. Monique Wittig's paper "One is Not Born a Woman" describes the common goal:

> Our fight aims to suppress men as a class, not through a genocidal, but a political struggle. Once the class 'men' disappears, 'women' as a class will disappear as well, for there are no slaves without masters.[23]

As a *Questions Féministes* editorial describes it, the first goal is self-determination and the next is an end to sexual categorization.

> Our top priority is the right to be autonomous (not to be 'objects of' or 'appropriated by' men); our second priority is the right to individuality without reference to sexual identity.[24]

The editorial speaks of destroying not individual men, but the idea of "man."

> ...At the same [time] as we destroy the idea of 'Woman,' we will also destroy the idea of 'Man.'[25]

The editorial is critical of those who criticize equality as a goal. Equality can still be a radical goal, the editorial says, if it is pursued with a radical understanding.

> Equality-with-the-oppressor, however, is a contradiction in terms. If there is equality between two beings, there is neither oppressor nor oppressed...But why do some people pretend to think that being 'equivalent' means for women to be *like* men *as they are now, before* equality?[26]

Integrative Feminism

Often, late 1970s and early 1980s radical feminist goals or solutions are expressed in somewhat less dramatic or militant terms than some earlier radical feminist goals or solutions had been. Adrienne Rich is one of many who could be said to use a milder tone.

Like Firestone, Rich connects the liberation of women with an integration of different kinds of thinking, such as the scientific and artistic or the rational and emotional. In *Of Woman Born*, Rich writes that "truly to liberate women, then, means to change thinking itself: to reintegrate what has been named the unconscious, the subjective, the emotional with the structural, the rational, the intellectual..."[27]

Rich's reaction to "artificial production of life" as a solution is ambivalent. Unlike Firestone, she briefly notes both the possibility of its being controlled by the patriarchy and the possibility for expanding women's choices.

> Ideally, of course, women would choose...between biological and artificial reproduction...But I do not think we can project any such idea onto the future—and hope to realize it—without examining...the shadow impression we carry out of the magical thinking of Eve's curse [traditional negative ideas about women's reproductive systems].[28]

Rich contends that Firestone is not "...taking full account of what the experience of biological pregnancy and birth might be in a wholly different political and emotional context. Her attitudes toward pregnancy ('the husband's guilty waning of sexual desire ...') are male-derived."[29]

Audre Lorde's goal is for a world that includes both independence and *inter*dependence, self-determination and responsibility.

> I work for a time when women with women, women with men, men with men, all share a world that does not barter bread or self for obedience, nor beauty, nor love. And in that world we will raise our children free to choose how best to fulfill themselves. For we are all jointly responsible for the care and raising of the young, since *that* they be raised is a function, ultimately, of the species.[30]

Lisa Leghorn and Katherine Parker's goal, expressed in *Woman's Worth*, is a matriarchal economy and a culture based on female values. That is, a non-competitive, sharing economy and a caring culture.[31]

> The economics of female values are implicit in the mothering role, where products such as cleanliness, standards of living and time are produced which improve the quality of life, where investment in these products is in their eventual independence (as with children) or sharing, rather than control and profit. These concepts of cooperation, sharing, and nurturance and pulling together as survival mechanisms, are very powerful when conceived of on a social and economic scale. The values underlying matriarchal economies would probably take the form of a non-growth model where surplus would be shared, where everyone's material needs would take priority over other potential expenditures, and decision-making as well as wealth would be collectivized.[32]
>
> ...In a matriarchal economy, the least specialized work would have to be mechanized or shared among all persons, so that everyone would have equal responsibility and power.[33]
>
> Such an egalitarian social structure would mean no differentiation in people's power on the basis of biology, and the integration of the public and private spheres.[34]

Leghorn and Parker emphasize changing the structure of all kinds of work—both traditional paid labor and housework—as both goal and tactic.

> What is actually needed is a synthesis of the two in our social and economic institutions: a more rational organization of housework, and a more human decentralization of industrial production.[35]

This "more rational organization of housework" could mean having more services provided collectively or for pay by the community. Their goal of shared work is similar to Atkinson's, although she would never call it "matriarchal."

Canadian radical feminist theorist Angela Miles writes about the goals of "integrative" feminists, with whom she identifies herself. ("Integrative" means that they emphasize both changes in the political realm and simultaneous changes within one's own life). The goal she suggests, like Leghorn and Parker's, is a change in values.

> ...A demand that the human values and concerns relegated to the sphere of personal life and restricted to women be general-

ized to all of society and become determining social values and concerns; that people's reproduction and self-realization begin to determine the structure of production, rather than the reverse (which is true in industrialism and late capitalism)...[36]

Like Leghorn and Parker, Miles emphasizes changing the structure of production and reproduction. She means that more men would have to become involved in child care, as well as women involved in paid labor, and that the systems of child care and paid labor be made more flexible and compatible.

Stated feminist goals show the influence of many systems of thought. The emphasis on ending oppression, abolishing class differences, and ending economic oppression comes from feminism's roots in marxism or socialism. The emphasis on ending power over others comes from root connections with anarchism. The emphasis on individual freedom and creativity probably is derived from liberalism and existentialism. The emphasis on self-determination may come both from liberalism and from the example of national liberation movements.

While the mixture of systems of thought from which feminists have consciously or unconsciously derived ideas may initially seem contradictory, they may be complementary. Each goal gains value from the presence of the others: What kind of individual freedom could there be in a classist, racist world? What kind of freedom or self-determination could there be in an authoritarian society, controlled from the top? What kind of collective or group freedom could there be without individual freedom, or individual freedom without collective freedom? Will greater individual autonomy or greater, more equal community and deeper bonding with women be the more powerful attraction to radical change?

Frankly, I see little viability in the acknowledgment of women's superiority by men as a goal. This goal seems least compatible with the other expressed goals. Radicals should remember that no one permanently accepts being ruled.

Even a brief look at these goals shows that many of them are more like expressions of values than plans of action.

Chapter 13

Strategies and Tactics: Taking Power?

Radical feminist and lesbian strategies and tactics differ as much as goals do. These differences have emerged in part, but not entirely, because goals differ.

Simone de Beauvoir did not really discuss strategies or tactics; unfortunately, many later feminists have followed that example. In *The Second Sex*, Beauvoir recognizes that women must work collectively to end their oppression, although she does not say much about how this is to be done.

> ...There is no other way out for woman than to work for her liberation.
>
> This liberation must be collective, and it requires first of all that the economic evolution of woman's condition be accomplished.[1]

The main tactic Beauvoir recognized in *The Second Sex*, then, was working for economic equality, which she believed was possible only in a socialist society. She does not suggest what kind of women's organizing should take place, other than working with socialist or communist parties.

In the years after Beauvoir, many differences on questions of strategy have come down to differences over direct confrontation versus indirect "working around" a problem or oppressor.

Feminist Concepts of Power

Feminists have different concepts of power, but many or most reject the concept of holding power over others. Very early in the movement, Ti-Grace Atkinson said that it was necessary to reject all claim to power over others.

> [The concept of power] is the 'answer,' the *conceptual* structure, on which all *political* structures are built. Without questioning this 'answer,' no fundamental change can occur.
>
> And, yet, how few are willing to give up the power relationship. Even the power*less* cling to the ideology, in the hope that as long as the *idea* exists they have hope of escaping power*less*ness by achieving *some* way, *some*how, power*ful*ness. Of course, as long as the conceptual framework of 'power' itself is valued (especially, if valued by the Oppressed!), *none* of us has *any* hope.[2]

In the first issue of *Quest* in 1974, socialist feminist Nancy Hartsock emphasized that power can mean being able to use our own capacity to act and create, rather than controlling others; although Hartsock was a socialist feminist (now she says she is no closer to socialist than to radical feminism), her concept of power is similar to that of many radical feminists. She says that power as capacity to act is feminists' aim. Hartsock quoted Bernice Carroll as saying, "power is first defined as 'ability, whether physical, mental or moral, to act.'" Hartsock continued,

> ...These understandings of power do not require domination of others: energy and accomplishment are understood to be satisfying in themselves.[3]

Although Hartsock's emphasis is on non-dominating power, she recognizes that other kinds of power might be necessary.

> While we have discussed only a few of the links among capitalism, patriarchy, and white supremacy, it is obvious that we cannot end any women's economic oppression and dependency without at the same time destroying those structures. Power as domination is fundamental to the three: taking power as domination appears to be the only way to take over and transform them.[4]

Feminists today still criticize the idea of power over others. Hooks wants to change "a world governed by politics of domination, one in which the belief in a notion of superior and inferior, and its concomitant ideology—that the superior should rule over the inferior"[5] and to create "a world where everyone can live fully and freely."[6]

Leghorn and Parker's "matriarchal concept of power" rejects power over others as much as possible and emphasizes voluntary cooperation and self-determination.

> A matriarchal concept of power has more to do with creativity and cooperation, the power to change that comes from the caring for others, than with coercion or control...To put such a matriarchal concept of power into form requires decentraliza- tion, with collective decision-making.[7]

Of course, not all radical feminists would agree with defining this concept of power as "matriarchal." Some, like Atkinson, would say that matriarchy implies rule by mothers rather than lack of power over others.

The radical feminist Atkinson, the socialist feminist Hartsock, and the "women's values" feminists Leghorn and Parker all say they wish ultimately to end power over others.

Most emphasis in feminist political writing has been on self-determination rather than on coercion of others. But is this self-determination to be achieved "by any means necessary"? Do most radical feminists assume, like traditional liberal theorists, that there is an ultimate harmony in realizing everyone's self-interests, if only everyone would understand their true self-interest? If there is no harmony of interests, if there are fundamental conflicts, how is the seeker after change to avoid using coercion? Even such pacific, liberal measures as desegrega- tion of public places have been achieved only through coercion. Although radical feminist writers often comment that men, like any dominant class, cannot be expected to give up power will- ingly, many also express reluctance to use coercion to divest them of power.

Some radical feminists caution that fear of obtaining too much power is premature to the point of being absurd. Charlotte Bunch wrote:

> Some argue that a revolutionary women's goal is the end of power—to create a world not based on power dynamics... Perhaps, ultimately, we can dream of an end to power. But before we can accomplish that, women must first gain enough control over society today to end patriarchal domination and destruction of the world. In that process, we hope, we can change the nature of power, but we cannot avoid or ignore it.[8]

What is 'Reform'?

On the other hand, radical feminists often have expressed a feeling that tactics can be flexible and should not be judged by pre-determined ideologies. As the "Principles" of New York Radical Women said in 1968, "We ask not if something is 'reformist,' 'radical,' 'revolutionary' or 'moral.' We ask: is it good for women or bad for women?"[9] The Redstockings Manifesto said, "We will not ask what is 'revolutionary' or 'reformist,' only what is good for women."[10]

Carrying on in that tradition, Charlotte Bunch wrote an article, "The Reform Tool Kit," in 1974, in which she rejected the dichotomy between reform and revolution and specified under what conditions reforms could lead to radical or revolutionary goals. (Bunch discussed "radical reform" a decade before Soviet leader Mikhail Gorbachev).

> When we probe these stereotypes [of 'reformer' or 'revolutionary'], we find that they primarily reflect *style* (how one lives or the comparative virtues of lobbying vs. shooting) and *surface content* (how far out or different it sounds from the way things are now) rather than *substantive content* (how the activity affects different classes of women and what happens to the women working on it) or *ultimate goals* (where the action leads in the long run and how it will get us there).[11]

Bunch writes that, "Reform or proposed changes can be part of any group's program, whether conservative or revolutionary in ideology...Reformism [on the other hand] assumes that the interests of women are not in fundamental conflict with the American system."[12]

In *The Politics of Women's Liberation*, the writer Jo (Joreen) Freeman, who became a feminist activist in Chicago in 1967, suggests that it is ironic that women who define themselves as radical often concentrate on their personal lives and on cultivating social and cultural networks and support services, such as shelters, which could be seen as part of women's traditional role—while those who work to change laws affecting such areas as women's wages are considered reformist.[13] Although Freeman's tone is sometimes uncomfortably disparaging of radicals, she does point out the dilemma: What does a radical feminist do? What is a radical action, and—even more important —what is a radical feminist strategy? Demonstrations, marches and sit-ins are perhaps the most obvious radical tactics—but can they constitute an entire strategy?

Bunch deals with this point with more sympathy for the radical feminist dilemma.

> One reason radicals have difficulty developing programs is our fear that reforms will coopt us or pacify too many women without overthrowing male supremacy.[14]
>
> Not knowing what to do with the immensity of what we question, we often become isolated, discouraged, and immobilized.
>
> Enter Reformism. Where radicals have failed, reformists have flourished. Reformist groups and activities attract many women primarily because such groups are well organized and provide involvement in programs of action that can produce immediate results and tangible—though limited—successes.[15]

Bunch suggests that radicals use the following criteria to determine whether a particular reform has radical potential and should be supported:

> 1) Does this reform materially improve the lives of women, and if so, which women, and how many? 2) Does it build an individual woman's self-respect, strength, and confidence? 3) Does it give women a sense of power, strength, and imagination as a group and help build structures for further change? 4) Does it educate women politically, enhancing their ability to criticize and challenge the system in the future? 5) Does it weaken patriarchal control of society's institutions and help women gain power over them?[16]
>
> Every reform will not necessarily advance all five criteria, but no reform that we undertake should be in opposition to any of these points.[17]

Bunch continues,

> Reforms should be judged by how they actually affect women; some sound good in theory, but work against women's material needs. For example, no-fault divorce...[18]

In other words, reforms that are proposed to counter the abstract idea of "sexism," rather than trying to help women overcome their class oppression, may not be helpful for women. The idea that women have had special rights that men, too, should share is likely to be used against women, as it has been in the area of child custody, as many men who try to obtain custody of their children are now obtaining it. (Criteria such as ability to afford care for the children, which of course men better fulfill, are creating a new disadvantage for women).[19]

Most radical feminists are too practical, too concerned about the concrete reality of women's daily lives, to accept the premise occasionally put forth by some leftists that reforms are dangerous because they placate the people into acceptance of their lot. Radical feminists certainly try to counter the idea that equality has already arrived, but they do not oppose all reforms for fear of strengthening the state. (However, some feminists do question particular reforms, such as the MacKinnon-Dworkin ordinance giving women the power to sue over damages done to them by pornography, on the grounds that that particular reform—or any that could involve restrictions on publications—would give the state too much power. [See pages 197-8, above]). Feminists generally assume that the more freedom women have, the more they will seek.

Reform may or may not involve confrontational politics. Lobbying often has a "respectable" style, but it is a means of dealing face-to-face with the class in power. Marching or sitting-in as an adjunct to lobbying makes it more confrontational.

Often radical feminists and (particularly) lesbian feminists have found it distasteful to deal with men in power directly in order to try to obtain reform. Asking for legislative change and, especially, being polite may seem to imply acknowledging their right to make rules. By the mid-1970s, the larger number of radical and lesbian feminists turned away from this type of politics.

Radical feminists have different perspectives on liberals: Some see them as potential radicals or as part of a spectrum which can appeal to all women. Others see liberals (or some of them) as diverting women from real feminism, because the liberals present feminism in a false light. In "The Liberal Takeover of Women's Liberation," Redstocking Carol Hanisch wrote:

> Today the women's liberation movement is in the hands of a group of liberal opportunists and therefore in the hands of the left/liberal male establishment. These women—*Ms.* magazine, some of the *Village Voice* writers, and the 'women's-lib ladies' in communities all over the country—are scrambling frantically after the few crumbs that men have thrown out when we radicals began to expose the truth and demand some changes. These are the women who have access to the press and money.

They are supposedly 'the leaders' of the women's movement, but they are leading us down the road to a few respectable reforms and nothing more.

...They refuse to name men as the enemy (oppressor) and talk endlessly about that vague monster 'society,' as being responsible for it all...They claim that women are brainwashed and damaged and consent to their own oppression and that men, poor things, treat women badly because they have been socialized into a 'role.'

...Further, they talk about women's liberation as a legal question, as if getting some legislation passed will solve our situation ...Never is it a question of the realities of power, real power—economic (who owns), military (whose physical strength) and political (who rules). It is never a question of what it means to take that power and distribute it among us all.[20]

Alternatives, Not Confrontation

In the early and mid-1970s, there was a turn by radical and lesbian feminists not only from working for legislated reforms but also from any sort of demonstrations or direct confrontation with the male power structure. Bunch's "Reform Tool Kit" article was an exception, not an indication of the most conspicuous practice. Creating independent projects—whether these were publications, bookstores, restaurants, record companies, credit unions or rape crisis centers—was seen by many as a more productive way of opposing the system. Creating an alternative system was seen as more radical than directly confronting the power structure. The alternative strategy is derived from the 1960s counterculture, but also ultimately from anarchist and utopian socialist principles.

Some radical feminists saw the turn to establishing alternatives as a diversion from radicalism and as triumph for liberals. However, even these feminists saw the need for an alternative press; they did not oppose all alternatives.

Radical feminist writer Brooke has criticized both feminist businesses and cultural feminism. She noted that feminist businesses cannot provide jobs for the majority of women.

Setting up 'alternative' situations doesn't really work. Most alternatives reach very few people...

Concentration on 'alternatives' causes a movement to renounce overthrow of the surrounding society for a peaceful coexistence with it.[21]

Brooke criticized cultural feminism, not the work of artists *per se*, but the idea that cultural change could bring about political change.

> The locus of women's oppression, therefore, is not culture but power, men's class power. Since women's oppression is a political matter affecting all women, it is necessary for women to create a mass, political women's movement to overthrow male supremacy.[22]

However, many revolutionary movements have viewed "cultural revolution" as an important part of the effort to mobilize people politically. The extent to which the content of music and art produced now is directed toward this goal is debatable. Artists such as Bernice Johnson Reagon, Alix Dobkin and Holly Near are consciously trying to spread a political message, but many others are not. Like many other sectors of the movement, feminists engaged in cultural work preach to the already converted.

The pressures on radicals to coexist with a given society are almost overwhelming. Part of the problem of maintaining one's radical identity and seeing beyond coexistence or cooptation is that the process of working for radical change can leave one exhausted and hopeless—"burned out." Cultural work that validates lesbianism and radical feminism can help mitigate isolation and, at best, inspire new action.

Lesbian feminist Susanna Sturgis, in response to a criticism of cultural feminism by Christine Delphy in 1984, wrote a letter to *off our backs* saying that "cultural feminism"—she points out that nobody calls herself a "cultural feminist"—is not the only possible form of escape for feminists.

> Maintaining feminist and lesbian spaces is a crucial form of political activism.
>
> Of course some women do use these spaces as 'their niche in the world,' as a permanent retreat. So...do some women use feminist theorizing and research to avoid the gut-wrenching demands of feminist activism. Others use their seven-night-a-week-meeting schedule to avoid thinking about what they are doing. Look around you. Theory and activism can be and are being used as escapes as successfully and destructively as are culture and spirituality.[23]

Do Some Tactics Reinforce Male Dominance?

Some lesbians have questioned whether strategies or tactics that could reinforce or salvage the institution of heterosexuality could be revolutionary. Abortion and birth control, for example, could be seen as perpetuating the institution of sexual intercourse of the standard variety, which has been developed around male desires. It may be necessary to secure the availability of abortion and birth control for women at the present time; but, once women have complete control over how and when their sexuality is expressed, abortion might become rare or unnecessary, according to these lesbian critics.

Jill Johnston writes:

> All the feminist issues—abortion, child care, prostitution, political representation, equal pay—are in relation to the man. In other words in relation to reproductive sexuality. Within which the woman remains trapped as a sexual nonentity.[24]

In other words, for Johnston, withdrawal of women's sexual and other services to men would be the most radical strategy, the only one that gives women a chance of real collective or individual independence. Under the present system, a reform such as freely available abortion can serve to make women more easily available as sexual objects for men or could lead to situations in which men forced women to have abortions. Under male supremacy, reforms are always open to abuse.

Johnston goes on to say,

> After there are proper child care centers and free abortions and easy contraception and equal pay and representation and job opportunities—then what? There'll still be a man. And biology is definitely destiny. The woman in relation to the man historically has always been defeated.[25]

This position sounds quite literally defeatist. "Biology is destiny" is the antithesis of Firestone and the radical feminists who agree with her.

Johnston's solution is the formation of a lesbian nation, or tribal grouping.

> Tribal groupings of such women, the fugitive Lesbian Nation, have begun and will continue to serve as sustaining support and psychic power bases within the movement.[26]

Are a tribal grouping and a nation the same thing? If one is seriously trying to establish a nation, how does one go about it? If one's goal is a lesbian or woman's state, obviously one cannot obtain it by direct demand from men.

> [It is] ... a state that woman cannot achieve by demand from the male bastion but only from within from exclusive woman strength building its own institutions of self support and identity.[27]

Johnston said she advocated matriarchy.

> By the matriarchate I mean in all cases a form of woman power, historically and futuristically, not necessarily akin at all to the patriarchy in its domination of one sex by another; I do mean that form of society in which women have complete control over their own bodies, destinies and produce.[28]

The term "matriarchy" is often used loosely. Johnston's definition sounds more like a definition of self-determination. However, she does suggest a return to some previous era. "We're moving backward now. We can't go back fast enough."[29]

Clearly, this emphasis on going backwards must be anathema to those radical feminists who believe that women always have been oppressed by men. Paradoxically, emphasis on the idea that "things were better once, under matriarchy," does not fit so well with the idea that men are biologically destined to be oppressors. Why would these biologically oppressive creatures have allowed matriarchy to develop?

Somewhat surprisingly, if one takes seriously her earlier comment that biology is destiny, Johnston suggests that society no longer be organized into "male" and "female" polarities. However, Johnston suggests that most of the changing must be done by men. (Why can't a man be more like a woman?)

> The aim is an end to the organization of society around the sexual polarities of 'male' and 'female.' An end, in other words, to sexual duality or the two-sex system and a gradual evolutionary movement through the massive liberation of homosexuality back to the true parthenogenic species. All men start off as women and that's the way they'll end up if they don't destroy us all first.[30]

Whether rule by women or mothers through matriarchy is consistent with turning men into "women" is questionable.

Finally, Johnston says that women deserve to rule because they are superior.

> The present urgent project of women is to reestablish harmony in the world by reclaiming the social prerogative which is in agreement with her natural biological position as parent prime.[31]

In other words, women deserve to rule. They deserve "prerogative." Is Johnston really suggesting ending the "male" and "female" principles, or establishing the superiority of "the female principle?"

> The order of the day for all women immediately is *psychic* parthenogenesis.[32]

In other words, Johnston suggests that psychic independence from men is the most crucial element in change, in addition to bonding with other women.

Without sharing all of Johnston's ideas, many lesbians did come to believe that trying to establish this kind of psychic independence was the fundamental building block on which all else must be created and that other issues had less significance.

Part of the appeal of this strategy, this focus on one's self and on forming bonds with other women, may be its non-violence.

What About Organizing? Downplaying Confrontation

Many radical and lesbian feminist writers simply have not discussed organization.

Like a number of other radical feminists writing in the late 1960s, Kate Millett says that change will come through coalitions, but she does not elaborate.

> The changes in fundamental values such a coalition of expropriated groups—blacks, youth, women, the poor—would seek are especially pertinent to realizing not only sexual revolution but a gathering impetus toward freedom from rank or prescriptive role, sexual or otherwise. For to actually change the quality of life is to transform personality, and this cannot be done without freeing humanity from the tyranny of sexual-social category and conformity to sexual stereotype—as well as abolishing racial caste and economic class.[33]

Shulamith Firestone's *The Dialectic of Sex* shows little sense of strategy or tactics. Although she was involved in demonstrations as an early radical feminist, she did not write about how to organize or demonstrate. She seemed to assume that change will come from technology—revolutionizing the childbearing process on one hand and changing the system of labor on the other.

(Many feminists are now more critical of the use of new reproductive technologies than Firestone was. In the 1980s, several books have challenged the use of these technologies as a possible way of giving men more control over reproduction—and women less control.)[34]

Firestone said that women's jobs will become more automated and many women will be forced out of the workforce.

> Massive unrest of the young, the poor, the unemployed will increase: as jobs become more difficult to obtain, and there is no cushioning of the cultural shock by education for leisure, revolutionary ferment is likely to become a staple. Thus, all in all, cybernation may aggravate the frustration that women already feel in their roles, pushing them into revolution.[35]

Firestone does not say how that revolution is to take place. Neither does she note that unemployed people do not necessarily become radicals of the Left. They may instead become radicals of the Right.

Firestone's understanding of revolution also can be called into question if one looks at her diagram, "3-D Revolution," which shows, for example, "Socialism's Dictatorship of the Proletariat" followed by "Self-Determination's 'Communist Anarchy'."[36] That is not what tends to follow proclaimed "dictatorships of the proletariat" historically; dictatorship by the strongest revolutionary party (e.g., the Bolsheviks over other leftists in the emerging Soviet Union), and by the elite of that party and its bureaucracy, tends to follow.

Firestone's frequent references to revolution seem to indicate that she expected that there would be some sort of confrontational and possibly violent change. It is less clear that feminists writing later in the 1970s expected such confrontation. Confrontational activism was not their major focus.

In *Of Woman Born*, Adrienne Rich describes the radical part of the movement as it developed.

> ...The extent and influence of the antipatriarchal women's movement is difficult to grasp. It is not defined by specific organizations, groupings, or factions, though these exist in abundance. It exists...as a network of formal and informal communications, as a growing body of analysis and theory...[37]

She says practically nothing about organizations. Like *Of Woman Born*, most other mid- and late-1970s feminist books don't discuss strategy and tactics, much less structure.

The Danger of Male-Defined Politics

Mary Daly emphasizes the dangers of accepting male or traditional definitions of politics and putting all of feminists' energy into fighting battles over issues that will give women only a small measure of control over our lives. In *Beyond God the Father*, Daly writes,

> Since, then, the experience of battling power structures head-on [e.g. churches, universities] invites an intensification of this kind of division of women against each other, many are coming to reexamine the problem of where to focus energy. I have just pointed out that there is a species of delusion involved in battling the objectified products of male externalization processes as if these were solid realities—not products, but immutable 'nature.' A central problem is to get to recognition of our own internalization of such soul-shrinking products and move toward externalizing our own being in objective social reality. This is another way of saying that the creation of new space involves facing nothingness and discovering power of being.
>
> Does this mean that there is no value in struggling on the level of political power? Such a conclusion would be simplistic. I would suggest that the point is to *avoid unrealistic expectations* concerning the outcome. The point is not to negate the value of the tremendous efforts made by women to obtain justice for women within sexist institutions.[38]

In other words, the institutions that oppress us are not the whole world—although they may control most of the world. If we always define ourselves in relation to our acceptance by churches, universities, the political system, etc., we will not change as much as we can by seeing their limitations and trying to create our own institutions.

Daly continues,

> The process of 'fighting,' then, has value as an educative and radicalizing activity, but there is a healthy cynicism that comes with recognition that a place in sexist society is not the goal...In fighting 'within' such space, we should allow it only

the minimal degree of power over our expenditures of energies that will serve our own purposes. As a cognitive minority, our war is on a deep level. It is with the prevailing sense of reality, according to which we must be relegated to nonbeing. Our self-recovery, in part, depends upon our refusal to take *this* 'reality' too seriously. To put this in another way, we have to learn to live *now* the future we are fighting for, rather than compromising in vain hope of a future that is always deferred, always unreal.[39]

As radical feminists, creating new ideas and organizations, we actually are creating new space and time, Daly says. We live in the future when we live with women as the center of our lives.

...For women entrance into our own space and time is another way of expressing integrity and transformation. To stay in patriarchal space is to remain in time past.[40]

Some other radical feminists might criticize this discussion of space and time on the grounds that it could discourage women from fighting to create change for all women. Now, some might say, living in women's space and time may be a privilege that many women cannot afford or to which they have little access. On the other hand, at least some poor women are able to center their emotional lives on women.

In *Gyn/Ecology*, Daly criticizes both the radical/lesbian and the reformist wings of the movement. Referring to the former, she suggests that at points during the 1970s there was too little fighting against patriarchy. She says that the change from the term "*the women's movement*" to "*the women's community*" is a "system of settling for too little, of settling *down*, of being too comfortable."[41] (Quite a few other feminists have made similar observations about that change in terms).

On the other hand, Daly was still most critical of accepting male establishment definitions of feminism and fighting only for goals which fall into legislative categories.

...Pseudo-feminism has been actively promoted by the patriarchs.

The real rebels/renegades have been driven away from positions of patriarchally defined power, replaced by reformist and roboticized tokens.[42]

Daly is particularly worried about tokenism or cooptation:

> As long as that...(system of [patriarchal] myths) prevails, it is conceivable that there be a society comprised even of 50 percent female tokens: women with anatomically female bodies but totally male-identified, male possessed brains/spirits. The myth/spell itself of phallocractism must be broken.[43]

In other words, Daly does not simply believe in challenging myths, but she believes that the whole intellectual and political framework of the world be changed. She challenges tokenism in many forms.

> ...Tokenism—which is commonly disguised as Equal Rights... yields token victories—deflects and shortcircuits gynergy, so that female power, galvanized under deceptive slogans of sisterhood, is swallowed by The Fraternity...When the oppressed are worn out in the game of chasing the elusive shadow of Success, some 'successes' are permitted to occur— 'victories' which can easily be withdrawn when the victim's energies have been restored. Subsequently, women are lured into repeating efforts to regain the hard-won apparent gains. [She cites the history of the struggles for abortion rights, affirmative action and the Equal Rights Amendment as examples.]
>
> Thus tokenism is insidiously destructive of sisterhood, for it distorts the warrior aspect of Amazon bonding both by magnifying it and by minimizing it. It magnifies the importance of 'fighting back' to the extent of making it devour the transcendent be-ing of sisterhood, reducing it to a copy of comradeship. At the same time, it minimizes the Amazon warrior aspect by containing it, misdirecting and shortcircuiting the struggle.[44]

Daly fears that token victories will de-radicalize women, that too much energy will be channeled into reforms. Daly does not, however, discuss when actions may be radical. She focuses on developing consciousness and bonding between women. She may envision other actions besides that, but she does not say what.

Daly suggests that large numbers may not be necessary for radical change. Perhaps that is why she does not discuss organization.

> Since we have been conditioned to think quantitatively, feminists often begin the Journey with the misconception that we require large numbers in order to have a realistic hope of victory. This mistake is rooted in a serious underestimation of the force/fire of female bonding.[45]

It is not clear what victory she believes can be achieved by small numbers of women. Is this a revolution by example?

On the other hand, Daly feels the absence of women who do not support radical feminists. She points out repeatedly that women who become truly radical often are hurt or attacked by other women, whose goals stop at tokenism.

> ...The Ultimate Irony [is] the desertion of courageous Searchers/ Spinsters by threatened pseudosisters, whose cowardice/absence casts strong women into the role of martyrs/scapegoats for feminism.[46]

Perhaps no other feminist has written so much about the pain caused by women who allow themselves to be used by men to control or hurt other women.

Despite her use of the Amazon warrior image, Daly's vision of change seems rather non-violent. It also seems non-confrontational. The focus away from confrontation seems to come not from fear of radicalism or desire to "help" men or not blame them, but from a fear of de-radicalization, a concern that battling on men's turf could be self-defeating.

Daly has said in an interview with *off our backs* that she does not think in terms of strategies and goals. However, she does not wish to be critical of women who are working on feminist actions.[47]

Daly suggests in *Pure Lust* that concrete goals are not very plausible in the midst of change. She suggests that there is something wrong with the question, "What kind of society do you propose for the year 2000?"

> What *is* wrong with such a question is its implied underestimation of the ineffable scope of a biophilic woman's Otherness in relation to all the prefabricated or imaginable shapes of patriarchal 'reality.' Such Otherness is underestimation by the questioner, so also is the enormity of the task of Shape-shifting. The *process* of Shape-shifting itself is short-changed in this patriarchal mode of questioning...[48]

Daly apparently is suggesting that life—especially a life with radical changes—does not develop in a set of actions directed by plans made in advance.

In her 1987 book *Going Out of Our Minds: The Metaphysics of Liberation*, Sonia Johnson carries Daly's idea of focusing on "be-ing" and concern over simply reacting against men, to the ultimate extreme. Johnson had been an activist in the National

Organization for Women, launched her own demonstrations to push for ratification of the Equal Rights Amendment, including a fast in the lobby of the Illinois legislature, and even ran for president of the United States in 1984. However, after her presidential campaign she turned against activism.

> I think we can trust women. When a whole nation full of women simply cannot get excited about protests, or about civil disobedience, we've got to take that judgment seriously. Because that's what it is, a judgment against reaction. Women don't want to do it...It seems to me that those out there who are determined to get women demonstrating and protesting and resisting have got to think hard about how much they trust other women's intuition...
>
> When we react, when we resist injustice, we are not free, we are bound to the perpetrators, dependent upon their every move, attached to them as if with puppeteers' strings: they pull our strings and we dance. It's as if there's a silent agreement, a contract. But if we refuse the contract, if we refuse the reciprocity—in our attitudes, in our feelings—if we disengage from their strings, no amount of pulling can make us dance. We're free.[49]
>
> *Feeling*, not doing, makes a movement. Our feeling at this moment is everything. The future lives in it. It is the *source* of the future...We can change patriarchy by changing our feelings, but we don't change for that reason. We change because we want to be our own genuine selves. It's not a process. It's *being* there.[50]

If one's own feeling is the whole movement, there is no movement. Perhaps working so much in, or confronting the legislative and electoral process—which might well engender a sense of futility—turned Johnson away from activism.

To say, as Johnson does, that if (most) women don't want to do something, it must be the wrong thing to do, assumes that all women fully understand what all of their options are, and what would be the consequences of all possible courses of action. If one has that much faith in women's ability to know what to do, why not say they must be right to be housewives? Johnson, who repudiated that life herself, clearly does not think that.

Strategically-Minded Feminists

Ti-Grace Atkinson

Ti-Grace Atkinson has discussed strategy and tactics more than many other radical feminist writers. No doubt this is linked to the fact Atkinson uses more specifically political language than other writers. "Oppressor," "oppressed," "class," "enemy," "strategy," and "tactics" are words that she uses more commonly than others do.

For example, in an essay in *Amazon Odyssey*, she wrote:

> If diplomacy fails, that is, if your enemy refuses to stop attacking you, you must force him to stop. This requires a strategy... including such basic information as
> 1. Who is the enemy?
> 2. Where is he located?
> 3. Is he getting material support? material? from where?
> 4. Where are his forces massed?
> 5. What's the best ammunition to knock them out?
> 6. What weapons is he using?
> 7. How can you counteract them?
> 8. What is your plan of attack on him to force diplomatic negotiation? program of action (including priorities) techniques?[51]

Atkinson fears that women will not confront men *enough*. Like Daly (of course, Atkinson's *Amazon Odyssey* was written earlier than Daly's major works), she fears that women will be derailed by reforms, but unlike Daly, she stresses confrontation as a counter-strategy.

> The master might tolerate many reforms in slavery but none that would threaten his essential role as master. Women have known this, and since 'men' and 'society' are in effect synonymous, they have feared confronting him. Without this confrontation and a detailed understanding of what *his* battle strategy has been...the 'Women's Movement' is worse than useless. It invites backlash from men, and no progress for women.[52]

Atkinson expresses concern that seeking reforms will be tactically unsuccessful and debilitating to the movement, insofar as this deflects women from working on more sweeping radical analysis and action.

> As for what the Movement labels 'civil rights' activities such as fighting job discrimination, it should be evident by now that

these are facets of women's oppression, are in that sense secondary, and reflect the roles assigned to women within the major sex institutions. Fighting job discrimination, as a primary attack on the oppression of women, is somewhat analogous to the blacks fighting 'job discrimination' as a primary attack on the oppression of blacks in the 1850s. Tactical suicide![53]

(In more recent years, African-American feminists have said they dislike the use of the condition of Blacks as a metaphor by white feminists, because it suggests that all women are white).

In *Amazon Odyssey*, Atkinson devotes a number of chapters to strategy, and illustrates these chapters with charts showing the movements of "rebels"—radical feminists—against the oppressors: men.

She does not trust all women to become feminists. There would be rebels, there would be a buffer of lesbians, outlaws and prostitutes who would bear the brunt of men's attacks, and there would be neutral women who could be won over. However, there would be anti-feminist women who could not really be won over.

Atkinson says that some anti-feminist women would be neutralized toward the movement only from prudence, not conviction. For some of these women, pressure would have to come from neutralized men. "Only men could modify these women, because the women's identification with men runs so very deeply throughout their personality."[54]

In other words, Atkinson thought that some men could be won over more easily than some women. Men, whom she defines as members of the oppressor class, were themselves sometimes oppressed by other men and could possibly become allies of radical feminists.

We must survey the *enemy's* territory for any *real* gains...

We must first look for factions within the oppressor class being denied certain rights by other factions within the oppressor class. These denied rights, for example, freedom of movement, economic freedom, life-style freedom, should, in some cases, coincide with crucial denied rights to members of the Oppressed in the sex class system...it could be that similar solutions are required...For example, where economic deprivation is the problem—whether it stems from *under-* or *un-*employment—free housing, free food, the nationalization of Con Edison and telephone service, free transportation, and other minimal living prerequisites, *could* be a common solution...[55]

Atkinson thought that a revolution would be led by or primarily composed of women, that it would be a socialist or anti-capitalist revolution, and that poor men and other oppressed men might join it or not oppose it.

> Any initial major first offensive, into the Oppressor via factions, should at least neutralize nearly a third of the Oppressor... some individuals would become openly Pro-Rebellion. Others of this third would be supportive to a degree. Others would simply no longer *oppose* the rebellion.[56]

In other words, Atkinson was an early exponent of the idea that radical feminists should work in coalition with other potentially radical groups. However, she did expect such coalitions to be continually re-evaluated.

> Did the coalition on disparate points (free housing, nationalizing Con Edison, et cetera) work?...
>
> If the overall experience of working together was positive... then a further solidification of this coalition is reasonable. At this point, rather than concentrate on disparate issues, we might coalesce them into one, such as a base guaranteed annual income...
>
> If steps were taken in this direction, the *battle*, within the sex class system as a whole, would shift in our favor at this point.[57]

Clearly Atkinson saw the battle against the sex-class system and the battle against capitalism as inseparable.

> The third offensive... The Rebels would fuse into a common Party, with some vision of humanity, and how society should support the full realization of the equal humanity of each individual... A full program would have to be detailed of rights and responsibilities...[58]

In writing of fusing into one Party, Atkinson did not even discuss the need for maintaining an independent women's power base after the revolution. Perhaps she took the existence of such a base for granted?

In addition to traditional revolutionary changes, Atkinson expected that women would change the system so that women's lives would no longer have to be a function of the system. Like

Firestone, Atkinson suggests that extra-uterine conception and incubation should be developed so that this could become "a truly optional method, at the very least."[59]

Many of the examples of radical action that Atkinson offers, such as taking over a utility company, are not necessarily violent —but they are far more confrontational and far closer to violent action than the tactics specifically advocated by most feminist writers. Atkinson thinks far more in classic revolutionary terms. She does not in any way disavow violence. (See Chapter 15 on "Violence and Non-Violence as Tactics," page 281 below).

Rita Mae Brown on Activism

Rita Mae Brown also wrote a considerable amount about strategy and tactics when she was more actively involved in the radical part of the movement. In 1970, Brown criticized reform as a diversion:

> The [Equal Rights] amendment is to defuse the revolutionary wing of the Women's Liberation Movement and to open vistas of establishment opportunity for professional women...Even when child care centers and abortion clinics are established across the land, the country will not be shaken. It will free more women to work for more rich men...before you know it, women will become as proficient at exploitation as men.[60]

As early as 1970, Brown said that the feminist movement needed a political party.

> ...We must be organized, we must be a party. We must concentrate our forces rather than scatter them.[61]

By the mid-1970s, Brown thought of a process through which feminists could begin a national organization; she outlines this process in her book *A Plain Brown Rapper*.

> Feminists in each state must create a Feminist Assembly so we can communicate to each other in a responsible fashion. The state system has its drawbacks but we will need to start at a state level because of the manner in which states' rights is currently being used to oppress women and gay people.
>
> The first Assembly should be in session for two weeks. Representatives should be paid. No more Lady Bountiful...

Each feminist group from all over the state should elect one representative. After the first session the representatives will have hammered out a more adequate system of representation. Your first assembly will strongly resemble the Constitutional Convention of the United States held at the end of the Eighteenth Century. You will need to solve the same problems. Do you elect representatives on the basis of the size of the group or do you elect one woman from each feminist group? Some states may pick one solution over the other, some may arrive at the same solution as the Convention; a House based on population and a Senate based on a set number for each group. It's vital for each state to find its own way.

The duties of the Feminist Assembly should be communicating the will of the feminist community, solving the problems of the various communities, ordering statewide political priorities both in terms of patriarchal politics (i.e., elections, strikes, equal opportunity employment, consumer revenge, etc.) and the priorities of feminist politics (i.e., creating separate spaces for women to go to in order to revive and be reborn, feeding our own people, developing programs to help women who aren't feminists and dispelling the patriarchal slander aimed at us). None of this is easy. Unanimous decisions will be extremely rare but once a decision is reached it is the duty of the representative and the community she represents to carry out the decisions of the Assembly.

The Assembly serves other functions. We create a counter-government to the existing government without directly *physically* challenging that government. That challenge may indeed come decades later but for now it is important to collect ourselves without wild claims that we represent the people and not the United States Senate. We develop skills that will enable some of us to get elected to the patriarchal government and work from the inside. We develop skills at solving our own problems. We learn to respect one another through contact, disagreement, compromise and hard work...

Each year, hopefully, the Assembly can meet for a longer period of time...

The question of what a feminist group is I also leave up to individual groups and the states. To me, a feminist group is any group pledged to advancing the cause of women, most especially gaining political power...

From state assemblies, in time, we move to regional assemblies and finally a national assembly...[62]

Brown does not ask whether developing a parliamentary system for the movement might lead to lawyers becoming the major leaders of the movement, or what the implications might be if they were. (Even without such a structure, lawyers have become increasingly prominent, in part because the American system grants lawyers a wider range of political moves—drafting laws and filing briefs can be political moves—than others. Prominent leaders on both sides of the highly adversarial controversy over pornography are lawyers: Catharine A. MacKinnon and Nan Hunter. Is it possible that the controversy would be less adversarial if it were not fought by lawyers in the terrain of the law?) Neither does she consider that giving groups weight in proportion to their numbers would allow the National Organization for Women (NOW), which already has considerable political power compared with other feminist groups, to dominate.

In addition to forming a party, Brown says the movement should provide services on a much more extensive scale.

> Women with economic privilege...should organize to meet the survival needs of women without economic privilege. This means food distribution centers, child care centers, health care centers, self-defense programs, skill centers, halfway houses...[63]

Brown frequently suggested that feminists should contribute their money to the movement to pay for full-time organizers as well as to help provide services. If each feminist gave part of her discretionary income, her extra money, the total would be quite significant. Brown gave consistently a percent of her income to the movement.

> If feminists put their money where their movement is we'd WIN.[64]

Brown now focuses on writing fiction, although she does still speak publicly on lesbianism and has worked against the Right and for (at this point, mostly liberal) issues such as abortion.

Many other feminists have discussed strategy and tactics only in passing. An exception is the 1981 book *Fight Back! Feminist Resistance to Male Violence*, edited by Frederique Delacoste and Felice Newman. The book, published by Cleis Press, presents a range of brief articles by feminist activists describing their projects and the problems they have faced. The actions discussed include everything from rape crisis centers and shelters for battered women to learning self-defense, opposing pornography, and protesting against militarism. Also, some articles chronicle women's resistance to situations where they have been beaten, sexually abused or harassed, and include everything from using caution, to leaving home, to screaming, to fighting back with weapons. The editors see resistance as a continuing aspect of women's lives.[65]

Since then, some other books have discussed ways to resist violence.[66]

Changing Sex Ratios as a Strategy

Those who believe that men are inherently more violent than women may have different strategies and aren't likely to endorse coalitions to implement them, as early radical feminists did. Some lesbian feminists have suggested that real change requires changing the ratio of women to men in society. Susan Cavin developed this idea, which envisions a higher ratio of women as both a strategy and a goal.[67] She also proposes other intermediate strategies and tactics.

> Since I do not think there is only one oppression of women, there is not only one liberation path for women...The plural oppressions of women demand plural liberations.[68]

Cavin's suggested possible strategies to end women's oppression include:

> ...All-female armies fighting for the military overthrow of the patriarchy...Female sexual separation...forming all-female colonies...Collective refusal of women to tell men who is the 'father' of their children...Collective female secession from established, nationalistic male political states to join an international collectivity of women...Collective female reproductive strikes... Female economic sabotage...Strengthening female social/political/economic organizations...Increased rates of female heterosexual frigidity and female celibacy, as well as lesbianism... Abolition of, and struggle against the patriarchal family, the state, private property, the patriarchal church...[69]

She does not suggest how these steps can be implemented. Women of many political affiliations may agree with the desirability of closer ties among women internationally; still, it is hard to imagine Third World (and Irish) women who are struggling against imperialism, seceding from their present countries to unite with women from countries such as the U.S., England, etc. Coalitions *across* these boundaries are, of course, necessary.

As for "heterosexual frigidity," does Cavin mean that women should stop pretending to feel pleasure they *don't* feel, stop showing pleasure they *do* feel, or stop feeling pleasure in sexual encounters with men? Feminist women who choose to stay with men are not likely to seek less pleasure in their sex lives.

Nor is it clear that these intermediate steps would lead to a change in the ratio of women to men—except that "forming all female colonies" would, of course, change the ratio in any such settlements.

Sally Gearhart took up Cavin's idea about sex ratios. Gearhart proposes in a 1982 article that *"the ratio of men to women must be radically reduced so that men approximate only ten percent of the total population..."*[70] She suggests this is necessary to save the earth from a nuclear war caused by male bonding.

> The real danger is in the phenomenon of male-bonding... If men were reduced in number, the threat would not be so great...[71]

Gearhart does not suggest reducing the ratio of men in society through violence. (Cavin does not either, although she does refer to an all-female army). Gearhart thinks that as women become freer they will choose to have fewer male children.

> ...If reproductive initiative were returned to women...then the natural ratio of females to males would be significantly higher.[72]

This plan sounds difficult to implement: If a lower ratio of men to women is a necessary condition of freedom for women, how could women in a society with about the same number of males and females have the freedom to decide to produce fewer male children? Gearhart ignores the likelihood that sex selection of infants in the present system means that parents would choose to have more sons than daughters. Feminists critical of new reproductive technologies have cited surveys that show this is the probable result.[73]

Gearhart admits that she may be wrong.

> ...We need to maintain ten percent males for the simple reason that I may be wrong; we may discover that violence does not

disappear with the reduction of males and that for the human species at least the present 47 percent ratio of males is more nearly appropriate.[74]

Nurturing as Strategy and Goal

It is possible to believe that women are profoundly, perhaps physiologically, different from men but to suggest strategies for change that are not militant. In the late 1970s, a New York City group called the Matriarchists suggested that women really are nurturers and that women's nurturance really could transform society if women were no longer under male control. An article by Elizabeth Shanklin in their publication, *The Matriarchist*, describes the basic idea.

> We are moved to liberate those who nurture and the power of nurturance from service to warrior institutions. We are moved by the desire to live in a matriarchy, a society in which the maternal principle, the nurturance of life, informs all institutions...
>
> Liberating women to nurture will entail the transformation of all patriarchal institutions: economic, political, sexual, educational and religious. Liberating women to mother is the key to the creation of a harmonious, nurturant society.[75]

Shanklin suggested that men would stop fighting if they were nurtured enough.

> Warrior society will end only when each individual can be nurtured as a trusting person.[76]

She did not note that if women were entirely free to nurture without regard to external constraints, they would also be free *not* to nurture. Nor does her argument consider what political roles men would have, but sees them as almost passive objects of nurturance, controlled by love. Not even a kitten is a passive receptacle for love and nurturance, returning good for good. Neither does Shanklin note that women have been nurturing men for a rather long time without ending violence. The existence of a class of nurturers, even if this is not an oppressed class, does not seem to be the condition for ending aggression.

If one assumes that male biology encourages or even forces men to oppress women, she may opt for pity towards men on the grounds that "men can't help what they do." Thus, rather than advocating mass murder—which some opponents of biological determinism suggest is the logical conclusion of the idea that women are better than men—proponents of female superiority may, ironically, suggest *milder* tactics towards men than women who believe that no one is biologically driven to oppression.

Lesbian writer Laurel Holliday, after citing many studies (by men) which say that male hormones are linked to aggressive behavior, suggests that somehow men can change. "MEN MUST CHANGE...WE MUST TRY TO HELP THEM CHANGE."[77] "Helping men change" does not sound like a very militant way of stating the problem. The idea of help assumes that women are obliged to "put energy into" individual men, and that collective, political solutions are not so important.

> If there is one lesson to be learned from the way men have botched the job of living on this planet, it is that *we cannot take power over men* in order to save them and ourselves... taking power over others inevitably leads to disharmony and destruction. We will have to help men change, but we cannot force them. We can make them excruciatingly aware of their limitations...We can set an example...We must speak to the highest idealism men are capable of; we must reward them generously when they show signs of understanding; and ultimately, although we may rightly hate almost everything they do, we must love them as we help them change![78]

That's rather a strange prescription from a lesbian writing to lesbians. Setting a good example, loving men even when their behavior is terrible and rewarding them when their behavior is good sounds very much like traditional female behavior. These ideas assume that men are incapable of taking responsibility for themselves and behaving as adults. If women still take care of men in this way, it is hard to understand what change can occur.

Holliday's solutions include providing better prenatal care (to prevent brain-damaged, aggressive males), good diet for children, discouraging men from drinking alcohol and encouraging marijuana use (which she sees as promoting peacefulness), and discouraging sugar and meat consumption.[79] A biological solution for a biological problem.

If one assumes that men are more limited or needy than women, then one can choose to ignore them or, like Holliday, one can be "motherly" (matriarchal?) and assume that this weakness means that men need *more* attention than women (which, of course, is what men generally have had). Holliday actually suggests giving male infants more attention than girls.

If the environment is limited...male children may develop more serious behavior defects...than females...

In order to assure 'equal handling,' a mother would have to cuddle her sons more than her daughters.[80]

In fact, Holliday assumed that it was acceptable and desirable to maintain differences between women and men. She did not see all "male" traits as negative:

We know that human males have developed peculiarities of body and mind...which are maladaptive to earth's synergy and to the evolution of consciousness. We could attempt to eliminate these propensities. But nature is never wasteful; we needn't assume that these qualities can only be used for harm.[81]

She even suggests that the division of labor supposedly based on biological differences continue:

Men have evolved to have greater physical strength than women. This too may have a right use. The work of production, now accomplished by the unconscious violence of machinery, which has come to take power over its very creators, can be successfully transferred back to the hands of men. This is not to say women will not participate in the process of physical work...[82]

How, then, are women to have any power? Holliday ignores the historical connection between men's control of various kinds of work with their control over women. Why should we suddenly assume that men would be more benevolent? Holliday also ignores the impact that technology has had in freeing women, through making physical strength a *less* important factor in many tasks and opening more jobs to women.

Holliday's strategy ignores *political* change, and does not discuss organizations. She is so concerned about eschewing power that she does not suggest ways that women's interests can be represented or safeguarded.

Chapter 14

Separatism: When and How Long?

A discussion of feminist goals, strategies and tactics must deal with the difference between those who see an autonomous movement as a strategy, but favor eventual integration with men — and those who see separatism as a goal.

All radical and lesbian feminists favor *some* degree of separatism. All believe that some independent, all-women's groups are necessary. The questions raised by lesbian separatists are whether it is necessary to be separate from men in all areas of one's life, whether separatism is a permanent goal, and to what extent lesbians will choose to work or live separate from women who are involved with men.

Temporary Separatism

Redstockings have insisted that separation of women from men is a *temporary* tactic. Barbara Leon wrote an article titled, "Separate to Integrate," in which she stated that in the 1960s, radical feminists had assumed they were forming separate women's political groups only to demand that women be fully integrated into society. She sees women who decided that they preferred to work and socialize only with women as a reactionary element.

In an ironic throwback to the old days of women's clubs, many women's groups began to be seen as ends in themselves—places for socializing, making friends and self-development.[1]

This view seems not only to disregard the interests of lesbians, but also to minimize the need for friendship felt by all women who are changing their lives to become radical feminists.

Leon expands the Redstockings' position that women should not form all-female groups except when they are working on specifically women's issues. In a quote from New York Radical Women, she says,

> Forming separate women's groups on issues other than women's rights and liberation is reactionary. It falls right within the male supremacist designs for keeping women segregated, excluded and 'in their place.' Only if the *stated* purpose of a women's group is to fight *against* the relegation of women to a separate position and status, in other words, to fight for women's liberation, only then does a separate women's group acquire a revolutionary rather than a reactionary character.[2]

This position points out the dangers of being ghettoized, but does not recognize that women who have come together to work on one set of issues may wish to keep working together—and may be most effective if they are together—on other issues.

It is true that in the late 1960s, radical feminists envisioned integration of women and men as the solution. Even the militant Ti-Grace Atkinson assumed that eventually women and men probably would be integrated, although she qualified this point.

> A separatist, technically, is someone who advocates a separate state for a particular group of people. I have never done that—yet.[3]

Atkinson has strongly criticized female "nationalism" as unrealistic tactically and said that nationalism was damaging to the Black movement.[4]

The boundaries between goals and tactics are not always clear. One woman's goal may be another woman's tactic. A separate community of women, for example, may be a goal for some women and a tactic for others. Or it may be a long-range goal for some and a short-range goal for others. Although these women may be able to work together, there may be conflict if one woman values a project as an end in itself, while the other sees it more as a means to an end.

Lesbian Views on Separatism

The earliest lesbian separatist statement may have come from *Spectre*, a 1971 and 1972 Ann Arbor, Michigan group that published a newsletter. The Washington, DC-based Furies began soon after, and published a newspaper of their own.

The question of lesbian separatism has been discussed almost since the idea of a distinct lesbian feminist politics was first formulated. Some lesbians have used the term "separatism" to mean as much separation as possible from men; others have used it to also mean separatism from women who are not lesbians. Some lesbians believe that it is preferable to avoid the problems of anti-lesbian attitudes in heterosexual feminists by working only with lesbians. Some lesbians felt that they had to leave the feminist movement and start a new movement of their own.

Furies member Ginny Berson wrote:

> Lesbians must get out of the straight women's movement and form their own movement in order to be taken seriously, to stop straight women from oppressing us, and to force straight women to deal with their own Lesbianism.[5]

However, lesbian feminists often have been ambivalent about separatism. In "Take a Lesbian to Lunch," Rita Mae Brown wrote,

> This is a call for a separatist movement of Lesbians? Yes and No. No,...because I do not want to be separate from any woman... Yes, because until heterosexual women treat Lesbians as full human beings...I have no option...[6]

Brown expressed ambivalence not only about lesbian separatism as a tactic, but also about separatism from men.

> Separatism is what the ruling rich, white male wants: female vs. male; black vs. white; gay vs. straight; poor vs. rich. I don't want to be separate from anyone—that just keeps the Big Man on top of all of us. But I can't work with people who degrade me, don't deal with behavior that is destructive to me and who don't share their privileges. The last thing I want is separatism. We can only achieve reformist changes for our sub-group if we remain separatists.[7]

In "The Future of Female Separatism," a 1975 article in *Quest: A Feminist Quarterly*, Lucia Valeska, who later chaired the National Gay Task Force (now National Gay and Lesbian Task Force), criticized separatism.

One of the hardest lessons for lesbian feminists to accept is that there are some straight feminists who are making a more vital contribution to women than some lesbians...

There has been a simultaneous realization that it isn't heterosexuality *per se* that must be conquered but the ideological and material base of support it gives to male supremacy... [a] lesbian feminist... analysis does not insist that all women become lesbians.

Choosing a modified course is not to admit defeat. In its purest form separatism doesn't work because you cannot cut yourself off from all sources of power and survive... But it is also dangerous to deny the strength of the initial analysis and move the other way altogether—into an anti-separatist position.[8]

Lucia Valeska says separatism helps lesbians create a sense of identity, but is not the only tactic to be used in social change. Not all changes, she feels, can best be accomplished through separatism. Even if she sees separatism as a tactic rather than a goal, she sees it as a long-term tactic.

To end separatism we must end the causes of it... Whatever your opinion of it, female separatism has just as long and viable a future as male supremacy. That's a long haul ahead.[9]

Some lesbians have been even more critical of complete separatism, both on tactical grounds and a feeling of commonality with other women. Rita Laporte wrote in the early 1970s:

As a Lesbian I especially fear a split between heterosexual women and Lesbians. Not only are Lesbians hated and feared by most women, but many Lesbians lose no love over their straight sisters...

I cannot see either Lesbians alone or straight women alone succeeding in the revolution for greater humanness in all people.[10]

Lesbian feminist writer Adrienne Rich also has expressed concerns about separatism. In a 1977 article in *Sinister Wisdom*, she wrote:

...Some lesbians have withdrawn or been forced into nonfeminist enclaves which reject or denigrate 'straight' women.[11]

For Rich, the term "separatist" emphasizes negation.

> It would be easier for some if all lesbians could be labelled 'separatists,' implying that our politics and self-definitions proceed first out of hatred and rejection of others (whether men or 'straight' women). It would be easier, but destructive to feminism, and finally a denial of our complexity. We have constantly to ask ourselves whether we are more concerned with what we are saying 'no' to than with the 'yes' we are saying to ourselves and to other women.[12]

A number of Women of Color have criticized separatism, both as a goal and as a tactic. There are Women of Color who are lesbian separatists, but few who are writers identify themselves as such. Exceptions are Anna Lee, a contributor to some lesbian publications, and Vivienne Louise, who has written in *off our backs* that she is working on "building a self-sufficient lesbian nation."[13] Anna Lee writes, "I claim and affirm under tremendous pressure all of who I am black lesbian separatist. To do so puts me in conflict with each of the groups from which I could reasonably expect support, nurturance and sustenance."[14] Half a dozen lesbians of Color contributed to the lesbian separatist anthology *For Lesbians Only*.

In that book, an essay by Naomi Littlebear Morena notes that white lesbians press her to assume a role she does not want.

> Look, I said, i wanna do C.R. and come out brown and proud, you know get down and angry about the truth about brown macho in the barrio loco, and i want a bumper sticker and a mother nature is a lesbian button. Well forget that shit. Here's your script sister and here's how it reads: 'Woman of Color meets Karl Marx, Woman of Color becomes politically correct, Woman of Color decides who to boycott and call racist in the community.'[15]

In a different note on separatism and ethnicity, the anthology also includes an essay from Naomi Dykestein, who says that her Jewish identity is connected with her lesbian separatism. "It's true: separatists are loud, angry, pushy, uncompromising, man-hating, and obnoxious—we do not shut up and we are not 'polite' womyn. But those 'criticisms' sound uncomfortably familiar—they're the same complaints made about Jews in general and Jewish womyn in particular. No coincidence, I think, considering the large percentage of Lesbian separatists who are Jews—which is something else I've come to realize is no coincidence. We came from a heritage of separatism—it's been one of the main ways my people have survived, and is an essential part of our culture(s).[16]

Criticisms of Separatism

Women of Color generally have seen separatism of any variety —both sexual and racial—as a pressure forcing them to split themselves into their component parts or give up some of them. Many have stated that they want to be and to act simultaneously as Black, Brown, Yellow and as women or as lesbians.

Merle Woo writes in her "Letter to Ma" in *This Bridge Called My Back*:

> Being a Yellow Feminist means being a community activist and a humanist. It does not mean 'separatism,' either by cutting myself off from non-Asians or men.[17]

Puerto Rican lesbian feminist socialist Juanita Ramos writes in *Compañeras: Latina Lesbians*:

> After many years of searching for 'a' movement where all parts of me would be accepted, I finally realized that each of these movements [Puerto Rican, gay, feminist] could not *by themselves* bring about the kind of society which would insure the eventual elimination of all forms of oppression. This is so because each of them tries to force us to prioritize issues and in this manner, to highlight some parts of our identity at the expense of others. I do believe these groups *must interact* with each other.[18]

The Combahee River Collective's "Black Feminist Statement" decries lesbian separatism.

> We also must question whether lesbian separatism is an adequate and progressive political analysis and strategy, even for those who practice it, since it so completely denies any but the sexual sources of women's oppression, negating the facts of class and race.[19]

In "Across the Kitchen Table: A Sister-to-Sister Dialogue" by Barbara and Beverly Smith, Barbara Smith criticizes those who practice separatism as their total politics. One of the authors of the Combahee statement, she suggests that complete lesbian separatism involves rejecting issues that affect many women and ways of working that might include a greater number of women.

> So seldom is separatism involved in making real political change, affecting the institutions in the society in any direct way. If you define certain movement issues as straight women's

issues, for example reproductive rights and sterilization abuse, then these identifiable sexual/political issues are ones you are not going to bother with. We have noticed how separatists in our area, instead of doing political organizing, often do zap acts. For example, they might come to a meeting or series of meetings, then move on their way...We sometimes think of separatism as the politics without a practice.[20]

Some feminists have suggested that lesbian separatism necessarily involves ignoring race and class. Sara Bennett and Joan Gibbs wrote:

...Lesbian separatism ignores or relegates to a secondary status race and class oppression, and negates the validity of a shared struggle by Third World women and men.[21]

However, a lesbian separatist group, the Furies, produced what was probably the first set of articles on the workings of class among feminists and lesbians, which were compiled in *Class and Feminism*, a book edited by Charlotte Bunch and Nancy Myron.[22]

Cathy McCandless, in her essay in the booklet *Top Ranking*, criticizes separatism on economic grounds.

What economic alternatives have we actually provided for women who really want to sever their connections with men or (much more to the point, I think) with the white male supremacist capitalist patriarchal system itself? Precious few... This is the crux of true Lesbian separatism...[23]

If separatism somehow were made available to all women who might want it, would there then be no objection to it? Is moving to the countryside the only possible kind of separatism?

McCandless continues:

Money can buy you a great deal of distance. Given enough of it, it is even possible never to lay eyes on a man. It's a wonderful luxury, having control over who you lay eyes on, but let's face it: most women's daily survival still involves face-to-face contact with men, whether they like it or not.[24]

She does not seem to recognize that many women make economic *sacrifices* in order to live or work only with women. Certainly not all separatists are wealthy. Some come from working-class backgrounds. Most of those who try to be economically separate from men must give up the potential or actual privilege of earning a high salary.

It is certainly true that not all women can afford to go and live on the land: Many have dependents to support. But neither can many poor women afford the time to become political activists, if they are burdened with a double day. Does this mean one should *not* be a political activist, because not every woman can be? Isn't it more appropriate to say that whatever a woman wants for herself—activism, a chance to work on art, a personal life separate from men—she should work to make it available to others who might want it also?

Nor do the critics of separatism always acknowledge that there are *degrees* of separatism. A woman can be a separatist in her personal life and political organizations, even if she knows she can't survive without a job that may bring her into some contact with men. She still can refrain from giving any of her deepest self to men.

In a 1981 *Sinister Wisdom* article, "What Does Separatism Mean?", Adrienne Rich discusses the history of separatism and questions about whether—or when—it is racist.

> I find myself wondering if perhaps the real question at issue is not separatism itself but how and when and with what kinds of conscious identity it is practiced, and to what degree any act of separatism is more than an act of withdrawing from difference with whose pain we can choose not to engage.[25]

All radical feminists are separatists to some degree. We all acknowledge the importance of doing at least some political work independently of men. Most lesbians (depending on how they define their separatism) are separatists in the sense that they do not sleep with or become romantically involved with men. Some separatists, however, reportedly have carried separatism to the point of criticizing other lesbians for occasionally seeing their fathers or brothers. I suspect that this degree of separatism is relatively uncommon.

Separatism which ignores the oppression of women who are not lesbians, or which rejects even lesbians who want to deal with the other oppressions they face (as workers, people of color, etc.), certainly could be criticized as short-sighted.

There is a considerable difference between saying, "I will not work closely with men" and saying "Black women should not work with men"—just as there is a difference between saying, "I believe that working with Third World men is important" and saying, "Any woman who will not work with any men, even if they are Third World men, is racist."

On the other hand, there can be times when it is legitimate to ask whether one is morally or politically obligated to work for particular ends on projects that may not be her usual ones.

Adrienne Rich asks,

> How will a decision to work against the Klan affect lesbian/separatist politics and strategy? Do these women have a choice, as young white lesbians on the land in the South, to join or not to join in anti-Klan activity?[26]

The urgency of a situation may determine when a woman decides to alter her political activities. Could a feminist turn away a man who needed to hide from people who might kill him because of his race or ethnicity? Surely not.

However, as Rich points out, separatism was not developed simply as a negative politics, but as an affirmation of one's own (oppressed) group.

> An act of separatism, separateness, can also be an act of connection. An all-female space is not definable simply as a space from which all males are excluded.[27]

It is only radical to be a separatist if one belongs to an oppressed group. White male separatists could not form a progressive movement.

Many African-American people have defined themselves as Black nationalists (or separatists). That was where lesbians got the idea.

Although it is clear that some Black feminists, hurt in working with both feminist and Black groups, have decided to form some groups that include only Black or Third World women, they do not define themselves as separatist. Often, they also work in other groups that include white women and/or Black men, and possibly even progressive white men as well.

Black feminist Bell Hooks criticizes all-Black feminist groups as separatist.

> Some black women who were interested in women's liberation responded to the racism of white female participants by forming separate 'black feminist' groups. The response was reactionary...
>
> Rather than black women attacking the white female attempt to present them as an Other, an unknown, unfathomable element, they acted as if they were an Other.[28]

However, most other Black feminists support or belong to such groups, and believe they are progressive and appropriate.

Many of the criticisms of total lesbian separatism mentioned in the 1980s are somewhat similar to criticisms raised earlier by other radical feminists such as Brooke, by former separatists such as Rita Mae Brown, and by those who see separatism as a valid but partial strategy such as Lucia Valeska. Although these earlier criticisms were not focused on race, they pointed out that total political lesbian separatism left little chance of reaching most women and organizing a women's liberation movement.

Criticism of separatism sometimes slips into separatist-*baiting*: Some feminists (including lesbians) accuse those who disagree with them over a particular tactic, of being "separatists" (and therefore, supposedly, obstructionist at best and racist at worst). Sometimes a lesbian may even criticize a heterosexual feminist as a "separatist" because the latter wants a particular event to be all-woman, while the lesbian does not.

Barbara and Beverly Smith on Separatism

African-American lesbian Beverly Smith notes, "...To begin to talk about being separate from men is viable. It has some worthwhile aspects."[29] Her sister Barbara Smith continues:

Many lesbians are separatists in that sense. You are very aware of the choice—that in being a lesbian you understand that you really don't need men to define your identity, your sexuality, to make your life meaningful or simply to have a good time. That doesn't necessarily mean that you have no comprehension of the oppressions that you share with men. And you see, white women with class privilege don't share oppression with white men. They're in a critical and antagonistic position—whereas Black women and other women of color definitely share oppressed situations with men of their race...[30]

In her introduction to the 1983 book, *Home Girls: A Black Feminist Anthology*, Barbara Smith finds the argument that white women's separatism from men means separation from *racist* men, inadequate as a defense of separatist politics:

I have often addressed the pitfalls of Lesbian separatism as practiced by mostly white women, which makes an ideology out of distance and the exclusion of the 'other,' even if that 'other' is ostensibly their white male oppressor.[31]

To Smith, separatism apparently implies seeing another group as a biologically constituted "other," rather than a group that may contain possible allies. Smith continues that separatism may most injure those who choose to separate: "The worst effect of separatism is not upon whomever we define as 'enemy,' but upon ourselves as it isolates us from each other."[32]

In the above passage, she is discussing Black women who reject other Black women for working with white women; but the perspective seems to be the same as her analysis of separatism generally. However, Smith does think there are times when members of a class (a socially constituted group) can appropriately choose to work only with each other, if they do not use this decision as a club against others who make a different choice.

> Black women can legitimately choose not to work with white women. What is not legitimate is ostracizing other Black women who have not made the same choice...[33]

Smith suggests that autonomy is different from separatism and more constructive.

> Autonomy and separatism are fundamentally different. Whereas autonomy comes from a position of strength, separatism comes from a position of fear. When we're truly autonomous we can deal with other kinds of people, a multiplicity of issues, and with difference, because we have formed a solid base of strength with those with whom we share identity and/or political commitment.[34]

Barbara Smith defines separatism, apparently, only as the total rejection of another group in all aspects of life—not as forming independent organizations that restrict membership by group. Some other feminists, such as Marilyn Frye, call the latter a form of separatism, while Smith calls it autonomy.

Bernice Johnson Reagon: 'There is No Hiding Place...'

Bernice Johnson Reagon, who has a long history of involvement in Civil Rights, Black, women's and other politics, suggested in a speech to the West Coast Women's Music Festival in 1981 that even separatism in the sense of providing separate places—like "women's space"—was obsolete and not constructive.

> We've pretty much come to the end of a time when you can have a space that is 'yours only'—just for the people you want to be there. Even when we have our 'women-only' festivals, there

is no such thing... There is no hiding place. There is nowhere you can go and only be with people who are like you. It's over. Give it up.[35]

(That festival was held in Yosemite National Park in California. The Michigan Women's Music Festival, which is held on land owned by the women who put it on and thus is easier to keep women-only, still draws thousands of women a year. Reagon, meanwhile, has been part of the group that started another women's music festival, Sisterfire, to which everyone is welcome.)

Reagon continues:

...In that little barred room where you check everybody at the door, you act out community. You pretend that your room is a world...

Of course the problem with the experiment is that there ain't nobody in there but folks like you, which by implication means you wouldn't know what to do if you were running it with all of the other people who are out there in the world. Now that's nationalism. I mean it's nurturing, but it is also nationalism. At a certain stage nationalism is crucial to a people if you are going to ever impact as a group in your own interest. Nationalism at another point becomes reactionary because it is totally inadequate for surviving in a world with many peoples.[36]

Like many Black feminists, Reagon sees separatism as nationalism and any form of nationalism as too limited.

Continuing Reaffirmation of Separatism

Estelle Freedman suggests in a 1979 article in *Feminist Studies* that separatism is a necessary component of successful integrationist strategies. She sees separate institutions, "a female public sphere," as necessary power bases.

At certain transitional periods, the creation of a public female sphere might be the only viable political strategy for women...

The creation of a separate, public female sphere helped mobilize women [in the nineteenth century] and gained political leverage in the larger society. A separatist political strategy, which I refer to as 'female institution building,' emerged from the middle-class women's culture of the nineteenth century. Its history suggests that in our own time, as well, women's culture can be integral to feminist politics.[37]

The kinds of institutions she suggests are "female interest groups and support systems." In other words, by separatism Freedman means separate political organizations and friendship networks for women. In the terms used by Barbara Smith, she is discussing *autonomy* rather than separatism. (See page 260, above).

Separatism is a theme in many feminist activities, Marilyn Frye writes; she defines it broadly and views it positively.

> The theme of separation, in its multitude variations, is there in everything from divorce to exclusive lesbian separatist communities, from shelters for battered women to witch covens, from women's studies programs to women's bars, from expansion of daycare to abortion on demand...The theme of separatism is noticeably absent or heavily qualified in most of the things I take to be personal solutions and band-aid projects, like legalization of prostitution, liberal marriage contracts, improvement of the treatment of rape victims and affirmative action.[38]

Frye writes about how the institution of heterosexuality and white women's connections with white men have been tied to racism in white supremacist society.

> White women's attachments to white men have a great deal to do with our race privilege, with our racism and with our inabilities to understand these. Race and racism also have a great deal to do with white women's attachment to white men.[39]

Frye points out there would be no white race (or perhaps race period) if women and men did not select sex partners at least in part on the basis of race.

> ...When the women start talking up feminism and lesbian feminism, we are very commonly challenged with the claim that if we had our way, the species would die out...What the critics are saying, once it is decoded, is that the white race might die out.[40]

Loyalty to white men in some circumstances may exclude the possibility for white women of loyalty to Women of Color. That is most obviously true when the men support or administer policies that keep Women of Color oppressed, but there may be more subtle variations on the theme, as when a white couple hires a Woman of Color as a domestic.

Frye does not specifically say that separatism *per se* combats racism, but she suggests that involvement with white men can be connected with certain forms of racism that a woman must learn to avoid.

Successive Waves of Separatists

In 1982, lesbian separatist Sidney Spinster wrote a history of separatism that noted that early separatists *did* think about race and class issues.

> The Lesbian Separatist Group in Seattle... [wrote that] white Dykes should not use our Separatism to be 'divisive' among third world people, when Women of Color have chosen to interact with men. Later they concluded, basically, that it was racist... not to credit Third World wimmin with the ability to see...the fundamental division between wimmin and men.[41]

Spinster points out that there is a difference between women who became separatists during the early 1970s, and those who became separatists in the late 1970s and early 1980s and were influenced by writers like Mary Daly and Marilyn Frye. Some of the remaining first-wave separatists were not satisfied with Daly's version of separatism.

> Many first wave Separatists bitterly resent *Gyn/Ecology* for publishing with a prick publisher (church-affiliated no less), and for ripping off a lot of Sep developed concepts and words while giving little credit in return. To many, the Radical Feminism of *Gyn/Ecology* was a candy-coated version of Separatism, minus any race and class analysis...
>
> [Daly's] redefinition of Separatism, which exorcised all the remaining Leftist mass-movement mentality and replaced it with an anachronistic personalized (womanized?) network of women in transition...[42]

Spinster says that the "purification" many (especially first-wave) separatists went through—giving away old possessions, severing ties with relatives and such, one of separatism's more controversial aspects—is "separate and distinct from Separatism *per se*." Eventually, she says, "most Lesbians loosen up their standards when the state of purity ceases to be a healing experience," or they "no longer define themselves as Separatists."[43]

The Separatists' Anti-Critique

In a 1985 series of articles in the journal *Lesbian Ethics*, Julia Penelope defended lesbian separatism. She now calls herself a lesbian rather than a lesbian feminist—because she believes the feminist movement is increasingly concerned with respectability and thus expects lesbians to be invisible, with their problems placed on the back burner.

Penelope particularly criticizes the Combahee River Collective's "Black Feminist Statement":

> ...In 'The Combahee River Collective Statement on Lesbian Separatism' [sic], a group of Black Socialists tried to negate Separatist analysis by claiming the superiority of their own analysis...
>
> By implicitly claiming that Separatists are white wimmin, they purposely ignore the fact that Separatists, like any group of wimmin, are racially and culturally diverse, and attribute to skin privilege the decision to work for and with wimmin only. In order to somehow validate their refusal to give first priority to their oppression as wimmin, they had to resort to distortion and omission.
>
> But that wasn't enough either to make their decision convincing. Having said that Separatism isn't 'a viable analysis or political' strategy for them, they felt perfectly justified in further asserting that Separatism isn't 'an adequate and progressive political analysis and strategy, even for those who practice it...' They might at least have left it up to us to decide whether or not Separatism is 'adequate' for us...[44]

In her 1984 book *Pure Lust*, Mary Daly counters the critics of separatism.

> Just as the label 'man-hater' in Woman-Hating Society functions to stop thought, so also the negatively charged use of the label 'separatist'...hinders women from Be-Friending.[45]

However, Daly wrote that the word *separatism* "does not emphasize the direction, or final cause, of our movement...but rather an essential condition of this movement under the conditions of patriarchy,...the whole point of feminist separation is biophilic communication/participation in Be-ing..."[46]

Some lesbians such as Marilyn Frye and the singer Alix Dobkin now prefer the term "lesbian connectionist" as describing their lives more accurately than "separatist." That is, their emphasis is on forming bonds with other lesbians rather than on the men from whom they are separating.[47]

In 1988, Sarah Hoagland said that separatism or withdrawal deserves recognition as an ethical or political choice.

...I realized that traditional ethics does not recognize with-drawal, separation, as a legitimate ethical option. Within a society of dominance, separatism is a non-choice. This judgment is reflected among lesbians. Too many lesbians hold the perception that separatism is not active, that separatists are hiding from reality and ignore the larger 'picture.' This judgment is an erasure of the moral and political function of separation.

We live within a system of values, a system which constructs what we perceive as fact...When we engage in that system, tacitly we agree to its values...We contribute by consensus to its underlying structure even when also challenging it by attempting to reform or deny such values...To withdraw or separate is to refuse to act according to the system's rules and framework and thereby refuse to validate its basic values...

Separatism is not recognized as a moral and political choice because those in power do not want us to perceive participation as a choice.[48]

Hoagland does not say that separatism is the only option, just that it is one option.

Within a given situation or at a given moment, there are often good reasons for either choice [separatism or direct challenge]. Further, both choices involve considerable risk; neither one comes with guarantees: while directly challenging something can validate it, withdrawing may allow it to continue essentially unhampered.[49]

Janice Raymond's Synthesis

Janice Raymond attempts a synthesis between separatists and non-separatists by calling for both separate connections between women, and work in the world. Raymond writes that some feminist separatists "have made dissociation from the world a political ideal and reality... Becom[ing] ignorant of conditions in the 'real' world... may militate against their very survival."[50]

Raymond suggests that becoming an "inside outsider" working in the world to change it, while not accepting prevailing values, is the most useful role for feminists. The inside outsider "...questions the man-made world but does not dissociate from it, assimilate to it, or allow it to define her as a victim in it. She demands her place in it as a woman whose affinities are with women."[51]

Raymond suggests that feminists can create their own *polis*, or political world that is not necessarily a geographical community, through friendships with women; this community can enable feminists to act in the outer world as well.

> Female friendship...creates a private and public sphere where happiness can become a reality.[52]

Coalitions

Women of Color's emphasis on activism has contributed to the revitalization of the feminist movement.

Bernice Reagon maintains that coalition politics is the only viable politics—but warns how difficult it is. Mutual trust cannot be a prerequisite for entering a coalition, she writes.

> I feel as if I'm gonna keel over any minute and die. That is often what it feels like if you're *really* doing coalition work...you feel threatened to the core and if you don't, you're not really doing no coalescing.
> ...You don't go into coalition work because you just *like* it. The only possible reason you would consider trying to team up with somebody who could possibly kill you, is because that's the only way you can figure you can stay alive.[53]

Barbara Smith suggests that coalition politics are necessary for a successful movement.

> What *I* really feel is radical is trying to make coalitions with people who are different from you. I feel it is radical to be dealing with race and class and sexual identity all at one time.[54]

Since Atkinson and Millett's early work, many radical feminists, especially those of the "classic" group, have suggested or assumed that coalition politics of some kind would be necessary at some point. But many worried that feminist issues would be ignored in coalitions.

Cellestine Ware, writing in the late 1960s, had less of a sense that coalitions were an appropriate strategy than many other Black feminists do now. This difference may reflect a difference between the Left then and the Left now.

> Their [the Boston group Bread & Roses] belief that women are united with poor and black men as oppressed people is irreconcilable with...the fact that women as a group have different interests from men.[55]

Ware ended her book *Woman Power* with a statement of relief that feminists were becoming less interested in coalitions.

> Best of all, a few coalitions with the New Left have disillusioned many feminists about the nature of their support from male groups. There may be no expedient concessions this time.[56]

Ware's wariness about coalitions was not based on an idea that coalitions were necessarily wrong in themselves—but that the leftist men involved would abuse them.

Both Separatism and Coalitions

Some lesbian separatists may have a broader definition of separatism than critics suggest. Some separatists have broadened or redefined their separatism in response to criticism by Women of Color.

Some women who define themselves as lesbian separatists may accept coalition politics and may already be engaging in it, especially in the anti-nuclear movement. A whole range of tactics, including perhaps confrontational ones, are possible for these lesbian separatists.

In one essay in the book *Fight Back*, Thrace mentions many possible tactics that lesbian separatists can use—including developing lesbian schools, lesbian centers, lesbian libraries, and lesbian clinics. She also suggests statewide meetings, saying that lesbians in Michigan have held such meetings since 1974. Other suggestions include homes for older dykes, halfway houses, self-defense and fighting groups.

The economic alternatives that Thrace suggests for lesbians include:

> We can pledge 5% of our incomes to collective Lesbian activities, institutions, services and political actions...teaching, services provided for free by Lesbians to each other...
>
> We need to openly support Lesbian job advocates [to fight discrimination]...[57]

Lesbian separatist Susan Cavin also has suggested forming economic networks. Cavin's proposed network also would include networking with underground economic exchange systems among other oppressed groups.[58]

Thrace's article on lesbian separatist tactics includes confrontational protest.

> I don't advocate reform politics so I'm not talking about electoral participation... I do not want to participate in or petition the patriarchy but rather use more revolutionary based, community organizing, mass protest kinds of tactics.
>
> We can protest the mistreatment of Lesbians by the police, schools, hospitals, mental 'health' industry, prisons, old people's homes, orphanages, and welfare.[59]

Although she defines her politics as separatist, Thrace says that lesbians can work with "womyn's groups who will respect Lesbian leadership." She mentions actions that might not appear on everyone's list of separatist activities: "issues such as the threat from Nazis, KKK & Moral Majority, attacks on labor unions... fire-bombings of Lesbian and womyn's centers and abortion clinics..."[60]

This kind of separatism amounts to coalition politics with a strong lesbian consciousness.

In a different approach, Sidney Spinster comments that some groups of men are oppressed under the patriarchy. She does not rule out coalitions between radical feminists and these men. However, she says, "phallocracy is to one degree or another in their interests."[61] Ultimately, she suggests working with these men in coalitions only "on single issue problems for a finite period of time."[62]

Coalitions with Whom?

The question is not only whether there should *be* coalitions, but what form such coalitions should take. Feminists must consider who should be included in coalitions and what organizational forms should be used.

In a conference on women meeting the challenges of the Right which was held at Johns Hopkins University in April 1981, socialist feminists Zillah Eisenstein and Barbara Ehrenreich suggested different directions for feminist organizing and coalitions. Eisenstein concluded, from her own research and experience, that liberal feminists are potentially radical, as they are already proceeding on the assumption that women are oppressed by men. Therefore, she proposed that radical and socialist feminists should concentrate on working with liberal feminists.

Barbara Ehrenreich disagreed, saying that forming coalitions with other socialists and self-identified radicals was more likely to be effective — since liberals have more of a stake in the system.

In a sense, this disagreement comes close to some old disagreements between radical feminists and socialist feminists, with Zillah Eisenstein taking a position similar to what is more commonly seen as a radical feminist position.[63] Should a movement for social change be based along the lines of sex class or economic class? Can we do both simultaneously, or must we tend one way or the other?

Often, coalition politics means coalitions with the leading activists in other political groups, rather than working directly with many people from the other groups. There are both advantages and disadvantages to this arrangement. One advantage is that it seems simpler for a few leading activists to cultivate a minimal sensitivity to the differences between the groups than for large numbers of people from very different backgrounds to be able to work together. It may be easier to find a few community activists who are capable of acting in ways that are not racist or heterosexist and do not offend each other — than, say, to create large groups in which many people of different races and sexual orientations will be working together.

A major pitfall of coalition politics is that it can make groups feel they are "reaching the people" when, in reality, they are only reaching a few other leaders. "Of course, we do outreach," activists may say. "We belong to a coalition. We met Wednesday night with leaders of Black and Hispanic groups." It is possible that these same activists have done virtually nothing to reach the people, even those belonging to "their own constituency" who have not yet been organized. If the other radical groups one is interacting with tend also to ignore the unorganized, the problem is compounded.

This type of coalition-at-the-top may reinforce the prestige of particular individuals from the various oppressed groups, while bypassing the people at the grassroots. If one Black woman, or white lesbian, or white or Black gay male comes to be seen as representing her or his "constituency" for a whole city, then it could be easier for leaders to stereotype or manipulate one another — while most of their "constituents" remain on the sidelines, unaffected by the existence of such a coalition.

Also, such activist leaders may have *more* sharply defined ideological differences among themselves than do other members of their groups, because the leaders may be more focused on ideology.

No doubt it is somewhat easier to deal with people who are already radical, but most North Americans aren't already radical. To ignore those who are not already radicalized is to be doomed to defeat.

Another question about coalitions is *when* they are appropriate —whether coalitions are appropriate on every issue, or only on some issues. Some feminists, for example, have felt that it is not appropriate to include men in marches against violence against women, since the marches are designed to emphasize that women can walk on the streets at night by themselves without fear. Other women who have worked on these marches believe that there should be a focus on educating and organizing men against rape and battering, and therefore men should participate in the marches. Some feminists and lesbians may be willing to march with men on some issues, such as opposition to the Reagan/Bush administration—but not on others, such as "take back the night" marches.

What Issues are Feminist?

Since the late 1970s, a number of socialist feminists and some radical feminists have urged a greater emphasis on civic issues that may be of particular concern to African-American and working-class women, although they are not primarily women's issues. Karen Kollias suggested that transportation policies should be a priority.[64] Nancy Hartsock suggested that transportation and utility rates are important issues for feminists.[65]

Sara Bennett and Joan Gibbs wrote:

> Such issues as public hospital closings, gentrification, police brutality, the rise of the Right, etc. are lesbian issues in our opinion, and the refusal to work on them or even recognize their importance is a manifestation of racism and classism.[66]

In other words, advocates of such a redirection of feminist tactics have not only suggested alternatives, but sometimes maintain that racism and classism are the only reasons why not all radical and lesbian feminists have adopted those suggestions.

Barbara Smith has suggested that feminists should choose issues to work on by looking at what women the issues will attract.

> What we've got to look at is what is the nature of those issues that get multi-oppressed women involved in movement work... Poor women have been involved in issues like tenants rights or welfare organizing...[67]

Feminists with a slightly different perspective contend that since our numbers are small and the amounts of time and energy we have are limited, issues that most specifically affect women as women, such as reproductive rights or violence against women, should receive priority. The argument for focusing on women's or lesbian issues generally is that if we don't, no one else will—which seems to be true. But it should be noted that early radical feminists such as Ti-Grace Atkinson expected feminists to work on a wide variety of issues, and gives the example of public utilities. (See page 240, above).

This is not to say that feminist work does not benefit poor women. Lobbying for Medicaid funding for abortions and working against workplace sexual harassment, for instance, clearly benefit many poor and working-class women.

While many feminists do focus on issues that affect *all* women (such as reproductive rights), middle-class feminists do not often focus on issues that primarily affect *poor* women. Reagan/Bush administration budget cuts that posed severe problems for poor women did prompt some lobbying against them by groups like the National Organization for Women; but radical, lesbian and socialist feminists did not go out to help organize demonstrations in local social service agencies. (There is much less of an active welfare rights movement to spur such actions than there was in the late 1960s and early 1970s—but that does not entirely excuse the absence of action).

White feminists are not serving even their own interests when they ignore issues that seem primarily to affect Women of Color. Problems that Women of Color face first, because of their more economically vulnerable situation, may hit white women later. In 1970, Cellestine Ware criticized white feminists for not focusing on teenage pregnancy and single mothers, because those were not perceived as white women's problems. "Scant attention has been paid by women's liberation to problems of women who head households," Ware wrote.[68] Now, the number of white single

mothers and pregnant teenagers has increased, and white feminists pay more attention to women in those situations.

African-American feminist June Jordan has noted,

> Most Americans have imagined that problems affecting Black
> life follow from pathogenic attributes of Black people and not
> from the malfunctioning of the state...
>
> I suggest that as long as state power serves the powerful,
> more and more of the people of this democracy will become
> powerless. As long as we have an economic system protected by
> the state rather than state protection against economic vagar-
> ies and depredations, then your and my welfare become expen-
> dable considerations.[69]

Several questions are involved in this debate. Is feminism a
political theory or set of ideas that can be used to analyze *every*
social problem, or an analysis that pertains only to issues that
most directly and obviously affect women differently than men
(reproductive rights, sexuality, violence against women, women's
employment and housework)? If one believes that feminism is a
general theory or perspective on the world, then there are
feminist perspectives on housing, transportation, militarism and
every possible social question. By many definitions, a radical
feminist perspective would seek solutions that involve the least
possible hierarchical or dominance structure and the greatest
amount of cooperative decision-making—for example, a housing
or transportation system that not only distributed housing or
transportation more equally, but that was controlled by those
who use it. The perspective would show how women are particularly harmed by inadequate housing, transportation, etc.

However, it is possible to have a general perspective that aims
at radical feminist goals on every issue, while focusing on fewer
issues for practical work. Most individuals have time for only one
major project and perhaps less intense or occasional work on
other projects (especially since most of us must support ourselves
in jobs that do not contribute directly to building the feminist
movement). Almost all of our projects are understaffed.

Almost any repressive or callous social policy will affect women
most severely because women are poorer than men. Women, especially women living without men, will have the worst housing and
transportation, will find it harder to pay grocery and utility bills,
and will face more assaults by men because they have less

adequate shelter or must walk further from transportation points. By forcing women to seek men for protection, women's poverty serves to reinforce the institution of heterosexuality. It makes life very hard for women who do not want a man or, for other reasons, do not have a man to provide "protection"—which many poor men may not be in a position to provide, anyway.

Responding to the 1980s

Feminists in the 1980s seemed to be more interested in tactics that could be called direct or confrontational, than many radical feminists and lesbian feminists were in the 1970s. To be sure, some radical feminists such as Atkinson and Redstockings, and lesbian feminists like Bunch, have supported a confrontational or activist politics even in years when many others did not. Now, many lesbian feminists whose emphasis has been on creating alternative institutions are perceiving a need for confrontational politics such as demonstrations, and for organizing political coalitions. Often, those who are shifting or broadening their tactics are not giving credit to and sometimes are not aware of those feminists who have expounded direct action tactics consistently.

Gradually, as the Equal Rights Amendment's ratification seemed threatened, more radical feminists joined the struggle for the ERA. Anti-abortion measures brought more radical feminists to lobby or demonstrate directly vis-a-vis legislators. Radical and lesbian feminists have also demonstrated against militarism and attacks on affirmative action, and for lesbian and gay civil rights.

There seem to be several reasons for a renewed interest in activism. One was the election of Ronald Reagan, a president who opposed the Equal Rights Amendment and abortion, and whose economic policies cut off government assistance to many low-income women. Even some previously separatist feminists decided there was a need to work in coalition with other groups against Reagan and his policies.

Also, political statements published by Feminists of Color, the vast majority of whom have supported a politics of direct engagement and of coalitions, have prompted many white feminists to rethink strategy and tactics.

Another, somewhat different source of renewed activism has been the growing movement against sexist violence and pornography. Feminists working on these issues are *not* trying to build traditional liberal coalitions—since many members of the liberal coalitions do not see pornography as a problem, nor do they focus on other forms of violence against women.

Rather, feminists who hold a variety of views—ranging from the belief that men are intrinsically more violent than women, to the belief that men are damaged by pornography but could have better sexual relations with women if pornography's influence were shaken—have demonstrated against violence against women and worked to provide services for women. These demonstrations include take-back-the-night marches or marches deploring violence against women, protests against films that make violence against women seem attractive, and protests at and zap actions against stores that sell pornography.

Somewhat less confrontational actions include holding workshops teaching children and adults that violence against women is wrong—and attempting to change laws on rape, battering and pornography, to make it easier for women to go to court when they have been treated violently. Sometimes these groups have sought to include men in their ranks, though more often they have not.

The renewed discussion of activist strategies has not brought much new organizing of women who are not already involved in feminism.

Some white feminist individuals and organizations have responded to the questions raised by Women of Color by trying to include at least some Women of Color in their networks. Some conferences, such as the National Women's Studies Association's annual meetings, make attempts to include Women of Color as speakers, participants, and, most important, as planners—often after a great of pressure from Women of Color has forced the issue.

There has been little movement from networking to organizing, however. It is not "just" that many feminists are not including Women of Color in their organizing efforts. The point is that there are virtually no general organizing efforts.

The most general organizing occurs when a major demonstration such as a march is planned. Usually, there is no follow-up afterwards to see that women who were contacted have some place to go to be in touch with the movement.

Perhaps one reason "networking" has been substituted for organizing is the conspicuous position in the movement of academic and other professional women, who need networking to be in touch with other women with their interests. (There is likely to be only one woman teaching, say, feminist theory, at a particular school).

Another reason for the prominence of networking over organizing may be that many white lesbian feminists, searching for a way to work with Women of Color and address issues raised for them by Reagan's presidency, have no prior history or interests in organizing; they feel unconnected with the organizing attempts of the (not very lesbian) radical feminist movement in the late 1960s.

Creating a broader network is a good thing, but it is not the same thing as organizing.

"Networking" has become a popular tactic, endorsed by everyone from Adrienne Rich to women in corporations, but what does it mean? In practice in the contemporary United States, "networking" can be used to mean increased contacts between middle-class professional women, with no aim but their individual or mutual professional advancement really in view. On the other hand, the term also is used to describe situations in which women depend on each other for their existence and use the network to resist their oppression as lesbians, poor women, Third World women, etc. I suggest that the term has been coopted by professional women who may or may not be feminists, and might as well be dropped.

Besides, not all women's networks are necessarily radicalizing, even though bringing oppressed people to connect with each other often can be radicalizing. Conservative women's groups such as the Daughters of the American Revolution are not potentially radicalizing.

Nationalism and Integrationism

Like some other social movements, the women's movement includes both those who would like to see the development of a kind of nationalism, and those whose politics could be called more integrationist (between women and men; feminists of all races give at least verbal support to the idea of racial integration). That is, the movement includes women who would like to see women as a group separate and independent from men, and others who feel that at some point, perhaps in the future, women and men should create a new society together, perhaps with no social distinctions between them.

This nationalist *vs.* integrationist distinction cuts across the pacifist *vs.* "by-any-means-necessary" distinction. Both women who advocate non-violence and women who believe that some use of force might be needed to change the social system could have an integrationist perspective on men. They might want to work with men in some present actions for social change, and/or they might believe that in a future society women and men should participate equally.

Similarly, nationalists could either advocate non-violent resistance, or struggle "by any means necessary." (But, in the women's movement, they almost always advocate non-violence).

There are several different possible scales for discussing militancy or radicalism. Some women may see militancy or radicalism linked with willingness to resort to violence; others might see radicalism in willingness to *renounce* violence. Some believe that militancy or radicalism is necessarily tied to abolishing gender differences in an integrationist (with men) context. Others would say that woman nationalism (some forms of separatism) is the true radicalism.

Although some revolutionaries like Karl Marx have rejected nationalist ideology as reactionary, revolutionary movements in many (if not all) countries have expressed at least some nationalist sentiments in order to enlist the support of their people.

Also, imperialism from Europe, the United States and the Soviet Union has generated and fueled nationalist feelings by imposing foreign political and economic systems on other peoples.

Oppressed people are at least as likely to embrace nationalistic sentiments as socialist ones—resenting the "foreignness" of the oppressors as well as their dominance. In fact, the same people often respond in both ways, both with somewhat nationalist feelings and somewhat socialist feelings.

(The reader may note that the words "national socialism" were used by the Nazis in Germany; undoubtedly, the term "nationalist" described them accurately, but "socialist" did not. Many very different political leaders—such as Josef Stalin in the Soviet Union, Jawaharlal Nehru in India, Mao Zedong in China, Joseph Broz Tito in Yugoslavia, Julius Nyerere in Tanzania and Fidel

Castro in Cuba—have drawn on both socialism and nationalism in some form to rally their peoples to change.)

Many people—including some white American feminists, some American feminists of Color, some Black men who are activists, and politically active women and men in countries oppressed by colonialism or neo-colonialism—are neither wholly nationalist, nor wholly integrationist/socialist in their politics. There are many positions along the spectrum.

Few of us are wholly nationalist or wholly socialist/integrationist, and yet we often conduct our political dialogue as if most of us were solidly one way or the other. Many of us are both nationalist and integrationist, both separatist and activist. All of our close associates may be women, while we work for a coalitionist strategy. We may attend both women's music festivals and conferences on occupational health. We may live in a household in which only women can visit and yet participate in a women's group in a mixed peace or civil rights demonstration. We may like to read both Mary Daly and Zillah Eisenstein. We may feel that our politics are perfectly clear, not seeing that some aspects of them could be contradictory. The contradictions in other women's lives may be easier to identify.

In a sense, this borrowing from a variety of sources may be intellectually incoherent. In a sense, it may be sane. Could a woman be entirely of a piece, a straight-line follower of one line of politics to the ultimate degree?

Perhaps if we realize what amalgams *all* of our politics are, we can be more tolerant of each other.

Surely it is preferable for us to be amalgams, than to refrain from reading books or even from knowing women who belong to different political tendencies.

Chapter 15

Violence and Non-Violence as Tactics

In the 1980s, there was not much discussion of whether violence should be a tactic for radicals. Feminists who joined the movement in the 1980s were sometimes surprised to learn that the use of violence as a revolutionary tool had been debated— though generally rejected even as an idea—by radical feminists who had been politically socialized in the 1960s, when such discussions were more common. Although there has been debate over this question, there hasn't been much—or any—actual violent action on the part of even those feminists who have defended it.

Against Violence

A number of radical feminists have explicitly disavowed violence. Kate Millett, for instance, believes in non-violence.

> We are speaking, then, of a cultural revolution, which, while it must necessarily involve the political and economic reorganization traditionally implied by the term revolution, must go far beyond this as well. And here it would seem that the most profound changes implied are ones accomplished by human growth and true re-education, rather than those arrived at through the theatrics of armed struggle—even should the latter

become inevitable. There is much reason to believe that the possession of numbers, dedication and creative intelligence could even render unnecessary the usual self-destructive resort to violent tactics. Yet no lengthy evolutionary process need be implied here, rather the deliberate speed fostered by modern communication, in an age when groups such as students, for example, can become organized in a great number of countries in a matter of two years.[1]

The implication is that Millett's strategy, although non-violent, is confrontational.

Lisa Leghorn and Katherine Parker generally are opposed to violence.

...The change must come about by explicitly female-value-based *means*, so as not to recreate patriarchal power dynamics in different forms...To use patriarchal means—such as centralized, hierarchical social organization, or violence—in either fighting patriarchal institutions or building matriarchal ones, is a contradiction in terms.[2]

For women to choose violence goes very much against the grain. But this represents a tremendous problem, given that men frequently respond to gains in women's power, with violence against women, on an individual and/or group level. [Women] have, for the most part, used violence only in self-defense, for their individual or group survival, from defending themselves against violent husbands, to participating in liberation movements fighting violent and oppressive regimes.

When women have used violent tactics, their violence has far more often been directed against property than people. Women's respect for life tremendously inhibits their ability to destroy it, and the fact that most property is owned by men clearly diminishes women's respect for it.[3]

Robin Morgan suggests violence and other traditional revolutionary tactics are "ejaculatory" or male behavior. Instead, she suggests using tactics based on what she considers to be the patterns of the female body.

Because if Man's revolutions have been premature in their readiness, ejaculatory in their abrupt style, and mostly impotent in bringing about real change, then the style of women might be:

• Long, tender, gradually increasing attention to detailed fore-play—which some would call careful organizing. This amounts to respect for oneself and one's partner(s), learning what is desirable and desired, learning what will *work*, learning how to advance and recede, and being open to experimentation. It also amounts to a delight in the process of communication *for its own sake* as High Serious Play, and not only for some distant result.

• Proceeding only when everyone concerned feels *ready* (or even eager)...[4]

Morgan may be suggesting a model of change that isn't viable. Can major changes happen if activists wait until "everyone concerned feels ready"? Who is everyone? All radicals? All women? Every person in a society?

Criticisms of Nonviolence

On the other hand, some feminists criticize the idea that women are inherently non-violent.

Bell Hooks points out that "...masses of women in the United States are not anti-imperialist, are not against militarism, and do not oppose the use of violence as a form of social control. Until these women change their values, they must be seen as clinging, like their male counterparts, to a perspective on human relationships that embraces social domination..."[5]

In *Our Blood*, Andrea Dworkin warns that women must not be non-violent in a submissive way.

...Any commitment to nonviolence which is real, which is authentic, must begin in the recognition of the forms and degrees of violence perpetuated against women by the gender class men...

As women, nonviolence must begin for us in the refusal to be violated, in the refusal to be victimized...

...We must not accept...male notions of what nonviolence is. Those notions never condemned the systematic violence against women.[6]

However, Dworkin dedicates the book to Barbara Deming, a well-known pacifist; Dworkin, therefore, does not believe that non-violence is necessarily submissive.

Ti-Grace Atkinson suggests that taking an absolutely non-violent position is masochistic: It simply emphasizes how much pain women can suffer without fighting back. Women may be non-violent because they have never believed that anything else was possible. The government does not fear feminists, because it has reason to believe that we won't do anything violent. Atkinson doesn't see anything good about this situation.

'Violence' is not a choice for us. Every woman is in it up to, and apparently *over*, her eyeballs. Violence for her friends, we all accept. Our enemies, we worry about...

We're in here talking about using violence, because we know we ain't got none to *use! First*, we got to get out into the street. Then, we got to get some direction. Then, all we got to do is *move*.[7]

'Violence' as a surplus energy or force is available as a *tactic* only to the oppressor class within any given system. I am not making any value judgment here but simply positing that, in political theory, 'violence' is by definition a class function. It is organized weight or pressure to maintain the *status quo*. As such, 'violence' is irrelevant as a concept and unavailable as a tactic to the oppressed...

Some people might suggest that this is why 'violence' is observed as a tactic of the Oppressed *primarily* when it is practiced *within* its own class.[8]

It is not agreed in all political theory that violence can be used only by the oppressors or the state, although radical theory often posits this.

The editors of *Questions Féministes* also considered the rejection of violence as a tool an unwarranted restriction on women's use of our capacities. Their argument follows the tradition of Beauvoir.

We should claim as ours all human potentialities, including those unduly decreed to be masculine, that is monopolized by men...For example, violence: it is up to us to choose its forms and objectives, but it is necessary to use it against the violence of oppression.[9]

Lesbian separatist Sidney Spinster agrees with Atkinson that pacifism for women may be self-sacrificing rather than radical. She questions why women absorb so much hostility from men harassing non-violent demonstrations. "...It could be because we're good at taking shit from men without fighting back. We're good at feminine self-sacrifice to the cause. This sort of self-sacrifice permeates non-violent defense methods."[10]

Lesbian feminist Jeffner Allen suggests that nonviolence is part of the female role imposed with the system of heterosexuality and that lesbians need to give up their allegiance to this role. The context of her consideration of violence is a discussion of a rape done to her.

> By assigning to women the projects of nonviolence, heterosexual virtue focuses the cause of women's victimization on women, blames the victim, tries to reform the victim, but never challenges the ideology of male entitlement which itself creates the construct of woman as victim.[11]

Allen cites Beauvoir's statement "Violence is the authentic proof of each one's loyalty to himself..." [Beauvoir had thought the ability to use violence was a positive thing for men and its lack detrimental to women]. However, Allen adds, "I would differentiate, however, as Beauvoir does not, between the male defined violence of patriarchy, which assumes the constant conjunction of violence and nonviolence, active and passive, powerful and powerless—and a liberating violence that is lesbian...

> A lesbian violence is neither anti-life nor pro-death, for it exhibits absolutely no equation between violence and destruction. *A lesbian creation and exercise of freedom, befriending and loving what is gentle and dear, is violence... A lesbian freedom is violence because it is dangerous to patriarchy, unrecoverable by it...*[12]

It is not clear that what Allen calls violence could be recognized by others as violence. Evidently, she means self-affirmation and self-defense.

It is notable that most feminists interested in self-defense are interested in the least violent form of self-defense, hand-to-hand combat—which is also the form in which women may be at the greatest disadvantage unless we are highly skilled.

Michaele Uccella and Melanie Kaye/Kantrowitz, in their article "Women's Capacity for Resistance," criticize the idea that women do not have the capacity for violence.

> ...Anyone who's been, or been around, an overwhelmed mother; who's hung out in a dyke bar; spent time on city streets; or sat up with a friend who's OD'd knows: we can be violent.

So why this fantasy that we are not violent, that they are the violent sex? ... The doctrine that idealizes us may be idealizing who *they* say *we* are; yes we are intrinsically nurturing, inherently gentle...

Such an analysis dooms us to inappropriate kindness and passivity; overlooks both our capacity for and our experience with violence; ignores in fact everything about us that we don't like...

The woman who is violent announces not only that things are intolerable (though her violent release may let her go on tolerating); she also announces that we are not who they say we are.... Women's violence ... sometimes serves women, sometimes not.[13]

Most radicals would agree that violence includes far more than direct physical attack; that creating a situation that systematically ensures that people will be hungry, unemployed, or unable to make basic choices about their lives is violent. The classic radical argument is that the violence of the oppressed is less violent, less pervasive and damaging, than that of the state trying to suppress them—although perhaps the rebels' violence is more obvious.

Is self-defense violent? What is self-defense? Is fighting back still self-defense if the violence is not breathing down one's neck? Few if any radical feminists are so absolutely pacifist that they would think a woman did not have the right to fight back against a would-be rapist who was grabbing her. However, even radical feminists differ about whether a woman has the right to fight back the day after an attack.

Feminists also might differ over whether helping someone else fight back is part of self-defense, or in what circumstances it is. Feminists probably don't all agree about whether carrying out actions against known rapists and woman-beaters is acceptable.

Radical and lesbian feminists rarely discuss full-scale armed rebellion. Probably, many would agree that there are circumstances where it could be justified, such as in Nazi Germany and perhaps present-day South Africa, even if they do not think it is appropriate or possible in the United States.

Why the Lack of Strategy?

Why don't most radical feminist writers discuss goals, strategies or tactics in detail? Surely it is a failure of the movement that so many do not. Is it because they are too subtle to write anything so blatant? Is silence really the best strategy? Is it true that we are brewing, stewing and percolating our goals and strategies and are simply much too clever to announce them until the brew is brewed and the people have drunk half the potion?

Or are radical feminists afraid of going to prison because our strategy would involve advocating violent overthrow of the government? Certainly not many radical feminists are advocating that.

Are radical feminists avoiding these questions, then, because we fear losing our jobs? Or are radical feminists afraid of sounding foolish, utopian? Or, have radical feminists simply been too lazy to think our thoughts through to their possible implications or conclusions?

On the other hand, is it possible that radical feminists have not talked much about strategies or goals because we have thought a great deal, and our conclusions are pessimistic? Perhaps we don't want to spread pessimism? Or have we become more pessimistic over the years than we were initially?

There are several possible forms that a radical feminist pessimism could take. Some of them may spring from the fear that perhaps women and men really *are* different by nature, that men won't change, and that women won't or can't force them to change.

Another possible fear is that, while men may not be different by nature, they have such a long history of power and have accumulated such an arsenal of weapons that they will not willingly change—and that women will not be willing or able to force them. Another variation on this is the fear that although men could change, they won't change in time, before a nuclear war. Some women might think that radical feminism could succeed if there was time—but fear there won't be.

Chapter 16

What We Want, and How to Get There

Feminists have not much discussed what sorts of power bases for women we want, beyond our interest in specific issues. For instance, do feminists want women's influence in making social decisions to be proportional to the stake that women as a group have in the outcome?

Feminists could seek collective power for women to decide issues that particularly affect women, such as abortion and rape. However, it is not obvious how such collective power could be institutionalized. At the present time, any body that could be created to speak for women, like the Ministry for Women's Affairs that existed under France's Socialist government for several years in the 1980s, would not be controlled by radical feminists and could be vulnerable to takeover attempts by conservative or right-wing women.

Even in a democratic, socialist society that was trying to move away from hierarchy, should we manage to achieve one, it is not obvious what sorts of organizations would best represent women's interests, or indeed, could say what women's interests are.

Plural Outcomes

In moving away from a society with a multiplicity of oppressions, it may be necessary to have multiple strategies for change and multiple changes. Socialists Michael Albert and Robin Hahnel have suggested that a plurality of outcomes—many outcomes, as well as a plurality of suggestions and of decision-makers—is possible when different people have different, but nonoppressive ideas and needs in a more democratic society.

> Under socialism, beyond a plurality of approaches, we also seek a pluralism of outcomes. The orientation that there is 'one right way,' a view common to patriarchy, racism and authoritarianism alike, is superseded. Diversity and the possibility of more than one valid policy... are the values socialists respect.[1]

For feminists, a plurality of outcomes could mean both a nonhierarchical, noncapitalist society in which women and men were more equal, with power bases for women, and more opportunities for community among women, including separate communities. Indeed, I do not see how our very plural feminism could lead to any outcome that was not plural, without ignoring the needs of many women. Whether or not we want a plurality of ideas and strategies, we have them.

Such an idea of plurality will not win complete acceptance. Radical feminist writer Brooke, for instance, has criticized the idea of pluralism in the movement.

> 'Militant plurality' (a term coined by Kirsten Grimstad and Susan Rennie in *The New Women's Survival Sourcebook*) besides echoing a very worn-out part of official U.S. ideology, essentially means *everything* is right, including outright counterrevolutionary endeavors... while a movement moves through diversity of views and infighting, in order to stay a movement it has to move in one direction. 'Militant pluralism' ends up moving in a circle. Being 'anti-correct line' assumes there is no correct, accurate way of perceiving a situation, which means there is no difference between telling the truth about a situation and lying about it... mass confusion and goallessness result, and where there is no goal, there is no movement.
>
> The real trick to this position is that being anti-party lines and anti-correct lines is a line... underneath the 'no-line' is a liberal party line...[2]

Although pluralism can mean liberalism, it does not have to reject radicalism. There are many radical groups in this country; there generally are several radical groups in *any* country, unless some of them are wiped out, as the Bolsheviks repressed other radical groups during their consolidation of power in the Soviet Union. There are plural oppressions in western society, plural interests in ending them and plural needs to meet and wrongs to redress.

Tactics: Linked to Goals?

Often, tactics cannot be directly linked with a particular long-term goal. Is a woman who believes that women and men ultimately can live together with autonomous organizational power for women, more likely to protest curbs on abortion than a woman who believes that a separate society for women or lesbians would be preferable? Perhaps, but not necessarily. Will the latter woman be more likely to organize a lesbian center than a women's center? Maybe, but either woman could make either choice. Will one of them be more likely to be involved in a demonstration against U.S. involvement in Nicaragua than the other? Not necessarily. In a demonstration against racism? Not necessarily. Will one of them be more likely to study or teach women about self-defense? Not necessarily. Could we say that the former might be more likely to operate a shelter for battered women, and the latter to teach women self-defense? Possibly. But even if the two women did choose those different tactics because of their different theories, the two actions seem complementary.

We probably can assume that a radical or lesbian feminist who believes that men are intrinsically more violent and that a separate women's nation is the most desirable goal is likely to be a lesbian and perhaps to stress organizing lesbians, but that is not necessarily so.

If one assumes that men are basically biologically flawed (more violent) and sees either a separate women's nation or rule by women as a goal, then it seems unlikely that she would choose tactics that involve trying to reform men, such as teaching men not to batter women. However, the assumption may not always be valid. Holliday, though she sees men as flawed, says women should try to change men. And most radical feminists, including a great many who do not believe that the biological differences between women and men are the causes of different behavior, do not emphasize working to reform men, but to organize women.

Of course, some tactics are better suited to some goals than to others. If one believes that a separate women's nation is the best goal, then she is not likely to participate in electoral politics. Those who anticipate revolution, either through violent or militant pacifist action, are not likely to become involved in electoral politics either. Those who believe that a feminist or socialist transformation can take place gradually in this society may, at times, participate in lobbying and electoral politics.

However, there are often exceptions to these general tendencies. Radical and lesbian feminists with widely differing goals may be willing to campaign against repressive governmental measures, such as proposals to discriminate further against lesbians and gays, and may be willing to campaign against politicians who espouse them. Feminists may also see opposition to racism as being so important that, whatever their eventual goals, they will work temporarily in reform coalitions to prevent the adoption of more racist policies. For example, some lesbians, like the New York group Dykes Against Racism Everywhere, worked for extension of the federal Voting Rights Act.

For a lesbian feminist, as opposed to a radical feminist who is a lesbian (to the limited extent that we can make these distinctions), lesbianism is one of the major strategies for changing women's lives and ending male supremacy, as well as being an end in itself. Lesbianism is a goal, a strategy, and a tactic, or working in support of lesbians is a tactic.

Different lesbian feminists put different emphases on this tactic. In the early 1970s, it was more common for lesbian feminists to focus on the promotion of lesbianism as their sole strategy and tactic; it is more common now to focus also on other issues and strategies as well, even though an emphasis on lesbianism and a critique of heterosexuality remain primary aspects of lesbian feminist analysis.

There are many reasons for cooperation between radical and lesbian feminists with different goals. For one thing, as I suggested earlier, even very different goals are not mutually exclusive. Separatist and mixed societies can coexist. For another reason, many women, even though they have different goals, are interested in similar tactics or strategies. If they are radical or lesbian feminists, presumably they often will be concerned about issues that involve sexuality or violence against women. Even when women are not involved in the same actions, their work may be complementary, as the example of shelters and self-defense courses illustrates.

Women's organizations, centers, publications, and demonstrations are needed; lesbian organizations, centers, publications, and demonstrations are needed. It is unfortunate that our small numbers sometimes seem to force these activities into competition for our time, since both are necessary.

In recent years, some of those who have been the readiest to think in terms of strategy and tactics have become less active in the movement—for instance, Ti-Grace Atkinson and Rita Mae Brown. (Atkinson now is involved in a study to learn why women have left the movement). Although there probably are many factors involved, one reason for women becoming less active may be the frustration of proposing specific tactics and finding that few, if any, women seem to be acting on these proposals.

Women leave the feminist movement for a variety of reasons. Women who see themselves as heterosexual sometimes leave because they feel the movement is too anti-male or too anti-heterosexual. Lesbians sometimes say they no longer want to call themselves lesbian feminists because heterosexual feminists are too reformist and oppressive of lesbians. Some women leave because they decide to focus on their personal careers or other aspects of their lives. Others leave because they find fights within the movement painful. (So do feminists who remain active).

Feminist Structures: Small Groups vs. Large Organizations

The anarchist tendency—which affects many women who do not think of themselves as anarchists as well as those who do—has had a major effect on radical and lesbian feminist group structures. The typical radical or lesbian feminist organization is a small group; very often, there are no specific leadership positions in the group. Responsibilities are shared. Tasks are shared in a roughly equal way, or rotated. Many, if not most radical and lesbian feminists have a strong commitment to this way of working.

A number of other radical feminists, such as Jo Freeman, have criticized these tendencies and have said the movement would be better organized if some form of responsible, accountable, and changeable leadership were accepted.[3]

However, the movement has proceeded without drastic changes in structure. Some groups such as the staff of the newspaper *off our backs* have thrived as collectives. A commitment to small, collective groups still is common, although some feminists have tried them and not liked them.

Questions about structure, such as whether there should be acknowledged feminist leaders, can be seen either as strategic or as more fundamental. Those who are committed to small groups or collectives are more likely to see the question as a fundamental issue of values, while others may be more likely to see the question as strategic.

What kind of organizations does the radical feminist movement need? Some feminists, particularly Rita Mae Brown, have suggested that a large national party should be formed, on the grounds that size really is necessary for "clout" in this country.

As it is, men, including those on the Left, tend to recognize only large organizations as legitimate. The lack of a large organization makes it easier for them to pretend we do not really exist. The government feels no need to negotiate with small groups; the Left outside the feminist movement does not either. For instance, socialist and other progressive groups sometimes invite the president of the National Organization for Women (NOW) and Gloria Steinem of *Ms.* magazine to speak for women, rather than inviting radical feminists; sometimes even socialist feminists are not included prominently.

It is possible that in order to have effective coalitions with the mixed Left, women's liberationists would have to have large groups of our own.

National, mass membership groups also would provide a place for greater numbers of women to join the radical feminist movement. A national organization that would be more radical than NOW might be able to draw both the more radical NOW members and many feminists who do not belong to organizations because nothing seems quite right. Such women may see many small groups as not action-oriented enough, but NOW as too conservative.

Yet radical feminists seem automatically drawn to forming small groups. This preference for small groups and for loosely structured ways of operating has become a major part of the political culture of radical feminism; it would not be easy (assuming that it was desirable) to change that orientation. Past attempts to form national radical feminist and lesbian feminist organizations have died very quickly. However, lesbians around the U.S. are now working on preparations for a national lesbian conference, probably in 1991, that may launch a national lesbian organization.

Another reason why larger groups have not developed, may be the dilemma over whether it is more appropriate to form a radical feminist or a lesbian group. Any time radical feminist lesbians form a group, this could be a question, but small-group projects often get off the ground anyway.

Is it more important to attract the largest possible number of women willing to accept a radical analysis and take radical actions and form radical feminist groups? Or is it more important to promote lesbian visibility and form lesbian feminist groups? Is it more important to reach women who see themselves as heterosexual, or lesbians who have not yet joined the feminist movement and perhaps would not join an organization unless it was called "lesbian"? Obviously, any answer to this question will be emotionally charged. Some radical feminists (including lesbians) do not want to put their time and energy into a lesbian organization, while some lesbians feel ripped off it they are working in organizations that are not specifically named as lesbian.

What would a national organization do, anyway, if its focus was not primarily on Congress and the federal government? Most national organizations seem to have a strong focus on legislation; probably, a radical feminist or lesbian organization would not have such a major legislative focus, but would be likely to take positions against repressive, and for useful legislation. A national organization could try to develop visibility in the establishment media, to draw more women into the movement. It could bring women together, sponsor demonstrations and training, and help local projects. It could serve as a forum for debate within the movement.

Also, it is possible to form local and state radical feminist or lesbian organizations that are either primarily membership organizations or coalitions of existing feminist and lesbian groups. In

Washington DC, for example, the DC Area Feminist Alliance was founded in 1977 as an organization composed of most of the feminist groups in the area. Each group was supposed to send a representative to the each meeting. Individual memberships also were allowed. Within a few years the groups stopped participating actively, and the Alliance became primarily an individual membership organization. The membership probably continued to be more diverse (in the number of groups whose members belonged) than it would have been if the Alliance had not had a history of group membership. However, the Alliance floundered and died in a few years.

If local alliances or coalitions thrived, such groups could form the basis for state or regional organizations, as Brown suggested. The alliances could form larger alliances. A national alliance could form from the grassroots up. Such connections could be formalized, or made in a less formal way.

One problem with coalitions, alliances and large organizations is that they tend to become somewhat parliamentary—that is, to emphasize formal debate and the writing of precisely worded principles. Moving from parliamentarism to action is not easy. Often, such groups may need to make and (perhaps) approve a proposal in one meeting, delegate members to work on it, then wait at least until the next meeting to approve plans for how the proposal will be carried out. By then, the situation that prompted the desire for action may have changed. For instance, a movie that a local group is considering whether to picket may have left town.

Also, in a large group there may be less room for the joking, the tangential political discussions, the informal way of speaking that often are present when the members of a feminist small group work well together. The informality and sense of immediate participation may be among the greatest attractions that the feminist movement has for its members.

Is it better to accept our small group orientation as a part of our radical feminist political culture that has a value of its own, and to devise all one's plans with this culture and structure as givens—or, to approach that orientation critically, seeing what sorts of politics it excludes as well as those it encourages, and perhaps trying to push ourselves to develop other sorts of organizations? I don't think the answer is clear.

If radical and lesbian feminists do not want to work in large organizations, does that mean there is something the matter with radical and lesbian feminists, or something the matter with large organizations? Is this emphasis on working mainly with a small number of people, whom one can get to know and with whom one can communicate rather freely the result of an anarchist wisdom, instinctively grasping the limits of other forms of organizing — or is it a withdrawal from reality? Or a bit of both?

Is it possible that federations or alliances of small groups can equal or improve on the political strength of traditional large membership organizations with powerful centers and relatively homogenous local structures?

In a way, the idea of smaller political units combining to form a larger one is similar to old, radical traditions such as organizing on the basis of the "cell." The cell could provide political support and a channel for self-expression. However, in many or most such radical parties, cell members had no knowledge of what was happening in other cells or voice in what happened at higher levels of the party or secret society. Such secretiveness breeds Soviet-style governments and is antithetical to the openness which is a highly valued, consciously chosen aspect of feminist political culture.

So, is the basic radical feminist small group more like a party cell, or like a New England town meeting? It is like the town meeting in not being controlled from above and in discussing matters freely, including revising decisions. But it is more like the party cell in having ideological prerequisites for membership—not anyone can belong, you have to be some sort of radical, lesbian or perhaps socialist feminist, roughly the same kind as other members of the group. These ideological requirements for membership are more obvious than the ideological criteria for membership in local Republican or Democratic party structures, in part because North Americans do not perceive acceptance of the current political system as an ideology.

Although there certainly have been radical political movements in U.S. history—including much of the earlier feminist movement —most North American women are not used to politics that are consciously and overtly based on theory or ideology. Given this, it is impressive that feminism has drawn as many women as it has.

There are aspects of radical feminist political culture that are not so different from the common North American political culture: Our emphasis on free communication and on self-determination could be seen as falling within the framework of the traditional value (theoretically, though certainly not always in practice) placed on independence and free speech. Our emphasis on men as a class and our anger at what has been done to women, however, are very different from general U.S. political culture, which plays down any kind of class conflict. (Of course, there is also a populist tradition that has not ignored class conflict).

I suspect that the informality and open expression of ideas in many of our meetings strikes a chord in many women. Our practice, although flawed, may have a wider appeal than our theory.

Our small group political culture may have more potential to spread than does the conventionally structured NOW, and may draw in far more women than we previously have, if only they knew it existed. There are few institutions in this society in which one can become an important member overnight, speak freely, discuss one's own life as well as more general issues, and not be controlled by some hierarchy. As women participate in this experience, we change.

In *Talking Back*, Bell Hooks notes how useful small groups can be (in her discussion, she is contrasting them with women's studies classes and conferences). "An especially important aspect of the small group setting is the emphasis on communicating feminist thinking, feminist theory, in a manner that can be easily understood. In small groups, individuals do not need to be equally literate or literate at all because the information is primarily shared through conversation...Reforming small groups would subvert the appropriation of feminist thinking by a select group of academic women and men, usually white, usually from privileged class backgrounds."[4]

If our small groups are an integral part of our politics or a valuable part of our political experience, then we need to spread them on a far wider scale. Also, if we build larger organizations, we may want to preserve small groups by keeping the small groups as integral members. The anti-nuclear alliances found ways of doing this, so feminists could also.

At this point, specialized segments of the feminist movement have developed connections between small groups and occasionally formed larger organizations. Groups working in the battered women's movement, for example, have conferences and networks, as do those in rape crisis centers and those working on pornography. There are also organizations for feminist and lesbian publishers, and feminist and lesbian printers.

However, the organizations in these different fields generally do not hold larger conferences, much less build organizations, in which *all* radical feminists can communicate, discover our common problems, and learn from one another. Have the women working against sexist violence, for example, learned things that the rest of us do not yet know? Are all feminists who relied on government funds or grants now in financial difficulties? Have certain types of feminist organizations been more repressive to lesbians than others—and, if so, is this just their problem, or is it a problem for the whole movement? (It has been reported that groups relying on government funding, particularly shelters, have required their lesbian members to be in the closet for fear of jeopardizing these funds.[5] Shouldn't the whole feminist movement be devising alternate solutions, perhaps raising money from alternate sources? The National Network of Women's Funds is one such attempt.)

Perhaps many of us resist organizing movement-wide conferences or organizations because we are afraid they would blow up in our faces, or come unravelled in disputes, rather than being constructive. Is our fear realistic, exaggerated, or cowardly? Or have we just been around long enough to see how frequently organizers get heavy criticism? (Much more immediate criticism and therefore more difficult to deal with than the sort of criticism that comes in a book review). These fears are not unrealistic, but how can we live and operate politically with such limitations?

Can a Radical Feminist Recruit?

The reasons for feminists' lack of emphasis on "recruiting" more women include a reluctance to "preach," to set themselves up as authoritative. Perhaps one way of overcoming this reluctance may be to emphasize that the ideas are what is important, and that women simply will not hear the ideas—at least not in a radical form—unless we communicate them. Women can receive or act on them as they think best, but first they must be clear on what the ideas are.

Even if all of us who currently are active feminists spent all of our time in active communication, and all of the women we reach spent all of their time in active communication, we would still be very far from reaching all women in the nation with our ideas.

Another reason why we do not spend more time in "outreach" is our personal vulnerability. The more radical that we become, the greater the number of women who will tune out whatever we say once they learn even the elementary facts of our lives. If we are lesbians, that is particularly true. The more radical our ideas, the more difficult it will be to communicate them in a way that women will be willing to hear. The more radical our ideas and lives are, the more chance we have of being rejected by the women we are trying to reach. It is not easy to speak to a group of women about lesbianism and be received by thunderous silence, a few defensive questions, and perhaps one or two comments afterward that you are "brave."

Feminists generally have an open political style. They do not operate like 1930s Communists in front organizations, hiding their most radical ideas in an attempt to "infiltrate." Most feminists would see such an approach as manipulative and patronizing.

Being rejected by other women because our politics are *too* pro-woman can seem intolerable. It can be hard not to become angry at mainstream women, not to feel that they are just collaborating in cutting their own throats and that they deserve no better if they are unwilling to hear our message. (It may be especially difficult not to feel that way after seeing that most white U.S. women voters chose Reagan in his second presidential election in 1984, after it was clear what sort of president he was—and many, though not a majority, voted for George Bush in 1988, despite his opposition to abortion).

Protecting ourselves from developing such bitter feelings toward other women is one reason we don't try harder to reach them. Perhaps the feelings are already there, latent, unacknowledged, and that is why we do not try harder. Perhaps we anticipate rejection too readily. Perhaps we are too pessimistic about other women. Perhaps reaching one woman is worth being apparently rejected by ninety-nine—if we can stand it.

There are many forms of communication we have not tried yet. Why not try standing on street corners and talking to women? It might not work. Then again, it might reach a few women. What does it mean to say that a tactic has worked? That thousands of people have read a message, or that one woman has become an activist?

We can speak, speak, speak whenever possible to all and (almost) any kinds of women's groups. Preferably, whenever we leaflet, speak, or demonstrate, we should mention some organization that women can attend, some way that they can join. We should let them know about feminist books, too.

Even going door-to-door to meet women and explain our ideas is possible. Bell Hooks mentions this as a possible tactic in *Feminist Theory: From Margin to Center*.[6] Yes, it sounds evangelistic. No, it doesn't sound either socially respectable or cool. But how else can we reach women? The mass media are not donating time or space to radical feminism.

Perhaps it may be harder for women to come to radical conclusions about their problems when they are living in conservative times. Those of us who became involved in the 1960s or early 1970s already were familiar with radical ideas, they were part of the air we breathed. We already were disenchanted with our government and our society. A woman today may not come to feminism with the same ideas or background that we had.

Consciousness-raising, for example, might lead to less radical conclusions for women who are not already radical. Perhaps it could be modified to include reading and discussion of feminist books so that the woman would at least be exposed to radical ideas. It is not insulting to provide aids for thinking: We all need them.

Some feminists have criticized the tactic of establishing services such as battered women's shelters and rape crisis centers as band-aid solutions to problems. However, it is vital that feminists show other women that we really care about them. It may seem obvious to feminists that feminists care about women, but it is not obvious to women who are not involved in the movement. Of course, if the services are taken over by government agencies, they no longer serve this purpose and may even provide the service in a repressive way (such as requiring women who are raped to report it to the police, even if they don't want to).

In the late 1970s, a number of feminists believed that violence against women might be a set of issues that would unite all women, because all women are affected by it. (Of course, they generally realized that the problem of violence against women must be confronted in a manner that explicitly refuses racist definitions and that recognizes most violence is done to women by men they already know). However, divisions over how to oppose violence, such as whether to include men in anti-violence work and whether pornography and sadomasochism constitute violence, have shown that fighting violence is not as unifying as feminists had hoped.

The workplace is another major area for feminist organizing. For instance, the campaign for "comparable worth" pay affects both clerical workers and professional women such as librarians and teachers. However, the difficulties of organizing are formidable. And trying to be at once an out lesbian on the job, an out radical feminist *and* an office organizer, is likely to endanger one's job. There are times when women can take those risks and other times when they cannot, or when they can only take some of them. Before taking the risk of trying to organize, it may be prudent to ascertain whether one's coworkers are also willing to take risks.

Many of us suspect that not all women are potentially reachable at this time. An increasing number of more or less conservative professional women in the United States are gaining careers in corporations or the government—or so it seems if one has lived in Washington DC during the Reagan administration. Those women are probably less reachable than liberal women with jobs, housewives, women on welfare, and students.

Perhaps a friendly, non-threatening approach to other women who are not yet feminists might help to make a radical message less frightening. One demonstration where a Washington DC group approached women by saying, "Happy International Women's Day," drew a more interested response than many other approaches.

Our weaknesses are not always a drawback. Women do not necessarily respond negatively to feminists who look insecure or occasionally hunt for words, or who admit that talking to them about radical subjects frightens us, too. Women may respond better to the real person than to a great orator.

We need to communicate the more deeply satisfying aspects of feminism as well as the horrors of patriarchy. If we only emphasize the violence and oppression that women face, women may feel that they need men for protection, Janice Raymond suggests.

One-dimensional emphasis on the 'State of Atrocity' in feminist literature...can inadvertently impress women with the fact... that woman is for man...[7]

Raymond emphasizes that feminists must make other women more aware that feminism involves—or can involve—affectionate, rewarding connection as well as political battles.

Many women have defined feminism only in political terms, accentuating struggle against male tyranny. They have failed to see that...feminism...must hold out to women the promise of happiness now.[8]

"What happiness?"—women familiar with intra-movement conflict may ask. It's true that disputes in the feminist movement often take a personal edge as women vent their pent-up rage at one another. It's true that long-term feminists usually have learned to heal or cope with scars inflicted within the movement as well as by patriarchy. It's true that feminists need to find more charitable ways of disagreeing with each other.

Nevertheless, there is a happiness in belonging to the feminist movement, even a flawed movement. A sense of purpose and direction and a connection with others who are at least somewhat like-minded provide a satisfaction that many women outside the movement lack. It really is more satisfying worrying about how to resolve political differences in the movement than about how to afford the latest consumer product. That's part of the message that feminists need to convey.

Conclusion

Can we reconcile the different radical feminist and lesbian feminist ideas? Does it make sense to identify oneself as part of a tradition that includes Ti-Grace Atkinson and Mary Daly or the Redstockings and the Furies?

If we look at theories of the origins of men's oppression of women, we see that all feminists believe that there are some biological differences between women and men and that men have used these differences both to suppress women's actions and to degrade or devalue those physical characteristics that are possessed by the beings called women. Virtually all feminist writers believe that men are capable in some way of modifying this behavior, willingly or unwillingly. All believe that women must obtain the power necessary to prevent their actions being controlled or their bodies being used against their wishes.

If we look at the theories of love and sexuality, we see at least a general agreement that sexuality in most societies has been defined by men, that historical and current relationships between men and women have been much affected by men's control of political, social and economic power, and that this unequal distribution of power should no longer continue. A sexuality based on male dominance is unacceptable to feminists. A sexuality that excludes the possibility of sexual commitment to women also is unacceptable.

If we look at goals, strategies and tactics, we see that all radical and lesbian feminists are (by definition) determined to end male supremacy. There is a common list of changes that we see as steps along the way: an end to violence against women; abolition of restrictions on reproductive freedom; economic independence for women; an end to capitalism, other forms of elite class economic and political domination, and white supremacy; and most of us now would add an end to the institutionalization of heterosexuality. There are many ways of working to accomplish these changes; and, of course, we won't all agree or always agree on the means.

One can see the point of the Redstockings' pro-woman line which says that everything women have done as survival tactics has been necessary and should not draw blame—and yet agree with the Furies that women can hurt or betray other women, in pursuit of a survival strategy that we must criticize. (I am sure that the Redstockings really do not believe that *every* survival strategy ever taken by a woman, including cooperation in maintaining fascism or racism, can be seen as acceptable).

It is difficult to reconcile the ideas of radical feminists such as Atkinson who use the word "strategy" and advocate direct action, with the ideas of those such as Daly who do not use the word "strategy" and who warn that women may become too involved in inconclusive actions over issues that men, ultimately, can manipulate. But one can see the wisdom of incorporating the latter view into an analysis of actions without giving up entirely on direct or confrontational action.

"The truth" is difficult to discover. We don't know exactly how male supremacy developed. We don't know exactly what love is.

We don't know whether the earth will survive, much less which of our goals can be accomplished. We don't know exactly what reaction each of our tactics will produce.

We don't know which of our ideas will be most appealing to women; but we do know that every idea appeals to some women.

Like others before us, we must act with less than perfect knowledge. We must try.

Reference Notes

Introduction

1. Zillah R. Eisenstein, editor, *Capitalist Patriarchy and the Case for Socialist Feminism*, Monthly Review Press, New York and London, 1979;

    Heidi Hartmann, "The Unhappy Marriage of Marxism and Feminism: Towards a More Progressive Union," in *Women and Revolution: A Discussion of the Unhappy Marriage of Marxism and Feminism*, edited by Lydia Sargent, South End Press, Boston, 1981;

    Alison Jaggar, *Feminist Politics and Human Nature*, Rowman and Allanheld, Totowa, New Jersey, 1983.

Chapter 1: Defining Ourselves

1. Maggie McFadden, "Anatomy of Difference: Toward a Classification of Feminist Theory," in *Women's Studies International Forum*, Vol. 7, No. 6, 1983, pp. 495-504.
2. Hester Eisenstein, *Contemporary Feminist Thought*, G.K. Hall & Co., Boston, 1983.
3. Catharine A. MacKinnon, "Feminism, Marxism, Method, and the State: Toward a Feminist Jurisprudence," in *Signs: A Journal of Women, Culture and Society*, Vol. 8, No. 4, Summer 1983, p. 639.
4. These books include: Bell Hooks, *Ain't I a Woman*, South End Press, Boston, 1981; Bell Hooks, *Feminist Theory: From Margin to Center*, South End Press, Boston, 1984;

    Cherríe Moraga and Gloria Anzaldúa, editors, *This Bridge Called My Back: Writings By Radical Women of Color*, Kitchen Table: Women of Color Press, Latham, NY, 1983 (originally published by Persephone Press in 1981);

    Barbara Smith, editor, *Home Girls: A Black Feminist Anthology*, Kitchen Table: Women of Color Press, Latham, NY, 1983;

    Evelyn Torton Beck, editor, *Nice Jewish Girls: A Jewish Lesbian Anthology*, The Crossing Press, Trumansburg, NY, 1982 (originally published by Persephone Press in 1981).
5. Juliet Mitchell, *Woman's Estate*, Vintage, New York, 1973, p. 94.
6. New York Radical Feminists, "Politics of the Ego," in *Radical Feminism*, edited by Anne Koedt, Ellen Levine, and Anita Rapone. Quadrangle Books, New York, 1973, pp. 379-383.

7. Dorothy Dinnerstein, *The Mermaid and the Minotaur: Sexual Arrangements and the Human Malaise*, Harper & Row, New York, 1976;

   Nancy Chodorow, *The Reproduction of Mothering: Psychoanalysis and the Sociology of Gender*, University of California Press, Berkeley, 1978.

8. Pauline Bart, review of Dinnerstein's book in *Contemporary Psychology*, Vol. 22, No. 11, 1977 and review of Chodorow's book in *off our backs: a women's news journal*, Vol. XI, No. 1, January 1981.

9. Andrea Dworkin, "Jews and Homosexuals," in *Right-wing Women*, Wideview/Perigree Books, New York, 1983, pp. 107-146.

10. Catharine A. MacKinnon, *Sexual Harassment of Working Women: A Case of Sex Discrimination*, Yale University Press, New Haven, 1979, pp. 219-220.

11. *Ibid.*

12. *Sisterhood is Powerful*, edited by Robin Morgan. Random House, New York, 1970, pp. 340-420;

   Radical Feminism, op. cit., edited by Koedt, Levine and Rapone, p. 81.

13. "Redstockings Manifesto," in *Sisterhood is Powerful*, p. 535.

14. "The Fourth World Manifesto," in *Radical Feminism, op. cit.*, p. 355.

15. Audre Lorde, "An Open Letter to Mary Daly," in *Sister Outsider: Essays and Speeches by Audre Lorde*, The Crossing Press, Trumansburg, NY, 1984, p. 70.

16. Adrienne Rich, foreword to *Blood, Bread, and Poetry, Selected Prose 1979-1985*, W. W. Norton & Co., New York and London, 1986, p. x.

17. "Redstockings Manifesto," in *Sisterhood is Powerful*, p. 535.

18. Nancy Hartsock, "Fundamental Feminism: Process and Perspective," in *Building Feminist Theory: Essays from Quest*, Longman, New York and London, 1981, p. 35.

19. Bell Hooks, *Talking Back: Thinking Feminist, Thinking Black*, South End Press, Boston, 1989, pp. 105-06.

20. *Ibid.*, p. 108.

21. Ti-Grace Atkinson, *Amazon Odyssey*, Links Books, New York, 1974, p. 111.

22. Mary Daly, *Gyn/Ecology: The Metaethics of Radical Feminism*, Beacon Press, Boston, 1978, pp. 30-31.

23. Firestone had not read Marx at the time she wrote *The Dialectic of Sex*, except for *The Communist Manifesto*. She derived her idea of marxism from reading Wilhelm Reich. (Personal communication from Ti-Grace Atkinson).

24. Vivian Gornick, *The Romance of American Communism*, Basic Books, New York, 1977.

Chapter 2: **The Sources of Feminist Theory**

1. Dale Spender, *Feminist Theorists: Three Centuries of Women Thinkers*, Pantheon Books, New York, 1983.

2. Ashley Montague, "The Natural Superiority of Women," in *The Saturday Review Treasury*, Simon & Schuster, New York, 1957;
   Robert Graves, *The White Goddess*, Farrar, Straus & Giroux, New York, 1948;
   Robert Briffault, *The Mothers*, Grosset & Dunlap, New York, 1963.

3. Dale Spender, *Feminist Theorists: Three Centuries of Women Thinkers, op. cit.*;
   Zillah R. Eisenstein, *The Radical Future of Liberal Feminism*, Longman, New York and London, 1981;
   Josephine Donovan, *Feminist Theory: The Intellectual Traditions of American Feminism*, Frederick Ungar, New York, 1985.

4. Adam Schaff, *Marxism and the Human Individual*, McGraw-Hill, New York, 1970, pp. 86-87.

5. Roger Garaudy, "Literature of the Graveyard," in *Existentialism versus Marxism: Conflicting Views on Humanism*, edited by George Novack. Dell Publishing Co., New York, 1966, p. 157.

6. Interview with Ti-Grace Atkinson: "Amazon Continues Odyssey," in *off our backs: a women's news journal*, Vol. IX, No. 11, December 1979, p. 2.

7. Jean-Paul Sartre, *Critique of Dialectical Reasoning*, translated by Alan Sheridan-Smith. New Left Books, London, 1976.

8. Michèle Le Doeuf, "Operative Philosophy, Simone de Beauvoir and Existentialism," paper for "*The Second Sex*: Thirty Years After" conference, New York University, September 1979.

9. *Ibid.*

10. *Ibid.*

11. Mary Daly, *Beyond God the Father: Toward a Philosophy of Women's Liberation*, Beacon Press, Boston, 1973, p. 23.

12. Temma Kaplan, "Other Scenarios: Women in Spanish Anarchism," in *Becoming Visible: Women in European History*, edited by Renate Bridenthal and Claudia Koontz. Houghton Mifflin Co., Boston, 1977, pp. 400-21.

13. Peggy Kornegger, "Anarchism: The Feminist Connection," in *Reinventing Anarchy*, edited by Howard Erlich, Carol Erlich, David De Leon, and Glenda Morris. Routledge and Kegan Paul, London, Boston and Henley, 1979, pp. 241-42.

14. Lisa Leghorn and Katherine Parker, *Woman's Worth*, Routledge and Kegan Paul, Boston, 1981.

15. Shulamith Firestone, *The Dialectic of Sex: The Case for Feminist Revolution*, William Morrow, New York, 1970, p. 13.

16. Kate Millett, *Sexual Politics*, Doubleday, Garden City, 1970, pp. 111-20.

17. Karl Marx, *Early Writings*, translated and edited by T. B. Bottomore. McGraw-Hill, New York, 1964. For criticism of Marx's mind/body dichotomy, see Mary O'Brien, *The Politics of Reproduction*, Routledge & Kegan Paul, Boston, 1981, pp. 37-40.

18. Catharine A. MacKinnon, "Feminism, Marxism, Method, and the State: An Agenda for Theory," in *Signs: A Journal of Women in Culture and Society*, Vol. 7, No. 3, Spring 1982, p. 515.

19. Lisa Leghorn and Katherine Parker, *Woman's Worth, op. cit.*; Christine Delphy, *Close to Home*, University of Massachusetts Press, Amherst, Massachusetts, 1984.

20. Zillah R. Eisenstein, *The Radical Future of Liberal Feminism, op. cit.*, p. 8.

21. *Ibid.*, p. 4.

22. Heidi Hartmann, "The Unhappy Marriage of Marxism and Feminism: Towards a More Progressive Union," in *Women and Revolution: The Unhappy Marriage of Marxism and Feminism*, edited by Lydia Sargent. South End Press, Boston, 1981, p. 33.

23. Juliet Mitchell, *Woman's Estate*, Vintage, 1973, p. 99.

24. Catharine A. MacKinnon, "Feminism, Marxism, Method, and the State: Toward a Feminist Jurisprudence," in *Signs: A Journal of Women, Culture and Society*, Vol. 8, No. 4, Summer 1983, p. 639.

25. Susan Griffin, "The Way of All Ideology," in *Signs: A Journal of Women in Culture and Society*, Vol. 7, No. 3, Spring 1982, pp. 642, 646, 654.

26. Chandra Malpede Mohanty, "The Politics of Colonization: Western Feminism and Women in Third World Countries," paper given at "After *The Second Sex*: New Directions Feminist Theory" conference, University of Pennsylvania, Spring 1984.

27. Caroline Whitbeck, paper given at New Directions Feminist Theory conference, University of Pennsylvania, Spring 1984.

Chapter 3: Against Gender

1. Simone de Beauvoir, *The Second Sex*, Alfred A. Knopf Inc., New York, 1968, p. xiv.

2. *Ibid.*, p. xiii.

3. *Ibid.*, p. 7.

4. *Ibid.*, p. xvi.

5. *Ibid.*, p. xvii.

6. *Ibid.*, pp. 64-65.

7. *Ibid.*, pp. xviii-xvix.

8. *Ibid.*, p. xviii.

9. *Ibid.*, p. xvix.

10. *Ibid.*, p. xix.

11. *Ibid.*, p. xxiv.

12. *Ibid.*, pp. 32-33.

13. Michèle Le Doeuf, "Operative Philosophy, Simone de Beauvoir and Existentialism," paper for "*The Second Sex*: Thirty Years After" conference, New York University, September, 1979.

14. Shulamith Firestone, *The Dialectic of Sex: The Case for Feminist Revolution*, William Morrow, New York, 1970, p. 8.

15. *Ibid.*, pp. 9-10.

16. *Ibid.*, p. 16.

17. *Ibid.*, p. 9.

18. *Ibid.*, pp. 16-17.

19. *Ibid.*, pp. 10-11.

20. *Ibid.*, pp. 82-83.

21. *Ibid.*, p. 83.

22. Kate Millett, *Sexual Politics*, Doubleday, Garden City, 1970, pp. 26-27.

23. *Ibid.*, p. 27.

24. *Ibid.*, p. 28.

25. *Ibid.*, p. 26.

26. *Ibid.*, p. 25.

27. *Ibid.*, p. 29.

28. *Ibid.*, p. 25.

29. "Redstockings Manifesto," in *Sisterhood is Powerful*, edited by Robin Morgan. Vintage, New York, 1970, p. 534.

30. Barbara Leon, "Separate to Integrate," *Feminist Revolution*, edited by Redstockings. Random House, New York, 1978, p. 155.

31. Roxanne Dunbar and Lisa Leghorn, "The Man's Problem," *No More Fun and Games*, November 1969, p. 26.

32. Roxanne Dunbar, "Female Liberation as the Basis for Social Revolution," *Sisterhood is Powerful*, *op. cit.*, pp. 479-480.

33. Ti-Grace Atkinson, *Amazon Odyssey*, Links Books, New York, 1974, p. xxii.

34. *Ibid.*, p. 54-55.

35. The Feminists, "The Feminists: A Political Organization to Annihilate Sex Roles," in *Radical Feminism*, edited by Anne Koedt, Ellen Levine, and Anita Rapone. Quadrangle Books, New York, 1973, pp. 368-369.

36. Atkinson, "Declaration of War," *Amazon Odyssey*, *op. cit.*, p. 53.

37. Atkinson, "Metaphysical Cannibalism," *Amazon Odyssey*, p. 62.

38. *Ibid.*, pp. 58-60.

39. *Ibid.*, p. 62.

40. Atkinson, "Radical Feminism and Love," *Amazon Odyssey*, p. 41.

41. Atkinson, "Metaphysical Cannibalism," *Amazon Odyssey*, p. 49.

42. Atkinson, "Radical Feminism and Love," *Amazon Odyssey*, p. 42.

43. Barbara Burris *et al.*, "Fourth World Manifesto," *Radical Feminism*, edited by Anne Koedt, Ellen Levine, and Anita Rapone. Quadrangle Books, New York, 1973, p. 355.

44. *Ibid.*, pp. 355-357.

45. Mary Daly, *Beyond God the Father: Toward a Philosophy of Women's Liberation*, Beacon Press, Boston, 1973, pp. 124-125.

46. *Ibid.*, p. 15.

47. *Ibid.*, p. 2.

48. Andrea Dworkin, *Woman Hating*, E. P. Dutton, New York, 1974, p. 34.

49. *Ibid.*, p. 156.

50. *Ibid.*, p. 158.

51. *Ibid.*, p. 162.

52. *Ibid.*, p. 166.

53. *Ibid.*, p. 167.

54. *Ibid.*, p. 174.

55. *Ibid.*, p. 175.

56. *Ibid.*

57. Andrea Dworkin, *Right-wing Women*, Wideview/Perigree Books, New York, 1983, p. 173.

Chapter 4: Male Biology as a Problem

1. Elizabeth Gould Davis, *The First Sex*, G.P. Putnam's Sons, New York, 1971, p. 335.

2. *Ibid.*, p. 336.

3. *Ibid.*, p. 335.

4. *Ibid.*, p. 330.

5. *Ibid.*, pp. 34-35.

6. *Ibid.*, p. 35.

7. *Ibid.*, p. 336.

8. *Ibid.*, p. 65.

9. *Ibid.*, p. 137.

10. *Ibid.*

11. *Ibid.*, p. 87.

12. *Ibid.*, p. 119.

13. *Ibid.*, p. 116.

14. *Ibid.*, p. 334.

15. Kathie Sarachild, "The Power of History," in *Feminist Revolution*, edited by Redstockings. Random House, New York, 1978, p. 29.

16. Jill Johnston, *Lesbian Nation: The Feminist Solution*, Simon and Schuster, New York, 1973, p. 187.

17. *Ibid.*, p. 173.

18. *Ibid.*, p. 175.

19. *Ibid.*, p. 190.

20. *Ibid.*, p. 207. Johnston here quotes Friedrich Engels, *The Origin of the Family, Private Property and the State*, International Publishers, New York, 1972, p. 120.

21. Jill Johnston, *Lesbian Nation, op. cit.*, pp. 207-208.

22. *Ibid.*, p. 173.

23. Valerie Solanis, excerpts from "The SCUM (Society for Cutting Up Men) Manifesto," in *Sisterhood is Powerful*, edited by Robin Morgan. Vintage, New York, 1970, p. 514.

24. "C.L.I.T. Statement #2," *off our backs*, Vol. IV, No. 3, July 1974, p. 13.

25. *Ibid.*, p. 12.

26. *Ibid.*, p. 11.

27. Rita Laporte, "Can Women Unite?", in *The Lavender Herring: Lesbian Essays from the Ladder*, edited by Barbara Grier and Coletta Reid. Diana Press, Baltimore, 1976, pp. 108-109.

28. Susan Brownmiller, *Against Our Will: Men, Women and Rape*, Simon and Schuster, New York, 1975, p. 13.

29. *Ibid.*, p. 254.

30. *Ibid.*, pp. 14-15.

31. *Ibid.*, p. 284-285.

32. *Ibid.*, pp. 285-286.

33. *Ibid.*, p. 16.

34. Adrienne Rich, "Compulsory Heterosexuality and Lesbian Existence," in *Blood, Bread, and Poetry: Selected Prose 1979-1985*, W.W. Norton & Co., New York and London, 1986, p. 42.

35. Susan Brownmiller, *Against Our Will, op. cit.*, pp. 17-18.

36. Susan Leigh Starr, "The Politics of Wholeness," *Sinister Wisdom*, No. 3, Spring 1977, p. 38.

37. Laurel Holliday, personal communication, Spring 1987.

38. Laurel Holliday, *The Violent Sex: Male Psychobiology and the Evolution of Consciousness*, Bluestocking Press, Guerneyville, California, 1978, p. 15.

39. *Ibid.*, p. 30.

40. *Ibid.*, p. 122.

41. See Dian Fossey, *Gorillas in the Mist*, Houghton Mifflin Co., Boston, 1983. Also, Jane Goodall, *In the Shadow of Man*, Houghton Mifflin Co., Boston, 1971.

42. Leila Leibowitz, "Perspectives on the Evolution of Sex Differences," in *Toward an Anthropology of Women*, edited by Rayna Reiter. Monthly Review Press, New York, 1975, pp. 24-25.

43. Laurel Holliday, *The Violent Sex, op. cit.*, p. 121.

44. *Ibid.*, p. 122.

45. *Ibid.*, p. 113.

46. *Ibid.*, p. 114.

47. *Ibid.*, p. 121.

48. *Ibid.*, p. 117.

49. *Ibid.*, p. 135.

50. *Ibid.*, p. 143.

51. *Ibid.*, p. 143.

52. *Ibid.*, pp. 99-100.

53. Susan Cavin, *Lesbian Origins*, ism press, San Francisco, 1985, p. 22.

54. *Ibid.*, p. 30.

55. *Ibid.*, p. 50.

56. *Ibid.*, pp. 50-60.

57. *Ibid.*, p. 90.

58. Jane Goodall, *In the Shadow of Man*, Houghton Mifflin Co.,
Boston, 1971;
    Dian Fossey, *Gorillas in the Mist*, Houghton Mifflin, Boston,
1983;
    Sarah Blaffer Hrdy, *The Woman That Never Evolved*, Harvard
University Press, Cambridge, Mass. and London, 1983.

59. Susan Cavin, *Lesbian Origins*, *op. cit.*, pp. 141-2. Emphasis
added.

60. *Ibid.*, p. 142.

61. Susan Griffin, *Woman and Nature*, Harper & Row, New York, 1979,
p. 5.

62. *Ibid.*, pp. 7-8.

63. *Ibid.*, p. 12.

64. *Ibid.*, p. 24.

65. *Ibid.*, p. 53.

66. *Ibid.*, p. 226.

67. Mary Daly, *Gyn/Ecology: The Metaethics of Radical Feminism*,
Beacon Press, Boston, 1978, p. 28.

68. *Ibid.*, p. 26.

69. *Ibid.*, p. 68.

70. Interview with Mary Daly, *off our backs*, Vol. IX, No. 5, May 1979,
p. 23.

71. Mary Daly, *Pure Lust: Elemental Feminist Philosophy*, Beacon
Press, Boston, 1984, pp. 350-351.

72. *Ibid.*, pp. 394-395.

73. Interview with Robin Morgan, *off our backs*, Vol. XIX, No. 4,
April 1989, p. 1.

74. Marilyn Frye, *The Politics of Reality: Essays in Feminist Theory*,
Crossing Press, Trumansburg, NY, 1984, p. 78.

Chapter 5: Men and Women: Same Species

1. Charlotte Bunch, "Lesbians in Revolt," in *Lesbianism and the
Women's Movement*, edited by Nancy Myron and Charlotte Bunch.
Diana Press, Baltimore, 1975, p. 32.

2. Charlotte Bunch, speech at "*The Second Sex*: Thirty Years After"
conference, New York University, September 1979.

3. The Combahee River Collective, "A Black Feminist Statement," in *Capitalist Patriarchy and the Case for Socialist Feminism*, edited by Zillah R. Eisenstein. Monthly Review Press, New York and London, 1979, p. 367. Also published in *This Bridge Called My Back: Writings by Radical Women of Color*, by Kitchen Table: Women of Color Press, Latham, NY, 1983, p. 214.

4. Andrea Dworkin, "Biological Superiority: The World's Most Dangerous and Deadly Idea," *Heresies* #6, Summer 1978, pp. 47-51.

5. Martha Shelley, "What is a Lesbian," *Sinister Wisdom* No. 3, Spring 1977, p. 14.

6. Toni Cade, preface to *The Black Woman*, edited by Toni Cade. Signet, New York, 1970, p. 8.

7. Toni Cade, "On the Issue of Roles," in *The Black Woman, op. cit.*, p. 103.

8. Michele Wallace, *Black Macho and the Myth of the Superwoman*, Dial Press, New York, 1978, p. 14.

9. Kay Lindsey, "The Black Woman as Woman," in *The Black Woman*, pp. 85-86.

10. Anita Cornwall, "Open Letter to a Black Sister," in *The Lavender Herring: Lesbian Essays from the Ladder*, edited by Barbara Grier and Coletta Reid. Diana Press, Baltimore, 1976, p. 229.

11. Cheryl Clarke, "Lesbianism: An Act of Resistance," in *This Bridge Called My Back: Writings by Radical Women of Color*, edited by Cherríe Moraga and Gloria Anzaldúa. Kitchen Table: Women of Color Press, Latham, NY, 1983, p. 131.

12. Bell Hooks, *Ain't I a Woman*, South End Press, Boston, 1981, p. 33.

13. Bell Hooks, *Feminist Theory: From Margin to Center*, South End Press, Boston, 1984, p. 35.

14. *Ibid.*, p. 86.

15. Bell Hooks, *Talking Back: Thinking Feminist, Thinking Black*, South End Press, Boston, 1989, pp. 19-20.

16. *Ibid.*, p. 20.

17. Cherríe Moraga, "La Güera," in *Loving in the War Years*, South End Press, Boston, 1983, pp. 56-57. Also published in *This Bridge Called My Back, op. cit.*, p. 32.

18. Juana María Paz, "The Ancient Matriarchy of Atlantis," in *For Lesbians Only: A Separatist Anthology*, edited by Sarah Lucia Hoagland and Julia Penelope. Onlywomen Press, London, 1988, pp. 297-303.

19. Janice G. Raymond, *A Passion for Friends: Toward a Philosophy of Female Affection*, Beacon Press, Boston, 1986, p. 21.

20. Adrienne Rich, *Of Woman Born*, W.W. Norton & Co., New York, 1976, p. 13.

21. *Ibid.*, p. 11.

22. *Ibid.*, p. 64-65.

23. *Ibid.*, pp. 58-59.

24. *Ibid.*, p. 60.

25. *Ibid.*, p. 72.

26. *Ibid.*, p. 85.

27. *Ibid.*, p. 283.

28. Adrienne Rich, conversation, April 1984.

29. Adrienne Rich, "Compulsory Heterosexuality and Lesbian Existence," in *Blood, Bread, and Poetry: Selected Prose 1979-1985*, W.W. Norton & Co., New York and London, 1986, p. 49.

30. Adrienne Rich, "Notes Toward a Politics of Location," in *Blood, Bread, and Poetry, op. cit.*, p. 217.

31. Mary O'Brien, *The Politics of Reproduction*, Routledge & Kegan Paul, Boston, 1981, p. 62.

32. *Ibid.*, p. 139.

33. Elizabeth Fisher, *Woman's Creation*, Anchor/Doubleday, New York, 1979, p. 5.

34. *Ibid.*, p. 9.

35. *Ibid.*, p. 259, 273, pp. 298-299.

36. *Ibid.*, p. 298.

37. *Ibid.*, p. 331.

38. *Ibid.*, pp. 194-195.

39. Gayle Rubin, "The Traffic in Women: Notes on the 'Political Economy' of Sex," in *Toward an Anthropology of Women*, edited by Rayna Reiter. Monthly Review Press, New York, 1975, p. 163.

40. Elizabeth Fisher, *Woman's Creation, op. cit.*, p. 215.

41. *Ibid.*, p. 34.

42. *Ibid.*

43. Gayle Rubin, "The Traffic in Women," *op. cit.*, p. 163.

44. *Ibid.*, p. 168.

45. *Ibid.*, p. 174-175.

46. *Ibid.*, p. 178-179.

47. Monique Wittig, "The Straight Mind," *Feminist Issues*, Vol. 1, No. 1, 1979, p. 108.

48. Gayle Rubin, "The Traffic in Women," *op. cit.*, p. 179.

49. *Questions Féministes* editorial, *Feminist Issues*, Vol. 1, No. 1, p. 5.

50. *Ibid.*, pp. 9-10.

51. *Ibid.*, p. 10.

52. *Ibid.*, pp. 12-13.

53. Christine Delphy, *Close to Home*, University of Massachusetts Press, Amherst, 1984, p. 17.

54. *Ibid.*, p. 144.

55. Monique Wittig, "The Straight Mind," *op. cit.*, p. 108.

56. Monique Wittig, "One is Not Born a Woman," *Feminist Issues*, Vol. 1, No. 2, Winter 1981, p. 48.

57. *Ibid.*

58. *Ibid.*

59. Margaret Simons and Jessica Benjamin, "Simone de Beauvoir: An Interview," *Feminist Studies*, Vol. 5, No. 4, Summer 1979, p. 345.

60. Joyce Trebilcot, "Male Orgasm and Male Domination," paper presented to the "After *The Second Sex*: New Directions Feminist Theory" conference, University of Pennsylvania, Spring 1984.

61. Jean-Paul Sartre, *Critique of Dialectical Reasoning*, translated by Alan Sheridan-Smith. New Left Books, London, 1976.

62. *Karl Marx: Early Writings*, translated and edited by T.B. Bottomore, McGraw-Hill, New York, 1984.

63. Interview with Ti-Grace Atkinson: "Amazon Continues Odyssey," *off our backs*, Vol. IX, No. 11, December 1979, p. 22.

64. Marilyn Frye, *The Politics of Reality: Essays in Feminist Theory*, Crossing Press, Trumansburg, NY, 1984, pp. 35-36.

65. *Ibid.*, p. 37.

66. *Ibid.*, p. 38.

67. Interview with Catharine MacKinnon on feminist theory, *off our backs*, Vol. XIII, No. 5, May 1983, p. 17.

68. Alison Jaggar, *Feminist Politics and Human Nature*, Rowman and Allanheld, Totowa, New Jersey, 1983, pp. 111 and 110.

69. Friedrich Engels, *The Origin of the Family, Private Property and the State*, International Publishers, New York, 1972, p. 237. Engels quotes Lewis Henry Morgan, *Ancient Society*, World Publishing Co., New York, 1973, pp. 561-2.

Chapter 6: Love: Can it be Good?

1. Simone de Beauvoir, *The Second Sex*, Alfred A. Knopf Inc., New York, 1968, p. 648.

2. *Ibid.*, pp. 650-51.

3. *Ibid.*, p. 643.

4. Simone de Beauvoir, *The Second Sex*, p. 643.

5. *Ibid.*, p. 644.

6. *Ibid.*, pp. 659-60.

7. *Ibid.*, p. 642.

8. *Ibid.*, p. 668.

9. *Ibid.*, p. 644.

10. *Ibid.*, pp. 646-64.

11. *Ibid.*, p. 657.

12. *Ibid.*, pp. 661-62.

13. *Ibid.*, p. 661.

14. *Ibid.*, p. 665.

15. *Ibid.*, p. 667.

16. *Ibid.*, p. 654.

17. *Ibid.*, p. 669.

18. *Ibid.*, p. 435-36.

19. *Ibid.*, p. 435.

20. *Ibid.*

21. Mary Evans, *Simone de Beauvoir: Feminist Mandarin*, Tavistock, London and New York, 1985, p. 25.

22. Shulamith Firestone, *The Dialectic of Sex*, William Morrow, New York, 1970, p. 143.

23. *Ibid.*, p. 144.

24. *Ibid.*, pp. 144-45.

25. *Ibid.*, p. 146.

26. *Ibid.*, p. 147.

27. *Ibid.*, p. 67.

28. *Ibid.*, p. 152.

29. *Ibid.*, p. 148.

30. *Ibid.*

31. *Ibid.*

32. *Ibid.*, p. 149.

33. *Ibid.*

34. *Ibid.*, p. 156.

35. *Ibid.*, p. 164.

36. *Ibid.*

37. *Ibid.*, p. 157.

38. *Ibid.*

39. *Ibid.*

40. *Ibid.*, p. 167.

41. Ti-Grace Atkinson, "Radical Feminism and Love," in *Amazon Odyssey*, Links Books, New York, 1974, pp. 43-44.

42. Ti-Grace Atkinson, "Metaphysical Cannibalism," in *Amazon Odyssey, op. cit.*, p. 62.

43. Atkinson, "Radical Feminism and Love," in *Amazon Odyssey*, p. 44.

44. Atkinson, "Lesbianism and Feminism," in *Amazon Odyssey*, p. 92.

45. Atkinson, "The Equality Issue," in *Amazon Odyssey*, p. 67.

46. Atkinson, "Vaginal Orgasm: A Mass Hysterical Response," in *Amazon Odyssey*, p. 7.

47. The Feminists, "The Feminists: A Political Organization to Annihilate Sex Roles," in *Radical Feminism*, p. 375.

48. Ti-Grace Atkinson, "Radical Feminism and Love," *Amazon Odyssey*, p. 44.

49. Interview with Ti-Grace Atkinson: "Amazon Continues Odyssey," *off our backs*, Vol IX, No. 11, December 1979, p. 3.

50. The Feminists, "The Feminists...," *op. cit.*, p. 376.

51. Kate Millett, *Sexual Politics*, Doubleday, Garden City, 1970, p. 50.

52. Kathie Sarachild, "Going for What We Really Want," *Feminist Revolution*, edited by Redstockings. Random House, New York, 1978, p. 158.

53. Barbara Leon, "The Male Supremacist Attack on Monogamy," *Feminist Revolution, op. cit.*, p. 128.

54. *Ibid.*, p.129.

55. *Ibid.*

56. Ellen Willis, "The Family: Love It or Leave It," in *New Political Science*, Fall 1980, p. 54.

57. *Ibid.*

58. *Ibid.*, p. 56.

59. *Ibid.*, p. 63.

60. Robin Morgan, "Lesbianism and Feminism," in *Going Too Far*, Random House, New York, 1978, p. 187.

61. Rita Laporte, "A Document," in *The Lavender Herring: Lesbian Essays from the Ladder*, edited by Barbara Grier and Coletta Reid. Diana Press, Baltimore, 1976, p. 144.

62. *Ibid.*

63. *Ibid.*

64. Rita Laporte, "Sex and Sexuality," in *The Lavender Herring, op. cit.*, p. 202.

65. *Ibid.*

66. Rita Laporte, "Sex and Sexuality," *op. cit.*, p. 203.

67. *Ibid.*, p. 213.

68. Rita Mae Brown, "It's All Dixie Cups to Me," in *A Plain Brown Rapper*, Diana Press, Baltimore, 1976, p. 198.

69. Mary Daly, *Beyond God the Father: Toward a Philosophy of Women's Liberation*, Beacon Press, Boston, 1973, p. 128.

70. *Ibid.*

71. Mary Daly, *Gyn/Ecology*, Beacon Press, Boston, 1978, pp. 372-73.

72. *Ibid.*, p. 342.

73. Mary Daly, *Gyn/Ecology*, *op. cit.*, pp. 319-20.

74. Simone de Beauvoir, *The Second Sex*, Alfred A. Knopf Inc., New York, 1968, p. 335.

75. *Ibid.*, p. 544.

76. *Ibid.*, p. 545.

77. Barbara Love and Elizabeth Shanklin, "The Answer is Matriarchy," in *Mothering: Essays in Feminist Theory*, edited by Joyce Trebilcot, Rowman and Allanheld, Totowa, NJ, 1983, p. 279.

78. Interview with Ti-Grace Atkinson: "Amazon Continues Odyssey," *off our backs*, Vol IX, No. 11, December 1979, p. 3.

Chapter 7: Sex: Will it Exist After the Revolution?

1. Anne Koedt, "The Myth of the Vaginal Orgasm," in *Radical Feminism*, edited by Anne Koedt, Ellen Levine, and Anita Rapone. Quadrangle Books, New York, 1973, p. 199.

2. Ti-Grace Atkinson, "The Institution of Sexual Intercourse," in *Amazon Odyssey*, Links Books, New York, 1974, pp. 13-14.

3. *Ibid.*, p. 18.

4. *Ibid.*, p. 20.

5. *Ibid.*

6. *Ibid.*, p. 21.

7. *Ibid.*, p. 23.

8. Dana Densmore, "Independence from the Sexual Revolution," in *Radical Feminism, op. cit.*, p. 107.

9. *Ibid.*, p. 108.

10. *Ibid.*

11. *Ibid.*, pp. 108-09.

12. *Ibid.*, p. 109.

13. *Ibid.*, p. 110.

14. Dana Densmore, "Independence from the Sexual Revolution," *op. cit.*, p. 111.

15. *Ibid.*, p. 113.

16. *Ibid.*

17. *Ibid.*

18. *Ibid.*, p. 114.

19. *Ibid.*

20. *Ibid.*, p. 117.

21. *Ibid.*, p. 118.

22. *Ibid.*, p. 117.

23. Mary Daly, *Beyond God the Father: Toward a Philosophy of Women's Liberation*, Beacon Press, Boston, 1973, p. 124.

Chapter 8: Lesbianism as a Politics

1. Simone de Beauvoir, *The Second Sex*, Alfred A. Knopf Inc., New York, 1968, pp. 411-12.

2. Claudia Card, "Lesbian Attitudes and the Second Sex," in *Hypatia*, special issue of *Women's Studies International Forum*, Vol. 8, No. 3, 1985, p. 209.

3. *Ibid.*, p. 210.

4. *Ibid.*

5. Shulamith Firestone, *The Dialectic of Sex*, William Morrow, New York, 1970, pp. 65-66.

6. Ti-Grace Atkinson, "The Sacrificial Lambs," in *Amazon Odyssey*, Links Books, New York, 1974, p. 25.

7. Ti-Grace Atkinson, "Lesbianism and Feminism," in *Amazon Odyssey*, p. 84.

8. *Ibid.*, p. 85.

9. *Ibid.*

10. *Ibid.*, pp. 85-86.

11. *Ibid.*, p. 87.

12. *Ibid.*

13. Atkinson, "Lesbianism and Feminism: Justice for Women as 'Unnatural'," in *Amazon Odyssey, op. cit.*, p. 132.

14. *Ibid.*, p. 133.

15. *Ibid.*, p. 134.

16. Atkinson, "Strategy and Tactics: A Presentation of Political Lesbianism," in *Amazon Odyssey*, p. 138.

17. Atkinson, "Lesbianism and Feminism: Justice for Women...," in *Amazon Odyssey, op. cit.*, p. 132.

18. Radicalesbians, "The Woman-Identified Woman," in *Radical Feminism*, edited by Anne Koedt, Ellen Levine, and Anita Rapone. Quadrangle Books, New York, 1973, p. 241.

19. *Ibid.*, p. 242.

20. Adrienne Rich, "Compulsory Heterosexuality and Lesbian Existence," in *Blood, Bread, and Poetry: Selected Prose 1979-1985*, W.W. Norton & Co., New York and London, 1986, p. 35.

21. Barbara Grier, "What is a Lesbian," *Sinister Wisdom*, No. 3, Spring 1977, p. 13.

22. *Ibid.*, p. 14.

23. Radicalesbians, "The Woman-Identified Woman," in *Radical Feminism, op. cit.*, p. 243.

24. Rita Mae Brown, "The Shape of Things to Come," in *A Plain Brown Rapper*, Diana Press, Baltimore, 1976, p. 110.

25. Radicalesbians, "The Woman-Identified Woman," in *Radical Feminism, op. cit.*, p. 245.

26. Charlotte Bunch, "Lesbians in Revolt," in *Lesbianism and the Women's Movement*, edited by Nancy Myron and Charlotte Bunch. Diana Press, Baltimore, 1975, p. 30.

27. *Ibid.*

28. Wilda Chase, "Lesbianism and Feminism," in *The Lavender Herring: Lesbian Essays from the Ladder*, edited by Barbara Grier and Coletta Reid. Diana Press, Baltimore, 1976, p. 101.

29. Martha Shelley, "Notes of a Radical Lesbian," in *Sisterhood is Powerful*, edited by Robin Morgan. Vintage, New York, 1970, p. 307.

30. *Ibid.*, pp. 307-08.

31. Mary Daly, *Gyn/Ecology*, Beacon Press, Boston, 1978, p. xii.

32. *Ibid.*, quoting from Marilyn Frye in *Sinister Wisdom*, No. 6.

33. Jill Johnston, *Lesbian Nation*, Simon and Schuster, New York, 1973, p. 172.

34. Charlotte Bunch, "Lesbians in Revolt," *op. cit.*, p. 31.

35. Ginny Berson, "The Furies," in *Lesbianism and the Women's Movement, op. cit.*, p. 18.

36. Rita Mae Brown, "The Shape of Things to Come," *A Plain Brown Rapper, op. cit.*, p. 110.

37. Jill Johnston, *Lesbian Nation, op. cit.*, p. 149.

38. Nancy Myron and Charlotte Bunch, introduction to *Lesbianism and the Women's Movement, op. cit.*, p. 13.

39. Rita Mae Brown, "Take a Lesbian to Lunch," *A Plain Brown Rapper*, *op. cit.*, p. 79.

40. Jill Johnston, *Lesbian Nation*, p. 90.

41. *Ibid.*, p. 166.

42. *Ibid.*, p. 185.

43. Monique Wittig, "One is Not Born a Woman," *Feminist Issues*, Vol. 1, No. 2, Winter 1981, p. 49.

44. Jill Johnston, *Lesbian Nation*, pp. 185-86.

45. C.L.I.T. Statement #2, *off our backs*, Vol. IV, No. 3, July 1974, p. 12.

46. Harriet Desmoines, "Go Tell Aunt Rhoddy," *Sinister Wisdom*, Vol. 1, No. 1, p. 70.

47. Bertha Harris, "The Lesbian, The Workmaker, The Leader," in *Quest: A Feminist Quarterly*, Vol. II, No. 4, p. 14.

48. *Ibid.*, p. 21.

49. *Ibid.*, p. 22.

50. *Ibid.*, p. 24.

51. Monique Wittig, "One is Not Born a Woman," *op. cit.*, p. 53.

52. Monique Wittig, "The Straight Mind," *Feminist Issues*, Vol. 1, No. 1, pp. 107-8.

53. Ariane Brunet and Louise Turcotte, "Separatism and Radicalism," in *For Lesbians Only: A Separatist Anthology*, edited by Sarah Lucia Hoagland and Julia Penelope. Onlywomen Press, London, 1988, pp. 451-54.

54. *Ibid.*, p. 456.

55. Sarah Lucia Hoagland, *Lesbian Ethics: Toward New Value*, Institute of Lesbian Studies, Palo Alto, 1988, p. 7.

56. *Ibid.*, p. 34.

57. Aimée Duc, "Are These Women?", in *Lesbian Feminism in Turn-of-the-Century Germany*, edited by Lillian Faderman and Brigitte Erickson, Naiad Press, Missouri, 1980, p. 11.

58. Martha Shelley, "What is a Lesbian?", *Sinister Wisdom*, No.3, Spring 1977, p. 14.

59. Brooke, "The Retreat to Cultural Feminism," in *Feminist Revolution*, edited by Redstockings. Random House, New York, 1978, p. 81.

60. *Ibid.*

Chapter 9: **The Critique of Heterosexuality**

1. Ti-Grace Atkinson, "University of Rhode Island: Movement Politics and Other Sleights of Hand," in *Amazon Odyssey*, Links Books, New York, 1974, pp. 103-04.

2. Atkinson, "Individual Responsibility and Human Oppression," in *Amazon Odyssey, op. cit.*, p. 122.

3. Atkinson, "Untitled: Some Notes Toward a Theory of Identity," in *Amazon Odyssey*, p. 115.

4. Atkinson, "The Political Woman," *Amazon Odyssey*, pp. 90-91.

5. Rita Mae Brown, "The Shape of Things to Come," in *A Plain Brown Rapper*, Diana Press, Baltimore, 1976, pp. 113-14.

6. Charlotte Bunch and Nancy Myron, editors. Introduction to *Lesbianism and the Women's Movement*, Diana Press, Baltimore, 1975, p. 12.

7. Coletta Reid, "Coming Out in the Women's Movement," in *Lesbianism and the Women's Movement, op. cit.*, p. 103.

8. Sharon Deevey, "Such a Nice Girl," in *Lesbianism and the Women's Movement, op. cit.*, p. 24.

9. Jill Johnston, *Lesbian Nation*, Simon and Schuster, New York, 1973, p. 167.

10. *Ibid.*, p. 165.

11. *Ibid.*, p. 174.

12. Andrea Dworkin, "Renouncing Sexual Equality," *off our backs*, Vol. IV, No. 9, November 1974, p. 2.

13. *Ibid.*

14. Coletta Reid, "Coming Out," in *Lesbianism and the Women's Movement, op. cit.*, pp. 96-97.

15. Barbara Solomon, "Taking the Bullshit by the Horns," *Lesbianism and the Women's Movement, op. cit.*, p. 42.

16. *Ibid.*, pp. 45-46.

17. C.L.I.T. Statement #2, *off our backs*, Vol. IV, No. 3, July 1974, p. 13.

18. *Ibid.*, p. 12.

19. *Ibid.*, p. 13.

20. Charlotte Bunch, "Not for Lesbians Only," *Quest: A Feminist Quarterly*, Vol. II, No. 2, Fall 1975, pp. 52-53.

21. Adrienne Rich, "Compulsory Heterosexuality and Lesbian Exis-
    tence," in *Blood, Bread and Poetry: Selected Prose 1979-1985*,
    W.W. Norton & Co., New York and London, 1986, pp. 50-51.

22. *Ibid.*, p. 67.

23. *Ibid.*, p. 51.

24. *Ibid.*, pp. 34-35.

25. Catharine A. MacKinnon, *Sexual Harassment of Working Women:
    A Case of Sex Discrimination*, Yale University Press, New Haven,
    Conn., 1979.

26. Adrienne Rich, "Compulsory Heterosexuality and Lesbian
    Existence," *op. cit.*, p. 42.

27. Ariane Brunet and Louise Turcotte, "Separatism and Radicalism,"
    in *For Lesbians Only: A Separatist Anthology*, edited by Sarah
    Lucia Hoagland and Julia Penelope. Onlywomen Press, London,
    1988, p. 455.

28. Marilyn Frye, *The Politics of Reality: Essays in Feminist Theory*,
    Crossing Press, Trumansburg, NY, 1984, pp. 156-57.

29. *Ibid.*, p. 172.

30. Joyce Trebilcot, *Taking Responsibility for Sexuality*, Acacia
    Books, San Francisco, 1983, pp. 11-12.

31. *Ibid.*, pp. 13-15.

32. Anne Koedt, "Lesbianism and Feminism," in *Radical Feminism*,
    edited by Anne Koedt, Ellen Levine, and Anita Rapone.
    Quadrangle Books, New York, 1973, p. 253.

33. *Ibid.*, pp. 254-55.

34. Alice Schwarzer, *After the Second Sex: Conversations with
    Simone de Beauvoir*, Pantheon Books, New York, 1984, p. 36.

35. Simone de Beauvoir, *All Said and Done*, Putnam, New York, 1974,
    p. 458.

36. Pat Mainardi, "The Marriage Question," in *Feminist Revolution*,
    edited by Redstockings. Random House, New York, 1978, p. 120.

37. *Ibid.*, p. 121.

38. *Ibid.*

39. *Ibid.*, p. 122.

40. *Ibid.*, p. 121.

41. Jessica Benjamin, "Starting from the Left and Going Beyond,"
    paper presented at *"The Second Sex*: Thirty Years After"
    conference at New York University, September 1979.

42. *Ibid.*

43. *Ibid.*

44. Mary O'Brien, *The Politics of Reproduction*, Routledge & Kegan Paul, 1981, pp. 207-8.

45. Robin Morgan, *The Anatomy of Freedom: Feminism, Physics and Global Politics*, Anchor Press/Doubleday, Garden City, NY, 1982, p. 165.

46. Interview with Robin Morgan, *off our backs*, Vol. XIX, No. 4, April 1989.

47. Vickie Leonard, "No Apologies from a Heterosexual," *off our backs*, Vol. IX, No. 9, October 1979, p. 13.

48. Carol Anne Douglas, "Confessions of an Ex-heterosexual," *off our backs*, Vol. IX, No. 9, October 1979, p. 13.

49. Jill Johnston, "Sexuality and All That," *The Village Voice*, July 31, 1979, p. 34.

50. Interview with Rita Mae Brown, *Washington Post*, August 13, 1981, Section C, p. 8.

51. Ti-Grace Atkinson, "On Violence and the Women's Movement," in *Amazon Odyssey*, p. 199.

52. Cellestine Ware, "Black Feminism," in *Radical Feminism, op. cit.*, p. 81.

53. Cellestine Ware, *Woman Power: The Movement for Women's Liberation*, Tower Publications, New York, 1970, p. 119.

54. *Ibid.*, pp. 31-32.

55. Toni Cade (later Bambara), "On the Issue of Roles," in *The Black Woman: An Anthology*, edited by Toni Cade. Signet, New York, 1970, p. 105.

56. Anita Cornwall, "Letter to a Friend," *The Lavender Herring: Lesbian Essays from the Ladder*, edited by Barbara Grier and Coletta Reid. Diana Press, Baltimore, 1976, p. 252.

57. Cheryl Clarke, "Lesbianism: An Act of Resistance," in *This Bridge Called My Back*, edited by Cherríe Moraga and Gloria Anzaldúa. Kitchen Table: Women of Color Press, Latham, NY, 1983, p. 128.

58. Ibid., p. 129.

59. Pat Parker, "Revolution: It's Not Neat or Pretty or Quick," in *This Bridge Called My Back, op. cit.*, p. 242.

60. Audre Lorde, "Uses of the Erotic: The Erotic as Power," in *Sister Outsider: Essays by Audre Lorde*, Crossing Press, Trumansburg, NY, 1984, p. 53.

61. *Ibid.*

62. *Ibid.*, pp. 54-55.

63. *Ibid.*, p. 56.

64. Barbara Smith, "Towards a Black Feminist Criticism," *Conditions Two*, Vol. 1, No. 2, October 1977, p. 40.

65. Michele Wallace, *Black Macho and the Myth of the Superwoman*, Dial Press, New York, 1978, p. 178.

66. Bell Hooks, *Ain't I a Woman*, South End Press, Boston, 1981, p. 102.

67. *Ibid.*, p. 191.

68. Bell Hooks, *Feminist Theory: From Margin to Center*, South End Press, Boston, 1984, pp. 154-55.

69. Bell Hooks, *Talking Back: Thinking Feminist, Thinking Black*, South End Press, Boston, 1989, p. 130.

70. *Ibid.*

71. *Ibid.*, p. 173.

72. Barbara Omolade, "Hearts of Darkness," in *Powers of Desire: The Politics of Sexuality*, edited by Ann Snitow, Christine Stansell and Sharon Thompson. Monthly Review Press, New York, 1983, p. 352.

73. *Ibid.*, p. 363.

74. Cherríe Moraga, *Loving in the War Years*, South End Press, Boston, 1983, p. 100.

75. *Ibid.*, p. 113.

76. Juanita Ramos, introduction to *Compañeras: Latina Lesbians* (an anthology), Latina Lesbian Herstory Project, New York, 1987.

77. Andrea Dworkin, "Renouncing Sexual Equality," *off our backs*, Vol. IV, No. 9, November 1974.

78. Andrea Dworkin, *Right-wing Women*, Wideview/Perigree Books, New York, 1983, pp. 53-54.

79. *Ibid.*, p. 61.

80. Andrea Dworkin, *Intercourse*, The Free Press, New York, 1987, p. 16.

81. Andrea Dworkin, *Right-wing Women, op. cit.*, p. 231.

82. Catharine A. MacKinnon, "Feminism, Marxism, Method, and the State: An Agenda for Theory," in *Signs: A Journal of Women, Culture and Society*, Vol. 7, No. 3, Spring 1982, p. 515.

83. *Ibid.*, p. 516.

84. *Ibid.*, p. 533.

85. *Ibid.*, p. 530.

86. *Ibid.*, p. 533.

87. *Ibid.*

88. Interview with Catharine A. MacKinnon on feminist theory, *off our backs*, Vol. XIII, No. 5, May 1983, p. 17.

89. *Ibid.*

90. Catharine A. MacKinnon, afterword to *Feminism Unmodified: Discourses on Life and Law*, Harvard University Press, Cambridge, Mass. and London, England, 1987, pp. 217-18.

Chapter 10: **Realignment in Feminist Sexual Politics**

1. Joan Nestle, "Butch-Femme Relationships: Sexual Courage in the 1950s," in *A Restricted Country*, Firebrand Books, Ithaca, NY, 1987, pp. 101-03.

2. Tacie Dejanikus, Carol Anne Douglas, Alice Henry, Fran Moira, "Towards a Politics of Sexuality," coverage of 1982 Barnard "Feminist and the Scholar" conference, *off our backs*, Vol. XII, No. 4, June 1982, p. 2.

3. Karla Jay and Allen Young, *The Gay Report*, Summit Books, New York, 1979, p. 510.

4. Amber Hollibaugh and Cherríe Moraga, "What We're Rollin' Around in Bed With: Sexual Silences," in *Heresies* #12, p. 58.

5. Ann Snitow, Christine Stansell, and Sharon Thompson, editors. Introduction to *Powers of Desire: The Politics of Sexuality*, Monthly Review Press, New York, 1983, p. 33.

6. Joan E. Biren, presentation at Lesbian Herstory panel, "Passages Conference on Lesbians and Aging," Washington DC, January 23, 1988.

7. Alice Echols, "The New Feminism of Yin and Yang," in *Powers of Desire: The Politics of Sexuality, op. cit.*, p. 446.

8. *Ibid.*, p. 449.

9. *Ibid.*, p. 450.

10. Amber Hollibaugh and Cherríe Moraga, "What We're Rollin' Around in Bed With: Sexual Silences," in *Heresies* #12, pp. 58-59.

11. *Ibid.*, p. 59.

12. *Ibid.*, p. 58.

13. *Ibid.*, p. 61.

14. Joyce Lindenbaum, "The Shattering of an Illusion: Competition in Lesbian Relationships," *Feminist Studies*, Vol. II, No. 1, Spring 1985, pp. 86-87;
    Alice Walker, "A Letter of the Times or Should This Sado-Masochism Be Saved," in *You Can't Keep a Good Woman Down*, Harcourt Brace Jovanovich, New York, 1981, pp. 118-19.

15. Ellen Dubois and Linda Gordon, "How Feminists Thought About Sex: Our Complex Legacy," paper presented at Barnard "Feminist and the Scholar" conference, April 1982.

16. Ann Snitow, Christine Stansell, and Sharon Thompson, introduction to *Powers of Desire, op. cit.*, p. 40.

17. Gayle Rubin, "The Leather Menace: Comments on Politics and S/M," in *Coming to Power*, edited by Samois, Alyson Publications, Boston, 1981, p. 213.

18. *Ibid.*, p. 222.

19. *Ibid.*, p. 213.

20. Alice Echols, "The New Feminism of Yin and Yang," in *Powers of Desire, op. cit.*, p. 453.

21. Mary Bailey, personal conversation.

22. Catharine A. MacKinnon, "On Collaboration," in *Feminism Unmodified: Discourses on Life and Law*, Harvard University Press, Cambridge, Mass., and London, England, 1987, p. 205.

23. Snitow, Stansell and Thompson, *op. cit.*

24. Ti-Grace Atkinson, "Why I'm Against S/M Liberation," in *Against Sadomasochism: A Radical Feminist Analysis*, edited by Robin Ruth Linden, Darlene R. Pagano, Diana E. H. Russell and Susan Leigh Starr, Frog in the Well, East Palo Alto, 1982, p. 91.

25. Bat-Ami Bar On, "Feminism and Sadomasochism: Self Critical Notes," in *Against Sadomasochism, op. cit.*, p. 74.

26. *Ibid.*, pp. 78-80.

27. Gayle Rubin, "The Leather Menace," *op. cit.*, pp. 222-23.

28. Marissa Jonel (pseudonym), "Letter from a Former Masochist," in *Against Sadomasochism*, pp. 16-22.

29. Audre Lorde and Susan Leigh Starr, "Interview with Audre Lorde," in *Against Sadomasochism*, pp. 67-68.

30. Mary Daly, *Pure Lust: Elemental Feminist Philosophy*, Beacon Press, Boston, 1984, p. 66.

31. Brief *Amicus Curiae* of Feminist Anti-Censorship Task Force, *et al.*, in American Booksellers Association *et al. v.* William Hudnut III, *et al.*, p. 31.

32. Adrienne Rich, "We Don't Have to Come Apart Over Pornography," *off our backs*, Vol XV, no. 7, 1985, p. 22.

33. Karen Lindsey, "Debate, Don't Excommunicate," in *Sojourner*, Vol. 8, No. 6, February 1983, p. 17.

34. Gayle Rubin, "The Leather Menace," *op. cit.*, p. 217.

Chapter 11: Love and Freedom

1. Tricia Lootens, "Lovers Who Don't Make Love," in *off our backs*, Vol. XIV, No. 2, February 1984, p. 6.

2. Joyce Lindenbaum, "The Shattering of an Illusion: Competition in Lesbian Relationships," *Feminist Studies*, Vol. II, No. 1, Spring 1985, pp. 86-87.

3. Simone de Beauvoir, *The Second Sex*, Alfred A. Knopf Inc., New York, 1968, p. 446.

4. *Lesbian Ethics*, Vol. 2, No. 3, Summer 1987.

5. JoAnn Loulan, *Lesbian Passion: Loving Ourselves and Each Other*, Spinsters/Aunt Lute, San Francisco, 1985, p. 196.

6. JoAnn Loulan, *Lesbian Sex*, Spinsters Ink, San Francisco, 1984.

7. Marilyn Frye, *The Politics of Reality: Essays in Feminist Theory*, Crossing Press, Trumansburg, NY, 1984, pp. 74-75.

8. Caroline Whitbeck, "Love, Knowledge and Transformation," in *Hypatia*, special issue of *Women's Studies International Forum*, Vol. 7, No. 5, 1984, p. 394.

9. *Ibid.*, p. 396.

10. *Ibid.*, p. 397.

11. *Ibid.*

12. *Ibid.*

13. *Ibid.*, p. 394.

14. Karen Lindsey, *Friends as Family*, Beacon Press, Boston, 1983.

15. Janice Raymond, *A Passion for Friends: Toward a Philosophy of Female Affection*, Beacon Press, Boston, 1986, p. 13.

16. *Ibid.*, p. 23.

17. *Ibid.*, pp. 23-24.

18. *Ibid.*, and pp. 238-39.

19. *Ibid.*, p. 152.

20. *Ibid.*, p. 199.

21. *Ibid.*, p. 223.

22. *Ibid.*, p. 225.

23. *Ibid.*

Chapter 12: What is the Goal, Anyway?

1. Simone de Beauvoir, *The Second Sex*, Alfred A. Knopf Inc., New York, 1968, p. 679.

2. *Ibid.*, p. 680.

3. *Ibid.*, p. 731.

4. Shulamith Firestone, *The Dialectic of Sex*, William Morrow, New York, 1970, pp. 270-71.

5. Women's Majority Union, Seattle, "Lilith's Manifesto," in *Sisterhood is Powerful*, edited by Robin Morgan. Vintage, New York, 1970, p. 529.

6. "Statement by Chicago Women's Liberation," February 1969, in *Sisterhood is Powerful, op. cit.*, p. 531.

7. Kate Millett, *Sexual Politics*, Doubleday, Garden City, 1970, p. 24.

8. *Ibid.*, p. 62.

9. Kathie Sarachild, leaflet for New York Radical Women, reprinted in *Feminist Revolution*, edited by Redstockings. Random House, New York, 1978, p. 154.

10. Ti-Grace Atkinson, "Radical Feminism: Declaration of War," in *Amazon Odyssey*, Links Books, New York, 1974, p. 48.

11. Atkinson, "Vaginal Orgasm as a Mass Hysterical Survival Response," in *Amazon Odyssey*, p. 6.

12. Atkinson, "Untitled—Some Notes Toward a Theory of Identity," in *Amazon Odyssey*, p. 111.

13. Atkinson, "Metaphysical Cannibalism or Self- Creativity," in *Amazon Odyssey*, p. 80.

14. *Ibid.*

15. Valerie Solanis, excerpts from "The SCUM (Society for Cutting Up Men) Manifesto," in *Sisterhood is Powerful, op. cit.*, p. 514.

16. *Ibid.*, p. 517.

17. *Ibid.*, p. 518.

18. *Ibid.*, pp. 518-19.

19. Elizabeth Gould Davis, *The First Sex*, G.P. Putnam's Sons, New York, 1971, p. 339.

20. Nancy Myron and Charlotte Bunch, editors. Introduction to *Lesbianism and the Women's Movement*, Diana Press, Baltimore, 1975, p. 12.

21. Mary Daly, *Beyond God the Father: Toward a Philosophy of Women's Liberation*, Beacon Press, Boston, 1973, p. 100.

22. Andrea Dworkin, "Renouncing Sexual Equality," *off our backs*, Vol. IV, No. 9, November 1974, p. 2.

23. Monique Wittig, "One is Not Born a Woman," in *Feminist Issues*, Vol. 1, No. 2, p. 50.

24. Editorial, *Questions Féministes/Feminist Issues*, Vol. 1, No. 1, p. 6.

25. *Ibid.*

26. *Ibid.*, p. 13.

27. Adrienne Rich, *Of Woman Born*, W.W. Norton & Co., New York, 1976, p. 81.

28. *Ibid.*, pp. 174-75.

29. *Ibid.*, p. 174.

30. Audre Lorde, "Man Child: A Black Lesbian Feminist Response," in *Conditions*, No. 4, Winter 1979, p. 35.

31. Lisa Leghorn and Katherine Parker, *Woman's Worth*, Routledge and Kegan Paul, Boston, 1981, p. 288.

32. *Ibid.*

33. *Ibid.*, pp. 288-89.

34. *Ibid.*, p. 287.

35. *Ibid.*, p. 289.

36. Angela Miles, unpublished dissertation, "The Politics of Feminist Radicalism: A Study in Integrative Politics," University of Toronto, 1979, p. 230.

Chapter 13: Strategies and Tactics: Taking Power?

1. Simone de Beauvoir, *The Second Sex*, Alfred A. Knopf Inc., New York, 1968, p. 627.

2. Ti-Grace Atkinson, foreword to *Amazon Odyssey*, Links Books, New York, 1974, p. xxii.

3. Nancy Hartsock, "Political Change: Two Perspectives on Power," *Quest: A Feminist Quarterly*, Vol. 1, No. 1, p. 15.

4. *Ibid.*, p. 20.

5. Bell Hooks, *Talking Back: Thinking Feminist, Thinking Black*, South End Press, Boston, 1989, p. 19.

6. *Ibid.*, p. 27.

7. Lisa Leghorn and Katherine Parker, *Woman's Worth*, Routledge and Kegan Paul, Boston, 1981, p. 287.

8. Charlotte Bunch, "The Reform Tool Kit," *Quest: A Feminist Quarterly*, Vol. 1, No. 1, p. 43.

9. "Principles of New York Radical Women," in *Sisterhood is Powerful*, edited by Robin Morgan. Vintage, New York, 1970, p. 520.

10. "Redstockings Manifesto," in *Sisterhood is Powerful, op. cit.*, p. 536.

11. Charlotte Bunch, "The Reform Tool Kit," *op. cit.*, p. 38.

12. *Ibid.*, pp. 38-39.

13. Jo Freeman, *The Politics of Women's Liberation*, David McKay Co., New York, 1985, pp. 241-43.

14. Charlotte Bunch, "The Reform Tool Kit," *op. cit.*, p. 40.

15. *Ibid.*, pp. 41-42.

16. *Ibid.*, pp. 45-46.

17. *Ibid.*, p. 48.

18. *Ibid.*, p. 49.

19. Phyllis Chesler, *Mothers on Trial: The Battle for Child Custody*, McGraw-Hill, New York, St. Louis, San Francisco, 1986.

20. Carol Hanisch, "The Liberal Takeover of Women's Liberation," in *Feminist Revolution*, edited by Redstockings. Random House, New York, 1978, p. 163.

21. Brooke, "The Retreat to Cultural Feminism," in *Feminist Revolution, op. cit.*, p. 79.

22. *Ibid.*, p. 80.

23. Susanna Sturgis, letter, *off our backs*, Vol. XIV, No. 4, May 1984, p. 26.

24. Jill Johnston, *Lesbian Nation*, Simon and Schuster, New York, 1973, p. 152.

25. *Ibid.*, p. 174.

26. *Ibid.*, pp. 181-82.

27. *Ibid.*, p. 278.

28. *Ibid.*, p. 265.

29. *Ibid.*, pp. 207-08.

30. *Ibid.*, pp. 189-90.

31. *Ibid.*, p. 257.

32. *Ibid.*, p. 258.

33. Kate Millett, *Sexual Politics*, Doubleday, 1970, p. 363.

34. Rita Arditti, Renate Duelli Klein and Shelley Minden, editors, *Test-Tube Women: What Future for Motherhood?*, Pandora Press, London and Boston, 1984;

    Gena Corea, *The Mother Machine*, Harper & Row, New York, 1985;

    Gena Corea *et al.*, editors. *Man-Made Woman: How New Reproductive Technologies Affect Women*, Indiana University Press, Indianapolis, 1987.

35. Shulamith Firestone, *The Dialectic of Sex*, William Morrow, New York, 1970, p. 230.

36. *Ibid.*, p. 217.

37. Adrienne Rich, *Of Woman Born*, W.W. Norton & Co., New York, 1976, p. 79.

38. Mary Daly, *Beyond God the Father*, Beacon Press, Boston, 1973, p. 137.

39. *Ibid.*, p. 138.

40. *Ibid.*, p. 43.

41. Mary Daly, *Gyn/Ecology*, Beacon Press, Boston, 1978, p. xv.

42. *Ibid.*, pp. xv-xvi.

43. *Ibid.*, p. 57.

44. *Ibid.*, p. 375.

45. Mary Daly, *Gyn/Ecology, op. cit.*, p. 379.

46. *Ibid.*, p. 346.

47. Interview with Mary Daly, *off our backs*, Vol. IX, No. 4, May 1979, p. 22.

48. Mary Daly, *Pure Lust*, Beacon Press, Boston, 1984, pp. 395-96.

49. Sonia Johnson, *Going Out of Our Minds: The Metaphysics of Liberation*, The Crossing Press, Freedom, California, 1987, p. 297.

50. *Ibid.*, p. 302.

51. Ti-Grace Atkinson, "Radical Feminism: Declaration of War," in *Amazon Odyssey, op. cit.*, p. 50.

52. *Ibid.*, p. 47.

53. Atkinson, "Rhode Island: Movement Politics and Other Sleights of Hand," in *Amazon Odyssey*, p. 105.

54. Atkinson, "Strategy and Tactics: A Presentation of Political Lesbianism," in *Amazon Odyssey*, p. 174.

55. *Ibid.*, p. 160.

56. *Ibid.*, p. 162.

57. *Ibid.*, p. 169.

58. *Ibid.*, p. 174.

59. Atkinson, "The Institution of Sexual Intercourse," in *Amazon Odyssey*, p. 20.

60. Rita Mae Brown, "August 26, 1976, N.Y.C.," in *A Plain Brown Rapper*, Diana Press, Baltimore, 1976, p. 55.

61. Rita Mae Brown, "The Shape of Things to Come," in *A Plain Brown Rapper*, p. 117.

62. Rita Mae Brown, "Conclusion," in *A Plain Brown Rapper*, pp. 218-21.

63. Rita Mae Brown, "The Shape of Things to Come," in *A Plain Brown Rapper*, p. 115.

64. Rita Mae Brown, "The Lady's Not for Burning," in *A Plain Brown Rapper*, p. 211.

65. Frederique Delacoste and Felice Newman, editors, *Fight Back! Feminist Resistance to Male Violence*, Cleis Press, Pittsburgh, 1981.

66. Pauline B. Bart and Patricia H. O'Brien, *Stopping Rape: Successful Survival Strategies*, Pergamon Press, London and Boston, 1985; Denise Caignon and Gail Groves, editors, *Her Wits About Her: Self-Defense Stories by Women*, Harper & Row, New York, 1987.

67. Susan Cavin, *Lesbian Origins*, ism press, San Francisco, 1985, p. 170.

68. *Ibid.*, p. 161.

69. *Ibid.*, pp. 169-72.

70. Sally Gearhart, "The Future—If There is One—is Female," in *Reweaving the Web of Life*, edited by Pam McAllister, New Society Publishers, Philadelphia, 1982, p. 280.

71. *Ibid.*, p. 281.

72. *Ibid.*, p. 283.

73. Roberta Steinbacher and Helen B. Holmes, "Sex Choice: Survival and Sisterhood," in *Man-Made Woman, op. cit.*, pp. 52-63.

74. Sally Gearhart, "The Future...," in *Reweaving the Web of Life, op. cit.*, p. 282.

75. Elizabeth Shanklin, "A Call to Matriarchy," *The Matriarchist*, Vol. 1, No. 1, p. 1.

76. *Ibid.*

77. Laurel Holliday, *The Violent Sex: Male Psychobiology and the Evolution of Consciousness*, Bluestocking Press, Guerneyville, California, 1978, p. 180.

78. *Ibid.*, pp. 180-81.

79. *Ibid.*, pp. 186-203.

80. *Ibid.*, pp. 62-64.

81. *Ibid.*, p. 212.

82. *Ibid.*, p. 213.

Chapter 14: Separatism: When and How Long?

1. Barbara Leon, "Separate to Integrate," in *Feminist Revolution*, edited by Redstockings. Random House, New York, 1978, p. 154.

2. *Ibid.*

3. Ti-Grace Atkinson, "The Political Woman," in *Amazon Odyssey*, Links Books, New York, 1974, p. 91.

4. Ti-Grace Atkinson, private conversations, 1979 to the present.

5. Ginny Berson, "The Furies," in *Lesbianism and the Women's Movement*, edited by Nancy Myron and Charlotte Bunch. Diana Press, Baltimore, 1975, p. 18.

6. Rita Mae Brown, "Take a Lesbian to Lunch," in *A Plain Brown Rapper*, Diana Press, Baltimore, 1976, pp. 94-95.

7. *Ibid.*, p. 95.

8. Lucia Valeska, "The Future of Female Separatism," *Quest: A Feminist Quarterly*, Vol. II, No. 2, p. 13.

9. *Ibid.*, p. 16.

10. Rita Laporte, "Can Women Unite?," in *The Lavender Herring: Lesbian Essays from the Ladder*, edited by Barbara Grier and Coletta Reid. Diana Press, Baltimore, 1976, pp. 110-11.

11. Adrienne Rich, "It is the Lesbian in Us...,"
Sinister Wisdom, No. 3, Spring 1977, p. 8.

12. *Ibid.*, p. 9.

13. Vivienne Louise, letter, *off our backs*, Vol. XVIII, No. 1, January 1988, p. 22.

14. Anna Lee, "A Black Separatist," in *For Lesbians Only: A Separatist Anthology*, edited by Sarah Lucia Hoagland and Julia Penelope. Onlywomen Press, London, 1988, p. 84.

15. Naomi Littlebear Morena, "Coming Out Queer and Brown," in *For Lesbians Only: A Separatist Anthology, op. cit.*, p. 346.

16. Naomi Dykestein, "One More Contradiction," in *For Lesbians Only: A Separatist Anthology, op. cit.*, p. 281.

17. Merle Woo, "Letter to Ma," in *This Bridge Called My Back: Writings by Radical Women of Color*, Kitchen Table: Women of Color Press, Latham, NY, 1983 p. 142.

18. Juanita Ramos, "Bayamón, Brooklyn y yo," in *Compañeras: Latina Lesbians* (an anthology), Latina Lesbian Herstory Project, New York, 1987, p. 96.

19. Combahee River Collective: "A Black Feminist Statement," in *Capitalist Patriarchy and the Case for Socialist Feminism*, p. 367. Also published in *This Bridge Called My Back*, p. 214.

20. Barbara and Beverly Smith, "Across the Kitchen Table: A Sister-to-Sister Dialogue," in *This Bridge Called My Back, op. cit.*, p. 121.

21. Sara Bennett and Joan Gibbs, "Racism and Classism in the Lesbian Community: Towards the Building of a Radical Autonomous Lesbian Movement," in *Top Ranking: Racism and Classism in the Lesbian Community*, edited by Gibbs and Bennett, February 3 Press, New York, 1980.

22. Charlotte Bunch and Nancy Myron, editors, *Class and Feminism*, Diana Press, Baltimore, 1976.

23. Cathy McCandless, "Some Thoughts on Racism, Classism and Separatism," in *Top Ranking: Racism and Classism in the Lesbian Community, op. cit.*, p. 109.

24. *Ibid.*, p. 108.

25. Adrienne Rich, "What Does Separatism Mean?," *Sinister Wisdom*, No. 18, Fall 1983, p. 90.

26. *Ibid.*, pp. 87-88.

27. *Ibid.*

28. Bell Hooks, *Ain't I a Woman*, South End Press, Boston, 1981, pp. 150-51.

29. Barbara Smith and Beverly Smith, "Across the Kitchen Table: A Sister-to-Sister Dialogue," *This Bridge Called My Back, op. cit.*, p. 121.

30. *Ibid.*

31. Barbara Smith, introduction to *Home Girls: A Black Feminist Anthology*, Kitchen Table: Women of Color Press, Latham, NY, 1983, p. xl.

32. *Ibid.*, p. xli.

33. *Ibid.*

34. *Ibid.*, pp. xl-xli.

35. Bernice Johnson Reagon, "Coalition Politics: Turning the Century," in *Home Girls: A Black Feminist Anthology, op. cit.*, p. 357.

36. *Ibid.*, p. 358.

37. Estelle Freedman, "Separatism as a Strategy: Female Institution Building and American Feminism, 1870-1930," *Feminist Studies*, Vol. V, No. 3, Fall 1979, p. 513.

38. Marilyn Frye, *The Politics of Reality: Essays in Feminist Theory*, Crossing Press, Trumansburg, New York, 1984, p. 96.

39. *Ibid.*, p. 121.

40. *Ibid.*, p. 124.

41. Sidney Spinster, "The Evolution of Lesbian Separatism," *Insider, Insighter, Inciter*, No. 7, April 1982, p. 18.

42. *Ibid.*

43. *Ibid.*

44. Julia Penelope, "The Mystery of Lesbians," *Lesbian Ethics*, Vol. 1, No. 1, pp. 19-20.

45. Mary Daly, *Pure Lust*, p. 364.

46. *Ibid.*, p. 363.

47. Alix Dobkin, public discussion on separatism, Washington DC, June 1984.

48. Sarah Lucia Hoagland, *Lesbian Ethics: Toward New Value*, Institute of Lesbian Studies, Palo Alto, 1988, pp. 3-4.

49. *Ibid.*, p. 1.

50. Janice Raymond, *A Passion for Friends*, Beacon Press, Boston, 1986, p. 153.

51. *Ibid.*, p. 232.

52. *Ibid.*, p. 238.

53. Bernice Johnson Reagon, "Coalition Politics: Turning the Century," in *Home Girls: A Black Feminist Anthology, op. cit.*, pp. 356-57.

54. Barbara and Beverly Smith, "Across the Kitchen Table: A Sister-to-Sister Dialogue," *This Bridge Called My Back*, p. 126.

55. Cellestine Ware, *Woman Power: The Movement for Women's Liberation*, Tower Publications, New York, 1970, p. 69.

56. *Ibid.*, p. 169.

57. Thrace, "Action Proposal for Lesbian Revolutionary Movement from a Lesbian Separatist's Position," in *Fight Back! Feminist Resistance to Male Violence*, Cleis Press, Pittsburgh, 1981, p. 302.

58. Susan Cavin, "Radical Feminism in the '80s," workshop presentation at "Women in Print" conference, Washington DC, October 1981.

59. Thrace, "Action Proposal...," *op. cit.*, p. 305.

60. *Ibid.*

61. Sidney Spinster, "Warriors of the Luniform Shield," in *Fight Back!*, *op. cit.*, p. 309.

62. *Ibid.*, p. 310.

63. Ellen Mutari, "Feminism and the Critique of Capitalism," *off our backs*, Vol. XI, No. 6, June 1981, p. 10.

64. Karen Kollias, "Class Realities Create a New Power Base," in *Building Feminist Theory: Essays from Quest, A Feminist Quarterly*, Longman, 1984.

65. Nancy Hartsock, "Feminist Theory and the Development of Revolutionary Strategy," in *Capitalist Patriarchy and the Case for Socialist Feminism*, edited by Zillah R. Eisenstein. Monthly Review Press, New York and London, 1979, p. 72.

66. Sara Bennett and Joan Gibbs, "Racism and Classism in the Lesbian Community" in *Top Ranking: Racism and Classism in the Lesbian Community*," *op. cit.*, pp. 28-29.

67. Barbara and Beverly Smith, "Across the Kitchen Table: A Sister-to-Sister Dialogue," *This Bridge Called My Back*, *op. cit.*, p. 116.

68. Cellestine Ware, *Woman Power: The Movement for Women's Liberation*, *op. cit.*, p. 97.

69. June Jordan, "Problems of Language in a Democratic State," in *On Call: Political Essays*, South End Press, Boston, 1985, pp. 27-29.

Chapter 15: Violence and Non-Violence as Tactics

1. Kate Millett, *Sexual Politics*, Doubleday, Garden City, 1970, pp. 362-63.

2. Lisa Leghorn and Katherine Parker, *Woman's Worth*, Routledge and Kegan Paul, Boston, 1981, p. 301.

3. *Ibid.*, pp. 299-300.

4. Robin Morgan, *The Anatomy of Freedom: Feminism, Physics and Global Politics*, Anchor Press/Doubleday, Garden City, NY, 1982, p. 79.

5. Bell Hooks, *Feminist Theory: From Margin to Center*, South End Press, Boston, 1984, p. 128.

6. Andrea Dworkin, "Redefining Violence," in *Our Blood: Prophecies and Discourses on Sexual Politics*, Wideview/Perigree Books, New York, 1976, pp. 71-72.

7. Ti-Grace Atkinson, "On Violence in the Women's Movement," in *Amazon Odyssey*, Links Books, New York, 1974, p. 203.

8. *Ibid.*, p. 200.

9. *Questions Féministes/Feminist Issues* editorial, Vol. 1, No. 1, p. 13.

10. Sidney Spinster, "Warriors of the Luniform Shield," in *Fight Back! Feminist Resistance to Male Violence*, Cleis Press, Pittsburgh, 1981, pp. 308-09.

11. Jeffner Allen, "Looking at Our Blood: A Lesbian Response to Men's Terrorization of Women," in *Trivia*, No. 4, 1984, p. 17.

12. *Ibid.*, pp. 20-21.

13. Michaele Uccella and Melanie Kaye/Kantrowitz, "Women's Capacity for Resistance," in *Fight Back!, op. cit.*, p. 321.

Chapter 16: What We Want, & How to Get There

1. Michael Albert and Robin Hahnel, *Marxism and Socialist Theory*, South End Press, Boston, 1982, p. 17.

2. Brooke, "Quicksand Politics: Some Liberal Arguments in the Women's Movement," in *Meeting Ground*, No. 1, January 1977.

3. Jo Freeman, *The Politics of Women's Liberation*, David McKay Co., New York, 1985, pp. 103-145.

4. Bell Hooks, *Talking Back: Thinking Feminist, Thinking Black*. South End Press, Boston, 1989, p. 24.

5. Susan Schecter, *Women and Male Violence: The Visions and Struggles of the Battered Women's Movement*, South End Press, Boston, 1982, pp. 267-71.

6. Bell Hooks, *Feminist Theory: From Margin to Center*, South End Press, Boston, 1984, p. 109.

7. Janice Raymond, *A Passion for Friends*, Beacon Press, Boston, 1986, pp. 237-8.

8. *Ibid.*, p. 23.

Bibliography

Albert, Michael and Robin Hahnel. *Marxism and Socialist Theory*, South End Press, Boston, 1982.

Allen, Jeffner. *Lesbian Philosophy*, Institute of Lesbian Studies, Palo Alto, Cal., 1986.

_____. "Looking at Our Blood: A Lesbian Response to Men's Terrorization of Women," in *Trivia*, No. 4, 1984, pp. 11-30.

Ascher, Carol. *Simone de Beauvoir: A Life of Freedom*, Beacon Press, Boston, 1981.

Atkinson, Ti-Grace. *Amazon Odyssey*, Links Books, New York, 1974.

_____. "Amazon Continues Odyssey," interview with *off our backs: a women's news journal*, Vol. IX, No. 11, December 1979, p. 2.

_____. "Why I'm Against S/M Liberation," in *Against Sadomasochism: A Radical Feminist Analysis* (anthology),* pp. 90-92.

Barry, Kathleen. *Female Sexual Slavery*, Prentice Hall, New York, 1979.

Bart, Pauline. Review of Dorothy Dinnerstein's book, *The Mermaid and the Minotaur*, in *Contemporary Psychology*, Vol. 22, No. 11, 1977.

_____. Review of Nancy Chodorow's book, *The Reproduction of Mothering*, in *off our backs*, Vol. XI, No. 1, January 1981.

Bart, Pauline B. and Patricia H. O'Brien. *Stopping Rape: Successful Survival Strategies*, Pergamon Press, London and Boston, 1985.

Bat-Ami Bar On, "Feminism and Sadomasochism: Self Critical Notes," in *Against Sadomasochism* (anthology), pp. 72-82.

Beauvoir, Simone de. *The Second Sex*, translated by H.M. Parshley. Alfred A. Knopf Inc., New York, 1968.

_____. *All Said and Done*, Putnam, New York, 1974.

_____. Interview with Margaret Simons and Jessica Benjamin. *Feminist Studies*, Vol. 5, No. 4, Summer 1979, pp. 330-345.

____

*For a complete alphabetical listing of the anthologies cited here, see page 349, below.

Benjamin, Jessica. "Starting from the Left and Going Beyond," paper presented at *"The Second Sex*: Thirty Years After" Conference at New York University, September 1979.

Berson, Ginny. "The Furies," in *Lesbianism and the Women's Movement* (anthology), pp. 15-19.

Biren, Joan E. (JEB). Presentation at Lesbian Herstory panel, Passages Conference on Lesbians and Aging, Washington DC, January 23, 1988.

Brief Amicus Curiae of Feminist Anti-Censorship Task Force, *et al.*, in American Booksellers Association *et al. v.* William Hudnut III, *et al.*

Briffault, Robert. *The Mothers*, Grosset & Dunlap, New York, 1963.

Brooke. "Quicksand Politics: Some Liberal Arguments in the Women's Movement," in *Meeting Ground*, No. 1, January 1977.

_____. "The Retreat to Cultural Feminism," in *Feminist Revolution* (anthology), pp. 79-83.

Brown, Rita Mae. *A Plain Brown Rapper*, Diana Press, Baltimore, 1976.

_____. Interview with *Washington Post*, August 13, 1981, Section C, p. 8.

Brownmiller, Susan. *Against Our Will: Men, Women and Rape*, Simon and Schuster, New York, 1975.

Brunet, Ariane and Louise Turcotte. "Separatism and Radicalism," in *For Lesbians Only: A Separatist Anthology*, pp. 451-55.

Bunch, Charlotte. "Lesbians in Revolt," in *Lesbianism and the Women's Movement* (anthology), pp. 29-37.

_____. "The Reform Tool Kit," *Quest: A Feminist Quarterly*, Vol. I, No. 1, pp. 37-51.

_____. "Not for Lesbians Only," *Quest: A Feminist Quarterly*, Vol. II, No. 2, Fall 1975, pp. 50-56.

_____. Speech at *"The Second Sex*: Thirty Years After" conference, New York University, September 1979.

Cade (Bambara), Toni. "On the Issue of Roles," in *The Black Woman: An Anthology*, pp. 101-110.

Card, Claudia. "Lesbian Attitudes and the Second Sex," in *Hypatia*, special issue of *Women's Studies International Forum*, Vol. 8, No. 3, 1985, pp. 209-214.

Cavin, Susan. *Lesbian Origins*, ism press, San Francisco, 1985.

Chase, Wilda. "Lesbianism and Feminism," in *The Lavender Herring: Lesbian Essays from the Ladder* (anthology), pp. 98-103.

Chesler, Phyllis. *Mothers on Trial: The Battle for Child Custody*, McGraw-Hill, New York, St. Louis, San Francisco, 1986.

Chodorow, Nancy. *The Reproduction of Mothering: Psychoanalysis and the Sociology of Gender*, University of California Press, Berkeley, 1978.

Clarke, Cheryl. "Lesbianism: An Act of Resistance," in *This Bridge Called My Back: Writings by Radical Women of Color* (anthology), pp. 128-137.

Cliff, Michelle. *Claiming an Identity They Taught Me to Despise*, Persephone Press, Watertown, Mass., 1980.

C.L.I.T. (Collective Lesbian International Terrors) Statement #2, *off our backs*, Vol. IV, No. 3, July 1974, p. 13.

Combahee River Collective. "A Black Feminist Statement," in *Capitalist Patriarchy and the Case for Socialist Feminism* (anthology), pp. 362-372. Also published in *This Bridge Called My Back: Writings by Radical Women of Color*, pp. 210-218, and issued as a Freedom Organizing pamphlet by Kitchen Table: Women of Color Press.

Corea, Gena. *The Mother Machine*, Harper & Row, New York, 1985.

Cornwall, Anita. "Open Letter to a Black Sister," in *The Lavender Herring: Lesbian Essays from the Ladder* (anthology), pp. 225-231.

_____. "Letter to a Friend," *The Lavender Herring* (anthology), pp. 249-255.

Daly, Mary. *Beyond God the Father: Toward a Philosophy of Women's Liberation*, Beacon Press, Boston, 1973.

_____. *Gyn/Ecology: The Metaethics of Radical Feminism*, Beacon Press, Boston, 1978.

_____. Interview with *off our backs*, Vol. IX, No. 5, May 1979, p. 23.

_____. *Pure Lust: Elemental Feminist Philosophy*, Beacon Press, Boston, 1984.

Davis, Elizabeth Gould. *The First Sex*, G.P. Putnam's Sons, New York, 1971.

Deevey, Sharon. "Such a Nice Girl," in *Lesbianism and the Women's Movement* (anthology), pp. 21-26.

Dejanikus, Tacie, Carol Anne Douglas, Alice Henry and Fran Moira. "Towards a Politics of Sexuality," coverage of 1982 Barnard "Feminist and the Scholar" conference, *off our backs*, Vol. XII, No. 4, June 1982, p. 2.

Delphy, Christine. *Close to Home*, University of Massachusetts Press, Amherst, Massachusetts, 1984.

Densmore, Dana. "Independence from the Sexual Revolution," in *Radical Feminism* (anthology), pp. 107-118.

Desmoines, Harriet. "Go Tell Aunt Rhoddy," *Sinister Wisdom*, Vol. 1, No. 1, pp. 69-70.

Dinnerstein, Dorothy. *The Mermaid and the Minotaur: Sexual Arrangements and the Human Malaise*, Harper & Row, New York, 1976.

Donovan, Josephine. *Feminist Theory: The Intellectual Traditions of American Feminism*, Frederick Ungar, New York, 1985.

Douglas, Carol Anne. "Confessions of an Ex-heterosexual," *off our backs*, Vol. IX, No. 9, October 1979, p. 13.

Dubois, Ellen and Linda Gordon, "How Feminists Thought About Sex: Our Complex Legacy." Paper presented at Barnard Feminist and the Scholar Conference, April 1982.

Duc, Aimée. "Are These Women?," in *Lesbian Feminism in Turn-of-the-Century Germany* (anthology), pp. 1-21.

Dunbar (Ortiz), Roxanne. "Female Liberation as the Basis for Social Revolution," *Sisterhood is Powerful* (anthology), pp. 477-492.

Dunbar, Roxanne and Lisa Leghorn. "The Man's Problem," *No More Fun and Games*, November 1969, pp. 25-7.

Dworkin, Andrea. *Woman Hating*, E. P. Dutton, New York, 1974.

——————. *Our Blood: Prophecies and Discourses on Sexual Politics*, Wideview/Perigree Books, New York, 1976.

——————. *Pornography: Men Possessing Women*, Wideview/Perigree Books, New York, 1981.

——————. *Right-wing Women*, Wideview/Perigree Books, New York, 1983.

——————. *Intercourse*, Free Press, New York, 1987.

——————. *Letter from a War Zone: Writings 1976-1989*, E.P. Dutton, New York, 1989.

——————. "Renouncing Sexual Equality," *off our backs*, Vol. IV, No. 9, November 1974, p. 2.

——————. "Biological Superiority: The World's Most Dangerous and Deadly Idea," *Heresies* #6, Summer 1978, pp. 47-51.

Dykestein, Naomi. "One More Contradiction," in *For Lesbians Only: A Separatist Anthology*, pp. 279-281.

Echols, Alice. "The New Feminism of Yin and Yang," in *Powers of Desire: The Politics of Sexuality* (anthology), pp. 439-459.

Eisenstein, Hester. *Contemporary Feminist Thought*, G.K. Hall & Co., Boston, 1983.

Eisenstein, Zillah R. *The Radical Future of Liberal Feminism*, Longman, New York and London, 1981.

Engels, Friedrich. *The Origin of the Family, Private Property and the State*, International Publishers, New York, 1972.

Evans, Mary. *Simone de Beauvoir: Feminist Mandarin*, Tavistock, London and New York, 1985.

Feminists, The. "The Feminists: A Political Organization to Annihilate Sex Roles," in *Radical Feminism* (anthology), pp. 368-378.

Firestone, Shulamith. *The Dialectic of Sex: The Case for Feminist Revolution*, William Morrow, New York, 1970.

Fisher, Elizabeth. *Woman's Creation*, Anchor/Doubleday, New York, 1979.

Fossey, Dian. *Gorillas in the Mist*, Houghton Mifflin Co., Boston, 1983.

"Fourth World Manifesto," in *Radical Feminism* (anthology), pp. 322-357.

Freedman, Estelle. "Separatism as a Strategy: Female Institution Building and American Feminism, 1870-1930," *Feminist Studies*, Vol. V, No. 3, Fall 1979, pp. 512-529.

Freeman, Jo. *The Politics of Women's Liberation*, David McKay Co., New York, 1985.

Frye, Marilyn. *The Politics of Reality: Essays in Feminist Theory*, Crossing Press, Trumansburg, New York, 1984.

Garaudy, Roger. "Literature of the Graveyard," in *Existentialism versus Marxism: Conflicting Views on Humanism* (anthology), pp. 146-164.

Gearhart, Sally. "The Future—If There is One—is Female," in *Reweaving the Web of Life: Feminism and Non-Violence* (anthology).

Goodall, Jane. *In the Shadow of Man*, Houghton Mifflin Co., Boston, 1971.

Gornick, Vivian. *The Romance of American Communism*, Basic Books, New York, 1977.

Graves, Robert. *The White Goddess*, Farrar, Straus & Giroux, New York, 1948.

Grier, Barbara. "What is a Lesbian," *Sinister Wisdom* #3, 1977, pp. 13-14.

Griffin, Susan. *Woman and Nature*, Harper & Row, New York 1979.

Griffin, Susan. "The Way of All Ideology," in *Signs: Journal of Women in Culture and Society*, Vol. 7, No. 3, Spring 1982, pp. 641-660.

Hanisch, Carol. "The Liberal Takeover of Women's Liberation," in *Feminist Revolution* (anthology), pp. 163-167.

Harris, Bertha. "The Lesbian, The Workmaker, The Leader," in *Quest: A Feminist Quarterly*, Vol. II, No. 4, pp. 12-18.

Hartmann, Heidi. "The Unhappy Marriage of Marxism and Feminism: Towards a More Progressive Union," in *Women and Revolution: A Discussion of the Unhappy Marriage of Marxism and Feminism* (anthology), pp. 1-41.

Hartsock, Nancy. *Money, Sex and Power: Towards a Feminist Historical Materialism*, Longman, New York, 1983.

——————————. "Feminist Theory and the Development of Revolutionary Strategy," in *Capitalist Patriarchy and the Case for Socialist Feminism* (anthology), pp. 56-77.

——————————. "Fundamental Feminism: Process and Perspective," in *Building Feminist Theory: Essays from Quest, a Feminist Quarterly*, Longman, New York and London, 1981.

——————————. "Political Change: Two Perspectives on Power," *Quest: A Feminist Quarterly*, Vol. 1, No. 1, pp. 10-25.

Hoagland, Sarah Lucia. *Lesbian Ethics: Toward New Value*, Institute of Lesbian Studies, Palo Alto, Cal., 1988.

Hollibaugh, Amber and Cherríe Moraga. "What We're Rollin' Around in Bed With: Sexual Silences," in *Heresies* #12, pp. 58-68.

Holliday, Laurel. *The Violent Sex: Male Psychobiology and the Evolution of Consciousness*, Bluestocking Press, Guerniville, California, 1978.

Hooks, Bell. *Ain't I a Woman*, South End Press, Boston, 1981.

——————. *Feminist Theory: From Margin to Center*, South End Press, Boston, 1984.

——————. *Talking Back: Thinking Feminist, Thinking Black*, South End Press, Boston, 1989.

Hrdy, Sarah Blaffer. *The Woman That Never Evolved*, Harvard University Press, Cambridge, Mass. and London, 1983.

Jaggar, Alison. *Feminist Politics and Human Nature*, Rowman and Allanheld, Totowa, New Jersey, 1983.

Jay, Karla and Allen Young. *The Gay Report*, Summit Books, New York, 1979.

Jeffreys, Sheila. *The Spinster and Her Enemies: Feminism and Sexuality 1880-1930*, Pandora Press, London, 1985.

Johnson, Sonia. *Going Out of Our Minds: The Metaphysics of Liberation*, The Crossing Press, Freedom, California, 1987.

Johnston, Jill. *Lesbian Nation: The Feminist Solution*, Simon and Schuster, New York, 1973.

_____. "Sexuality and All That," *The Village Voice*, July 31, 1979, p. 34.

Jonel, Marissa. "Letter from a Former Masochist," in *Against Sadomasochism* (anthology), pp. 16-22.

Jordan, June. *On Call: Political Essays*, South End Press, Boston, 1985.

Kaplan, Temma. "Other Scenarios: Women in Spanish Anarchism," in *Becoming Visible: Women in European History* (anthology), pp. 400-421.

Koedt, Anne. "The Myth of the Vaginal Orgasm," in *Radical Feminism* (anthology), pp. 198-207.

_____. "Lesbianism and Feminism," in *Radical Feminism* (anthology), pp. 246-258.

Kollias, Karen. "Class Realities Create a New Power Base," in *Building Feminist Theory: Essays from Quest, a Feminist Quarterly*, Longman, 1984.

Kornegger, Peggy. "Anarchism: The Feminist Connection," in *Reinventing Anarchy* (anthology), pp. 237-249.

Laporte, Rita. "Can Women Unite?" in *The Lavender Herring: Lesbian Essays from the Ladder* (anthology), pp. 107-115.

_____. "A Document," in *The Lavender Herring* (anthology), pp. 138-148.

_____. "Sex and Sexuality," in *The Lavender Herring* (anthology), pp. 197-219.

Le Doeuf, Michèle. "Operative Philosophy, Simone de Beauvoir and Existentialism," paper for "*The Second Sex*: Thirty Years After" conference, New York University, September 1979.

Lee, Anna. "A Black Separatist," in *For Lesbians Only: A Separatist Anthology*, pp. 83-92.

Leghorn, Lisa and Katherine Parker. *Woman's Worth*, Routledge and Kegan Paul, Boston, 1981.

Leibowitz, Leila. "Perspectives on the Evolution of Sex Differences," in *Toward an Anthropology of Women* (anthology), pp. 20-35.

Leon, Barbara. "The Male Supremacist Attack on Monogamy," in *Feminist Revolution* (anthology), pp. 128-9.

Leon, Barbara. "Separate to Integrate," in *Feminist Revolution* (anthology), pp. 152-157.

Leonard, Vickie. "No Apologies from a Heterosexual," *off our backs*, Vol. IX, No. 9, October 1979, p. 13.

Lindenbaum, Joyce. "The Shattering of an Illusion: Competition in Lesbian Relationships," *Feminist Studies*, Vol. II, No. 1, Spring 1985, pp. 85-103.

Lindsey, Karen. *Friends as Family*, Beacon Press, Boston, 1983.

——————. "Debate, Don't Excommunicate," in *Sojourner*, Vol. 8, No. 6, February 1983, p. 17.

Lindsey, Kay. "The Black Woman as Woman," in *The Black Woman* (anthology), pp. 85-89.

Lootens, Tricia. "Lovers Who Don't Make Love," in *off our backs*, Vol. XIV, No. 2, February 1984, p. 6.

Lorde, Audre. *Sister Outsider: Essays by Audre Lorde*, Crossing Press, Trumansburg, NY, 1984.

——————. *A Burst of Light*, Firebrand Books, Ithaca, NY, 1988.

——————. "Man Child: A Black Lesbian Feminist Response," in *Conditions*, No. 4, Winter 1979, pp. 30-36.

——————. Interview with Susan Leigh Starr, in *Against Sadomasochism* (anthology), pp. 66-71.

Louise, Vivienne. Letter, *off our backs*, Vol. XVIII, No. 1, January 1988, p. 22.

Loulan, JoAnn. *Lesbian Sex*, Spinsters Ink, San Francisco, 1984.

——————. *Lesbian Passion: Loving Ourselves and Each Other*, Spinsters/Aunt Lute, San Francisco, 1987.

Love, Barbara and Elizabeth Shanklin. "The Answer is Matriarchy," in *Mothering: Essays in Feminist Theory* (anthology), pp. 275-83.

MacKinnon, Catharine A. *Sexual Harassment of Working Women: A Case of Sex Discrimination*, Yale University Press, New Haven, 1979.

——————. "Feminism, Marxism, Method, and the State: An Agenda for Theory," in *Signs: A Journal of Women in Culture and Society*, Vol. 7, No. 3, Spring 1982, pp. 515-544.

——————. "Feminism, Marxism, Method, and the State: Toward a Feminist Jurisprudence," in *Signs: A Journal of Women, Culture and Society*, Vol. 8, No. 4, Summer 1983, pp. 635-658.

——————. Interview on feminist theory with *off our backs*, Vol. XIII, No. 5, May 1983, p. 17.

MacKinnon, Catharine A. *Feminism Unmodified: Discourses on Life and Law*, Harvard University Press, Cambridge, Mass., and London, England, 1987.

_____. *Toward a Feminist Theory of the State*, Harvard University Press, Cambridge, Mass., 1989.

Mainardi, Pat. "The Marriage Question," in *Feminist Revolution* (anthology), pp. 120-122.

Marx, Karl. *Early Writings*, translated and edited by T. B. Bottomore, McGraw-Hill, New York, 1964.

McCandless, Cathy. "Some Thoughts on Racism, Classism and Separatism," in *Top Ranking: Racism and Classism in the Lesbian Community* (anthology), pp. 103-115.

McFadden, Maggie. "Anatomy of Difference: Toward a Classification of Feminist Theory," in *Women's Studies International Forum*, Vol. 7, No. 6, 1983, pp. 495-504.

Miles, Angela. "The Politics of Feminist Radicalism: A Study in Integrative Politics," unpublished dissertation, University of Toronto, 1979.

Millett, Kate. *Sexual Politics*, Doubleday, Garden City, 1970.

Mitchell, Juliet. *Woman's Estate*, Vintage, New York, 1973.

Mohanty, Chandra Malpede. "The Politics of Colonization: Western Feminism and Women in Third World Countries," paper given at After *The Second Sex*: New Directions Feminist Theory Conference, University of Pennsylvania, Spring 1984.

Montague, Ashley. "The Natural Superiority of Women," in *The Saturday Review Treasury*, Simon & Schuster, New York, 1957.

Moraga, Cherríe. *Loving in the War Years*, South End Press, Boston, 1983.

Morgan, Elaine. *The Descent of Woman*, Stein and Day, New York, 1972.

Morgan, Robin. *Going Too Far*, Random House, New York, 1978.

_____. *The Anatomy of Freedom: Feminism, Physics and Global Politics*, Anchor Press/Doubleday, Garden City, New York, 1982.

_____. Interview with *off our backs*, Vol. XIX, No. 4, April 1989, p. 1.

Mutari, Ellen. "Feminism and the Critique of Capitalism," *off our backs*, Vol. XI, No. 6, June 1981, p. 10.

Nestle, Joan. *A Restricted Country*, Firebrand Books, Ithaca, New York, 1987.

New York Radical Feminists. "Politics of the Ego," in *Radical Feminism* (anthology), pp. 379-383.

O'Brien, Mary. *The Politics of Reproduction*, Routledge & Kegan Paul, Boston, 1981.

Omolade, Barbara. "Hearts of Darkness," in *Powers of Desire: The Politics of Sexuality* (anthology), pp. 350-365.

Parker, Pat. "Revolution: It's Not Neat or Pretty or Quick," in *This Bridge Called My Back: Writings by Radical Women of Color*, pp. 238-242.

Paz, Juana María. "The Ancient Matriarchy of Atlantis," in *For Lesbians Only: A Separatist Anthology*, pp. 297-303.

Penelope, Julia. "The Mystery of Lesbians," *Lesbian Ethics*, Vol. 1, No. 1, pp. 7-33.

Questions Féministes editorial, *Feminist Issues*, Vol. 1, No. 1, pp. 3-21.

Radicalesbians. "The Woman-Identified Woman," in *Radical Feminism* (anthology), pp. 240-245.

Ramos, Juanita. "Bayamón, Brooklyn y yo," in *Compañeras: Latina Lesbians* (An Anthology), pp. 89-96.

Raymond, Janice. *A Passion for Friends: Toward a Philosophy of Female Affection*, Beacon Press, Boston, 1986.

Reagon, Bernice Johnson. "Coalition Politics: Turning the Century," in *Home Girls: A Black Feminist Anthology*, pp. 356-368.

"Redstockings Manifesto," in *Sisterhood is Powerful* (anthology), pp. 533-536.

Reid, Coletta. "Coming Out in the Women's Movement," in *Lesbianism and the Women's Movement* (anthology), pp. 91-103.

Rich, Adrienne. *Of Woman Born*, W.W. Norton & Co., New York, 1976.

――――――――――. *Blood, Bread, and Poetry: Selected Prose 1979-1985*, W. W. Norton & Co., New York and London, 1986.

――――――――――. "It is the Lesbian in Us...," *Sinister Wisdom*, No. 3, Spring 1977, pp. 6-9.

――――――――――. "We Don't Have to Come Apart Over Pornography," *off our backs*, Vol XV, No. 7, 1985, p. 22.

Rubin, Gayle. "The Traffic in Women: Notes on the 'Political Economy' of Sex," in *Toward an Anthropology of Women* (anthology), pp. 157-210.

――――――――――. "The Leather Menace: Comments on Politics and S/M," in *Coming to Power* (anthology), p. 213.

Sarachild, Kathie. "The Power of History," in *Feminist Revolution* (anthology), pp. 13-43.

_____. "Going for What We Really Want," *Feminist Revolution* (anthology), pp. 158-160.

_____. Leaflet for New York Radical Women, reprinted in *Feminist Revolution* (anthology), p. 154.

Sartre, Jean-Paul. *Critique of Dialectical Reasoning*, translated by Alan Sheridan-Smith. New Left Books, London, 1976.

Schaff, Adam. *Marxism and the Human Individual*, McGraw Hill, New York, 1970.

Schecter, Susan. *Women and Male Violence: The Visions and Struggles of the Battered Women's Movement*, South End Press, Boston, 1982,

Schwarzer, Alice. *After the Second Sex: Conversations with Simone de Beauvoir*, Pantheon Books, New York, 1984.

Shanklin, Elizabeth. "A Call to Matriarchy," *The Matriarchist*, Vol. 1, No. 1, p. 1.

Shelley, Martha. "Notes of a Radical Lesbian," in *Sisterhood is Powerful* (anthology), pp. 306-311.

_____. "What is a Lesbian," *Sinister Wisdom #3*, Spring 1977, p. 14.

Simons, Margaret and Jessica Benjamin. "Simone de Beauvoir: An Interview," *Feminist Studies*, Vol. 5, No. 4, Summer 1979, pp. 330-345.

Smith, Barbara and Beverly. "Across the Kitchen Table: A Sister-to-Siter Dialogue," in *This Bridge Called My Back: Writings by Radical Women of Color*, pp. 113-27.

Smith, Barbara. "Towards a Black Feminist Criticism," *Conditions Two*, Vol. 1, No. 2, October 1977, pp. 25-44.

_____. Introduction to *Home Girls: A Black Feminist Anthology*, pp. xix-lvi.

Solanis, Valerie. Excerpts from "The SCUM (Society for Cutting Up Men) Manifesto," in *Sisterhood is Powerful* (anthology), pp. 514-519.

Solomon, Barbara. "Taking the Bullshit by the Horns," *Lesbianism and the Women's Movement* (anthology), pp. 39-47.

Spender, Dale. *Feminist Theorists: Three Centuries of Women Thinkers*, Pantheon Books, New York, 1983.

Spinster, Sidney. "The Evolution of Lesbian Separatism," *Insider, Insighter, Inciter*, No. 7, April 1982, p. 18.

Spinster, Sidney. "Warriors of the Luniform Shield," in *Fight Back! Feminist Resistance to Male Violence* (anthology), pp. 306-311.

Starr, Susan Leigh. "The Politics of Wholeness," *Sinister Wisdom* No. 3, Spring 1977, pp. 36-44.

Steinbacher, Roberta and Helen B. Holmes. "Sex Choice: Survival and Sisterhood," in *Man-Made Woman: How New Reproductive Technologies Affect Women* (anthology), pp. 52-63.

Sturgis, Susanna. Letter, *off our backs*, Vol. XIV, No. 4, May 1984, p. 26.

Thrace. "Action Proposal for Lesbian Revolutionary Movement from a Lesbian Separatist's Position," in *Fight Back! Feminist Resistance to Male Violence* (anthology), pp. 301-305.

Trebilcot, Joyce. *Taking Responsibility for Sexuality*, Acacia Books, San Francisco, 1983.

―――――. "Male Orgasm and Male Domination," paper at the "After *The Second Sex*: New Directions Feminist Theory" conference, University of Pennsylvania, Spring 1984.

Uccella, Michaele and Melanie Kaye/Kantrowitz. "Women's Capacity for Resistance," in *Fight Back! Feminist Resistance to Male Violence* (anthology), pp. 321-324.

Valeska, Lucia. "The Future of Female Separatism," *Quest: A Feminist Quarterly*, Vol. II, No. 2, pp. 2-16.

Walker, Alice. *You Can't Keep a Good Woman Down*, Harcourt Brace Jovanovich, New York, 1981.

Wallace, Michele. *Black Macho and the Myth of the Superwoman*, Dial Press, New York, 1978.

Ware, Cellestine. *Woman Power: The Movement for Women's Liberation*, Tower Publications, New York, 1970.

―――――. "Black Feminism," in *Radical Feminism* (anthology), pp. 81-84.

Weinbaum, Batya. *The Curious Courtship of Women's Liberation and Socialism*, South End Press, Boston, 1978.

Whitbeck, Caroline. "Love, Knowledge and Transformation," in Hypatia, special issue of *Women's Studies International Forum*, Vol. 7, No. 5, 1984, pp. 393-405.

Whitbeck, Caroline. Paper given at feminist theory conference, University of Pennsylvania, Spring 1984.

Willis, Ellen. *Beginning to See the Light: Pieces of a Decade*, Alfred A. Knopf, New York, 1981.

Wittig, Monique. "The Straight Mind," *Feminist Issues*, Vol. 1, No. 1. 1979, p. 103-111.

_____. "One is Not Born a Woman," *Feminist Issues*, Vol. 1, No. 2, Winter 1981, pp. 47-54.

Woo, Merle. "Letter to Ma," in *This Bridge Called My Back: Writings by Radical Women of Color*, pp. 140-147.

Anthologies

Against Sadomasochism: A Radical Feminist Analysis, edited by Robin Ruth Linden, Darlene R. Pagano, Diana E. H. Russell and Susan Leigh Starr. Frog in the Well, East Palo Alto, 1982.

All the Women are White, All the Blacks are Men, But Some of Us are Brave, edited by Gloria T. Hull, Patricia Bell Scott, and Barbara Smith. The Feminist Press, Old Westbury, NY, 1982.

Becoming Visible: Women in European History, edited by Renate Bridenthal and Claudia Koontz. Houghton Mifflin Co., Boston, 1977.

Black Woman, The, edited by Toni Cade (Bambara). Signet, New York, 1970.

Capitalist Patriarchy and the Case for Socialist Feminism, edited by Zillah R. Eisenstein. Monthly Review Press, New York and London, 1979.

Class and Feminism, edited by Charlotte Bunch and Nancy Myron. Diana Press, Baltimore, 1976.

Coming to Power, edited by Samois. Alyson Publications, Boston, 1981.

Compañeras: Latina Lesbians, edited by Juanita Ramos. Latina Lesbian Herstory Project, New York, 1987.

Existentialism versus Marxism: Conflicting Views on Humanism, edited by George Novack. Dell Publishing Co., New York, 1966.

Feminist Revolution, edited by Redstockings. Random House, New York, 1978.

Fight Back! Feminist Resistance to Male Violence, edited by Frederique Delacoste and Felice Newman. Cleis Press, Pittsburgh, 1981.

For Lesbians Only: A Separatist Anthology, edited by Sarah Lucia Hoagland and Julia Penelope. Onlywomen Press, London, 1988.

Her Wits About Her: Self-Defense Stories by Women, edited by Denise Caignon and Gail Groves. Harper & Row, New York, 1987.

Home Girls: A Black Feminist Anthology, edited by Barbara Smith. Kitchen Table: Women of Color Press, Latham, NY, 1983.

Lavender Herring, The: Lesbian Essays from the Ladder, edited by Barbara Grier and Coletta Reid, Diana Press, Baltimore, 1976.

Lesbian Feminism in Turn-of-the-Century Germany, edited by Lillian Faderman and Brigitte Erickson. Naiad Press, Missouri, 1980.

Lesbianism and the Women's Movement, edited by Nancy Myron and Charlotte Bunch. Diana Press, Baltimore, 1975.

Man-Made Woman: How New Reproductive Technologies Affect Women, edited by Gena Corea *et al.* Indiana University Press, Indianapolis, 1987.

Mothering: Essays in Feminist Theory, edited by Joyce Trebilcot. Rowman and Allanheld, Totowa, New Jersey, 1983.

Nice Jewish Girls: A Jewish Lesbian Anthology, edited by Evelyn Torton Beck. The Crossing Press, Trumansburg, NY, 1982.

Powers of Desire: The Politics of Sexuality, edited by Ann Snitow, Christine Stansell, and Sharon Thompson, Monthly Review Press, New York, 1983.

Radical Feminism, edited by Anne Koedt, Ellen Levine, and Anita Rapone. Quadrangle Books, New York, 1973.

Reinventing Anarchy, edited by Howard Erlich, Carol Erlich, David De Leon, and Glenda Morris. Routledge and Kegan Paul, London, Boston and Henley, 1979.

Reweaving the Web of Life: Feminism and Non-Violence, edited by Pam McAllister. New Society Publishers, Philadelphia, 1982.

Sisterhood is Global, edited by Robin Morgan. Anchor Press/Doubleday, New York, 1984.

Sisterhood is Powerful, edited by Robin Morgan. Random House, New York, 1970.

Take Back the Night: Women on Pornography, edited by Laura Lederer. William Morrow, New York, 1981.

Test-Tube Women: What Future for Motherhood?, edited by Rita Arditti, Renate Duelli Klein and Shelley Minden. Pandora Press, London and Boston, 1984.

This Bridge Called My Back: Writings by Radical Women of Color, edited by Cherríe Moraga and Gloria Anzaldúa. Kitchen Table: Women of Color Press, Latham, NY, 1983.

Top Ranking: Racism and Classism in the Lesbian Community,
edited by Sara Bennett and Joan Gibbs. February 3 Press, New York,
1980.

Toward an Anthropology of Women, edited by Rayna Reiter. Monthly
Review Press, New York, 1975.

*Women and Revolution: A Discussion of the Unhappy Marriage of
Marxism and Feminism,* edited by Lydia Sargent. South End Press,
Boston, 1981.

Feminist and Alternative Publishers of Works Cited in Text

Alyson Publications
40 Plymptom Street
Boston, MA 02118

International Publishers
381 Park Avenue South
New York, NY 10016

Cleis Press
P.O. Box 8933
Pittsburgh, PA 15221

ism press
P.O. Box 12447
San Francisco, CA 94112

Crossing Press
P.O. Box 1048
Freedom, CA 95019

**Kitchen Table:
Women of Color Press**
P.O. Box 908
Latham, NY 12110

Firebrand Books
141 The Commons
Ithaca, NY 14850

Latina Lesbian Herstory Project
Box 627, Stuyvesant Station
New York, NY 10009

Frog in the Well
25A Buena Vista Terrace
San Francisco, CA 94117

Monthly Review Press
122 West 27th Street
New York, NY 10001

Institute of Lesbian Studies
P.O. Box 60242
Palo Alto, CA 94306

Naiad Press
P.O. Box 10543
Tallahassee, FL 32302

New Left Books/Verso
6 Meard Street
London W1V 3HR
England

Pergamon Press
Maxwell House
Fairview Park
Elmsford, NY 10523

New Society Publishers
4527 Springfield Ave.
Philadelphia, PA 19143

South End Press
116 St. Botolph St.
Boston, MA 02115

Onlywomen Press
38 Mount Pleasant
London WC1X 0AP, England

Spinsters/Aunt Lute
P.O. Box 410687
San Francisco, CA 94141

Pandora Press
imprint of Unwin Hyman
8 Winchester Place
Winchester, MA 01890

Index

About the Author

I was born in New Rochelle, New York, but my parents transplanted me to Los Angeles when I was nearly seven. I was very annoyed, because I was sure I was meant to be an Easterner rather than a Westerner. I went to grade school and high school at the Catholic school Marymount, where I learned to enjoy being around women—although I'm afraid the school will sue me for writing that.

I went to UCLA for college and my master's degree in political science, because it had a curriculum that permitted me to learn about all areas of the world, not just the United States and Europe. At that time I did a little, but not much, work in the civil rights and anti-war movements.

I moved to Cambridge, Massachusetts because it seemed both radical and Eastern. There I learned about feminism. An article by Mary Daly in the liberal Catholic magazine *Commonweal* convinced me that abortion was a woman's right, thus enabling me to become a feminist. I joined Boston Female Liberation in 1972 and worked briefly on the feminist magazine *The Second Wave*.

That same year I moved to Washington, D.C. to study at Catholic University, because it was the only school where I could get a teaching assistantship. I did all of the course work for a doctorate in political science and passed the comprehensive exams—but never wrote the dissertation because of the pressures of feminist work, family illness, and this book, and the difficulty in finding a topic that was acceptable both to me and the department. My means of support is a reporting job for a nonprofit magazine.

In July 1973, I joined the staff of the feminist newspaper *off our backs*, and fell in love with the newspaper. I have continued to work (unpaid, except for a year as office worker) for it ever since. In my work on the paper, I have focused on feminist theory and on international women's news.

I have taught women's studies courses at George Washington University and American University. For many years, I have taught feminist theory courses to women in the community— first through the Washington Area Women's Center and, after the center closed, on my own. Teaching feminist theory gave me the framework for writing *Love and Politics*.

I am a lesbian, single at the moment of writing this bio. I live in an apartment in the District of Columbia (and support statehood for the District!), and spend as much time as possible in the woods, mountains, and marshes.

—*Carol Anne Douglas*, March 1990

Lesbian Origins

by *Susan Cavin, Ph.D.*

Janice Raymond, writing in *The Women's Review of Books* (March 1986), calls *Lesbian Origins* "a creative and innovative approach to lesbian feminist theory, specifically because it dares to deal with the whole question of origins in a new yet rigorous way. Much feminist theory has deliberately avoided exploring the origins of society, or relegated it to an insignificant part of the history and theory of women's oppression and liberation. In addition, Cavin's work... fills a gap in Feminist Studies—the dearth of good lesbian feminist theory..."

Cavin bases her theory on sociological data drawn from a broad range of cultures around the world. She holds that original human societies were woman-centered, with females greatly outnumbering males; the latter were marginalized from women's societies. When armed men overthrew the women's societies, they integrated themselves into society, breaking women's social power.

"...What is so intriguing and powerful about Cavin's work on incest and incest taboos, and also her empirical work on sex ratios, female sexuality and sex segregation, is that she provides actual feminist material conditions for the transition from gynosocieties to patriarchies...," Raymond continues. "...Susan Cavin's book should be discussed widely and seriously; it should be required reading in every feminist theory course."

288 pages, including 31 illustrations and 55 anthropological tables.

Paperback...ISBN 0-910383-15-4...$12.
Hardcover...ISBN 0-910383-16-2...$18.

(To order, see next page)

ORDER FORM

Amount

☐ Send me _____ copy/ies of
Love and Politics at $12.00 each . . . . $_____

☐ Send me _____ copies
(5 or more copies) at $10.80 each . . . . . . $_____

☐ Send me _____ copies of the
hardcover edition at $18.00 each . . . . . . $_____

☐ Send me _____ copy/ies of
Lesbian Origins at $12.00 each . . . . $_____

Add postage: $1 for one book,
25¢ for each additional book . . . . $_____

California residents add 7¼% sales tax
(87¢ for one paperback copy) . . . . $_____

Total payment . . . . $_____

Name _____

Address _____

City, State & Zip _____

Make check or
money order out to: **Ism Press, Inc.**
P.O. Box 12447
San Francisco, CA 94112